For the

CONSERVATION *of* EARTH

WORLD WILDERNESS INVENTORY

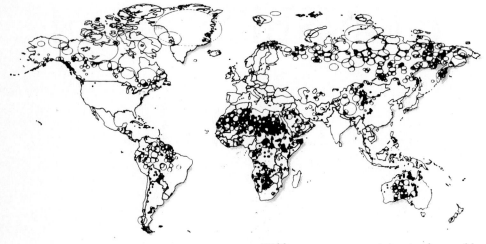

Wilderness areas remaining in the world

The result of inventory conducted for
the 4th World Wilderness Congress.

For the
CONSERVATION
of
EARTH

Vance Martin
Editor

Book and Cover Design by
Jody Chapel
Cover to Cover Design

Library of Congress Cataloging-in-Publication Data

World Wilderness Congress (4th: 1987: Denver, Colo.)
    For the Conservation of   Earth

        1. Nature conservation—Congresses.   2. Natural areas—
        Congresses. 3. Wilderness areas—Congresses.
        I. Martin, Vance.   II. Title.

QH75.A1W67 1987   333.78'2   88-16319
ISBN 1-55591-026-2

Printed in the United States of America
10 9 8 7 6 5 4 3 2 1

CONTENTS

II. NATIONAL CASE STUDIES

III. ECONOMICS, DEVELOPMENT AND ENVIRONMENT

ACKNOWLEDGMENTS

The 4th World Wilderness Congress was made possible by the dedicated work of many highly qualified people, virtually all of whom gave their services freely, and by financial support from a wide range of organizations, agencies, corporations and individuals. The International Wilderness Leadership Foundation and the 4th WWC Executive Committee offer sincere appreciation to each and every one who helped in any way. A special acknowledgment goes to the College of Forestry and Natural Resources at Colorado State University, which provided the Secretariat offices during the four years of planning and implementing the 4th World Wilderness Congress.

Special thanks are also due to all of the participants in the 4th World Wilderness Congress whose work is published in this volume, to co-editor Darby Junkin, and for the help of Jack Armstrong, Craig Sarbeck, Alice Hubbard, Gina Magnum, Allison Tyler, Kenneth Player, Karen Groves, Kate Farren and Felicia.

From an idea in the Zululand wilderness grew the
World Wilderness Congress

Dedicated to
Sir Laurens van der Post, C.B.E.,
who understood what we were trying to do

"You are tired with years of civilization.
I come and offer you what? A single green leaf."
—Grey Owl, 1930

The symbol of the International Wilderness Leadership Foundation and the World Wilderness Congress is the three-pointed *Erythrina caffra* leaf. It expresses three relationships of man to his surroundings: Man to Man, Man to God and Man to Earth, and bespeaks the essential hope that man can reconcile the driving force of development with the sustaining power of the environment. Only in this way will we honor the spirit of all life and assure human survival.

FOREWORD

Dr. Ian Player, Founder
World Wilderness Congress

When the 4th World Widerness Congress was finally over there were many emotional farewells. Differences in status, colour, nationality and religion had been put aside for a week in a search of answers for a common future for mankind. Friendships had been forged that would last a lifetime. The interlinking of science, art, music, politics and finance, poetry, religion and psychology as well as tribal lore had been powerfully demonstrated. There had been some unpleasantness and many crises, but we are human, after all.

I went for a short hike up into the mountains at Estes Park when all the delegates had gone. I sat looking over the splendid vista of the great Rocky Mountain National Park. It was a still day and in my secluded spot I was protected from the winds sweeping over the snow. I lazed in the warmth of the day and watched the golden leaves of aspen trees dance in the sun. Around me were high rock pinnacles and in my imagination I saw the feathered headdress of North American Indians watching me, or were they watching the herds of bison that once roamed in the valley below?

My mind drifted over the events of the past week and journeyed back through the years. I remembered how in 1955 I was a young game ranger stationed at Umfolozi game reserve with my companions Ken Tinley and Jim Feely. We talked often of the future of game reserves and conservation in southern Africa. We were a small, tightly knit, often lonely band of men in close contact with Zulu game guards such as Magqubu Ntombela, Gqakaza Ntombela, Mdiceni Mtetwa. It was the game guards who bore the brunt of the fight against poachers.

In many ways our task seemed hopeless. There was little money for the game reserves and our own salaries were a pittance. There was great hostility to conservation from Zulu tribesmen and white farmers. One could not blame them since they had suffered losses of cattle from a disease carried by the tsetse fly. The courts were most unsympathetic because for years there had been an official slaughtering of game in order to try and wipe out the tsetse fly. Now here we were taking poaching cases to court. Magistrates imposed ridiculous fines: 10 shillings ($1 in those days) for killing a warthog within the game reserve. The capture of poachers meant waiting throughout days and nights in the cold, wet bush, only to face a fierce fight with spear or gun. Frequently guards were badly injured. We were up against officials in government departments who had no sympathy for the game reserves or for conservation. They regarded both as a joke, at times a nuisance. We were subjected to delegations who came to discuss how the land would be used for other purposes such as cattle farms or settlements.

There was always some crisis or another and our morale was often at a low ebb. But after a few days walking out on long patrols and seeing the rhino, wildebeest, zebra, bushbuck and other animals, and after sleeping next to campfires while the jackal screamed and hyena whooped in nearby valleys, we would return to our main camp revitalized and ready to fight on for a cause we knew to be honest and just. We would have long conversations deep into the night, discussing how we could win public opinion to our cause.

One day Jim Feely, nicknamed "The Brain," because he had such an inexhaustible supply of knowledge, showed me the 10 fundamental principles of the wilderness concept in an American book on wildlife management. The words reverberated through my brain. Never before had I been so excited by the written word. Here before me was what I had experienced in the bush of Umfolozi, the rivers of northern Zululand and the coastal lakes with flamingo, crocodile and hippo. For years the wilderness had worked its magic upon me, but I had never been able to express it. Now here was the inner understanding, written down.

Jim Feely and Ken Tinley were scientists in the true sense of the word and their contribution to the science of conservation had already begun. My forté was in the political and administrative aspects of conservation and I immediately knew that there was a key to public opinion in the wilderness concept. I began corresponding with Howard Zahniser, the secretary of the American Wilderness Society, and he sent me the hearings by the senate on the National Wilderness Preservation Act. It became the most precious reference book I possessed. It inspired me to begin the protracted battle to have wilderness areas set aside within our game reserves and to initiate treks, which were called wilderness trails, into the area.

Slowly but surely, the people of South Africa began to walk the trails. They realized that here was a resource of enormous value to the country. We had begun making friends for conservation and many of those who walked the trails were touched by the same magic that had inspired Jim Feely, Ken Tinley and me.

I conceived the idea of the Wilderness Leadership School. The Natal Parks Board who employed me allowed me to use the wilderness areas of the Umfolozi and Lake St. Lucia to organize trails of leaders from the community. I found myself taking wilderness treks for the Natal Parks Board in official time and then for the Wilderness Leadership School during my holidays. It was exhausting work and I knew that we were contributing to a new conservation ethic.

For 22 years I served the Natal Parks Board, slowly climbing through the ranks, stationed in different game reserves in Zululand engaged in tasks that varied from the capture and translocation of the then rare and endangered white rhino, to surveys of hippo populations and bird-breeding colonies on Lake St. Lucia. There were also piles of official files to be attended to and correspondence and memoranda that never seemed to end. As I rose higher in the ranks, the administrative burden grew in proportion and field work became infrequent. There were official visits to the United States where I gained more knowledge of wilderness conservation. Magqubu Ntombela, the down-to-earth Zulu companion, guide and mentor of my early years was always there for me to consult and provide guidance.

In 1974 I left the Natal Parks Board to work full time with the Wilderness Leadership School and the International Wilderness Leadership Foundation. Laurens van der Post, a friend since 1969, came home frequently to South Africa, and he, Magqubu and I walked in the wilderness of Umfolozi game reserve. We sat around the fire of acacia logs and talked at great length until the early hours of the morning. We heard the jackal screaming and saw a leopard in the moonlight, moving from shadow to shadow, stalking an impala. We watched the sun rise and set and heard Magqubu say, "There arises from the ears of an elephant the sun." We heard how the old people used to say the sun has a very old blanket, full of holes, and when it goes to bed at night it pulls the blanket over itself and the stars are the light shining through the holes.

We walked for days in complete silence, feeling the changes in diurnal rhythms and seeing the ancient landscape where the brooding mysterious spirit of early man still lingers in hidden valleys guarded by the baboons, lions and snakes. The tribal people of Africa have guided our steps and we have realized that the world must learn from this ancient treasure house of a different kind of knowledge.

We boiled the billy can in the shade of the giant sycamore fig trees and drank tea from enamel mugs and talked about C.G. Jung who said, "Africa is God's own country." We agreed that the major task of the Wilderness Leadership School was to continue to bring people of all races and creeds into the wilderness of Africa, to meet in an atmosphere conducive to a better undertanding of ourselves and the world in which we live. It was from the small *indabas* (gatherings) of six people at the end of a trail and a conversation Magqubu and I had that the idea emerged of an *indaba-nkulu* (great gathering) of those who knew the wilderness and what it could do for mankind. This led to the 1st World Wilderness Congress in Johannesburg, South Africa in 1977; Cairns, Australia in 1980; Inverness, Scotland in 1983; and Denver and Estes Park, Colorado in 1987.

These were the thoughts that passed through my mind as I looked down across the valleys of Estes Park to snow-covered peaks of the Rocky Mountains. It had been a long haul since the reading of the 10 fundamental principles of the wilderness concept at Umfolozi game reserve in 1955. The wheel had turned the full circle.

INTRODUCTION

Vance G. Martin, Executive Director
4th World Wilderness Congress

The environmental problems we face today no longer concern only individual species or the deterioration of local and regional natural areas. A wider, more dangerous scenario is beginning to emerge. Our global biological and environmental support systems—those natural processes that supply or help purify our air and water and which build the soil—are deteriorating rapidly because of our increasing abuse and neglect. We face an undeniable degradation of our basic life-support systems.

There have been successes. Occasionally the force of reason, personal commitment and political will have combined to help make progress on some of our conservation challenges. These have usually been too little or too late in order to offset the cumulative effects of overpopulation, deforestation, unwise industrialization and the proliferation of toxins and waste products in the global environment. Sadly, the solution of environmental problems has too often been hampered by politics or by professional and cultural differences. In virtually all cases, conservation remedies have been limited by lack of available finances or thwarted by prevailing economic theory. Clearly, new approaches are needed.

The World Wilderness Congress (WWC) is a response to this need for new approaches to the conservation and development dilemma. A project of the International Wilderness Leadership Foundation (IWLF), the WWC is an ongoing, worldwide forum which involves all aspects of professional and public conservation efforts. It has met on four occasions: South Africa (1977), Australia (1980), Scotland (1983) and the United States (1987). Each WWC has had a different emphasis with unique objectives, but the three general goals which help to guide each Congress are:

• To achieve practical results in specific environmental objectives, in order to stimulate new initiatives in worldwide conservation and sustainable development;
• To integrate wild land values and the protection of wilderness into all natural resource, economic and social development programs;

- To emphasize and demonstrate how a holistic approach to problem solving is necessary to deal successfully with increasingly complex conservation challenges.

A lot of work went into the 4th WWC. Four years of planning by a highly qualified executive committee were required to clarify the objectives and to develop the program. In addition, the funds to plan and implement the Congress had to be raised by the IWLF. In order to maintain its stance as an independent forum in the field of international conservation, the WWC is funded through a wide range of public- and private-sector support and from individual donations. The IWLF accomplishes a great deal with modest financing.

The 4th World Wilderness Congress met in Colorado, USA, September 11 through 18, 1987, with some 1,700 participants from 65 countries. True to the form of previous congresses, these participants included not only the scientists and natural resource managers that one expects to find at such a gathering, but also a wide range of other individuals who increasingly have a conservation mandate in their fields, including bankers, businessmen, politicians, educators, artists, cultural figures, psychologists and native peoples. Beyond the diversity of the participants, another unique and important aspect is that the WWC is a public forum: it is open to everyone.

We achieved a great deal together. A consensus emerged from the speakers, all leaders in their fields, and from all other participants throughout the eight days of global overview presentations, scientific symposia, educational demonstrations, workshops and cultural events. Four major points were emphasized.

First, because the environmental challenges facing us are increasingly interrelated with economics, agriculture, industry and health, a whole new perspective and type of planning is needed. The environmental challenges facing us demand more and better-directed information, applied through new methods of system-wide management at a global level.

Second, in the words of Maurice Strong, it is time for an "eco-convergence," a synthesis between economic planning and ecological thinking which can create new avenues for building, maintaining and conserving our world. While agreement was unanimous that conservation and development are inseparable partners in shaping our future, interpretation of their respective roles is open to debate. James Baker, U.S. Secretary of Treasury, insisted that "economic growth is essential for conservation." Conversely, Chief Oren Lyons, who spoke for native peoples, said that "conservation is a necessity, and development is a matter of choice."

Third, the solutions needed depend increasingly upon concerted action by non-governmental organizations and individual citizens. People everywhere must realize that the future is in their hands and is shaped by their actions and decisions. In an era when governments find themselves increasingly bound by budgetary considerations and bureaucratic structures, public involvement is a key to finding workable, effective answers. Governments alone cannot solve the worsening environmental crisis; it requires attention by all individuals.

Fourth, there is a fundamental need for cooperation, which can only spring from new attitudes and perspectives. While at first this may seem somewhat simplistic, it may in fact be the most challenging task of all. In our increasingly global society, biological systems or ecological problems themselves show us the way to formulate solutions. Ecological systems and pollution pay no heed to national boundaries, skin color or religious differences. A new, cooperative approach must integrate national identities, professional or self-interest perspectives and cultural differences into a cohesive, collective response, unhindered by greed and politics, in order to assure human survival. Respect for all people, selflessness rather than self-interest, innovation and good stewardship of natural resources are not clichés; they are critical elements of an urgently needed approach.

The WWC is a demonstration of how this critically important need for information and effective global action can be addressed. It is a model for the new thinking and planning, and is evidence of the strength in cooperation, enthusiasm and concerted action which can be generated by such an approach. Practical solutions emerged from the discussions such as a World Conservation Bank (International Conservation Finance Program). These are presented in the following pages.

For the Conservation of Earth is structured to provide you with a variety of information and avenues for action. It brings to you, in edited and selected form, the unique proceedings of the 4th WWC, including global overviews by world leaders, specific case studies from a variety of developing nations, and the philosophical, practical wisdom of tribal peoples. It also offers information and addresses to enable you to become involved immediately in worldwide conservation.

Finally, as proceedings of the previous World Wilderness Congresses have been, this book is a benchmark against which future generations can measure the success—or failure—of our commitment to the survival of nature and of the human race.

We encourage you to use this book. Contact the people and organizations listed. Information, technical assistance, financial and other types of involvement are necessary to create cooperative, effective solutions. Worldwide conservation is an essential part of our lives and determines our future. It depends upon each of us.

THE DENVER DECLARATION

Preamble

Our earth is unique. All living things depend on its life-supporting, natural processes for survival. Over the millennia, self-regulatory processes inherent in its design have maintained a productive balance of natural resources as well as providing an inspirational foundation for human culture. Today, Earth's destiny is largely in our hands—where once humanity was surrounded by wilderness, now wilderness is surrounded by humanity. Only as we understand, respect and cooperate with the self-regulatory dynamics of Earth will we and future generations be capable of maintaining and restoring its processes which support all life.

The 4th World Wilderness Congress recognizes, in accord with the recent findings of the World Commission on Environment and Development, that:

• There is a direct connection between healthy natural ecological systems and the economic and political stability of all nations;
• The productivity of Earth's natural resource base is rapidly deteriorating, as evidenced by desertification, deforestation, accumulation of toxic wastes, polluted drinking water and oceans, diminution of wilderness habitat and loss of genetic diversity. It is clear that, under the demands of increasing human population, the overall situation will continue to deteriorate;
• While qualitative similarities and differences exist in the environmental problems of the nations of the world, there is an uneven capability among nations to redress this situation;
• Financial and development institutions (public and private), non-governmental organizations and all citizens have a significant role to play in defending and restoring the productivity of natural systems and environmental quality, working with governments to provide basic human needs for an expanding population.

A new initiative is needed in worldwide conservation:

• To halt the destruction of the Earth's remaining wild lands and its natural resource base, and to assist ecological processes in being restored to healthy balance;
• To ensure that development is sustainable by incorporating long-term natural resource concerns into economic development programs of all countries;
• To promote conservation education activities as well as cooperative exchange of knowledge, technology and financial assistance to meet global conservation challenges;

We therefore recommend that:

• The natural environment be recognized as a source of knowledge, well-being and inspiration essential to the highest achievements of mankind.
• Non-governmental organizations and the private sector should join forces with governments in a major effort to stimulate educational, political and technical actions for sustainable development and an enhanced environmental ethic. These coalitions would support mutual actions which respond to the recommendations of the World Commission on Environment and Development, under such established programs as the World Conservation Strategy, the World Charter for Nature and others.
• To strengthen the efforts of existing international institutions working in those countries whose natural resource base is in the greatest decline, a World Conservation Corps or similar service should be established which would enhance the international sharing of conservation information, technology and experience.
• Because new sources of funding must be mobilized to augment the expansion of conservation activities, a new International Conservation Banking Program should be created to integrate international aid for environmental management into coherent, common programs for recipient countries based on objective assessments of each country's resources and needs.

—Denver, Colorado, USA
September 1987

The
GLOBAL
CHALLENGE

"If current trends continue, the atmosphere will warm by about 1.5° to 4.5° C by the year 2030. Warming of just 2° C will take the earth out of the range of anything that has been experienced in the last ten million years."

—Dr. Irving Mintzer
World Resources Institute

POLICY

OUR COMMON FUTURE

Gro Harlem Brundtland, Prime Minister of Norway

The 4th World Wilderness Congress is a vivid and strong response to the call for action of the World Commission on Environment and Development. *Our Common Future* is also your report. It was formed through an open process as the WCED heard and received hundreds of submissions from people and their organizations in all parts of the world. The public hearings were as important as the private deliberations. Without continuous interaction with the people who cultivate the land, live in the slums, direct the companies, do the research, hold high political office, work in the media, and others, the report would not have been the same.

The process through which the report was formed has been of vital importance to its message and perspective. Bill Ruckleshaus, Minister Salim of Indonesia, a Soviet member of the Academy of Science, the Finance Minister of Zimbabwe, a Chinese and a Saudi Arabian scientific director, a Colombian environmentalist, and Maurice Strong, to mention but a few, all agreed on a common analysis, on shared perceptions and concrete recommendations addressed to the global community.

As the commission worked, nationalism and artificial dividers receded. In their place emerged a common concern for the planet and for the interlocking ecological and economic threats facing humanity. This experience is one that must be shared by millions of people around the globe. Only if mutual understanding can replace mutual mistrust, and only if mutual respect and solidarity can prevail will we be able to take the necessary corrective action. The commission offers its own consensus as one on which the international community can build.

Through the history of man a number of great political changes have taken place which have proven to be irreversible. Even temporary setbacks cannot detract from the fact that universal suffrage, large-scale decolonization and the establishment of a universally recognized set of fundamental human rights stand out as such great historic achievements.

The present world situation calls for new leaps forward. The world's political map and agenda have changed. The environment—previously viewed as a theme of protection—has now become a theme of survival. We must recognize that the interrelated issues of environment and development belong at the very top of the international political agenda, on a par with the vital issues of disarmament and security. If the commission succeeds in establishing this world agenda, gaining an irreversible foothold for this work, it will indeed have fulfilled its mandate.

There are many tragic examples of unsustainable practices that are the direct consequences of economic and social conditions and of mismanagement of natural resources: the slash and burn of vegetation; the felling of forests; the overuse of lands, causing soil erosion and desertification and ultimately threatening the carbon dioxide cycle which in turn threatens to alter the global climate. The excesses of affluence in the North, the burning of fossil fuels, the use of chemicals and treatment of industrial wastes threaten lakes and soil and cause damage to human health. The atmosphere's ability to absorb our emissions is approaching its limits. And all these phenomena interact across national borders and between continents.

Clearly these trends demonstrate that we have come to a point in our history where we can no longer act primarily as citizens of any single nation state. We have to behave as world citizens. We are entangled in the same destiny, and we have been brought closer together—so much closer that we no longer have the option of placing more distance between us—even though some gaps between us are widening.

We are drifting farther apart as the gaps between the rich and the poor are widening. But we have been brought closer through communications, capable of bringing news about people's life and destiny from around the globe in seconds. This gives hope of building identification and feeling of human responsibility. We have become closer through the sheer force of numbers. One hundred million people are added to the global population every year. We have come so much closer that we run the risk of ruining our future, but together we can also save it.

Since the Stockholm Conference, frustration has been growing over our collective inability to deal effectively with crucial environment and development issues. We have had a number of political conferences, but sufficient political action has not been forthcoming.

The establishment in 1983 of the WCED as an independent body reflected the high priority assigned to environment and development issues by the General Assembly of the United Nations. This happened at a time when we experienced the paradox of decline in international cooperation and multilateralism parallel to an obvious increase in global interdependence.

Our Common Future covers the entire political agenda. It discusses the international economic relations system, food security, industry, energy, the urban challenge, the protection of genetic resources and international institutions. How can we assure enough food for a growing world population, while at the same time avoiding environmental damage from large-scale agriculture? How can industry produce all the goods required to remove poverty and squalor without depleting the world's natural resources? How can we meet the growing energy requirements of developing countries without a global environmental breakdown? How can we curb rapid urbanization and get rid of urban slums? Is it within our reach to protect the genetic resources of the planet's plants and animals?

The international imbalances which are at the root of the deadlock between environment and development must now be corrected. In a world ridden by poverty, only economic growth can offer hope for a better life for the poor who now number close to 800 million and create the capacity to solve environmental problems. The overriding political concept of the Commission's report is, in fact, a new concept for economic growth and we have called for a new era of growth. This new growth must be substantial but its content needs to be changed. The ability of future generations to meet their needs can be compromised as much by affluence—the excesses of industrial and technological development—as by the environmental degradation which is the result of underdevelopment. A new era of growth must be supported by a broad process of change, of policy reforms across the spectrum of human imagination. It requires more equal access to knowledge and to resources. It requires a more equitable distribution within and among nations. There are not limits to growth itself, but it can and must be managed in such a way as to enhance the resource base on which we all depend.

To pursue a new era of economic growth, we need to breathe new life into the multilateral approach to problem solving. There is no alternative to concerted and coordinated action. Deteriorating terms of trade, soaring interest rates, protectionism, declines in financial flows, and debilitating debts strangle development potential in the Third World and threaten to destroy our environment. Clearly, the developing countries will have real opportunities to follow sustainable paths of progress only when external conditions offer them reasonable hopes for a better future. We in the industrialized countries must do more to ensure that the international economy serves the interests of developing countries rather than leaving them behind in the poverty trap.

Consequently, commodity prices must be further increased and interest rates must come down. The debt crisis must now be seriously addressed, taking due account of the legitimate interests of both lenders and borrowers. Increased capital transfers and development assistance are clearly necessary, and new funds must be forthcoming for projects that aim at sustainable development.

Sustainable development is possible through a more equitable international economic regime. We must establish a world order based not only on equal rights among nations and people, but on more genuinely equal opportunities.

The reports analysis is clear. Environment is not a separate sector distinct from key economic sectors such as industry, agriculture and energy. It is not a question of environment or development. It is both or none. Ecology and economy will have to merge. Environmental concerns must become an integral part of decision making at all levels. These goals will require changes also in the policies of the international organizations responsible for trade, aid, technological and financial assistance. Further re-orientation of the policies of the World Bank, the IMF, the regional development banks, GATT, UNCTAD, UNDP, WHO and FAO, to mention a few very key agencies, will be at the core of the process we call for.

During the international debate this year about the commission's report, some skepticism has been voiced about certain implications of the commission's call for incorporation of sustainability criteria into international financing. Applied to North-South issues, this has been perceived by some as implying a new form of conditionality, a constraint imposed on the developing countries from outside—an asymmetric burden-sharing, since the North would seemingly be exempted.

It must be noted, however, that the commission was emphatic in coupling its call for higher quality in aid and lending with substantially increased financial flows. Recipient countries bear an obligation equal to that of lenders and donors as regards setting their development priorities on the basis of long-term sustainability criteria. The notion is not one of unilateral conditionality, but of solidarity and equality among nations. It is one of common pursuance of mutual self-interest.

This integration of sustainability criteria into the decision-making process must be made operational by governments themselves as part of their national strategies. Developing countries will need external assistance from UNEP and other organizations in order to increase their capacity to manage this integration in practice. Such assistance must come from the international community at the request of the countries concerned.

When *Our Common Future* was launched in April, the commission had worked together for 900 days. Since then a broad public outreach programme has been conducted. The response and the interest generated by this work have strengthened us in the conviction that it is possible to reach the minds and hearts of people irrespective of where they live or their economic situation. All of the commissioners have a strong sense of dedication.

The report has been presented and discussed with governments and NGOs in Eastern and Western Europe. It has also been presented in China and Latin America, in south Asia, Africa and in North America. *Our Common Future* offers motivation and challenge to governments and peoples alike. It sounds a message of warning and of hope and has set in motion a process which will motivate governments to act. And act they will, if presented with enough broad public pressure to that effect.

In Norway, a broad campaign of information and education on environment and development has been launched as a joint venture between private organizations and public authorities. The Norwegian government has also asked all ministries of finance, justice, defense and others not normally perceived to be close to these issues, to review and study the commission's report and compare our domestic and foreign policies against its principles and recommendations. They have been asked to note where our present policies differ and, if they do, to consider what steps can be taken to bring them into line with the report's recommendations.

The commission has called on the United Nations General Assembly to transform its report into a UN Programme of Action and Sustainable Development in the belief that responsible action by the world organization will strengthen its standing and authority. The United Nations can breathe new life into the multilateral approach to international cooperation and has a unique opportunity to demonstrate leadership in making a fundamental commitment to sustainable development. The secretary general himself should be the pivotal force for environment and development. What could be more appropriate than international civil servant number one taking responsibility for the basic elements of human survival, peace, environment and development?

Critics of the UN have long dominated the debate on its role, and it is true that there have been setbacks due to inefficiency, bureaucracy and lack of support. But at this juncture, where multilateral cooperation is at a low ebb, we need a renewed commitment to multi-lateralism and we need governments infused with a moral vocation which goes beyond pursuance of national interests. The time has come to restore the authority of the international institutions we have created. My work on the Commission has further strengthened my own conviction that we need the United Nations now, more than ever before.

We should ask ourselves: What happens next? Who should do what? What is my role in this? What can my organization do? My appeal to all of you is this: Use your influence. Do whatever is possible to create awareness and promote change.

Our report places a powerful tool in the hands of all interested citizens' groups, institutions, trade unions, businesses, executives, company boards, nations, the media, and not least, individuals. I call upon each of you to use that tool. We all face a challenge and opportunity. Sustainable development should be taken out of books and reports and implanted into decision-making processes. Sustainable development will depend on a decision-making process capable of securing effective citizen participation. It is the concerned public that can put environment and development issues onto political agendas.

We must build on present momentum. In particular we must build on the enthusiasm of young people. We must all do our part in launching a global campaign of information and education. We need a new motivation for a global transition to sustainable development. We must secure a constructive debate to persuade public opinion to heighten its pressures and hold governments, institutions and policy makers responsible and convince them of the merits of our overriding goal of sustainable development.

In light of the critical thresholds we are already approaching, the next decades are crucial. This one very finite earth must provide food and energy and meet the needs of double the world population. It may be required to sustain a world economy five to ten times as large as the present. It is quite clear that this cannot be done by multiplying present patterns. Changes are needed. Decisions are due now. We must chart a sustainable course of action.

To secure our common future, we need a new international vision, one which looks beyond narrow, short-sighted, national and entrepreneurial ambitions. We must have a "new deal" in international cooperation. The time is urgent. The environment/development crisis is real. We must all join forces in a new partnership and start acting together. We are all dependent on one another and we share a common future.

THE THREE TIERS OF ACTION

Mostafa K. Tolba

There is something very wrong with the way modern man views the wilderness. We love it, and yet we often take a puerile delight in despoiling that heritage. At best, it seems, we are callously insensitive to the land we spend so much time extolling.

It is worth reflecting on the heroes of the American western frontier—Daniel Boone, Davy Crockett, Buffalo Bill and even Theodore Roosevelt. They were men who loved the wilderness, but much of their joy was derived from senselessly vandalizing the land they loved. William Cody slaughtered the plains game. When he didn't kill for food, he killed for fun.

On the other side of the Atlantic we find a similar paradox.

In the Federal Republic of Germany, 70 percent of all males, according to a recent poll, would like to be a forester. No less a figure than the German chancellor has said that the forests are the soul of the German nation. But the cars and power stations of the same Germans are destroying their beloved forests with the cocktail of pollution we call acid rain.

There are many such contradictions. If the wildernesses we hold in such high regard are to be conserved, short-term sacrifices will be required. And the most urgent priority will be the transfer of enough resources to give hard-pressed Third World communities incentives to safeguard wild areas for the benefit of all humanity.

The economic, aesthetic and cultural value of our remaining wild areas are many. They protect inland drainage systems, offer refuge to the five to 10 million species alive today and to beleaguered indigenous cultures, they generate income through tourism and their almost limitless value as providers of the genetic material for new crops, medicines and industrial products.

We need no longer justify why wild areas need to be conserved. We do need to sound the alarm among governments and the public at large that unless drastic steps are taken, humanity will preside over a holocaust which could remove one-tenth of the world's species before the end of this century. Most important, the environment and development communities need to be united on how we should go about persuading others to take these "drastic steps."

Perhaps most vital of all, we need to leave decision makers and the public in general with a firm impression that there are no simple solutions.

As H.L. Mencken, America's modern-day sage, put it: "For every problem there is a solution that is simple, direct and *wrong*."

Putting up fences around threatened wilderness areas is the wrong solution. Survival of wild places depends on putting to work the recommendations best and most cogently expressed in the World Conservation Strategy and the World Commission on Environment and Development.

I will briefly outline what UNEP is already contributing to the reconciliation between development and the conservation of natural habitats and then indicate what we perceive to be the drastic steps needed to keep wilderness areas intact.

While UNEP recognizes and regrets that, in the industrialized world, wild areas remain at risk from acid rain, clearance for farmland, urban development and replacement of indigenous tree species with "mono-forests," it also recognizes that there is a level of awareness and action which, for example, has left tree felling in rough balance with tree planting. I am fully aware that tree planting does not equate reconstructing a forest, but while we appreciate the value of northern habitats as sanctuary for wild species, we also recognize that their genetic value pales in comparison with the open and closed tropical forest.

The savanna and rain forest environment of the poor world is where the holocaust is happening. At the most conservative estimate, at least 225 million more hectares will be cleared or degraded before the year 2000.

Harsh experience has shown what ecologists have known for a long time, namely that the soils in rainforest areas are poor and usually unsuited for intensive cultivation. In countries like Costa Rica, Indonesia, Brazil and Ivory Coast, areas of tropical forest have been reduced to near desert.

The challenge facing the global community is to help give countries like these proper incentives to manage their forest resources sustainably; to ensure that tree growth is equated with economic growth.

UNEP is supporting a wide-ranging programme aimed at achieving this objective.

We have been working closely with our sister UN agencies to respond to the crisis. With UNESCO we are helping to establish and support protected areas, and there are now more than 250 biosphere reserves which permit various types of land use in all but the core area. With FAO, UNEP is playing a supportive role in the Tropical Forest Action Plan. Good progress is being made toward realizing commitments of up to $8 billion from many governments and agencies to stabilize and strengthen tropical sustainable forestry efforts.

Also with FAO and the International Board for Plant Genetic Resources (IBPGR), UNEP is participating in more than a dozen projects to conserve genetic resources. These include on-site stands in Africa and Asia and five pilot projects for the conservation of endangered animal breeds in five key countries.

UNEP is also involved with IUCN in a range of protected and wildlife initiatives. This includes providing secretariats for CITES and the Migratory Species Convention and core financing for the Conservation Monitoring Center which publishes the Red Data books.

Under our Earthwatch programme, UNEP is gathering and disseminating reliable environmental information. As governments were quick to acknowledge at our recent Governing Council, the data collected and distributed by our Global Environmental Monitoring System (GEMS) is a key element in sustainable planetary management.

There was similar recognition for the indispensible role our regional seas programme—now encompassing over 120 nations—is playing in conserving marine and coastal areas.

In a sense, it is invidious to single out any single UNEP activity as being more important in the preservation of the planet's wild areas than any other, be they within protected areas or outside their boundaries. Our programme is conceived and managed on an unshakable recognition of the realities of environmental interdependence.

We should be doing far more. But with a budget of just over $40 million each year, there are severe limitations on what UNEP can be expected to achieve. Nevertheless, we are urgently working on ways and means to make our initiatives better targeted.

We recognize even more acutely that environmental interdependence is inseparable from economic interdependence. Again I will not rehearse the now familiar arguments which overwhelmingly favor the marriage of ecology and economic development. What I will say is that unless drastic steps are taken to move our ideas for sustainable development into action, the work of UNEP and our partners in the conservation movement in general will be discounted.

Let us not doubt that the natural habitats in the South will continue to disappear unless the major forces of destruction are tackled. A partnership between North and South is needed to head off catastrophe. I am talking of the need for highly organized environmental groups in the North to do much more to convince governments, industry, the development finance institutions and the commercial banks that new funding must be mobilized.

I am suggesting three tiers of action:
• Cooperative assistance to developing nations—UNEP and its partners need to step up their hands-on assistance to developing countries and to work in closer partnership with each other. We won't solve the crisis, but we can lead by our examples.
• Cross-Sectoral Response—There has been enough talk. We need to get the big-spending government agencies and the banks to take the environment much more seriously. We need to be vigilant to ensure the reforms announced by the World Bank and other institutions have the intended impact and to be mindful that loans by the development finance institutions build confidence for investment by commercial banks at four to five times their present level.

Ideal rallying points are: The Tropical Forest Action Plan; the international Tropical Timber Trade Agreement (which has yet to make an impact); the campaign to safeguard the world's threatened wetlands; the regional seas treaties, full of good intentions but seriously underfunded; and the new move UNEP is starting to establish a complementary network of riverain agreements.
• Changes in Global Economy—In the last analysis, the conservation of the world's wild areas depends on a global resolve to reform regressive terms of trade, alleviate the debt burden and slow down the arms race. These are the real motors of environmental destruction.

The environmental movement has had little influence in macro economic planning. But there are signs of radical change as the case for fair and sustainable development becomes overwhelming. Governments have seen how environmental cooperation can create goodwill and they are increasingly receptive to the idea that policies must be designed to effect change without bankrupting the environment.

There is a growing recognition from all quarters that if the industrialized countries want their poorer neighbors to conserve wild areas, ways and means will have to be found to assist them to do this. At our most recent Governing Council, I floated the idea that one 'way' and 'mean' would be to reschedule debt in favor of conservation. Would it not be possible for the creditor nations to recycle part of the debt repayments to finance conservation projects?

Other specific ideas I would like to see considered are:
• How can support to the 5,000 or so NGOs now involved in forestry be increased?
• How can we do more to interest the private sector in management of wild areas?
• How can developed nations be persuaded to pay, even partially, for the invisible benefits they get from the Third World's wild areas?
• And how can UNEP's efforts be better coordinated with our partners to ensure maximum impact?

Our time is now. We must all consider a partnership of different groups to step up the momentum. We have the sympathy of the public—modern mass media coverage has seen to that—and we have an increasingly receptive cadre of decision makers who are eager not to repeat the mistakes of the past.

When we recognize that we need a new ethic for a new wilderness, then we will have made progress. When we realize that the wilderness that William Cody took to be infinitely vast and infinitely wild is actually fragile and threatened, then we will have made progress. When we learn to tread lightly on this earth, we will have begun to turn from the path of destruction.

© Ted Kerasote/Sports Afield

WORLD WILDERNESS INVENTORY

A RECONNAISSANCE-LEVEL INVENTORY OF WORLD WILDERNESS AREAS

J. Michael McCloskey and Heather Spalding

Almost everyone acknowledges that not all parts of the planet Earth should be developed. A balance must be sought between "man and nature," between the areas developed to sustain humanity and the areas where nature predominates. How to strike this balance may tax human wisdom; even to attempt the task requires that our species know something about where we are in the process of development and how much land still remains wild.

There are atlases which show how much land is arable. There are estimates of how much of the native tropical rain forests survive, and there are inventories of how much land around the world is protected in reservations for various public purposes. But there have been no inventories of how much of the world is still undeveloped—of how much is still primarily influenced by the forces of nature.

That such inventories have not been done should not entirely surprise us. Most of the world has been preoccupied with development and still is. Wilderness is generally appreciated when most of it is gone. And the task is Herculean: How do you get the data on a consistent basis, in enough detail, and from all nations regardless of their interest? And, of course, who is prepared to undertake the task?

Believing that no more time should be lost waiting for others to step forward, we at the Sierra Club decided to undertake a first approximation of how much of the land surface of the globe still remains wild. Ours is a reconnaissance-level inventory that we think can be useful in providing a broad overview of where the major blocks of wild land still can be found.

In a rough sense, this inventory represents the opportunity to balance the equation between nature and development. It is from this inventory that reservations of major new protected areas can be made. Some have called for a trebling of the amount of land protected in nature reserves.[1] This inventory shows that this can be done.

Specific judgments still need to be made about the future of given blocks, but at least the question may now be asked whether the block should be preserved or not, in whole or in part. Inquiries can be organized into the specific values of each block and, most importantly, people around the world can watch to see what decisions are made and how they are made. This land will no longer be anonymous backcountry and bush which is nibbled away with impunity.

The remaining wild land is the patrimony of the world—of all living things, and of all generations to come. With this inventory, we can start to track what is happening and to mark trends as subsequent inventories reveal changes. Humanity can decide whether it is losing too much wild land and where.

As a reconnaissance-level inventory, this undertaking represents an approximation, which is probably accurate in the aggregate, but will be shown to have specific shortcomings. That probability is implicit in the methodology used, and we invite interested parties around the world to work with us to perfect the detail. The findings need to be verified on the ground—to be "ground checked." We would like to stimulate collaboration around the world to develop an increasingly accurate inventory. The results of such perfected inventories can be presented when each World Wilderness Congress convenes.

In our research, we looked for wilderness tracts in 195 political entities plus Antarctica. The basic methodology we employed was to analyze a common set of highly detailed maps of the globe to look for "empty quarters"—areas showing no development, areas of so-called de facto wilderness. We used the Jet Navigation Charts and Operational Navigation Charts, at a scale respectively of 1: 2,000,000 and 1:1,000,000, of the U.S. Defense Mapping Agency. These maps, used for commercial and military aeronautical navigation, show increasing levels of detail on human constructs to provide orienting landmarks as areas become sparsely settled and remote. Their information on such constructs is provided on a consistent basis around the globe. In our search for "empty quarters," we eliminated all areas showing roads, settlements, buildings, airports, railroads, pipelines, power lines, canals, causeways, aqueducts, major mines, dams and reservoirs, and oil wells. While the maps did not always show areas subject to agricultural development or logging, these activities occur in proximity to roads and settlements. We identified areas removed from such developments.

Moreover, we only identified *major* blocks of so-called "empty quarter" land, land in blocks of at least one million acres, or 400,000 hectares. This limitation arose primarily out of the practical need to make the project manageable. We did not have the time and resources necessary to search for smaller blocks. Moreover, our maps may not always have shown high levels of development detail for smaller blocks in areas closer to major settlements. We were also mindful of the fact that the larger blocks are probably of greater world significance because they are likely to harbor more viable ecosystems. Under theories of island ecology, which some have suggested may apply to islands of wilderness on large land masses, more of the habitat niches are likely to be occupied in larger units, and if preserved, such units may be able to sustain more biological diversity. Because of their size, 400,000 hectare units are less likely to have been destroyed since the last Jet Navigation Charts were published. Finally, we remembered that both Aldo Leopold and Bob Marshall had suggested that a wilderness area should be large enough for somebody to travel in for two weeks "without crossing his own tracks."[2] Such an area would have to be at least a million acres in size.

In limiting this initial effort to searching for units of 400,000 hectares or more, we do not want to suggest in any way that preservation of smaller areas is not important. It is, and this first effort would be far more complete and meaningful if it could have included all areas over 100,000 acres, or 40,000 hectares. Undoubtedly, the inventory of wilderness would be somewhat higher with these smaller units included, but it is impossible to know whether it would be 10, 20, or 30 percent higher. In any event, an expansion of this inventory will have to arise from a second phase which can best be undertaken by interested parties around the world who may wish to cooperate with us. Refined local data and maps are needed to identify such areas, as well as up-to-date information on adverse development.

The inventory attempted here basically seeks to identify undeveloped land and uses an approach similar to that used by the U.S. Forest Service in its RARE I and II inventories.[3] These inventories were conducted under the legal framework of the Wilderness Act of the United States and sought to identify areas that were roadless and undeveloped without initially making any judgments about the suitability of the areas for status as potential protected areas.

Our world inventories are of such a broad level, though, that they do not need to be drawn into debates over fine points of defining exactly what wilderness is. By implication, our approach identifies more with the biocentric than the anthropocentric approach to defining wilderness since no criteria involving suitability for recreation (e.g., grandeur, ruggedness, etc.) were used.[4] Flat tracts of desert, tundra and ice are included in our inventory, which few backpackers may ever want to visit. However, our inventory does look at land of all kinds, without regard to how much or how little biomass it may support or biological diversity it may have. We are identifying wildness per se.

Our inventory does draw upon the approach of the U.S. Wilderness Act in the way it looks at the present appearance of the land in determining what is wilderness, rather than at the historical reality of how the land has been used.

Land is classified as wilderness if it looks like wilderness, even if it once had been developed. This inventory operates in the spirit of the U.S. Wilderness Act when it characterizes land as wilderness if it "generally appears to have been affected primarily by the forces of nature, with the imprint of man's work substantially unnoticeable."[5] Under that act, wilderness is an area where man and his works do not dominate the landscape. Unlike the U.S. Wilderness Act, however, our inventory undoubtedly includes areas inhabited by traditional, indigenous peoples and in some cases peoples practicing traditional pastoralism. In our inventory, it is only modern man who is a visitor who does not remain.[6]

In the sense just described, it would appear that about one-third of the land surface of the globe is still wilderness. We found five billion hectares (50,887,300 square kilometers) of undeveloped land in over a thousand (1,050) tracts. The tracts were located in 78 countries plus Antarctica. The countries with the biggest aggregations of "empty quarters" are: the Soviet Union (39 percent wilderness), Canada (65 percent wilderness), Australia (33 percent wilderness), Brazil (28 percent wilderness), China (Tibet) (24 percent wilderness), Denmark's Greenland (99 percent wilderness), Algeria (64 percent wilderness), the Sudan (37 percent wilderness), Mauritania (74 percent wilderness), and Saudi Arabia (30 percent wilderness). One hundred and eight countries did not appear to have any of these large wilderness tracts.

Under our definitions, the continents with the most wilderness are Antarctica, Asia, Africa and North America. See TABLE I.

TABLE I

	Wilderness Sq. Km.	Percent Wild	No. of Areas
Antarctica	13,209,000	100%	2*
Asia	11,864,000	27%	306
Africa	9,177,700	30%	437
North America	9,006,700	36%	89
South America	4,222,700	24%	91
Oceania and Australia	2,666,300	30%	94
Europe	741,000	7%	31
World	50,887,400	34%	1,050

* This is really one contiguous block divided in two only for purposes of biogeographical classification.

In terms of the relative amount of wilderness, most of the settled continents are still between one-quarter and one-third wild, Europe being the exception. The European wilderness is largely in northern Scandinavia and European

Russia. Wilderness blocks on most continents average between 21,000 and 46,000 square kilometers in size, with the average being larger in North America (101,000 sq. km.), probably because of Greenland's inclusions in its totals.

If one looks at all of this wilderness plotted on a map of the world, the patterns are clear and in broad outlines match one's intuitive sense of where wilderness would be: Antarctica and Greenland are mostly wild; then one sees a broad band of wilderness sweeping across the northern latitudes of Alaska, Canada, and the Soviet far north. A diagonal band then is seen to run southwesterly from the Soviet far east down through Tibet, Afghanistan, and Saudi Arabia to Africa, where a distinct east-west belt runs through the Sahel. A scattering of units also runs southward through Africa. In South America, as one might expect, the blocks are concentrated in the Amazon, with a scattering southward along the Andes. In Australia, a band runs north-south through the middle of the continent. Somewhat surprisingly, almost no wilderness in one million-acre blocks shows up in the United States. The frontier was lost long ago.

To analyze this inventory data in terms of its biological significance, we have overlaid it on Miklos Udvardy's classification system[7] for the biogeographical provinces of the world. Using his system to look at our data, it is arrayed in TABLE II:

TABLE II

	Wilderness Sq. Km.	% of Total Wilderness	No. of Areas
Palearctic Realm (Europe, North Africa, and Asia, except India and S.E. Asia)	16,774,400	33.0%	514
Antarctic Realm (including New Zealand)	13,249,300	26.0%	7
Nearctic Realm (North America and Central American highlands)	8,968,700	17.6%	84
Afrotropical Realm (sub-Saharan Africa and Madagascar)	4,786,400	9.4%	239
Neotropical Realm (South America, Caribbean, and lowland Central America)	4,260,700	8.4%	96
Australian Realm	2,516,500	4.9%	82
Indomalayan Realm (India, S.E. Asia, Philippines, and most of Indonesia	221,800	0.4%	21
Oceanian Realm	109,500	0.2%	7
Total	50,887,300	100.0%	1,050

Running across all of these realms are biomes representing predominant vegetative cover types. When the wilderness data is arrayed by biomes under Udvardy's system, it is easier to see the distribution of wilderness by climate and habitat zones. Forty-two percent is in the high Arctic or Antarctic; 20 percent is in the warm deserts; 20 percent is in temperate regions; about 12 percent is in the tropics; nearly 4 percent is in mixed mountain systems; 3 percent is in the cold winter deserts; and only a fragment is in the island regions. By biomes, the inventoried wilderness is distributed in TABLE III:

TABLE III

	Wilderness Sq. Km.	No. of Areas	% of Total Wilderness
1 Tundra Communities	21,321,600	104	41.9%
2 Warm Deserts	10,158,600	391	20.0%
3 Temperate Needleleaf Forests	8,893,300	126	17.5%
4 Tropical Humid Forests	3,532,300	78	6.9%
5 Tropical Dry Forests	1,723,800	120	3.4%
6 Cold Winter Deserts	1,630,300	51	3.2%
7 Mixed Mountain Systems	1,463,900	75	2.9%
8 Tropical Grasslands	768,000	33	1.5%
9 Temperate Rainforests	457,700	15	0.9%
10 Temperate Broadleaf Forests	332,000	20	0.7%
11 Temperate Grasslands	310,000	23	0.6%
12 Evergreen Sclerophyllus Forests	186,200	7	0.4%
13 Mixed Island Systems	109,500	7	0.2%
Total	50,887,300	1,050	100.0%

Of the various provinces, the ones with the largest concentrations of wilderness, i.e., having over one million square kilometers or 100 million hectares of wilderness, are in Table IV:

TABLE IV

	Wilderness Sq. Km	No. of Areas
Maudlandia (Antarctica)	9,324,000	1
Sahara	4,382,000	197
Canadian Taiga	3,981,400	29
Marielandia (Antarctica)	3,885,000	1
Low Arctic Tundra	3,067,300	64
East Siberian Taiga	2,672,600	68
Arctic Desert & Icecap	2,348,600	13
West Sahel	1,997,100	45
West European Taiga	1,767,700	25
Amazonian	1,339,000	14
Madeiran (S. America)	1,152,400	15
Central Desert (Australia)	1,093,200	24
Arabian Desert	1,014,200	31

A comparison of the aggregate amount of wilderness within each realm or province with the amount of land now protected in that realm and province suggests something about the opportunity to establish more protected areas. And it offers some perspective on how good a job has been done of protecting remaining wilderness. Existing protected areas were not deducted from the areas inventoried. The comparison of the total amount of land in the inventory with that protected in a number of continents is interesting. Superficially, it suggests that 20 percent of the Nearctic Realm's remaining wilderness is protected; that 18 percent of the Afrotropical Realm's wilderness is protected; and that 12 percent of both the Neotropical and Australian Realms' wilderness is protected.[8]

This comparison, however, is somewhat misleading because comparable concepts are not being looked at. Many protected areas are not roadless at all and thus will not show up in the wilderness inventory. Moreover, most protected areas embody blocks smaller than 400,000 hectares, and the totals for protected areas usually aggregate many such smaller units. Furthermore, the wilderness inventory fails to show the opportunity to protect blocks of less than 400,000 hectares. For all of these reasons, the figures for Africa show that only 6.6 percent of the protected areas plot within the wilderness inventory.

Where the wilderness inventory shows land totals far in excess of the amount now protected, there clearly is the opportunity to protect more land in large blocks. Where no opportunity is shown, there may still be opportunity to protect smaller blocks should they be identified in other inventories.

With this inventory showing that generally less than 20 percent of the remaining wilderness is being protected, one is prompted to ask what the prospects are for the rest of this wilderness surviving without protection.

TABLE V—DISTRIBUTION OF WILDERNESS BY REALMS AND BIOMES (IN SQ. KMS.)

Biomes	Realms								Total
	Afrotropical	Antarctic	Australian	Indomalayan	Nearctic	Neotropical	Oceanian	Palearctic	
Cold-winter deserts	0	0	0	0	0	7,700	0	1,622,600	1,630,300
Evergreen sclerophyllous forests	0	0	186,200	0	0	0	0	0	186,200
Mixed island systems	0	0	0	0	0	0	109,500	0	109,500
Mixed mountain systems	89,100	0	0	107,000	191,500	360,300	0	716,000	1,463,900
Temperate broadleaf forests	0	0	0	0	0	0	0	332,000	332,000
Temperate grasslands	0	0	0	0	0	0	0	310,000	310,000
Temperate needleleaf forests	0	0	0	0	4,453,100	0	0	4,440,300	8,893,300
Temperate rain forests	0	40,400	8,800	0	152,400	256,200	0	0	457,700
Tropical dry forests	1,338,900	0	258,700	29,400	0	96,800	0	0	1,723800
Tropical grasslands/savannas	0	0	251,400	0	0	516,600	0	0	768,000
Tropical humid forests	533,100	0	10,900	53,800	0	2,934,500	0	0	3,532,300
Tundra communities	0	13,209,000	0	0	4,155,300	0	0	3,957,300	21,321,600
Warm deserts/semi-deserts	2,825,300	0	1,800,500	31,600	16,400	88,600	0	5,396,200	10,158,600
Totals	4,786,400	13,249,300	2,516,500	221,800	8,968,700	4,260,700	109,500	16,774,400	50,887,300

This research effort did not attempt to determine what the threats are to this wilderness and how imminent they are. However, by their location one can deduce that the wilderness of the Nearctic Realm (principally in Alaska and northern Canada) is likely to disappear primarily in response to pressures for more oil and gas development and other mineral development. In the Palearctic Realm, the wilderness of the Soviet far north is disappearing under similar pressures and deliberate settlement policies, with logging important in certain areas too. In the Afrotropical Realm, population pressures may be the biggest factor, though ironically spreading desertification may be creating new wilderness in the Sahel. In the Neotropical Realm, Amazonian rainforests are disappearing in response to a cluster of development initiatives: massive land clearance schemes for grazing, huge hydroelectric projects, mineral development and logging. In the outback of Australia, mining provides the impetus to break up wilderness blocks, and the same is likely to be true of Antarctica. In the Indomalayan Realm, planned land settlement programs, logging and oil development are pressing the remaining wilderness blocks. In much of the developing world, smaller wilderness blocks (not identified in this inventory) are undoubtedly also disappearing in response to pressures from shifting cultivators who gain access to the wild land via new development roads.

METHODOLOGY

In developing the inventory, we used Jet Navigation Charts (JNCs)[9] at a scale of 1:2,000,000. There are 65 of these maps for the world. In remote areas, these maps show a great deal of cultural data, such as the location of isolated shrines in the Sahel.

Basically, the approach taken was to draw lines around areas devoid of recorded development in polygons and irregular loops. The lines were set back at least four miles (6.4 km) from developed features such as roads and settlements to allow space for developments that may not have been recorded on the maps or new developments that may have occurred since the maps were prepared. The four-mile setback was chosen arbitrarily on the basis of judgment as sufficient for such purposes (representing about one-fourth of an inch on such maps). The setback could have readily been a little more or less. However, any errors in estimation based on unknown developments impinging on a wider band than this in some localities may be offset in the aggregate by the absence of any such developments in many other setback zones. In fact, it is likely that the use of such a wide setback may have led more to underestimation of the amount of wilderness than overestimation.

Additional information on development was obtained from the Operational Navigation Charts (ONCs) at a scale of 1:1,000,000. There were 212 of these, and they generally showed a greater level of detail. Deference was given to whichever map showed evidence of development in a given area. In a few cases where these ONC maps were dated, other maps were used to provide supplementary information. This was done particularly for Australia where the Reader's Digest Atlas of Australia was used; prepared at a scale of 1:1,000,000, its maps provided highly detailed information.

Other map data was also used to spot check information, including various maps in the Cartographic Collection of the U.S. Library of Congress. The map collection of the World Bank was also made available to us to update information on recent development projects, such as in the Amazon.

The data on human culture on the maps dated on the average from the early 1980s, though in a limited number of instances went back well into the 1970s. Whenever the data on human culture dated before 1980, supplementary maps were used to check the findings. This was done particularly for Australia, Borneo, Canada, China, Greenland, Indonesia, Mongolia, Papua New Guinea, and the Soviet Union. Also because of the rapid pace of development in Brazil's provinces of Rondonia and Acre, World Bank maps were used to verify our results there. Supplementary maps were also used to verify results in several desert areas of North Africa.

The areas identified on the base maps were measured with a planimeter and given code designations by country. For purposes of further identification on smaller scale maps, the coordinates of the center of each tract were plotted. Also the biogeographical realm, biome and province were noted for each tract. The boundaries of each area were then digitized through use of equipment at the World Bank and can be readily revised and compared with data in UNEP's GRID system.

Early in the genesis of the project, we considered using NASA's LANDSAT images for this work, but concluded they were more appropriate for detailed investigations of a given area. A reconnaissance-level survey of the globe could not be easily accomplished if every LANDSAT image had to be studied. Because of the complexity of interpreting data on them and the way in which some developments are obscured in their images, it was much more workable to use maps based on interpretations of their data. Moreover, the budget for this project did not permit acquiring LANDSAT images. If, however, certain units in our inventory cannot be ground-checked by cooperators, we may be able to explore using LANDSAT images to verify findings in a limited number of instances.

A number of special problems arose in connection with the inventory. In some places such as the Amazon and Borneo, settlements appear along rivers where no roads are evident. In some instances where there was reason to believe that other development might cluster along the rivers between settlements (even though none is shown on the maps), these riverside areas were excluded from the inventory. In Iceland, four-wheel drive tracks are shown through the center of the island; these tracks were excluded. In the Soviet far north, corridors were excluded along arctic river systems spotted with settlements; this exclusion will probably eliminate rivers used for summer barge traffic. Moreover, the maps show the routes of winter ice-roads across tundra; these areas were also excluded. In Paraguay, small airfields were shown peppered across otherwise roadless areas; these areas too were excluded. However, areas with ruins and isolated water wells, as in north African deserts, were not always excluded. And in a number of instances where we found traces of development in the midst of large wild tracts we often drew "holes in the donut," i.e., we excluded only the immediate developed area. In a few cases, inventoried wilderness areas straddled national boundaries. In those cases, the areas were disaggregated to show the portions of the wilderness in each country in their national totals, but the area by name is listed only in the country with the larger portion of the tract.

The inventory effort also faced the problem of how to regard land uses and occupation by traditional societies. For instance, portions of the Tibetan plateau may be in the inventory that are used by pastoralists who graze sheep and yaks at elevations up to 5,000 meters.[10] They do so in areas devoid of roads and listed settlements. While we have eliminated areas of heavy use for this purpose, undoubtedly some such use occurs within units in this inventory. Such areas meet the criteria of this inventory in that they appear to be generally influenced primarily by the forces of nature. However, it is likely that small huts are found in the areas and that some change in vegetation has been induced by long-standing grazing. These vegetative changes are even more likely to have progressed in lower elevation steppe and desert areas because of pastoralism over the centuries.[11] No effort has been made to remove such areas from the inventory, but it is likely that the areas subject to the most evident change will not appear in the inventory because of the encroachment of roads and settlements. An extreme example of this is that none of the western American desert in the United States, where sagebrush has replaced grass because of excessive grazing, shows up in the inventory.

A related issue arises with respect to bands of traditional indigenous peoples in places like Papua New Guinea, Borneo and the Amazon. Undoubtedly, such people occupy areas within inventoried units. We did eliminate small settlements recorded along river systems in these places, and indeed inventoried units are sparser than one might imagine in these places, particularly in New Guinea and Borneo. Where no settlements were recorded, we assumed that the impact of such occupants was so slight as to leave the areas appearing to be generally influenced primarily by the forces of nature. However, it is quite likely that some use of motors, particularly on boats, occurs in these areas. This issue arises particularly in western Alaska where native peoples now widely use motorboats and snowmobiles. Since such use is transitory and leaves no lasting marks on the land, we did not assume any impact on the inventory. It is likely too that the areas where such use is heaviest are near recorded settlements and thus will not show up in the inventory.

A final issue concerns routes of passage by traditional societies. These can be trade or caravan routes in the desert or routes for taking flocks from summer to winter pastures in Tibet. A few such routes are recorded on our maps as "tracks" in Tibet and north Africa. They were eliminated from the inventory, though others undoubtedly exist and may not be precise in alignment. Moreover, indiscriminate vehicular use in flat desert areas and on steppes makes it hard to know which areas should be disqualified. Again, following definitions used in the United States for wilderness inventories done by the Bureau of Land Management in desert areas, we eliminated only areas showing constructed roads, not areas showing evidence of mere vehicular passage. On-the-ground checks of units in the inventory may suggest removal of areas marred by too much cross-country vehicular use.

In conclusion, this inventory represents the first time in history that humanity has been able to look at how far it has gone in subjugating the Earth and bending it to its use. Two-thirds of the land of the planet is now dominated by our species.

But with one-third of the land still dominated by nature, there is still a chance to maintain some measure of balance between "man and nature." But this balance will not occur by accident. At least half of the remaining stock of wilderness is not self-protecting by virtue of its forbidding nature. Through encroachment it can slip away easily, with little notice, as billions more are added to the human population.

This inventory needs to be firmed up to provide a useful yardstick to measure what is happening and to prompt conscious decisions with regard to the fate of the wilderness that remains. The boundaries of the units need to be verified by those with access to better information in every country. We need to add data on units of less than 400,000 hectares, and we need to revise the information continuously.

We invite the collaboration of interested conservationists around the world to build this into a tool which can play a central role in maintaining a balance between our world and the world of nature.

FOOTNOTES

1. See, e.g., Edward C. Wolf, "On the Brink of Extinction," (Worldwatch Institute, Washington, D.C., June 1987). Wolf calls for increasing the amount of protected land from 425 million hectares to 1.3 billion hectares.

2. See Roderick Nash, Wilderness and the America Mind (New Haven: Yale University Press, 1967), pp. 4-5 for Aldo Leopold's suggestion that an area be large enough "to absorb a two week's pack trip"; See also James Glover, A Wilderness Original: The Life of Bob Marshall (Seattle, the Mountaineers, 1986), p. 147.

3. RARE stands for Roadless Area Review and Evaluation. The RARE II process was completed in 1979.

4. For a recent discussion of the differences between the anthropocentric and biocentric approaches to defining wilderness, see R.G. Leslie and S.G. Taylor, "The Wilderness Continuum Concept and Its Implications for Australian Wilderness Preservation Policy," Biological Conservation 32 (1985), pp. 311-313.

5. See Sec. 2(c) of 16 U.S.C. 1131-1136 (1965); reprinted and discussed in Michael McCloskey, "The Wilderness Act of 1964: Its Background and Meaning," 45 Oregon Law Review 288 (1966).

6. Ibid.

7. Miklos D.F. Udvardy, *A Classification of the Bio-geographical Provinces of the World* (Morges, IUCN Occasional Paper 18, 1975).

8. For a convenient tabulation of this data, see Table 21.2 in *World Resources* (Washington, D.C., World Resources Institute, 1987).

9. For a discussion of the indications of data on human culture shown on these maps, see U.S. Defense Mapping Agency, *Product Specifications for Jet Navigation Charts* (1980), Chapter 1 Sec. 700.

10. See, e.g., Robert B. Ekvall, *Fields on the Hoof: Nexus of Tibetan Nomadic Pastoralism* (New York: Holt, Rinehart and Winston, 1968), Chapters 1 and 2.

11. For a discussion of these changes, see Pierre Bonte, "Ecological and Economic Factors in the Determination of Pastoral Specialization," in *Change and Development in Nomadic and Pastoral Societies,* ed. by John G. Galaty and Philip Carl-Salzman (Leiden, E.J. Brill, 1981), p. 33.

THE GEMS/GRID TOOLBOX

H. Croze and M.D. Gwynne

It was the dramatic views from spacecraft which showed for the first time the planet as a whole, floating in the emptiness of space, that finally brought home to most people the realization that our earth is a single entity—an entity in which all the elements are interconnected and what happens in one area can have consequences in others. Prior to these pictures the concept of the global whole was held by relatively few—mainly concerned scientists and environmentalists. At the time of the UN Conference on the Human Environment in 1972—which established the United Nations Environment Programme (UNEP)—these few, farsighted people realized that we simply did not have enough information on the global environment and what was happening to it. They called, therefore, for the establishment of an Earthwatch Programme, which was to be the environmental assessment process of UNEP. At the heart of Earthwatch was to be GEMS—the Global Environment Monitoring System.

GEMS gathers data on the state and trends of the world environment and identifies, as far as possible, the causes of these, so that corrective counteractions can be taken. The information monitored, therefore, must be of good quality and of a nature that allows data from different areas and sources to be compared. Co-ordinated by a Programme Activity Centre in UNEP, GEMS works with and through international and national agencies and organizations. So far there are

GEMS activities of one sort or another in 142 different countries—all in cooperation with the governments of those countries.

There are in GEMS, to date, 22 global monitoring networks in the fields of pollution, climate and renewable natural resources. Mention of a few will give you the feel of the GEMS programme. Urban air contamination—dirty air in cities—is a world wide problem. GEMS-Air, run by UNEP and the World Health Organization, looks at the sulphur oxide and suspended particulate content of city air. GEMS-Water, again a joint UNEP/WHO network, is concerned with the water quality of rivers, lakes and aquifers. Carefully chosen representatives sites allow the global picture to be kept under review. In order to determine the background or baseline levels of contamination in an ecosystem, UNEP, UNESCO and the World Meteorological Organization run an integrated monitoring programme in very remote areas to determine the pollutant content of organisms and their environment. One such station is in the Torres del Paine area of extreme southern Chile. Global atmospheric contaminants are looked at through the UNEP/WHO Background Air Pollution Monitoring Network which has stations in very remote areas—such as the South Pole, Cape Grim in Tasmania, and Point Barrow in Alaska. These determine the lowest levels of atmospheric pollutant content. Against these results, measurements made of a global network of regional stations allow the local levels to be viewed relative to the basic levels for the planetary atmosphere near the ground.

In renewable natural resources, GEMS' concerns are with soils, forests and other constituent resources of the living world, including habitat and the state of rare and endangered species. As you will have realized, work with the latter is done through the International Union for Conservation of Nature and Natural Resources (IUCN) and the Conservation Monitoring Centre. The natural resources area of GEMS is most relevant to the work being conducted on the World Wilderness Inventory.

Wilderness and protected areas are now perceived to be a global, and no longer just a national, patrimony. This is why it is presumed possible to discuss from afar the possible management and potential fate of land areas in some 150 other countries. The presumption is justified by the mandate given to those organizations which were conceived and mandated by the world community, such as UNEP and IUCN. I sense, however, a persisting gap between the "internationalists" and the well-informed and sponsored NGOs on the one hand, and the actual owners of the land on the other. We must not lose sight of the essential need to close that gap, quickly, before the wilderness areas are put to other, perhaps less sustaining and sustainable uses.

But let us be optimistic and assume that our concern will find an ear with the national decision makers and that a mechanism can be found among the tangle of global economy which will allow the message to be taken to heart. As the *I Ching* says, "It is common for travellers on the same road never to meet."

If our plans for wilderness and protected areas are to be coherent and coordinated and, therefore, credible and effective, they must be based on common data sets and common data handling techniques so that data collected at one scale can be compared to and married with those collected at another. Most of our questions and concerns are about particular places on the earth's surface. Geographical location is the common denominator: all the areas have measurable characteristics—soil type, topography, a spectrum of plant and animal species, land use, an hydrology regime—all of which we can now capture, analyze and display using the toolbox of Geographical Information System (GIS) technology.

A GIS is a special set of computer hardware and software systems which is designed to deal with that which can be located on a map. One of the most powerful GIS functions is "overlaying," in which "layers" of geo-referenced data are superimposed to produce a picture and richness of information far greater than any of the data sets on their own. Deforestation, for example, is not just a question of trees. If we are to truly understand—and therefore, be able to alleviate the problem—we have to combine information on trees with data on soils, topography, climate, vegetation cover, land use and the like to produce a composite picture of the interaction of these factors which manifests itself in the symptoms of deforestation.

The need for such technology, as well as the need for environmental data in useful and usable forms, led us to establish GRID, the Global Resource Information Database, within the GEMS Programme at UNEP headquarters in Nairobi. GRID was established in a two-year pilot phase with generous donations from governments and private organizations of hardware, software, facilities and seconded professional staff. GRID is designed to be a distributed, networked system, and already there are three communicating nodes—GRID-Control in Nairobi, GRID-Processor in Geneva, and a technical support node at NASA's Earth Resources Laboratory in the southern United States. A regional node for southeast Asia in Bangkok is planned for early next year, and GRID nodes for other regions are under discussion.

GRID's main objectives are to provide data, to develop methodologies for handling global data sets, and to provide access to GRID's GIS technology. The three functional areas are data collation, data supply and technology transfer. The technology transfer task of GRID is especially important because GIS is quite new. Thus we have regular major training courses for Third World experts sponsored by the Swiss government. In this way, we hope to create a global-user community for GRID peopled by national practitioners and not just western experts.

The initial work of GRID has concentrated on two scales: global and continental, and national. A number of global data sets have been obtained, georeferenced and made available within GRID. Thus data sets are now available for: global elevation, which can be extracted in any subset and overlayed with any other geo-registered data on a global or continental scale; global ozone distribution and surface temperature of the earth's crust, which are also available for scientists to model global processes; and the FAO-UNESCO soils map of the world, which is now available in digital form as a basic data layer for small-scale studies of natural resource states and trends.

The beauty of the GIS is that it allows merging of resource data from many sources: maps, monitoring stations on the ground, or satellites. Thus, we have added a global vegetation index to the database, which shows the amount of green biomass present at any particular time.

While building a repository of global data in readily usable GIS form, we are at the same time providing help to developing countries with national-scale case studies to demonstrate GIS capabilities and provide training for national experts. For example, a comprehensive environmental database was constructed for the entire country of Uganda to examine, among other things, the erosion hazard. Thus, a model was developed by GRID using all available information from thematic maps of topography, climate, soils, land use and population pressure.

It was also possible to examine land-use change during the turbulent years in Uganda. Land use in 1964 was digitized into GRID from a map of the colonial period. From a mosaic of satellite images, land use in 1973 was derived, analyzed and interpreted by a team of Ugandan experts with firsthand knowledge of conditions on the ground. Then it was compared to a similar interpretation from 1986 data. In GRID's computers, the time periods were "subtracted" from one another to show change in land use during the period. It was possible to detect many areas of significant change. Many intensive agricultural areas have reverted to woodland for the most unfortunate and tragic of reasons.

The agricultural potential of Uganda was also analyzed for a wide range of crops, such as the major cash crop, *Robusta* coffee. GRID also allowed us to examine the potential consequences of global climate change, showing that the potential for *Robusta* would diminish should there be a climate warming.

The results of the Uganda national database (which took five months to construct) were presented to the prime minister of Uganda and his ministers, who immediately saw the potential of the GIS approach for resource management and land-use planning and requested that we assist them in establishing a national GIS capability.

A GIS thus allows us to merge data, model their interactions, and thereby provide a greater understanding of cause and effect. One can combine basic resource data sets for the entire continent—soils, topography, climate, number of rain days, wind speed, vegetation and so on, to attempt to point to areas at risk from desertification.

The model is, of course, preliminary and imperfect. The use of a computerized GIS means that we do not stick our necks out and produce a map of desertification, for example, which is an historical document as soon as it is printed. We invest instead in a process which, by its very nature, accommodates improvements in both the basic input data as well as the model rules themselves. In the case of desertification and soil degradation, UNEP is doing both at the moment with its agency partners.

GRID's philosophy is not to wait for perfect data because, if we wait, decisions will certainly be taken with no data at all. Thus, we obtain the best available, such as early vegetation maps of Africa which were first used in the desertification exercise. Then we explored with the world experts ways and means of improving the data set. We carefully qualify data sets, and caution users in their reliability and limitations.

Thus, GIS capabilities allow us to move from simple description to analyses: We not only need to know where things are, but how they interact to produce the symptoms we observe. We believe that the assessment and husbandry of wildlife, wild lands and protected areas require both the kinds of resource data and the GIS toolbox offered by GRID. We need to plan our campaign of deploying parks and protected areas against not only the current expanse of wilderness, but also against the realities of species distributions and ecological constraints as typified, for example, in a synthetic ecological classification such as that of Udvardy. There are many examples in Africa alone which can illustrate how overlying the data set of current protected areas with that of the habitat of a particular endangered species can show us a great deal.

Threatened animals, such as the Crested Mangabey, have a relatively restricted distribution confined to central African forest zones. It is evident, however, that this threatened species is little helped by current deployment of protected areas. The aardvark, or African antbear, though rarely seen because it is nocturnal, is widespread, albeit thinly, throughout Africa covering a wide range of habitat types and is well represented in many protected areas. The Namibian desert rose is highly restricted both spatially as well as ecologically. Fortunately, it appears to enjoy congruency with a large national park. *Embelia schimperi* is a medicinal shrub used by local herders for deworming themselves and their stock: It is localized but widespread, and it occurs over a range of arid zones, but is not particularly well represented within protected areas. Such information would help us plan a campaign for preserving this particular genetic resource.

It is also possible to zoom in on particular parts of GRID's African database for more detailed analysis of IUCN data. For example, the protected areas of east Africa can be overlaid on Udvardy zones and a good ecological distribution can be seen. Focusing on Tanzania, we can ask the computer to pull out these areas— the Serengeti, Mkomazi and the Selous—and then look at their potential protective effect on the distribution of seven endangered bird species provided to us by the Conservation Monitoring Centre. It would be apparent that those particular species do not derive much benefit from the protected areas.

Recently, GRID helped direct the search for an endangered tree species. The world's musicians may be running out of the basic ingredients for woodwind, the heartwood of the *Mpingo (Dalbergia melanoxylon)*. Before starting a search of all of central Africa, experts visited GRID-Control in Nairobi and outlined the *Mpingo's* requirements in terms of soil type, vegetation zone, and rainfall. The result was a "road map" of where most profitably to begin the search in Tanzania for potential in situ remnants of this very special genetic and cultural resource.

Finally, GRID has a potential for even more complex conservation modelling. For several decades, individuals and organizations have been compiling information on the distribution of the African elephant. The extent of elephant range is now quite well known, and the data on range were recently updated and reviewed by the African Elephant and Rhino Specialist Group at Nyeri, Kenya in May 1987. Current data concerning elephant numbers are less comprehensive than range data. Although numerous aerial surveys, ground counts and other estimates have been made, there remain many areas for which elephant numbers are unknown. This lack of information hampers the ability of planners to manage and conserve the species.

In conjunction with World Wildlife Fund and the Elsa Wild Animal Appeal, GEMS has attempted to fill in missing information by using the analytical powers of GRID. First, the existing estimates of elephant populations were combined with other datasets in order to perform analyses to determine the relationship between elephant density and factors such as human population density, effectiveness of protection, GNP and vegetation type. A model was developed from which elephant densities were extrapolated for the section of range which were lacking in estimates.

In the course of the analyses, effective protection emerged as the factor with the highest correlation to elephant density. This suggests that increased protection could play an important role in the conservation of elephants. We therefore updated IUCN's latest protected areas map for the continent with national-scale maps to produce a detailed picture of the continent's protected areas with a categorization of effectiveness: from one (very good) to four (virtually nil).

Finally, we combined these data on protected areas with the data on elephant distribution. By examining the results, one can determine which sections of elephant range are not well protected and plan conservation management strategy accordingly. These data were, in addition, presented to the last meeting of CITES as a basis for the establishment of realistic elephant quotas.

Everyone in the conservation community is reaching for common goals— let us work together to achieve them. We in UNEP in Nairobi watch with concern our own east African back garden, where at least half a dozen conservation bodies trip over each other while doing more or less the same thing. The examples of application of GRID technology demonstrate how cooperation can occur and help break down sectorial barriers toward a common end. Eventually, perhaps we will all share a common resource data heritage and talk to each other more often, if only through our networked computer terminals.

As a gesture toward continued, increasing cooperation and integration, UNEP will make a concrete offer. We are prepared to make both GRID data and the GRID toolbox available to the conservation community. Provide your data and experts and let them come and work on an existing system to do the necessary analyses leading to comprehensive and workable conservation campaigns.

ACHIEVING A WORLD NETWORK OF PROTECTED AREAS

Kenton Miller

Wild lands are protected for a variety of reasons. In some countries the main concern is to maintain natural scenery, sites of grandeur and places for outdoor recreation and education, while in others the protection of watersheds, marine fisheries and habitats for endangered species are paramount. These differing goals vary with the needs of conservation and the requirements perceived by people. The connection between protected areas and the needs of local peoples has become increasingly important, particularly in developing countries.

In recent years, science and resource management have shown that underlying these considerations are fundamental biological concerns which require careful consideration. Maintaining maximum biological diversity, for example, and ensuring future access to plant and animal genetic materials of value for medicines, food crop development and industrial chemicals are two such considerations.

These and similar concerns have led conservation managers to ask ever more complex questions as they select and plan national parks and other reserves: How many areas, of what size, are needed to ensure that as many plant and animal species as possible are retained into the twenty-first century and beyond? Can areas bear various kinds of uses and still retain their diverse species?

In dealing with these complex questions, conservation scientists and managers have realized that, in order to achieve the conservation of nature, various kinds of reserves need to be established, which provide different types of management and a sufficient habitat for the long-term survival of our natural heritage. Achieving conservation goals through protected areas requires careful and professional planning, international cooperation and coordination with surrounding development within the ecosystem and adjacent land and water uses.

The International Union for the Conservation of Nature and Natural Resources (IUCN) was established as a non-governmental organization (NGO) in 1948 to deal with these and other conservation challenges. In 1959 the Economic and Social Council of the United Nations (ECOSOC) mandated IUCN to monitor the status and trends of the world's national parks and other types of reserves. In response, the Commission on National Parks and Protected Areas (CNPPA) was established. In the early years, all data collection and analyses were done by hand by such pioneers as Jean-Paul Harroy and Fred Packard. As technology became available, IUCN established its Conservation Monitoring Centre in the United Kingdom, with a specialized Protected Areas Data Unit (PADU).

In 1980, in partnership with UNEP and WWF, IUCN launched the *World Conservation Strategy.* UNESCO and FAO were important collaborators in the long process of consultation. This landmark document was prepared by world-wide participation of scientific experts, political leaders, resource managers and citizen conservation groups from all continents. It provides the policy framework for a strategic perception of reality whereby "there will be no conservation without sustainable development, and development cannot become sustainable without conservation." Working within this global framework, IUCN and its partners have found the following approach helpful in achieving the worldwide network of protected areas:

• *A network of professional managers,* scientists and conservation supporters provides the expertise and the synergy required to study and prescribe needed action;
• *A data management center* gathers, organizes and publishes information on the status and trends of protected areas, and highlights problems warranting international attention;
• *Regional working sessions* of the network are held on a regular schedule, in all parts of the world, to analyze the status of protected areas, the challenges facing managers in achieving their goals and to assist their search for solutions to local problems. These sessions are backed by extensive field work and site visits;
• *Strategies for action* are prepared which outline the activities required to achieve the global network of protected areas, guiding investments toward sites of highest priority for maintaining maximum biological diversity and other conservation goals;
• *Cooperation* is established with partner organizations to design programmes and projects, seek funding and support actual tangible implementation. This usually includes joint efforts with banks, industry, various levels of government, NGOs, funds and foundations, development aid agencies, private landowners and resource user groups;
• *Integration* with other actors and sectors involved is essential. The National Conservation Strategy enables resource managers to work with lawyers, economists, scientists, agronomists, foresters and political leaders to formulate a strategic plan for conservation and development. This normally includes activities in education and training and linkages with ongoing international programmes and conventions.

No one organization could begin to implement this approach alone. For IUCN this depends upon the cooperation of UNEP, WWF, UNESCO, FAO, the 590-member governmental and non-governmental organizations including the U.S. Park, Forest, and Fish and Wildlife Services, NOAA, Environment Canada and over 3,000 volunteer professionals from around the world.

Since the Yellowstone National Park was established in 1872, the global system of protected areas has increased to over 3,500 areas covering 425 million hectares, an area larger in size than the whole Indian subcontinent. Information on these areas and the species they contain is managed by IUCN's Conservation Monitoring Center, which publishes the United Nations List of National Parks and Protected Areas and the Red Data Book Series.

Most countries in the world have some form of protected-areas system. One can best assess how well these established systems protect biological diversity by looking at their distribution within each country and by assessing coverage within each biogeographical province or region. Within the world's protected-area system, particular significance is attached to those areas which, although set up nationally, are given a degree of recognition under an international convention or through their participation in an international programme. Ninety-six countries are now party to the World Heritage Convention, and within these countries 70 natural sites have been inscribed on the World Heritage List. Forty countries have acceded to the Convention on Wetlands of International Importance, listing some 350 sites amounting to well over 10 million hectares. Seventy nations have set up 266 biosphere reserves under UNESCO's Man and Biosphere Programme.

The rate of growth of the protected area network is encouraging, particularly over the past 25 years in many developing countries. But, based upon principles from the science of conservation biology, there are serious concerns over inadequate size of many individual areas. Conservation of biological diversity and preservation of wilderness values rely upon the establishment of relatively large areas. Currently the vast majority of established areas are less than 100,000 hectares in size. At the other end of the spectrum there are more than 30 areas greater than two million hectares in size, including the immense North East Greenland Park and Australia's Great Barrier Reef.

Within the last few years, IUCN and UNEP have assessed the protected-areas systems in three of the four major tropical regions: Africa, Indo-Malaysia, and Oceania. Africa provides a good case study.

Today there exist some 88 million hectares of land in 426 protected areas in sub-Saharan Africa. This is an area equivalent in size to California, Oregon and Washington combined and equal to the total amount of land under protection in Canada and the USA. Of these, 174 are national parks or equivalent reserves.

Virtually every country in Africa has established parks and reserves, with the result that fully 4 percent of the biogeographic region is devoted to nature protection. Scientific documentation of all these reserves is contained in IUCN's recently completed Directory of Afro-tropical Protected Areas.

The growth of Africa's system of protected areas began in 1885 with the establishment of the Umfolozi and St. Lucia Game Reserves. Since the end of the colonial era in the early 1960s, African governments have effectively doubled the number of areas that have been established. Although the majority of Africa's protected areas are less than 100,000 ha in size, there are 20 areas over one million, with eight exceeding two million ha. The single largest national park is Salonga in Zaire, which is roughly four times the size of Yellowstone National Park.

IUCN and UNEP have recently completed a four-year continent-wide assessment of the system of protected areas in Africa. Conservation biology principles were used to answer three basic questions:

- What are the most important areas in Africa according to biological diversity criteria?
- How well do existing protected areas cover the full range of Africa's diverse natural heritage?
- Where are the underrepresented bio-units and the gaps in the system?

In other words, all protected areas in Africa were rated as to their importance to conservation on strictly biological grounds. Among the areas that stand out are:

- The Salonga National Park and World Heritage Site in Zaire, Africa's largest national park;
- The Tai National Park of the Ivory Coast, also a World Heritage Site and the last remnant forest of its type;
- The Virunga Volcanoes in Zaire, Uganda and Rwanda;
- The Bale Mountains National Park in Ethiopia;
- The proposed Ras Tenewi Coastal Park in Kenya.

There is still much to do. Of Africa's 17 bio-units, only four are regarded as having sufficient area under protection. At the other extreme, four others stand out as needing a much greater conservation effort. These units, which lack sufficient area under protection, are some of the most biologically rich in all of Africa and also are sites with high species conservation programmes to date.

Despite Africa's impressive record in establishing 88 million hectares of land for conservation, we also recognize that the stewardship and security of the existing estate is increasingly beset by a variety of threats. Within the context of the World Charter for Nature and the World Heritage Convention, IUCN annually compiles a register of Threatened Protected Areas of the World. This list, supported as well by UNEP, now numbers 76 sites, 24 of them in Africa.

The case of Sudan's Dinder National Park illustrates the problem. This park, established in 1936, has suffered a gradual loss of biological diversity caused by five interrelated pressures:

- Loss of access to wet season habitat by migratory species. Much of this area has been turned over to settlement and agriculture.
- Poaching in the park and heavy hunting pressure in the adjacent area have resulted in the loss of at least five major species in the past 20 years. Even giraffes have been eliminated, and the large herds of gazelle have now disappeared with only scattered individuals remaining.
- Heavy domestic stock grazing in the park has resulted in competition, loss of

cover, introduction of diseases, excessive trampling and soil erosion. Regular, uncontrolled wildfires set by local people exacerbate the problem.
• Surrounding land-use pressures on the park have built up over the years. The park now stands as a desertified island in the middle of a degraded landscape dominated by subsistence use.
• Despite early advisory reports of FAO wildlife experts and others, there has been no commitment to implementing a management regime in the park. Fundamental park facilities such as boundary markers are not in place. Patrols are rarely carried out, there are no extension programmes to gain support of local people and almost no tourism.

Although every park has its management problems, Dinder's are so severe that its very viability as a conservation area is being lost and its existence in the twenty-first century is in doubt.

The root causes of the threats to Africa's protected areas, such as Dinder in Sudan, are imbedded in historical, social, environmental, economic and political factors. Corrective actions that are required are outlined in the *Action Strategy for Protected Areas in the African Realm.* This document, prepared over the course of several years at the working sessions of IUCN's Commission on National Parks and Protected Areas, is a bottom-up assessment of what needs to be done to ensure more adequate coverage and more effective management of Africa's protected areas. Some 244 specific recommendations are made for the 45 countries involved. The document stresses that it is the human dimension in conservation planning which requires the greatest thrust in years to come as rural populations of Africa intensify their dependence on wild living resources.

Effective management needs to be consciously designed and implemented to provide people with the benefits for which the protected area was established. Implementation implies that the application of our concepts and principles in the field is dependent on a supportive public and a trained and committed cadre of staff, such as those trained at the College of African Wildlife Management. The complexity of the task and the full range of talents involved were reviewed at the Third World Congress on National Parks, held in Bali, Indonesia in 1982 and published in basic reference manuals on management of protected areas in both terrestrial and marine environments. These are practical how-to manuals that outline experience from park and reserve managers worldwide.

Many organizations are implementing conservation field projects in Africa. One specific example in Tanzania's Ngorongoro/Serengeti region is noteworthy. Here, assistance from Norway's bilateral aid and the World Heritage Fund is being used to help the Ministry of Natural Resources to strengthen management not only of the national park, but also of the surrounding controlled hunting areas and pastoral buffer zone. Initially a workshop was held involving individual experts and government agencies concerned. A planning process is now under way. Training workshops are being held, relations with local people are being strengthened, and regional resource-use schemes including harvesting of wildlife and improving livestock and range management are being proposed. An overall aid package amounting to $6 million is now being sought to restore and retain this internationally important ecosystem.

This case study of Africa's protected areas illustrates four conservation programming needs:

• Database management on species and protected areas;
• Networking among experts in the region and through local and international cooperation;
• Preparation of plans and strategies, including the identification of opportunities for integrated regional development; and finally,
• The actual execution of projects designed and managed in cooperation with national governments to strengthen conservation activities on the front line.

Although one can make plans and develop activities which strengthen park systems or improve and support their management, this should be set within the context of the whole picture of conservation and development at the national level. Our experience shows that this can best be accomplished by preparing a National Conservation Strategy to ensure that both conservation and development are sustainable. This is the *World Conservation Strategy* in action.

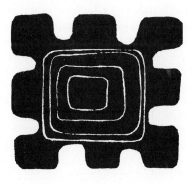

SCIENCE AND MANAGEMENT

THE NEW RESOURCES MANAGER

Walter J. Lusigi

It is just a little over a century since the first protected area was set aside at Yellowstone in the United States of America, marking the beginning of the present modern conservation movement. If the participants of that crucial campfire meeting who made the decision to set aside Yellowstone would, by some miracle, come back today, they would definitely be horrified at what we have made of the world since that time. As predicted by authors of *The Global 2000* report to the president of the United States in 1980, the world is presently more crowded, more polluted, less stable ecologically and more vulnerable to disruption than the world they lived in at that time. Despite greater material output, the world's peoples are poorer today. These clearly visible stresses of population, resources and the environment are a definite concern to conservationists, especially inasmuch as they were predicted for year 2000 and it is only 1987 now.

The biggest danger from the growth of the human population to the natural resource base does not result directly from the increased demand on the resources due to the numbers, but from the lack of understanding and sympathy of the greater part of the population to the cause of conservation. Conservation has remained the concern of a few despite the rising human population of the world. Those who were originally responsible for creating the system of protected areas like those in the United States were a few foresighted, unselfish and idealistic men and women who foresaw the national need and got the areas established and protected in one way or the other. They were, in fact, attempting to establish buffers against the greed and rapacity of their fellow citizens, fighting public inertia and selfish commercial interests at every step. Today the added population to the globe, which is more urbanized, either lacks the understanding for conservation, or is not the slightest concerned about the fate of man. Inasmuch as the democratic processes demand popular support for any resource conservation measures, those charged with responsibility of managing natural resources must make a bigger effort to bring about this understanding and sympathy.

The problem regarding the widening gap between conservationists and other resource managers could sometimes be blamed on the conservationists as much as the other parties. It is unfortunate that conservationists have, at times, been overprotective of natural resources. We have frequently interpreted too strongly the saying "wise use without abuse." We have sometimes forgotten that the values of many renewable resources can be enhanced by proper use. We have laid ourselves open to the claims of many that conservationists can be equated with preservationists. There is a need for a common ethic for all managers of land-based natural resources.

As a concept, conservation seems to be well accepted as a sound guideline for resource exploitation and use. But two major problems usually arise when attempting to implement the concept. First, there is a mistaken presumption that conservation represents a single philosophy or school of thought and action. On closer examination, profound differences in means and goals separate the many organizations and institutions bearing the conservation label. Second, with goals and objectives defined, there is no assurance that conservationists themselves perceive the same thing. This has been perhaps the biggest weakness of the conservation movement because different resource managers have been known to apply different management strategies for even the same piece of land. This has not only sometimes led to clashes between various conservation groups, but it has also led to confusion within the populations who are expected to take conservation advice.

In order to alleviate the above concerns, and in order to ensure effective conservation of our natural resources in the face of various pressures, I submit that there is an urgent need for the development of what could be referred to as the "New Resources Manager." It is unfortunate, but true, that although the complexity of the problems of natural resources use has been more appreciated in the last few decades, and the multidisciplinary approaches to the solution of these problems recognized, many approaches have still remained sectoral, falling within the traditional disciplines such as forestry, wildlife management, agriculture and fisheries. To overcome the complex, present-day problems in resource management, a new, more broadly based manager will have to emerge. There are major and key problems in resource management which will need to be addressed by the new resources manager, and numerous ways in which we can stimulate development of such a new function.

POPULATION PRESSURES ON NATURAL RESOURCES

Predictions about the state of the world in the short term—the next 20 years—are uniformly disquieting. By the year 2000, the projected growth in human population can be expected to create enormous economic and political pressure for making more productive use of the world's remaining "natural" ecosystems. However, because thus far the world has always been able to feed itself, and because more improved production practices and technology could expand food production even more, the concern of conservationists and those charged with the management of the world's natural resources should go much farther than human statistics, supply and demand. We should also be concerned with the level of understanding of the increased population and its sympathy for the conservation of our natural resources. Wherever there exists a human population, it is certain that there will exist also a complex of ethnic, biological and social influences which, unless they are understood and incorporated in resource management plans, will introduce an unpredictable element into a desired outcome.

I am convinced that the majority of people who are being added to the world's population today neither understand nor sympathize with conservation. Although the number of conservation organizations and their members has increased, the percentage has gone down in terms of the total population.

In the last five decades since the industrial revolution, the majority of the people, especially in the industrialized nations, have been largely concentrated in urban centers where their occupations are largely in the industrial, commercial and administrative sectors of the economy rather than in land-based resources. The attachment of these people to the land keeps becoming more and more remote. Those born and brought up in urban centers even have a fear of the natural environment—nature is supposed to be insecure and primitive. Indeed because of the petty crimes which take place in natural parks surrounding urban centers, the city dwellers have come almost to resent the wild. These populations, however, wield a lot of political and economic power. The natural resources manager must have full understanding of this group, its thinking, its structure and how it operates. This group must be made to understand the importance of natural resources in supporting life within the urban ecosystem— clean water and air. Although this group might never visit a national park or a natural area, if they have this broad understanding they will be able to vote in the right direction when it comes to important conservation decisions.

Most of the highest recorded population growth rates are in developing countries, or the so-called Third World. Although now there is a strong tendency toward urbanization and industrialization, most of the population in the Third World is rural-based and derives all or most of its livelihood from the land. Land-use practices in the Third World are also still largely traditional and mainly for subsistence. The large-scale commercial exploitation of natural resources is still relatively minimal and land use also fulfills cultural traditions which form the pillars of those societies. The Third World, however, has some of the most valuable natural resources in terms of both natural areas, minerals and, perhaps, oil. There is now growing opportunism from entrepreneurs from the developed world encouraging some wanton exploitation of these resources. There is also an increasing tendency, because of the bad state of most of the Third World economies, to overexploit certain resources in order to meet the increasing demand for food and other essential products for survival. Since most Third World countries are relatively desperate and have limited resource bases other than the land, they must develop the full potential of the land. But development must take the form most suited to the prevailing circumstances and the purposes to which an area is best adapted. The development of faunal resources is as important as the development of any organic natural resource and should be undertaken to the maximum extent consistent with its perpetuation. The natural surplus can be legitimately used and tourism can be instituted without detriment to the continuation of the resource.

The resource manager needs to be well acquainted with the various cultures in these areas and how they affect natural resource exploitation. He will have to learn to have certain tolerance and understanding of other viewpoints which might not necessarily be in agreement with his own. He has to develop an understanding of the constraints on resource exploitation in certain situations and have the capability to design alternatives that can improve resource exploitation without necessarily destroying it. It is only with improved land-use practices that recognize limitations of the land and the significance of the lives that depend on it that conservation will succeed and become a reality to millions of people.

There is further evidence of need for a new resources manager. The fact that most major world ecological systems are unstable or in some form of deterioration does seem to give clear evidence that present resource managers have had some shortcomings or that the management systems being implemented are not working.

Tropical forests are an example. What happens to tropical forests affects the whole ecological stability of the globe, yet decisions regarding their exploitation lie with individual states. This points out a new orientation needed by the resource manager. He must first understand the forces at work in the exploitation of tropical forests, including political, cultural and economic forces. He should be able to address himself to all of these concerns. Biologically, the resource managers should start addressing themselves to the problems of the restoration of stability. As most of the tropical forest ecosystems across the globe are in some form of instability, their restoration should take priority in all research and management.

What has been said about tropical forests is also true for temperate forests. Temperate forests have had the longest history of pressure from modern man through increased population growth and industrialization. Because of their structure and limited species diversity, they are fragile and vulnerable to many kinds of malpractice. Solutions which have been applied to the management of temperate forests have been largely sectoral. Either the forests are being managed for the sustained production of timber, or as a hunting reserve for a specific group, or as a water catchment, for example. In many instances these utilizations are not usually coordinated to realize that the forest is one whole ecological system. Individual states, especially in Europe, have also had different approaches to the management of their bit of the forest, although it is one continuous belt. The latest threat through acid rain has clearly pointed out the need for new thinking and the evolution of new strategies for the management of this ecological system.

The instability of river systems, lakes and oceans is also another factor of concern to the survival of man on this planet. Those charged with the management of these systems are realizing how limited they are in the face of clear signs of pollution, overexploitation of fish resources and threats through offshore drilling of oil and accompanying threats of spills—to mention only a few. Yet here again, one finds all kinds of managers who are preoccupied with their specific bits of the resource. For example, the marine specialist starts at the shore of the ocean when it is clear that part of his problem starts in the mountains where the river originates. Likewise, the river manager seems not to take note of the forester at the source of the river or the agriculturalist who is applying chemicals and eroding the land. The new manager should have a better overview of the entire functioning of the ecological system and be less biased toward resource managers. He can only do this if he thoroughly understands other land management concerns.

One other example, which demonstrates the need for new approaches, is the world's arid lands. The deterioration of the world's arid lands has been the subject of world concern in the last two decades largely because of the droughts which have led to the starvation and death of millions of people. As it has clearly been pointed out by experts in this area, drought alone is not to blame for this situation. The situation arises from the cumulative effects of long-term abuse and misuse of the resources of the arid lands which have completely destabilized these ecological systems. The challenge that confronts the arid lands resource manager is to restore human dignity that has been undermined through starvation and poverty and then to design land-use systems that would restore the stability of the land and balance resources use in this area in both the short and long term.

Finally in this regard, let me take a look at the threat to the world's fauna and flora. Experts estimate that we are now losing at least one species per day and that by the end of the 1980s we could be losing one species per hour. Another estimate suggests that, if present trends continue, at least 500,000 of the 3 million to 10 million species of animals and plants now present on earth will be extinguished during the next two decades. The major cause of these extinctions will be the disruption and degradation or destruction of natural habitats, particularly in the forested areas of the tropics. To have any chance of preempting such predictions, two main problems need to be tackled: first, that of providing a sound scientific basis for the planning and management of protected areas; and second, that of convincing land planners and resource users, particularly at the local level in developing countries, that conservation is not necessarily inimical to their daily social and economic needs.

These are but a few examples of the major ecological systems, the management of which must be thoroughly understood by the new resources manager. The list is long and includes concerns for the ozone layer and nuclear winter, the Arctic and the Antarctic, all of which have a bearing on the ecological stability of the planet.

ECONOMICS AND RESOURCE CONSERVATION

Modern society as we know it today is almost wholly run by various economic forces. This is an outgrowth of prevailing values of the Western world. The Western world is a human-oriented society, in which it is believed that reality exists only because humans can perceive it; that the cosmos is a structure erected to support the human race—its pinnacle—and that man exclusively is divine and has been given dominion over all things. Indeed since the Industrial Revolution, nature seems to have always presented a challenge which modern man has always tried to overcome. Development seems to be equated to overcoming nature and making man-made systems. But development is not bad per se. What causes concern to conservation is the waste that accompanies development. It is not until natural systems started giving in and human welfare was threatened that a few individuals started to see the necessity for conservation.

There is another aspect of economics as it affects conservation. Even in the wealthiest nations that have high conservation consciousness, not enough fiscal resources are devoted to conservation. Budget allocations to conservation are a drop in the sea compared to spending on things like defense. It is depressing that we never hear of environmental issues being on the top of the agenda when heads of the six most wealthy nations usually meet.

In the Third World the economic picture is grave and, in some instances, hopeless. As Jon Tinker of Earthscan said, "The African crisis can be summed up in two words: 'environmental bankruptcy.'" The term is useful because it stresses that the problem is caused by both environmental and economic factors, and that bankrupt environments can only lead to bankrupt nations. The somber reality is that the cancer of ecological collapse is eating away at nearly every country in sub-Saharan Africa.

What we are now seeing, from Ethiopia through Chad to the Atlantic and down to Mozambique and the Bantustans of South Africa, may well be the biggest disaster of our generation. There is probably no way of saving millions from a miserable death. It is increasingly clear that these deaths will be the direct result, predictable if not predicted, of foolish agricultural and environmental policies on the part of both African governments and of Western and international aid agencies. The seeds of environmental bankruptcy have been sown by government policies and watered by three decades of misdirected foreign aid.

The most obvious symptom of this failure is hunger and starvation. The ultimate failure of African development has been to convert the continent, in three short decades' independence, from a region which could by large feed itself into one that is increasingly dependent on grain imports, which ultimately come mainly from the United States.

This example of the African situation could with various exceptions apply to the greater part of the Third World. Its implication on conservation is obvious—that a poor man cannot conserve. It seems necessary that to even talk about conservation, one must start by developing means by which people can adequately feed themselves. The economies of these countries must be strengthened and only then can they develop realistic conservation policies.

The new resource manager has two challenges in this regard. First, to assist in developing realistic consumption and resource utilization patterns in the developed world while bringing about the necessary change in the economic yardsticks for measuring development. There is no reason why the new resource manager should not be a highly qualified economist or banker, but we must not be required by economic forces to quantify the unquantifiable in order to be recognized in a world dominated by powerful economies. Second, in the Third World the new resources manager should understand the root causes of poverty and help alleviate the present disparity. To do this he must assist in developing policies that will improve people's welfare through proper resource use. They should work with governments to set realistic targets for economic growth and acknowledge countries that have to base their development on agriculture alone will never be able to develop in quite the same way as the Western world.

POLITICS AND RESOURCE CONSERVATION

All final decisions with regard to the implementation of resource management policies lie with the legislative authorities of individual nations. These legislative authorities are usually composed of politicians. There are two objectives toward which a resources manager should work: to make the politicians and the political process more understanding and sympathetic to conservation, and to be involved in that process themselves by being politicians.

Many times resource managers have considered the political process to be something almost out of their control. They have many times preferred to withdraw to the rural communities and enjoy the protected areas "while they last." It is almost a defeatist attitude. Rather, they should see that it is quite possible, with the right training and attitude, for resource managers to participate actively in the political process. Only then can we be sure that conservation is appropriately taken care of in decision making.

In the Third World, one cannot be so optimistic since stable political systems have not yet quite evolved. In Africa, for example, the wave of independence was followed by a bewildering wave of violence, manifested in coup d'etats, secession and tribal clashes, which swept across the continent from east to west. The past three decades have been characterized by ever-changing policies and political systems, and this trend is still going on today. These political upheavals are taking their own toll on the protected areas and on efforts to enforce a realistic conservation policy. Amid warring factions, wildlife has of necessity often been the only source of food for hungry soldiers. And wildlife and other valuable resources from protected areas have often been made to supply the quick gains needed by the ones who emerge as the temporary winners in these struggles. It is a simple fact that a civil war undermines resource conservation and food production.

It is impossible to say when the situation will stabilize, but conservationists should not only hope for the best but also prepare for the worst. Resource managers should, therefore, try to develop policies that can maintain the wholeness of protected areas against this background. As mentioned earlier, it seems to me that the only hope is for the conservationists to turn their attention to the rural populations that live around protected areas. If such populations can be brought to realize the benefit of these protected areas, they will be able to hold them against any army.

INTERNATIONAL COOPERATION IN CONSERVATION

"In the 5,000 days between now and the end of this century, over a billion people will be added to the planet. During the next century another two to seven billion people could be added before the size of the human family stabilizes at somewhere between eight and 13 billion people. Thus we and our children must plan to squeeze perhaps two new human worlds into only one Earth. We must plan to support them with the same ecosystems from which we today draw our food, fish, energy, wood products, minerals and other materials." This message is from the authors of *Only One Earth* from which I would like to view this section. It is also the message that is given to us by the Brundtland Report, *Our Common Future*.

With the increase in the world population and improved communication, the world is much smaller than it ever was before. One can fly from Africa to Colorado on the Concord in just four hours. We can communicate by telex, photo copying, electronic mail and telephone directly to any part of the world. Decisions made in New York on resources use can be implemented in Indonesia thousands of kilometers away at the same time. The approach to international cooperation in the field of conservation should be based on the principle that the unique resources we are seeking to conserve, although they are contained within the national boundaries, are of significance to mankind as a whole. Furthermore, the distribution of strategic resources is not equal. There are some states that are more endowed with resources than others. This calls for a concerted spirit of sharing—experiences, expertise and resources—and for helping each other in every way to conserve the resource base for human survival.

Faced with financial problems and bare survival, it is unlikely that conservation will be a priority for many countries of the Third World. It is unfortunate but true that many Third World nations will not afford the bill for conservation when their foreign debt keeps rising and amount of aid escalates. The report of the independent commission on international humanitarian issues on famine in Africa, 1985, indicates that in sub-Saharan Africa as a whole, official annual aid per person amounted to $18 a year in 1982. In the low-income, semiarid countries, aid has, since the famine in the mid-1970s, reached more than $44 per person. In south Asia, aid amounts to only $4.80 per person. In Africa, aid finances from 10 percent of gross domestic investment up to 80 percent for low-income, semi-arid countries. Between 1973 and 1982 sub-Saharan Africa's debt increased fivefold. In the two years 1980-82 following the oil price increases and a slump in world trade, Africa borrowed heavily to maintain its level of imports of essential goods. Public-debt service payments amounted to $9.9 billion in 1984 and are expected to rise to $11.6 billion this year. It's against this grim picture that we must look at cooperation in conservation, since despite this these countries still harbour some of the world's most strategic resources, for example tropical forests and wildlife. Can the countries of South America afford to protect the Amazon Forest, or Zaire the Congo Forest or Tanzania the Serengeti? Yet if these areas are destroyed, is it these countries only that will lose or suffer?

As the authors of *Only One Earth* put it, "The problems we face as a world community are planetary, but not insoluble. Our two greatest resources, land and people, can still redeem the promise of development. If we take care of nature, nature will take of us. But the huge changes sweeping over us and our biospheres demand fundamental changes in our attitudes, our policies and in the way we run our societies."

For the past 20 years the world community has perceived periodically a need for long-term analysis of problems relating to natural resources, population or the environment. For the most part responses have come too late when faced with a crisis like drought and flood. The result is that too many organizations have been created to deal with each individual crisis while there has been insufficient recognition of the interrelationship within the environmental crisis. Also, most of the responses have been national, whereas the harmful effects of population growth, resource consumption and pollution spread across borders and oceans. These are the challenges that confront the new manager. He must have a broad understanding that encompasses all these problems and help work out realistic solutions to them. A comprehensive reform of international economic relationships is essential and environmental crisis must form a new basis for cooperation among nations for their survival. This may require powerful institutions with adequate resources and political backing to do the job.

THE NEW RESOURCE MANAGER

Although we have realized the complexity of the problem and the need for a multidisciplinary approach, in practice we have been reluctant to depart from the conventional or traditional disciplines like forestry, outdoor recreation, soil schemes, agriculture and geology. Whenever a new threat to a resource has developed, we quickly adjusted to that need by developing a course in the existing disciplines or an altogether new course dealing with that specific threat, but within existing institutions. We have been reluctant to think of a new institution that would be based on a completely revised thinking on the whole problem of the deterioration of natural resources. This perpetuates the continued segmentation, and each discipline jealously guarding its territory to the extent of being hostile to other disciplines.

Conservationists have tried to solve the problem of natural resource deterioration with professionals who are very competent in their own biological fields, but largely weak in the broader realities of how society functions. The new resources manager should be a broadly educated person with equal emphasis in social as well as biological sciences. Of increasing importance, the new resources managers will have to be shrewd economists and politicians. They should be able to develop economic models and make legislation that they themselves can see and sponsor through to the end. They must be able to lobby in legislative chambers and corridors.

The present conservation efforts have succeeded in delineating various tracts of land, which have been put into some form of protection or the other. What is needed now is how to manage these lands considering the realities of the present state of the world. There is no place in the present world for resources which are not properly managed. If this cannot be done for the areas under protection, it is simply only a matter of time before other interests could exceed the value of the resource. We would then stand the danger of losing these resources. Present resource managers have been too shy and have locked themselves within the boundaries of the protected areas and thrown the blame at others. The new resource manager will have to be more outward looking and lay emphasis on managing the whole region where the resource is situated. This will mean dealing with people of all walks of life as well as other resource managers and new resource management strategies being implemented at the regional level.

In the past decades, we have addressed ourselves to various threats to the natural resources base by creating new organizations to address specific threats. Because of the number of organizations involved, it has been difficult to gather resources to support the organizations. The result has been the existence of thousands of organizations which have virtually been weak and ineffective. The new resource manager will have to help reorganize the existing institutions which will make a visible impact in solving the resource management problems that confront us today and help design new strategies to mobilize more resources for conservation.

We must look at the world as one. The new resource manager should have a thorough understanding of other cultures and people, resource-use strategies in other cultures and how to exchange good ideas on resource management between cultures. The problems confronting the Third World will need a special understanding by the new resources manager and he should assist in designing strategies to reverse the downward trend and reduce suffering in those areas.

It is doubtful that the new resource manager can come out of existing institutions, although many could claim to be doing exactly just this. The biases which also presently exist in these institutions for various approaches, and the identities which have been developed, prevent the development of such a discipline which will be acceptable to all concerned. A new postgraduate institute is needed, one which would accept students who do not necessarily have a biology bias but have a good first degree in any discipline. The only other qualification should be a commitment to the cause of natural resources conservation. The program should, therefore, be organized to produce resource managers who can be plugged into various institutions—finance, administration, business, etc., according to the original bias of the first degree. The most important thing is that they will be resource managers wherever they are. You do not necessarily have to be sitting or standing on a specific resource to be a resource manager.

Last but not least, the solution to the crisis confronting the world's natural resources today needs to be treated as an emergency. We cannot afford to lose any more time in debate. We know where the problems lie and we have seen what can happen if we don't act, so let us act now.

THE RAMSAR CONVENTION AND WETLAND PROTECTION

George Archibald

Wetlands are often thought of as wastelands, habitats for mosquitoes, crocodiles, and schistosomiasis. They are difficult to traverse. And, to most people, they are out of sight, out of mind and destined for development. This is particularly true in temperate climates where, once a wetland is drained, its rich soil provides excellent agricultural land, minus the mosquitoes. Consequently, wetlands have been ruthlessly destroyed and their merits largely unknown and ignored. It is estimated that one-half or more of earth's wetlands have been lost to date and that most of the destruction has taken place in this century. In the USA for example, 50 percent of the wetlands in colonial times have disappeared between the mid-1950s and mid-1970s. In the USA, 200,000 hectares of wetland are lost each year and 87 percent of this loss can be attributed to agricultural development.

But, wetlands are important. They provided the biological soup from which the first vertebrates moved to dry ground. In temperate zones, wetlands support the greatest biological diversity and productivity. Some wetlands can produce up to eight times as much plant material as an average wheat field of equal size.

There are many types of wetlands with a diversity of functions. Fresh water wetlands help prevent floods as well as maintain streams. They act like enormous sponges absorbing water in seasons of high rainfall and melt. In periods of drought, the wetland's stored water is slowly released. Wetlands are also enormous filters acting as cleansers transforming turbid and polluted runoff into clear, clean water. Coastal salt marshes are huge nurseries where two-thirds of the world's fish are harvested. They subdue wave action, minimize erosion and protect inland regions during storms. Wetlands are also home to a wide variety of colorful aquatic birds that have inspired and fed mankind since times untold.

If one individual might be selected as the father of wetland conservation, it would have to be Sir Peter Scott. Fascinated since childhood by the waterfowl of his native Great Britain, Sir Peter maintained a private collection of free-flying, semi-captive ducks, geese and swans at his country home near an estuary where large numbers of wild waterfowl spent the winter. His collection of birds and his passion for wild animals and wild places were the ingredients that led to the founding of the Wildfowl Trust at Slimbridge.

After World War II, hunters and other conservationists in western Europe were concerned about the welfare of waterfowl. It was this concern that led to the founding of the International Waterfowl and Wetlands Research Bureau (IWRB). Its first director was Dr. Edward Hindle of the London Natural History Museum. From 1962 to 1969, its headquarters were in Camargue, France, where Dr. Luc Hoffmann was director. In 1969 when professor Geoffrey Matthews became director, IWRB headquarters moved to Slimbridge.

Still headquartered at Slimbridge, IWRB is the leading organization for wetland conservation. Supported by grants from member nations and private organizations, particularly the World Wildlife Fund (WWF), IWRB's small but industrious staff coordinates waterfowl research and helps stimulate wetland conservation in many nations. It is an international, non-government body that encourages annual waterfowl counts, draws up inventories of wetlands of international importance, and convenes meetings of its members—often at a location where there are pressing conservation problems. It supervises and encourages the activities of 14 research groups, each of which specializes in a particular type of wetland bird family or problem.

Although many nations collaborated closely with IWRB, there remained a need for a formal intergovernmental agreement, a convention that these nations might adhere to in advancing the conservation of wetlands. There had never been an international conservation convention, however, and some parties were skeptical that such a convention be restricted to just one type of habitat—wetlands. Realizing the importance of international cooperation in the conservation of migratory birds and the vulnerability of wetlands, the International Council for the Conservation of Nature (IUCN), and the International Council for Bird Preservation (ICBP) joined forces with IWRB and cosponsored meetings of governmental delegates in France (1962), Scotland (1963), Netherlands (1966) and USSR (1968) to draft an agreement for wetland conservation. Their nine years of labor, masterminded by IWRB Director Professor Geoffery Matthews, resulted in an historic meeting in the city of Ramsar, Iran in 1971. Delegates from 18 nations advanced a document known as the Ramsar Convention, or the Convention on Wetlands of International Importance, especially as waterfowl habitat.

A wetland was defined as areas of arch, fen, peatland or water, whether natural or artificial, permanent or temporary, with water that is static or flowing, fresh, brackish or salt, including areas of marine water the depth of which at low tides do not exceed six meters. The convention further recommended that nature reserves be established for important wetlands in signatory nations and that these wetlands be wardened to assure their preservation and the welfare of the waterfowl. The convention was careful not to infringe upon the sovereign rights of member states. To join the convention would be a declaration of intent which involves a strong moral obligation to wetland conservation.

In 1971, the documents of the Ramsar Convention were deposited with the United Nations Economic, Scientific and Cultural Organization (UNESCO). IUCN became responsible for "continuing bureau functions" (i.e., secretariat duties) under the Convention and IWRB, the scientific advisor. IUCN's Conservation Monitoring Center in England maintained the List of Wetlands of International Importance. In 1975, the Ramsar Convention was officially accepted by seven nations and it became a legal entity, the first of its kind to address the conservation of a single type of habitat. From the start, the Ramsar Convention has been administered on a shoestring budget. The Ramsar List of Wetlands grew as member nations developed a new interest in wetlands and as more nations were encouraged to join the convention. Budget constraints, however, limited the productivity of the convention.

The first official conference of governments belonging to the Ramsar Convention was at Cagliari, Italy in 1980. The topics discussed included conservation measures taken at sites designated for the List, and the conference established criteria to guide member states in what constitutes a wetland of international importance. Criteria based on unique or representative wetlands and on the general importance of wetlands to fauna and flora were supplemented with quantitative criteria related to waterfowl and were agreed upon. Waterfowl were considered as "indicators" of wetlands. On the northern continents, most waterfowl migrate and require a series of wetlands between their breeding and wintering habitats. The Ramsar Convention encouraged member states to protect their links in those chains. These wetland areas to be added to the Ramsar List should have at least one percent of the population of a migrating waterfowl species that uses that wetland.

The Cagliari conference also addressed the need to amend the text of the Convention. The 1984 conference, held in Groningen, Netherlands, once again reviewed the status of listed Ramsar sites and established a task force to advise on a secretariat, a budget and a standing committee. At the latest round of meetings in Regina, Canada in May/June 1987, a further Extraordinary Conference adopted amendments to the Convention Text which allow a budget to be established, while the third ordinary meeting approved the level of the budget and set up a permanent bureau (or secretariat and a Standing Committee). It is proposed that member nations would provide an annual budget of U.S. $400,000 with developing countries paying as little as $41. For the first time since its inception, the Ramsar Convention now has stable funding and a formal secretariat with two sections, one attached to IUCN headquarters in Switzerland and one at IWRB headquarters in Slimbridge. Today 45 nations are party to the Ramsar Convention, and 380 wetland sites are listed, thereby assuring a safer future for some 27 million hectares of wetland, an area the size of New Zealand, or larger than the whole of U.K.

All sites initially listed are still listed. Being included on the list helped thwart development plans for wetlands in Italy and Great Britain and curbed commercial fishing at a site in Pakistan. Unfortunately, one Ramsar site in Spain has been affected by drainage, 11 sites in Greece are seriously damaged and sites in four other western European nations are threatened. Some countries have listed sites that are already strictly protected, while others strive to expand wetland protection by listing sites that need better protection.

The Ramsar Convention had its birth in Western Europe and initially concerned itself with migratory waterfowl. Wetlands are worldwide, however, and there is a need to include more developing nations in the convention and to expand the criteria for identifying wetlands of international importance. Particularly in tropical regions, wetlands are the basis of the livelihood for millions of local people living near the water. Great flocks of migratory waterfowl may be entirely absent from these wetlands, and the local waterfowl are usually widely scattered in small groups. A major topic for discussion at the Regina meetings was the wise use of wetlands—the conservation of wetlands so that they will benefit both man and wildlife. We must promote wise use defined as "their sustainable utilization for the benefit of humankind in a way compatible with the maintenance of the natural properties of the ecosystem."

Joining the Ramsar Convention indicates national interest in and commitment to wetland conservation and international cooperation. Wetlands gain status as important regions that should be protected. Member nations benefit from the expertise and motivation of wetland researchers and conservationists from many nations. Issues that require the cooperation of several nations, challenges ranging from migratory waterfowl to watershed and waterways, can be addressed and perhaps resolved through the convention. Signatory nations are stimulated to make inventories of their wetlands and resources within the wetlands and then to take stronger steps to protect the wetlands. The Ramsar Convention is not expensive to join, and it has no authority over sovereign rights.

The secretariat of the Ramsar Convention soon hopes to be in a position to influence technical and financial assistance from developed nations and international aid agencies to help assure that environmentally damaging projects are curtailed. The Ramsar Convention has matured and is now able to help nations meet the challenges of wetland conservation. Every nation has much to gain by being party to this Convention.

GLOBAL CLIMATE CHANGE AND ITS EFFECTS ON WILD LANDS

Irving Mintzer

Modern industrial and agricultural activities release gaseous pollutants that are changing the composition and behavior of the atmosphere. The release of some of these chemicals into the atmosphere is affecting the earth's radiation budget. The continuing release of these pollutants represents a giant uncontrolled experiment that threatens to alter the climate of the planet.

If current trends continue for the next several decades, the atmospheric buildup of greenhouse gases is likely to change global climate more than any other event during the period of written human history. The changes in regional climates that result from this buildup will have profound implications for economic societies, for managed ecosystems, and in particular, for wild lands. The following discussion explores five basic questions about the buildup of greenhouse gases, its effect on global climate and implications for wild lands. The key questions are:

• How is the atmosphere being changed by human activity?
• How large are the changes that have occurred so far?
• How much additional change is already in the pipeline from activities?
• How much additional change is already in the pipeline from activities that have taken place within the last hundred years?
• What are the likely consequences of these changes?
• To what extent can policy choices made today affect the timing and the magnitude of the damages which result?

It is important to note that the greenhouse problem does not exist in isolation from other important international environmental issues. Much popular rhetoric would suggest that there is one atmosphere with an acid-rain problem today, and at some future time, perhaps in the lives of our grandchildren, there will be another atmosphere with an ozone-depletion problem and with regional climates altered by the greenhouse effect. Many would suggest that these air-pollution problems are unrelated to the more dramatic problems of tropical deforestation and species loss. This is both false and misleading.

In the last several years, the leaders of the international scientific community have come to recognize that there are strong and pervasive linkages between these important problems. The three atmospheric problems—global climate change due to the greenhouse effect, modification of the stratosphere due to ozone depletion, and the complex modifications of tropospheric chemistry that are commonly referred to as acid rain—are all linked at several important levels. Fig. 1 illustrates some of these linkages.

Figure 1

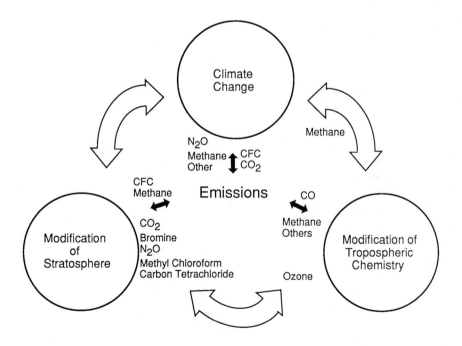

The three problems are linked at the level of emissions, since many of the same chemical pollutants participate concurrently in several of the effects. They are linked economically because the same industrial activities that produce the emissions contribute simultaneously to all three problems. They are linked politically because policy choices made today to try to relieve the pressures of any one set of effects will inevitably affect the others. In particular, the timing and severity of each of these problems will be strongly affected by the energy strategies chosen today and implemented over the next several decades. For example, efforts to limit the damages due to acid rain by putting sulfate scrubbers (i.e., flue gas desulfurization equipment) on power plant exhaust stacks will accelerate the rate of climate change and the rate of ozone depletion by increasing emissions of CO_2 and N_2O.

THE GREENHOUSE EFFECT

Fig. 2 illustrates the greenhouse effect schematically. Most of the light that comes in from the sun is in the visible part of the electromagnetic spectrum. A large portion of it is reflected back out into space but much of it is absorbed at the surface of the planet. In order to keep the earth from getting continuously hotter (and eventually melting), an equal amount of energy must be constantly reemitted into space in the form of infrared radiation. Certain chemicals, called "greenhouse gases," are transparent to incoming solar radiation, but absorb the long-wave, infrared radiation emitted from the earth's surface, warming the atmosphere.

Figure 2

EARTH'S TEMPERATURE IS RAISED BY EXISTING GREENHOUSE GASES

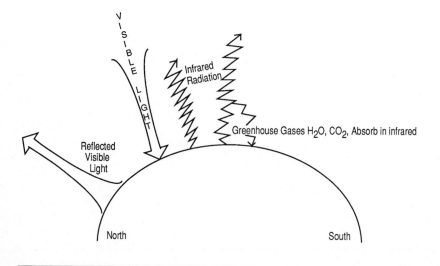

The greenhouse effect was not always a problem for human societies and natural ecosystems. In fact, it was one of the key phenomena in earth's history that permitted the evolution of familiar forms of life. Early in our planet's history, background concentrations of naturally occurring greenhouse gases, especially water vapor and carbon dioxide, absorbed some of the incoming solar energy and trapped it near the earth's atmosphere. This natural greenhouse effect caused the planet to be about 33° C warmer than it would otherwise have been.

Today, the average surface temperature of the planet is approximately 15° C. Without warming due to the natural background concentrations of greenhouse gasses, average global temperature would be minus 18° C. This difference has allowed water-based organic chemistry to evolve into a rich fabric of life.

THE HISTORIC BUILDUP OF GREENHOUSE GASES

In the last century, the greenhouse effect has been transformed from an important natural phenomenon into a global environmental problem. Steadily increasing concentrations of greenhouse gases in the atmosphere are altering the thermal emissions' spectrum of the planet. It represents the band of wavelengths through which infrared radiation can escape the earth's atmosphere, maintaining the earth's radiation balance with outer space and keeping the planet from melting. Industrial and agricultural activities are releasing increasing amounts of gases that absorb in this wavelength band. These gases are muddying up the window and causing more and more radiation to be trapped close to the earth's surface. If current trends continue, the increasing concentrations of greenhouse gases threaten to alter global climate more rapidly than economic societies or natural ecosystems can adapt to successfully.

Five families of gasses are principally responsible for covering up the atmospheric window. The compounds which have historically contributed the most to the risk of global climate change are: (1) the chlorofluorocarbons (CFCs), the halons (brominated relatives of the CFCs), methane (CH_4, commonly known as natural gas), nitrous oxide (N_2O, known in the U.S. as laughing gas) and carbon dioxide (CO_2). Each of the first four amplifies the warming due to CO_2 alone.

All five also affect the concentration and the distribution of ozone in the atmosphere. Figure 3 summarizes these linked affects. The chlorofluorocarbons, important industrial chemicals that do not occur naturally, contribute to the greenhouse effect while they reside in the troposphere and increase the rate of ozone depletion when they percolate up into the stratosphere. The Halons, a related family of man-made chemicals used principally in fire extinguishers, also contribute to global warming and accelerate ozone depletion. Similarly, increasing atmospheric concentration of N_2O warms the troposphere and depletes ozone from the stratosphere. Methane buildup, by contrast, counters some of the effects of stratospheric ozone depletion, although it does amplify the tropospheric warming. The steady buildup of CO_2 warms the troposphere, but ultimately because it causes the stratosphere to cool, reduces the rate of ozone depletion by slowing down the reactions that catalytically destroy ozone.

WARMING EFFECTS OF MAJOR COMPOUNDS

Compounds	Stratospheric Ozone	Global Temperature
Chlorofluorocarbons	Depletes	Increases
Halons (Bromine)	Depletes	Increases
Methane (CH_4)	Counter Depletions: Adds Ozone (Troposphere)	Increases
Nitrous Oxide (N_2O)	Depletes	Increases
Carbon Dioxide (CO_2)	Slows Depletion	Increases

Figure 3

Substantial emissions of these greenhouse gases have occurred during the industrial era. Measurements of air samples trapped in ice cores removed from glacial areas of Greenland and Canada indicate that the concentration of carbon dioxide in the atmosphere has increased by approximately 25 percent over the last century, from about 280 parts per million by volume (ppmv) in the pre-industrial period, to about 346 ppmv today. For the period since the International Geophysical Year (i.e., since 1958), substantially more accurate CO_2 concentration measurements are available. The carbon dioxide concentration of the atmosphere has been growing even more rapidly during this period, increasing by more than 10 percent in the last 30-year period.

Similar increases in atmospheric concentrations have been observed for the other principle greenhouse gases. Based again on ice core measurements, scientists now believe that the concentration of N_2O has risen about 10 percent since the beginning of the industrial era. Atmospheric concentration of methane remained stable for about 10,000 years, but it has increased by a factor of two in just the last 200 years. Recent changes in the concentration of methane in the atmosphere have followed an exponential growth curve with a rate of growth equal to about 1 percent per year. The change in the concentration of methane is a little bit more puzzling to the atmospheric science community than is the growth in other greenhouse gases. Although the sources of methane emissions are known, other factors resulting from human activity also affect its concentration. For example, automobiles, woodstoves, the burning of tropical forests and other activities emit carbon monoxide (C). These emissions reduce the ability of the atmosphere to cleanse itself by eliminating hydroxyl (OH) radicals, the natural cleansing agent that would otherwise combine with methane and remove it from the atmosphere.

Not all human activities contribute equally to the risks of global warming and ozone depletion. For example, although all fossil fuel combustion adds CO_2 to the atmosphere, not all combustion contributes equal amounts of CO_2. Table 1 illustrates the range of CO_2 emissions per unit of energy supplied for a range of commercial fuels. Natural gas releases about 14 million tons of carbon as CO_2 per exajoule or per quadrillion of heat supplied. By contrast, burning coal releases about twice as much CO_2 per unit of energy and burning synfuels derived from coal releases three to three and one-half times as much CO_2 as natural gas per unit of energy supplied.

Furthermore, the contribution to global warming of non-CO_2 chemicals also varies substantially. Some pioneering investigations conducted at the National Center for Atmospheric Research (NCAR) have explored the impact of a one part per billion by volume (ppbv) increase in the atmospheric concentration of many greenhouse gases. The work done at NCAR has demonstrated that the greenhouse problem is not a problem of CO_2 alone, and has revealed that almost half of the current contribution to future global warming is the result of emission of non-CO_2 trace gases. The NCAR analysis suggests that if current trends continue, the atmosphere will warm by about 1.5° to 4.5° C by the year 2030.

Although this sounds like a small and insignificant effect, it is, in fact, an absolutely unprecedented rate of change. An average global warming of just 2° C will take the earth beyond the range of anything that has been experienced in the last 10,000 years. It will thus take us outside the range for which human societies have any written record of how they adapted in the past. Such a warming will stress the ability of organisms and ecosystems to adapt and evolve rapidly. And it will certainly put great strains on wild lands and nature preserves. But even this level of warming is not the most extreme possibility.

THE EFFECT OF TODAY'S POLICIES ON
THE ATMOSPHERE OF TOMORROW

Recent research at the World Resources Institute has investigated the effect of various policy options on the rate and timing of future global warming. Four different policy scenarioswere considered, each supporting the same population and the same rates of regional economic growth. Two criteria are used to compare the effects of policies implemented in each scenario. The first criterion is the timing of commitment to a warming of 1.5° to 4.5° C, a warming equivalent to the effect of doubling the pre-industrial concentration of CO_2 with all other gas concentrations held at their pre-industrial levels. This is the benchmark that is used in the atmospheric science community as a common measure of climate change. The second criterion is the total commitment to future warming due to all projected emissions between the present and 2075.

The studies conducted at the World Resources Institute indicate that if current trends continue, the world will be committed to a warming of 1.5° to 4.5° C by 2030 and to a warming of about 3° to 9° C by 2075. On the other hand, in a high emissions scenario in which policies to expand the use of coal and the use of coal-based synfuels are implemented, the rapid-cutting destruction of tropical forests is encouraged and the use of the most dangerous chlorofluorocarbons increases, the planet could be committed to a warming of 1.5° to 4.5° C as early as 2015, less than 30 years from today. In this scenario, by 2075 the total warming commitment has increased to between 5° and 15° C. By contrast, in the WRI slow buildup scenario, in which strong and aggressive measures are taken to improve energy efficiency, to reduce the use of the most dangerous chlorofluorocarbons and to protect the tropical forests, the date at which the planet is committed to a 1.5° to 4.5° C warming could be postponed to well beyond 2075. The difference between the results in the high emissions and the slow buildup scenarios, a shift from 2015 to 2075 in the date of commitment to a 1.5° to 4.5° C warming, may seem insignificant, but it represents an important window of opportunity for human societies and ecosystems in which adaptive responses can develop to that part of the climate change that can't be avoided.

Unfortunately, however, there are no options that will allow the planet to avoid all future global warming. The earth is now committed to a significant global climate change—committed by actions that have already taken place as well as by the industrial infrastructure that is in place throughout the world. The best recent analyses suggest that emissions from 1880 to 1980 have committed the planet to a warming of approximately 0.7° to 2° C.

Although some future warming cannot be avoided because of past and present emissions, the resulting damages and dislocations can be minimized if the available time is used wisely. By slowing the rate of growth in future emissions, it may be possible to slow the rate of change enough to develop and implement adaptive responses that protect the most vulnerable societies, species and geographic areas. In order to identify what such prudent responses might entail, however, it is necessary to look beyond the globally averaged warming discussed above and focus some attention on the regional distribution of the expected impacts.

IMPACTS OF A GREENHOUSE GAS BUILDUP

The global warming and the stratospheric ozone depletion that accompany a buildup of greenhouse gases in the atmosphere will not be uniformly distributed. The greatest warming will occur at the poles, in the vulnerable high-latitude areas of arctic communities and in high-latitude countries. The warming in the polar regions is expected to be two to three times the global average. The concurrent warming of tropical areas is expected to be only 50 to 75 percent of the global average.

The latitudinal distribution of warming effects is critical to the ecological impacts that will result. By changing the natural thermal gradient of the earth between the poles and the equator, the greenhouse effect will weaken the great heat engine that drives the global weather machine. It is this heat engine which generates the rains, winds and the ocean currents, and is responsible for the familiar patterns of regional climate.

The principal effects of a global warming are likely to be: 1) a rise in sea levels, varying in magnitude between regions and communities; 2) changes in winds and ocean currents; 3) changes in precipitation and water resources; and 4) changes in the frequency of extreme events. These physical changes will have major implications for the earth's wild lands and unmanaged ecosystems.

For example, a warming of 1.5° to 4.5° C is expected to cause a rise in sea level of 20 to 140 centimeters. The effects of this sea level rise are likely to be important not only for ecosystems but for human communities as well. Human populations and wetland ecosystems in low-lying areas and river deltas, such as the Ganges-Bhamaputra system, the Nile, the Mississippi and the Yangtze are especially vulnerable to rises in sea level. In these regions, much of the population is concentrated in a broad alluvial delta area that is flat and close to sea level.

It is important to note that the effects of sea-level rise can place devastating pressures on wild communities and on ecosystems. Sea-level rise can push coastal wetland habitats up against the edge of human development, giving their inhabitants no place to run and little area in which to hide. This problem is especially important for the migratory birds and other animals who must use critical habitat areas that are spread over large geographic ranges.

In addition, sea-level rise can lead to saltwater intrusion into aquifers and deeper saline penetration into tidal estuaries. These effects can cause severe disruption to the ecosystems that require the presence of fresh water in these areas.

Changes in ocean currents could affect the presence and distribution of sea ice and the upwelling of nutrients that feed oceanic and aquatic ecosystems. Shifts in the location of major currents are likely also to affect the polunias, the open water oases of the arctic region. If high latitude areas are warmed by the greenhouse effect, these areas could become greatly enlarged, altering the balance among local species. Such changes are likely to be a mixed blessing— good for some, perhaps for fish and whales, while potentially creating great difficulty for mammals and certain other species. The migratory patterns of these latter inhabitants of the arctic wild lands would be severely disrupted if they could not move from one ice island area to another in the winter.

Changes in the frequency and distribution of precipitation could also have important impacts on wild lands and unmanaged ecosystems. Precipitation and temperature combine to effect both evapotranspiration and soil moisture.

Recent analyses with large-scale computer models indicate that a global average warming of 1.5° to 4.5° C might be accompanied by a decline of as much as 40 percent in summer soil moisture in the Great Plains of the United States and in the grain belts of the Soviet Union, Australia and in Central Europe. In addition, the models suggest that these changes could occur simultaneously in a way that would be extremely disruptive to the world food system. In a world with growing human populations, any failure of the global grain economy would increase pressure for poaching and harvesting of wildlife to meet constantly increasing demands for food and fodder. While modelling exercises have produced some-what different estimates of the regional distribution of changes in rainfall and soil moisture, unfortunately, one of the biggest weaknesses in atmospheric science today is the limited ability to predict changes in regional climate with the same degree of certainty that we can forecast changes in global climate.

The enormous changes in the earth's thermal gradient described above are likely to produce some predictable alterations in regional climates and some potentially surprising effects. For example, as a result of global warming, the warm waters of the Gulf Stream current could move as much as 300 kilometers to the west. If this occurred, the warm climates of Iceland and the United King-dom, both anomalies for their latitude, would grow much colder even as the rest of the world warmed rapidly.

Another type of expectable surprise likely to accompany a greenhouse warming is an increase in the frequency of extreme weather events. These will include heavy rains and heavy snowfalls occurring at untimely periods, droughts and severe storm surges in coastal areas.

The kinds of impacts these events will cause have already been observed. Along the polar bear paths that cross the Canadian Yukon, an unseasonably heavy, early and wet snowfall in 1973 severely disrupted the species balance. It resulted in the untimely deaths of 75 percent of the local muskoxen and two-thirds of the caribou in the area. Similarly, heavy storms in the Bay of Bengal in 1972 created a national disaster. One particular storm produced a great surge into the Ganges Delta that resulted in extensive flooding and the deaths of 100,000 people.

The United States has recently observed some indications of the kinds of effects that changes in climate would have upon our society. These include the drought in 1986 in the southeastern United States, the rise in the waters of the Great Lakes and the floods on the edges of the Great Salt Lake. Although not necessarily caused by global climate change, these events dramatize the kinds of disruptive impacts that could be expected to occur as the world warmed.

CLIMATE CHANGE AND THE MANAGEMENT OF WILD LANDS

Climate change will alter habitat boundaries and inter-species relations in ways which will effect wildlife refuges and unmanaged ecosystems. Many spe-cies now have limited access to suitable habitats. Like others more generously endowed, they face the natural random genetic events that decimate populations. With changes in global and regional climate due to the greenhouse effect and human encroachment upon their limited habitats, they will be severely at risk. Birds and other migratory species which must periodically use widely dispersed yet critically important habitat areas will be especially vulnerable.

Robert Peters of the Conservation Foundation has provided several useful examples of the potential impacts of changing climate on natural habitat. Figure 4 illustrates schematically how these changes might affect the habitat of an imaginary species. The line in the middle of the figure bounds the suitable habitat range for this species. The white area represents the unsuitable habitat and the shaded area is the range in which the species survives and prospers. The hexagon is the sight of a future reserve. As climate changes, the limit of the range shrinks around the reserve, reducing the buffer zone that protects the inhabitants or the preserve area from human society and its pressures. As local climate shifts, the natural inhabitants are pushed closer to the periphery of the suitable range. At some future time, the entire former reserve, though originally suitable to protect the vulnerable population, exists outside the limits of the now-suitable range. The lesson here is simple: In the selection of preserve sites, ample consideration must be given to the effects of changes in climate patterns on the ability of the reserve to support the vulnerable species the preserve is meant to protect.

Species at high latitudes and species in mountain communities are vulnerable in yet another way. Figure 5 illustrates the ranges of four species A,B,C,D in a mountain reserve before a climate change. As the world warms and species retreat to suitable habitats at higher altitudes, the range available to species A has disappeared entirely. Species B has been forced to move to the top of the first mountain and off the second mountain. Species C has now colonized the second mountain and the base of the third and species D, which was outside the original frame of reference, now dominates the area at the bottom of the illustration.

Climate change, ozone depletion and acid rain will present new challenges to the management of wild lands and to the selection of sites for preserve areas. Those concerned with the successful management of wild land preserves may ask how present species

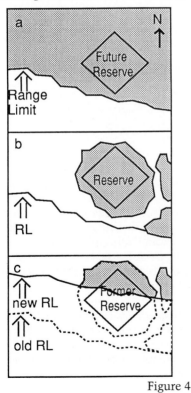

Figure 4

and ecosystems could possibly respond successfully to future global warming. Unfortunately there is no simple formula; small steps may improve the resilience of those species which dwell in the reserves whose sites are being planned.

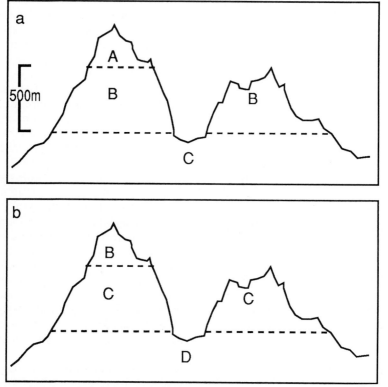

Figure 5

Figure 6 illustrates some of the geometric principles of preserve design developed by Dr. Jared Diamond of the University of California at Los Angeles. 1.) Because the number of species that can be supported in a preserve is a function of size, where the option exists a large site is better than a small site and one large site is often better than several small sites. 2.) Because they increase the likelihood of successful migration as conditions change, contiguous or closely spaced sites are preferable to widely separated locations. 3.) Sites which are symmetric around a point are preferable to locating all sites in a linear array because of the danger of isolation of sub-groups at the extreme edge of a range, where it is not possible to choose contiguous sites. 4.) It is better if the sites are connected rather than separated because land bridges will increase the likelihood of migratory success in the face of changing conditions, if the sites must be stretched out along a line (as when all available land borders a highway). 5.) If only one site can be chosen, round is preferable to linear, as this will again decrease the probability of isolating pockets of inhabitants in untenable micro-climates.

Figure 6

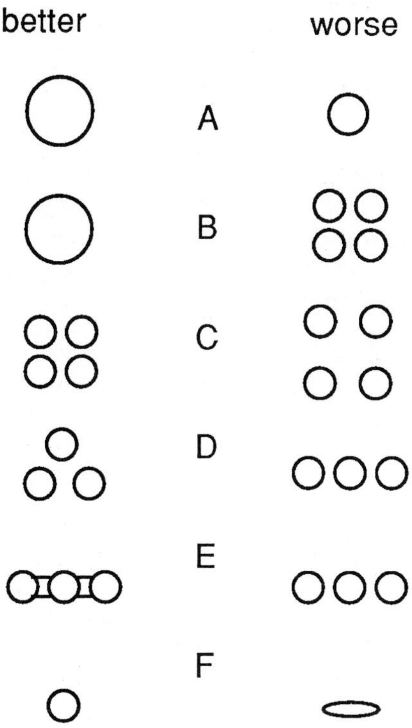

better

worse

A

B

C

D

E

F

CONCLUSION

It is reassuring to note that with enough time, whole communities and even major biomes have, in the face of past global warmings, moved great distances. The critical factor is not just the magnitude but the rate of change in climate. If current trends continue, the rate of global warming over the next 50 years will exceed that of the last 10,000 years. Under these conditions, the rate of change for the next century will exceed the rate for the last million years. And, if policies now under consideration to increase the use of coal and cut down the remaining tropical forests are implemented, over the next several decades the rate of change in climate could be even greater.

Fortunately, the results from recent studies at the World Resources Institute indicate that the earth is not locked into the worst of these hot-house futures. Policies to improve the efficiency of energy use, to shift the balance of commercial fuels away from coal toward less carbon-intensive fuels and to limit the rate of tropical deforestation can substantially slow the rate of greenhouse gas buildup and ozone depletion. Equally important, such strategies can buy time for human societies and natural ecosystems to adapt to those aspects of climate change which cannot be avoided. There are two principal challenges for those who would preserve our heritage of biological diversity through the careful management of the earth's wild lands. The first is to stimulate the choice of energy and industrial policies that can sustain economic growth while they slow the rate of growth in emissions of greenhouse gases. The second is to choose carefully the sites of future preserves and the management strategies with which they are operated to maximize the resilience of vulnerable species to the stresses of a changing and uncertain environment.

CONSERVATION, LAND USE AND SUSTAINABLE DEVELOPMENT

Raymond F. Dasmann

We are trying, in this Congress and in our collective work, to confront the issues of conservation and development, specifically as they refer to wilderness.

If I were to sum up my ideas in one sentence it would be this: Beware of bankers bearing gifts. They are unnatural, like pigs with wings. Now I don't want to disparage any particular banker, I am only using them to illustrate a concern. When conservationists deal with developers, the odds are not even. Wealth and power tend to be concentrated on one side only. I worry that in the new alliance between conservation and development, the conservation forces will give away too much and get little in return. There was a saying in my family that "He who sups with the devil should use a long spoon." It may apply here as well. If I may extend my imagination a bit further, there was a short film going around in the early 1970s which may apply to this situation. It was called "Bambi meets Godzilla." I don't have to remind you who Bambi is.

There is a great deal of information on the need for growth and development. But the people who are involved in these areas don't always mean the same thing when they use these words. If we hear the term economic development, we must always ask: Development of what? In what way? For the benefit of whom? At whose expense? Development of resources for the benefit of the elite at the expense of the poor is not going to work for very much longer. Similarly, there can be no sense in talking about continuing economic growth unless we recognize that there are limits to growth imposed not only by the physical realities of our planet, but by our human desire to keep the planet a fit place for all species to live. This desire itself may express a physical necessity of limitation.

There are some kinds of development that can go on forever, without known limits, such as development of knowledge and understanding, development of human potential or the human spirit. Development can be applauded whole-heartedly if it moves toward those goals, not just for the elite but for all.

There are many ideas offered about sustainable development, but we must once again question the meaning of this term. Sustainable development must mean ecologically sustainable development, and that implies that it will take care of all of our essential life support systems—our air, water, soil and vegetation. Sustainable development must be based on the preservation of biological diversity—not in a deep freeze or a seed collection, but out there where it belongs, in its native habitat. Sustainable development must also, first of all, take care of the needs of the poorest people. Not by giving them food, but by restoring their ability to look after themselves. By helping them to return to what they always used to be: self-reliant. Sustainable development must always move toward ecological sustainability, using living resources only in ways that maintain or increase their renewability.

That kind of sustainable development is compatible with wilderness conservation. In fact, the two go hand in hand. But don't buy any other brand. Look under the label. Be cautious. Remember Bambi.

Global generalities must always be put into practice locally. Several years ago, a few of us began a study of the Santa Cruz mountains in California, intending initially to answer the question, "Why are the mountains wild?" And, leading from that, "How do we keep them that way?"

This mountain system extends from San Francisco for a distance of 75 miles to the Pajaro River in the south. The total area is close to 1,400 square miles, of which about 1,000 square miles are not urbanized. They are not particularly high or precipitous (the highest elevation is near 3,800 feet), yet they are a barrier to urban development. They stand between the five million residents of the San Francisco Bay metropolitan area and the small towns on Monterey Bay and the Pacific Coast. Visually they give the impression of an extensive area of wild land, mostly covered by redwood or mixed evergreen forests. The question of why they are still wild becomes significant when we realize that there is no extensive federal presence—no national forests or parks. Most of the land is privately owned.

In the absence of a federal presence, state and local governments have taken a more active role. There are six state parks, mostly established to protect the last of the old-growth redwoods, starting with Big Basin State Park in 1901. However, only 40,000 acres are included in this system. There is also an important state fish and game refuge protecting the watershed of the San Andreas and Crystal Springs lakes. There is an impressive network of county parks and two university reserves. However, even in the aggregate these protected areas do not explain the wild quality of the mountains.

Unquestionably, natural phenomena affect development. The California climate features wet and dry cycles—flood years and drought years. In flood years those who have built on unstable slopes or in river bottoms see their houses washed away. In drought years, forest and brush fires often sweep through the mountains, destroying houses built on vulnerable sites. One could say the mountains defend themselves against excessive development. However, it is the attitude of people toward growth and development that is more important. This is particularly evident in Santa Cruz County, on the ocean side of the mountains. People come to Santa Cruz for its beaches and spectacular scenery and to escape the big-city confusion of the San Francisco Bay area. But once they have arrived in Santa Cruz, their tendency is to shut the door behind them and say "no more room" to those who would come later. This leads to antigrowth legislation at the city and county level.

Thus, to attempt to protect the wild country of the mountains, one must confront one of the major global issues of today: the issue of population growth.

The more manageable side of the population problem is the one resulting from an excess of births over deaths. But the growth of population in the San Francisco Bay area does not result from San Franciscans breeding like rabbits. It is immigration from other areas. Declining birth rates are matched by increasing immigration rates. This is a problem confronting governments in many parts of the world, and in a democratic society or even a loosely controlled autocracy, it is difficult to deal with. There seem to be two directions that are being followed. The first "leave it to the market" approach is popular today. Land and housing prices are allowed to increase to the point where enclaves of the rich develop and the poor are pushed to the margins, often into the remaining wild land. The other approach involves increasing governmental control over land use through planning, zoning and strict regulation of permits to build or develop. This has not been highly successful in protecting choice agricultural land. It seems less likely to succeed in protecting wild land of more indeterminate value.

There are two other approaches to this problem that show some promise of reinforcing the ability of local governments to control growth and development. One of these is the Pinelands National Reserve model which is being tested in New Jersey. In this, a core area of wild land, the Pine Barrens, is protected by a state park. Other areas are protected as prime agricultural land. Other sites are determined to be suited for development, for industry, commerce, roads, housing, etc. The federal government is more actively involved. Both reinforce the ability of local governments. Growth is not prevented, but channeled in appropriate directions.

The other approach that is also being used in the pinelands is that of a Biosphere Reserve. This is an international designation derived from the UNESCO Man and Biosphere (MAB) program. It has no strict legal status in this country, but indicates a commitment of the federal government to meet international standards of protection, management and research. It places an international layer of protection over the existing federal, state and local authorities.

Ultimately none of these approaches, or any others, will work unless the local people are behind them. But the local people, by themselves, cannot protect wild country or wilderness when the forces acting against such protection originate outside of the local area and override local controls. Thus, it is important to always question the meaning of growth and development. Let us be careful in joining the new alliance of development and conservation.

OCEAN WILDERNESS— MYTH, CHALLENGE OR OPPORTUNITY?

Nancy Foster and Michele H. Lemay

In the months preceding the 4th World Wilderness Congress, the organizers of the Ocean Wilderness Seminar and colleagues in the marine conservation community were confronted with several questions:

• Does the concept of "wilderness" apply to ocean areas and, if so, what is ocean wilderness?
• And how does a country or a region provide for wilderness in its national agenda for ocean resource management?

The discussion that followed our early inquiries provided insights into the value of the concept of wilderness for integrated marine resource management. Simultaneously, the rapidly growing experience of countries that have established marine protected areas raised questions concerning the practical, legal and political aspects of ocean wilderness. The discussion culminated in a resolution at the 4th World Wilderness Congress which marks initial progress in placing the idea of ocean wilderness in a broader context. The following is a brief account of the thinking that led to this collective statement.

The century of thought that has gone into defining wilderness on land provides a starting point for understanding ocean wilderness. At first glance, the physical attributes of terrestrial wilderness seem to have little relevance in an ocean environment. For example, we could argue that since ocean areas seldom show permanent visible impact of human activity and since people are always transient, these areas all qualify as wilderness. Alternatively, ocean systems are completely open to external processes and impacts and cannot be viewed as pristine in the conventional sense. It is also doubtful whether the absence of mechanical transport, a criterion used for terrestrial wilderness, applies to ocean areas. Given the scale and openness of ocean systems, it is unlikely that many of the physical criteria used to define land wilderness will apply to the ocean.

However, philosophers have explored the concept of wilderness in much broader terms than its physical characteristics. Many have pointed out that wilderness is also a driving force which has led to significant changes in Western society's attitudes and beliefs. In the early 1900s, wilderness evolved as an ideology which was instrumental in the development of grassroots environmental movements and which ultimately led to legislation now considered the foundation of our land conservation ethic. In the process, areas such as Yosemite

National Park in the United States and Banff National Park in Canada gained unprecedented societal value.

Hence, while it may not be possible to apply totally the terrestrial concept of wilderness to ocean areas, it is valuable to examine wilderness as an evolving relationship between people and natural areas which serves as a catalyst for institutional change. For those now working toward raising awareness and appreciation for ocean areas, it is clear that today's public support for marine conservation has to evolve to a point where it can motivate the grassroots activism necessary to change the way institutions manage ocean environments. And there are important lessons in understanding the role played by the Yosemites of the ocean in triggering that change, whether in the Great Barrier Reef in Australia, Lancaster Sound in Canada, or the Waddensea in western Europe.

OCEAN WILDERNESS AND MARINE PROTECTED AREAS

For the past 30 years, the world's network of protected areas has helped the exchange of information among nations administering wilderness areas. This network has led to the development of improved guidelines for land and wildlife management, and most importantly, increased the international commitment to wilderness as an essential ingredient for sustainable development.

Marine protected areas have played a limited role in this global experiment, due partly to their small numbers and recent acceptance. At the 1982 World Congress on National Parks and Protected Areas in Bali, participants observed that marine protected areas were still at an early stage of development and lagged behind terrestrial sites in worldwide coverage. There has been considerable progress since that time. By 1985, 430 marine protected areas had been proclaimed by 69 nations, with another 298 proposals under consideration. Early attempts to manage marine protected areas have led to a more practical understanding of ocean wilderness. There is now a growing recognition that ocean wilderness represents one end of the spectrum of marine protected areas ranging from multiple-use areas to strict nature reserves. Taken in its entirely, this spectrum is the key to achieving sustainable development in ocean areas.

Countries that are establishing national networks of marine protected areas are already facing many challenges that relate to the question of ocean wilderness. One of the first challenges has been the identification and delineation of marine areas that are representative of an ocean region and that function so as to maintain the integrity of the system being managed. Unfortunately, drawing boundaries in the ocean has never been easy. However, some of the pioneering work in large marine ecosystems may hold the key to designating workable areas that are representative and functional. This work represents a significant step away from the single-species focus of conventional fisheries management. The research may suggest management strategies that can adapt to the variability of ocean systems.

In the meantime, managers need to recognize that marine protected areas are part of variable systems closely linked to other coastal and inland habitats.

As the emphasis in many countries, including the United States, is shifting from simply identifying sites to making marine protected areas fully operational, many other challenges are being faced. Agencies responsible for marine protected areas are confronted with the harsh reality that ocean areas are a common property resource administered by an array of sectoral jurisdictions. When a site is designated as a marine protected area, the people whose livelihood depends on that common property resource, and the layers of government agencies that manage economic activities (fisheries, transport, tourism), still remain. The ability of sectoral agencies to deal with shared management processes has been limited, but long-term arrangements are emerging at the community level.

This recognition leads to a basic principle emerging from the experiences of small developing islands of the Caribbean and the Pacific. These small island nations are undertaking integrated programs for marine conservation that have to balance objectives for resource protection, food production (fisheries and aquaculture), traditional lifestyles and economic development. In the context of a small island, the management of marine protected areas and ocean wilderness involves a broad social responsibility to local communities. Management plans must involve these local stakeholders and be implemented with a view toward the objective of long-term community well-being.

Another lesson is that one fundamental mission of marine protected areas is to encourage community involvement in marine conservation. The voluntary marine reserves of the United Kingdom and the municipal reserves of the Philippines offer convincing evidence of this principle. In both instances, local users recognized the importance of responsible resource management to ensure their continued use and enjoyment of the marine habitat. The marine protected area provided the opportunity to become involved through special projects such as volunteer naturalist programs, community-based habitat management, volunteer patrols and participation in field inventories.

OCEAN WILDERNESS AND INTEGRATED
MARINE RESOURCES MANAGEMENT

Clearly, those committed to marine protected areas and ocean wilderness cannot ignore the greater task at hand: long-term, wise use and management of ocean ecosystems. Although marine protected areas and oceanic wilderness are certainly part of the agenda, how do they contribute to the development of integrated marine resource management?

If such questions are left unanswered, governments may well grow content with designating relatively small portions of their territorial waters as "protected"—assuming that conservation objectives for marine areas have been adequately addressed. Yet the ocean systems that support world fisheries, for example, are much larger than any area that could be contained within such legal boundaries.

There are several initiatives addressing this problem that deserve international attention. The Antarctic Treaty System (ATS), including its more recent developments, represents one attempt to implement a regional conservation regime for marine resources. The ATS is a complex array of international agreements, management guidelines and cooperative efforts which focus systematically on protected species, populations, habitats and harvesting of renewable resources. Recent scientific research which demonstrates how the Southern Ocean is best understood (and therefore managed) as a large marine ecosystem has been instrumental in the elaboration of some of these agreements, particularly the Convention for the Conservation of Antarctic Marine Living Resources (CAMLR). While the ATS is not without flaws, it has shown that we have reached the point where protected species, protected areas and sustainable use must be linked together.

Canada has been moving in similar directions with the formulation of its Arctic Marine Conservation Strategy. In a broad and comprehensive policy, Canada's Department of Fisheries and Oceans has outlined six strategies for sustainable use of the Arctic: Science for Management; Shared Management; Integrated Resource Planning and Management; Marine Environmental Quality; Public Knowledge; and International Considerations. Marine protected areas are understood to be one of the many tools available to achieve the goals of the policy.

The United States has made preliminary attempts to integrate formerly isolated objectives into marine resource management. While much of the work is still in its infancy, it is possible to anticipate a time when fisheries management, marine mammal protection, marine habitat management and marine protected areas will be understood as part of an integrated framework for resource management.

OCEAN WILDERNESS: CHALLENGE AND OPPORTUNITY

Though not easily defined, the concept of wilderness applied to ocean areas holds some promise. It is not a myth to the extent that it can serve as a catalyst of new ocean policies. However, it offers both a challenge and an opportunity to the marine conservation community. Non-governmental organizations need to broaden grassroots support for, and involvement in, responsible marine resource management. This support must evolve from its current focus on a few "flagship" species to an ethic for the stewardship of ocean areas. Governments need to take on the chief institutional challenge of the decade as identified by the World Commission on Environment and Development by focusing on sustainable development rather than short-term economic benefits and by making shared management work at the local, national and international levels.

WILDLIFE VALUES

Joyce M. Kelly

Each of us has had special wildlife experiences in his lifetime. Those experiences which capture and recall my wildland experiences include the eerie tremolo of a loon on a northern lake, which I thrill to no matter how many times I have heard it. The staccato beat of the pileated woodpecker on dead timber, the grizzly lumbering along on the mountainside well above me, battling a 21-pound northern pike into a boat in northern Saskatchewan. Or the experience I hope to have, to hear the rich crescendo of a wolf's howl and the wild echoing response of a pack member in Yellowstone National Park. Experiences, memories and visions we cherish. They are experiences which enhance our appreciation and emotional ties to wilderness, ecosystem preservation and wildlife.

Those same wildlife experiences must be used to build public support for wildlife which is critical to our own survival. If we continue to limp along with our recovery efforts, not only will we impair the value of these laws such as the Endangered Species Act (ESA) and the Convention on International Trade in Endangered Species in Wild Flora and Fauna (CITES), we will have failed to translate our feelings and commitment to wildlife into action.

Wildlife is important to our health and well-being. Wildlife has aesthetic values; subsistence values to native peoples; medicinal values which benefit all mankind; and commercial values, trade or tourism which benefit the economics of states, regions and countries.

Survey results here in the United States indicate a growing interest in the preservation of natural areas and in what is termed watchable wildlife or non-game uses. The President's Commission on Americans Outdoors, which recently completed its report, found that 87 percent of the American public supported the preservation of natural areas and were willing to pay extra to protect and maintain these areas. The U.S. Fish and Wildlife 1985 Survey of Fishing, Hunting and Wildlife Associated Recreation revealed that:

- 46.6 million, or more than one in four, adult Americans fished.
- 16.7 million, or about one in 10, adult Americans hunted.
- 109.7 million of all adult Americans, actively participated in non-consumptive wildlife related activities such as feeding, observing or photographing wildlife.

It is clear that recreational interest in wildlife is growing. To a large extent this interest has been stimulated by U.S. wildlife conservation groups, each of which originated in response to a wildlife crisis. The challenge before us is to translate this awareness and concern into action to protect and recover species and their habitats.

The ESA and CITES are matters of national and international pride. They reflect the idea that wildlife is important to us and that we suffer a loss when a species of wildlife vanishes from the earth. Both provide the tools for preservation and recovery: good biology, good planning and effective consultation.

For recovery to succeed, which is the goal of both the ESA and CITES, those who are most affected by these laws must be included in the decision-making process. Sociopolitical and economic considerations are as important as good biology in the decision-making process and may be more important in ensuring effective implementation.

Both CITES and ESA were signed in 1973 in response to the concerns over species decline and the rapid escalation in species extinctions. They were both established to protect species: the ESA primarily through conserving ecosystems upon which threatened and endangered species depend; CITES through regulating the buying and selling of endangered wildlife. They both established systematic processes of identifying those species in danger of extinction and providing for their recovery.

The ESA also authorizes a program to protect the habitats of endangered and threatened species, hence the critical importance of maintaining wilderness areas.

The United States was the first country to ratify CITES with enactment of the ESA, which also implements U.S. participation. Thus, the successes and difficulties of the ESA are illustrative of administrative and legislative history.

CITES' philosophy now is to manage, not prohibit, trade in wildlife products and thereby strive to create financial incentives for saving species and preventing overexploitation. It does this by:
• prohibiting commercial trade by its parties in species threatened with extinction,
• controlling trade through permits in those species that may become threatened unless commerce in them is strictly regulated, and
• providing for a secretariat, biennial Conference of Parties and direct communication among Management Authorities and Scientific Authorities of Parties. By recognizing the economic value of species, CITES acknowledges an important source of income to wildlife producing countries.

The 1987 CITES meeting held in Ottawa, Canada had the largest participation of Third World countries in the history of CITES. This is particularly significant because the developing countries have most of the world's wildlife and secondly, to quote Eugene Lapointe, Secretary General of CITES, "their presence brings developed country delegates and environmentalists closer to the realities of endangered species problems in Africa, Asia and Latin America."

A great many specific issues were discussed:
1. Strong support was expressed by all the delegates and non-governmental organizations for the principle that endangered species can be saved from extinction largely through their rational exploitation.

2. Canada and others expressed concern that:

    a. Proceedings need to become more scientific and rational; too large a number of species are placed in appendices without meeting criteria (no evidence the species is threatened by illegal trade). For example, trade in hummingbirds basically stopped in the 20th century, yet a decision was made to list 350 species in Appendix II.

    b. Advice of IUCN and Traffic is disregarded too often.

3. Downlisting activities of note included:

    a. Report by animal experts that leopard numbers are sufficiently healthy to allow controlled commerce; this was a reaffirmation of a quota resolution adopted at an earlier meeting.

    b. Renewed commitment and support for the quota system on elephant ivory that gives profits from the legal sale of the tusks to African governments and people, instead of to poachers and illegal traders.

    c. Downgrading the vicuna so the animal can be sheared, its wool woven into cloth and legally sold outside Peru and Chile.

4. A resolution was adopted banning all trade in rhinoceros horns both in international trade as well as domestic commerce and destruction of existing stocks of rhino horns. This led to the first withdrawal of a country, the United Arab Emirates, from the convention.

5. There was overwhelming support from the delegates, wildlife user groups and wildlife conservation organizations to increase the budget for CITES.

6. There was considerable discussion over reported infractions. In a report the secretariat was directed to prepare, three countries were singled out for criticism. There was increased willingness by many members to take note of each other's reported infractions and request explanations.

There are interesting parallels between the ESA and CITES in terms of problems and successes. Unfortunately recovery of species under both the Act and the Convention has been painfully slow. The Endangered Species Act and CITES both seek to protect species and recover them, using different tools. The crises inhibiting effective recovery know no national boundaries and include:

1. Habitat destruction and illegal hunting.

2. Wildlife trade.

3. Few recovery efforts, some plans, but few being implemented.

4. Overemphasis on listing.

5. Not enough funding.

6. States' right, the argument that states must be able to manage wildlife within their own jurisdiction as they see fit.

7. Lack of administrative leadership and enforcement.

8. Failure to involve more affected publics in the decision-making process, to build the awareness necessary to ensure viable wildlife populations.

While funding is a critical need and must be at reasonable levels, we also know that there will never be enough funds available to stop extinctions or recover all those species in need. I do not believe the future of either CITES or the ESA is in serious jeopardy in spite of the extremely difficult financial situation they both currently find themselves in. The public commitment to wildlife preservation is too strong to let either effort vanish.

Of the crises listed I believe the greatest challenge is recovery. We need to determine which endangered wildlife are the most significant with respect to critical land-use decisions being made at the national and international levels and move to protect and recover those species quickly. While the listing process is an important first step, I believe we have let ourselves fall into the trap of focusing too much attention on the listing process to the exclusion of the recovery process.

The greater and more difficult challenge is in the recovery of species. Recovery is more political and requires tougher decisions, hence requires more time and effort. As one well-known wildlife manager said to me: "To list you just have to sign a bureaucrat's name. To recover requires funds for habitat acquisition, time, and planning. To be sure, the listing process lends itself to litigation which gives it more appeal than the tough negotiating and decision making that is required for recovery."

Let's look at a few facts drawn from the U.S. experience. Recovery plans are being written at a much slower rate than the rate at which species are being listed. Only 57 percent of the total U.S. species listed had recovery plans at the end of 1986. The funding is minimal at best. It has been roughly $6 million per year since 1981. In a review currently being done of 18 recovery plans, actual expenditures are running approximately 0 to 1 percent of the estimated three-year costs for listed priority tasks. The priority tasks are:

1. Forestall extinction.
2. Stabilize the populations.
3. Bring the species to recovery.

The recovery efforts, however, do not proceed in that order. The funding is directed very often at Level II tasks, which involve habitat acquisition, prior to Level I.

It would cost $75 million per year to accomplish the Level I tasks currently stated in completed plans. Sadly, but realistically, funding at that level is not, nor will it be, available in the near term. I am not suggesting we should be satisfied with the current dollar levels, but given the limited funds available, we must do a more responsible job of determining how to best utilize those funds.

There has been little hard assessment of how successful the recovery process is, and whether the dollars are being used as effectively as possible. The economics of recovery appears not to be a question even asked. While the right biological questions are perhaps being asked, the economic, social and political questions are not. Perhaps this is why the ESA is being increasingly viewed as a repository of lists with little real effort or interest in "delisting." Because of this, economic interests, which might be enlisted in support of the Act's intent, become wary and see the legislation as an attempt to lockup lands for aesthetic wildlife values with no intent to ever delist. CITES faces a similar problem. By appealing to the emotional and the aesthetic and ignoring the legitimate economic values of wildlife and wilderness, we are losing constituencies, not winning them.

If we are unable to demonstrate the values of recovery, we will have failed. Let us face it— economic arguments have considerable merit and appeal. By proving the value of recovery, we will be in a stronger position to win broader support and acceptance of the entire listing and recovery process and obtain more funding. After all, early in this country's history we had two billion passenger pigeons and no chickens. Now the situation is reversed, we have two billion chickens and no passenger pigeons. Economics did play a part. In fact, we probably know more about the health and welfare of chickens than we do about people. I wish we could say the same about Florida panthers and timber wolves, to name a few.

I am using economic or market values here in their broadest context. For example, I may choose to visit Glacier over another national park on the chance that I may see a wolf or a grizzly bear. That decision has an economic value—a value that more and more communities are beginning to recognize, albeit slowly. The recovery of the peregrine falcon has brought excitement to many of our major cities. The trials and tribulations of Scarlett, Baltimore's famed city falcon, did much for the corporate image of US Fidelity and Guarantee as well as for the potential of city release elsewhere. Market value? Of course. We also need to look at the question of whether collective or public ownership of the habitat is the most effective way to protect endangered species. It may not be in all instances. After all, the black-footed ferret was found on private land.

CITES, perhaps of its overt economic goals, has been successful in obtaining funding from non-governmental sources. I realize there are many who will question whether or not CITES has been successful in recovery. But by giving enhanced economic value to species which can survive trade (5 billion in export income is no small number), CITES has provided an incentive to people to protect habitat and indirectly to protect numerous other species.

I doubt there is any disagreement with the premise that conservation is an indispensable element of sustainable development, including tourism. You may or may not agree that we have been slow to point up the economic values of wildlife conservation. I believe we have been, partly because we are uncomfortable in accepting market values in the environmental arena generally.

The agreement at the Ottawa CITES conference to permit Peru and Chile to sell vicuna cloth is an excellent example of how safeguards for a species can combine with their economic use. In the past the vicuna was overexploited, trade was restricted and the population subsequently recovered to the point where its wool can be harvested, as sheep's wool is harvested. This will benefit those nations' economies in several ways: wool production, cloth manufacture, export and the species will be able to survive indefinitely.

Using economic incentives through the legal harvest of elephant ivory, the quota system provides a reason for the poor in Africa to protect the elephant that uses coveted land. While conflicts continue over competing use of the land and poaching, there is now an incentive for positive action on the part of the population directly impacted to conserve the resources and reduce the illegal intake. In addition, the economy benefits directly as opposed to indirectly from illegal, black market operation. Will the quota system succeed in protecting the elephant? It is still too early to tell. Hopefully, yes.

Some of the African nations recognized early the increasing economic value and importance of wild resources for external trade and tourism, as well as for internal consumption. In the United States the value of wildlife as a "financial resource" is only beginning to be recognized. Its contributions to state treasuries and the U.S. treasury are not small. In recent remarks, the Colorado State Wildlife director recognized the critical contributions wildlife is making to the state economy. Fishing and hunting contribute a billion dollars a year to the state economy, not even considering the expenditures of those engaged in nonconsumptive wildlife uses.

Those kinds of dollars should lead to a policy of land use that promises and enhances fish and wildlife opportunities and then recovery and protection. It also means it is time to look creatively at the concept of wildlife market value.

This may mean taking a new look at the potential for game ranches. Under CITES there is a mechanism which permits captive breeding of endangered animals for economic purposes, as occurring in Zimbabwe with Nile River crocodile ranches. Will it be allowed to work? Can we say that the sea turtle is made more secure by prohibiting sea turtle ranching—a recent CITES issue?

In the United States in one area instance due to what I will call enlightened management, the American alligator is ranched. The law enforcement agents developed a way of marking hides that prevented illegal hides from being "laundered" and which followed the hide through to the finished product. It was a rational approach that worked; the species won.

If recovery is to work, it is important to carefully select species to which limited resources can be devoted. I suggest that this be a collaborative process to determine what criteria should be used to select species for limited recovery dollars. While we can't totally objectify the process, it can be vastly improved through greater administrative leadership and institutional awareness which may have to come from outside government. The process must build on good biology, but involve other considerations.

Obviously it won't be easy to draw the line between those species which may need the efforts the most and those species where you can achieve the greatest good. The process does need some order. Focusing on achievable goals would be a good first step. While existing legislation provides considerable flexibility, we may also need additional legislation simply to get the attention devoted to recovery that is desperately needed.

All governments must be persuaded to invest in recovery now, for their own long-term benefits. It is a form of insurance. The financial needs of CITES and ESA exceed what the governments are now putting into them to list and recover species, to adequately enforce existing regulations and legislation and to determine which species, populations and habitats may be at risk and how best to manage and conserve them. Control is still hampered by poor enforcement, scientific uncertainty and disputes about where to draw the line between safe exploitation of a species and dangerous pillage. Private groups, both profit and nonprofit, have done much to contribute funds and provide monitoring. But we need to do more.

We must also enlarge the organized constituency for wildlife. For instance, opportunities exist to link hunters with nonhunters. While our respective motivations to preserve species may be different, we share the same goal, species preservation. Trade associations provide another opportunity for cooperation. While they may be operating in terms of enlightened self interest in maintaining the resource base, aren't we all? Let us not forget, exploitation is in the eye of the beholder. The challenge is too great to continue to emphasize our differences at the risk of losing wildlife. To the extent we do broaden our constituency base, there will be greater acceptance of and support for the process and results.

Developing nations, which possess 80 percent of the world's wildlife resources, have a valuable asset. The United States can provide technical expertise and management experience. We certainly do not have a corner on all the right answers. We can hope that others can learn from our own mistakes and that we can learn from the mistakes and successes of other nations.

We know wildlife is critical to our own survival. So how can we ensure that we both survive? Sometimes strict "protectionism" helps wildlife far less than it helps the illegal traders, smugglers and poachers. We need to look at creative new arrangements involving nontraditional alliances, utilizing and not rejecting entrepreneurial skills, and developing new operating definitions for wildlife market values. The Rockefellers and Du Ponts created values for a number of goods which were considered valueless before their involvement, like the early Americans. Why can't we find and utilize those same talents to create market values for wildlife preservation? There does not need to be a conflict over environmental values and the market; the public good and private ownership can work synergistically.

No one will dispute the important values of wildlife, whether we are talking about subsistence values for native peoples, or the aesthetic values of wildebeest surging over the African plains, or the Porcupine caribou streaming down from the mountains to the Arctic coast in northern Canada and Alaska. What we clearly need is a stronger demonstration of our commitment—in terms of funding, institutional awareness and political leadership. Each of those requires action from the government and the private sector. CITES and the ESA owe their births and effectiveness to the private sector; it is time to strengthen our political leverage to prove that recovery works.

We cannot let the ESA or CITES become simply listing documents; they must remain broad wildlife management tools used to solve problems.

We should take heed of what Chief Seattle of the Suwamish tribe of the state of Washington wrote in a letter to the president of the United States, in 1855:

"If all the beasts were gone, men would die from great loneliness of spirit, for whatever happens to the beasts also happens to the man. All things are connected. Whatever befalls the earth befalls the sons of the earth."

FURS—AN ENVIRONMENTAL ETHIC

Alan Herscovici

(*Editor's Note:* This presentation was prepared by Alan Herscovici for the International Fur Trade Federation.)

The word "ecology" was coined by the German naturalist Ernst Haeckel in 1866 to describe the interdependence of living organisms with their environment. This concept had little impact on laymen until 100 years later, with the publication in 1962 of Rachel Carson's *Silent Spring*, an expose of the indiscriminate use of pesticides. The book made the interdependence of life clear: DDT moved up through the food chain, accumulating in ever-higher concentrations, and resulted in egg shells too thin and weak to support the nesting birds.

Rachel Carson's *Silent Spring* was a turning point and signaled the birth of the modern environmental movement. By the late 1960s, attempts were being made to assess the extent of the damage caused by a century of extremely rapid growth and to legislate controls.

In the field of wildlife conservation, it was estimated in the 1960s that about half of the animal species which had become extinct in the past 2,000 years had disappeared during the first 60 years of this century. At least one-tenth of all remaining plant and animal species were now endangered.

This alarming balance sheet led to the drafting of the Convention on International Trade in Endangered Species of Wild Flora and Fauna (CITES) in 1973 to monitor and regulate commercial traffic in wildlife at the international level. Ninety-five nations are now parties to this agreement.

Controlling trade, however, is only half the battle. By itself, this can accomplish little so long as wildlife habitat is being steadily eroded. Endangered species, in fact, are usually only a symptom of more profound environmental degradation. In 1980, scientists under the auspices of the International Union for the Conservation of Nature (IUCN) began work on a comprehensive World

Conservation Strategy, which confirmed that conservation and development are inextricably linked.

A fundamental objective of conservation strategy is to achieve sustainable use of renewable resources. In other words, we must learn to live within our means. We may use the interest made available by the inherent productivity of nature, but we must refrain from squandering our environmental capital.

It is estimated that close to one-third of the world's arable land will be lost by the end of this century. The extent of tropical forests will be halved. Up to one million species of animals, plants and smaller species (especially invertebrates like mollusks, insects and corals which promote the productivity of the land and oceans) will become extinct, largely because of habitat destruction. Meanwhile, in this same period, world human population is expected to rise by almost 50 percent—to some 6,000 million.

Despite our impressive advances in agriculture and industry, wild plants and animals still provide us with food, medicines, clothing, building materials and fuel. They provide a gene pool from which our domestic plant and animal breeds are improved and strengthened, to resist parasites and disease. They are also the models or building blocks for many of our most important technological innovations.

The principles of the World Conservation Strategy may be summarized in three main objectives: maintenance of essential ecological processes and life-supporting systems; preservation of genetic diversity; and sustainable utilization of species and ecosystems.

Sustainable management of wildlife and animal products, by the fur trade or any other industry, must clearly support these objectives if the best ends of conservation are to be served.

One way to measure adherence to these objectives is by the concept of reciprocity, which could be adapted as the creed of true conservation effort. Whenever we take from nature we must give something back. Our relationship with nature must be reciprocal, for despite our scientific and technological advances, we remain part of nature and dependent on it, ultimately, for our very survival.

The modern fur trade is a well-controlled industry that provides a high quality, natural product. It is also more ecological than most industries—making use of renewable resources without polluting or damaging wildlife habitat.

From the woodcraft of American Indian trappers to the art of the dresser and the fur artisan, the trade encompasses the expertise of a remarkable range of cultures. It also provides income for tens of thousands of people, often in rural or remote regions where alternative employment may be rare or nonexistent. As an industry based upon the responsible use of a valuable natural resource, the modern fur trade has an important role to play—and a direct interest—in promoting the protection of wildlife habitat and the natural environment as a whole.

From an ethical perspective the fur trade clearly has special responsibilities because it uses animals. The reciprocity of the fur trade may be explained in four main areas:

1. *Respect for the land.*

Habitat destruction is the single greatest threat to the survival of many plant and animal species (67 percent of all endangered vertebrate species are threatened by habitat degradation). It is, for now, a more immediate problem on land than in the oceans, where overharvesting is still the main threat to the survival of many fish and other marine species.

There are numerous ways in which the fur trade, with other responsible wildlife use, can help to protect habitats.

• Wildlife use as a sensor to call attention to environmental damage:

At the grassroots level, wildlife use serves as an important environmental sensor. It was sports fishermen, for example, who first brought acid rain to the attention of scientists—when it was noticed that fewer fish were being caught in lakes which had once been productive. Many wildlife biologists and managers depend on hunters, trappers and others who live by the land as their best sources of information. While the plight of endangered animals often sounds alarm bells, it should be remembered that their threatened habitat also supports thousands of less glamorous plant and animal species, many of which are found nowhere else.

• Wildlife use protects habitat—and may be more productive than agriculture in some areas:

The destruction of natural habitat for agriculture is a major threat to wildlife throughout the world. Almost 90 percent of the large mammals are estimated to have already disappeared from Africa, mostly during this century. And the destruction is escalating, pushed on by the growth of human population.

In the second edition of his book, *Animals and Man* (1985), Richard Van Gelder, of the American Museum of Natural History, describes two regions of Kenya where wildlife is still plentiful. In one, elephants, lions, giraffes and other large mammals are strictly protected as an attraction for the tourist industry, which is now that country's second-largest producer (after agriculture) of foreign income. In another, gazelles, hartebeest, impala and other animals are harvested in an orderly way—as on any other ranch—so that their meat may be sold in Nairobi. Here are two clear cases where well-regulated commercial "use" of wildlife has ensured the preservation of their habitat and, hopefully, the long-term survival of many different species.

But then Van Gelder describes a less happy situation: "Fifty miles to the northeast of this ranch is another area I know. Fifteen years ago, I used to see giraffes, gazelles, zebras, ostriches and hartebeest there; today, there are no animals except a few donkeys pulling water carts. The land is divided into small farms, but they are bare and barren, because the area is suffering from one of the periodic droughts that is characteristic of this area. The farms are failing and producing nothing; the people are starving; and the wild animals are no longer present. All has been lost in this place.

"It is still my philosophy that wildlife can be utilized for the benefit of human beings without jeopardizing the existence of the wild species and without destroying their habitat. It is just another form of harvest and human enterprise.

"Some parts of the world produce agricultural products; other parts of the world can use their lands, unsuited for farming, for the production of cash crops from wildlife, be they skins, meat or passive tourism, with which they can purchase the surplus food from other lands. This, to me, is the way of the future and the hope for both humans and animals. But it does require intelligence. . . "

• Wildlife use can help control the impact of existing agriculture on surrounding habitat.

In western Canada (as in many parts of the world), up to 95 percent of the available fresh water is used for agricultural purposes. Agriculture could use the remaining 5 percent as well, to produce more wheat and cattle. But this water now supplies marshes and wetlands that are prime habitat for many wildlife species. Without the income which now comes into the province from hunters, fishermen and trappers, biologists would have difficulty convincing administrators (and taxpayers) to resist the higher productivity promised by agriculture.

• Wildlife use protects habitat from industrial development.

Sometimes wildlife use can prevent habitat destruction from occurring. In the Northwest Territories of Canada, native Indian communities lobbied successfully in the late 1970s to block construction of a gas pipeline, which they feared might disrupt habitat and wildlife through the Mackenzie Valley. Their efforts were successful largely because the communities could show that livelihoods were still highly dependent upon subsistence hunting and furtrapping.

• Wildlife use provides an opportunity to repair damage caused by industrial projects.

In regions disrupted by industrial activity, the possibility of using wildlife may ensure that at least some habitat is restored. The construction of the Bennett hydroelectric project, in the Canadian province of British Columbia, reduced spring flooding downstream and resulted in the drying of marshlands in neighboring Alberta. Efforts are now being made in the Fort Chippewayan and Peace-Athabaska Delta regions to restore some of this prime wildlife habitat. The work is economically and politically viable because it will provide local Indian communities with income from the cultivation of wild rice and muskrat trapping. Other ways the fur trade can help protect habitat include:

• Wildlife use may encourage other resource industries to employ methods which are more compatible with the needs of wildlife.
• Wildlife use can prevent habitat damage from the population cycles of certain species.
• Wildlife use permits "mixed" use of habitat. In a world where wildlife often must survive in close contact with human endeavors, natural controls on wildlife populations may not be adequate or may no longer be present.

3. *Respect for wildlife species.*

Despite worldwide threat of extinction to more than a thousand species and sub-species of vertebrates, one fact stands out strikingly: no species used in the fur trade today is endangered by overexploitation. Nor has this happened by accident. This has been achieved through careful education, controls and legislation, at both national and international levels.

• Protecting wildlife species: National controls—Furs are recognized as a valuable renewable resource and all of the major producing countries have management regimes to ensure that harvesting is conducted at sustainable levels. Exploitation is regulated through a variety of measures: controlled trapping seasons, quotas, licensing, biological monitoring and other techniques.
• Preserving wildlife species: International controls—International trade is now monitored and controlled under the provisions of CITES. The goal is to provide a safety net for national conservation programs by controlling international markets for these products. With literally thousands of plant and animal species threatened in various parts of the world, the difficulty of monitoring and enforcing international controls is evident. As far as the fur trade is concerned, however, the system has been overwhelmingly successful.
• Protecting habitat and wildlife from introduced species—IUCN estimates that almost one-in-five endangered vertebrates are threatened by competition from species which have been introduced, intentionally or otherwise, into their environment.
• Protecting wildlife from "non-target" captures—For the effective management of fur resources, the capture of furbearing species should be quite "selective." It must be possible to avoid nonfurbearing species, or furbearers which are protected by closed seasons or restricted harvesting quotas. Trapper training manuals explain in detail the techniques which allow specific species to be taken. A quick-kill "Conibear" trap for marten or fisher, for example, can be set on a narrow, inclined log or tree bough, making it inaccessible to overly-curious dogs. A sprig of pine placed over the "set" allows birds which are attracted by the bait to land without triggering the trap.

4. *Respect for individual animals.*

An environmental ethic must also take into account the interests and welfare of the individual animals we use. Recently, certain philosophers and authors have taken this argument to its extreme, suggesting that we have no right to ever confine or kill any animal, even if little suffering is caused. The problem is that a philosophy of never harming or killing other creatures simply cannot be realized.

We may choose, for example, to stop eating meat, but habitat will still be taken for cities and farmland. Animals will still be killed to protect our crops. Similarly, well-controlled fur trapping may actually enhance habitat protection. In fact, many of the industrial and technological processes which supposedly liberate us from the need to kill animals have proven far more damaging to wildlife and its habitat than hunters ever were. Animal welfare is a more useful concept: i.e., the recognition that our use of animals imposes upon us an obligation to minimize unnecessary suffering.

In the past century, humane societies have contributed to improving conditions for livestock, for animals used in research and product-safety testing and in many other fields. The fur trade has encouraged important advances in humane-trap research and development and research and codes of practice for the care and handling of farmed furbearing animals.

• Humane-trap research and development—Since any method of restraining a wild animal is likely to cause stress, government research in Canada has been directed primarily toward identifying effective quick-killing traps. More than 90 percent of the animals taken for fur in Canada can now be captured in quick-killing traps or sets. Canada has adopted a National Standard for Humane Traps, the first of its kind. Efforts are also being made to establish international standards, since animal populations must be controlled (e.g., to protect crops), even in countries where there is no fur trade.

Research is continuing under the auspices of the Fur Institute of Canada, a national grouping of government, trade, conservation and animal-welfare representatives. The goal is to further refine the effectiveness of quick-killing traps, as well as to investigate various soft-holding devices for the larger predators. (e.g., wolf, fox, coyote and lynx) for which no adequate quick-killing trap has yet been developed. This research includes that first attempt to measure the psychological stress experienced by animals when they are restrained in the new live-holding traps. Preliminary results (for foxes) suggest that this stress may not be much higher than that experienced during normal activities in the wild, such as running, hunting or eating.

Other moral considerations: Three additional concerns should be considered when animals are being utilized humanely and at sustainable levels.

• Avoiding "waste." It might be considered wasteful to kill an animal if only one part (the fur) is to be used. Native Canadian trappers, however, use the main furbearing animals (e.g., muskrat and beaver) for food as well. It has been estimated that the value of this food is often double what they receive for the furs. But without the cash income furs provide, few could afford to remain on the land. Even if meat is not consumed by the trapper and his family, it is not necessarily wasted. Trappers generally return carcasses to the woods as bait. Hunger reigns in the bush through the winter and this meat helps assure the survival of not only many furbearers, but also of birds, mice and other animals. Only the fur has been removed from the environment that produced it. Farmed fur animals are also recycled to produce fertilizers and other products. There is very little waste.
• Fur products are not frivolous items. Well cared for, a good fur coat will last from 10 to 20 years, far longer than most other materials. Unlike cloth and

synthetics, furs can easily be remodeled; their utility is not limited by the whims of fickle fashion. And unlike synthetics, a fur coat is produced from a renewable natural resource—its production doesn't use up scarce materials or burden the environment.

5. *Respect for the diversity of human cultures.*

A large part of the world's population still lives on the land, in small villages, working as farmers, nomadic herders, coastal or inland fishermen and hunters. No development or conservation plan is complete if it ignores the store of knowledge that such people have accumulated about their own environment.

Scientists are stepping back from earlier assumptions that Western models of development can or should be applied everywhere. Experiments have shown that many traditional cropping systems produce high yields, conserve nutrients and moisture and help suppress pests. Native wild herbivores are adapted to make use of natural grazing land without causing deterioration, and in extreme conditions, may be the only species which can do so.

The continued importance of wildlife in many parts of the world has been consistently underestimated. This is unfortunate, for were the true nutritional values and the uses made of wild plants and animals appreciated by governments, they might be more ready to encourage these resources to be managed sustainably and take steps to retain their habitats.

In parts of west and central Africa, up to three-quarters of animal protein in the human diet still comes from wild animals and wild plants are used for food and medicines. Across much of the North—Canada, the Soviet Union and Greenland—Indian and Inuit people still depend upon land and sea mammals for much of their food, as well as for the cash income they need to support a basically subsistence-oriented economy.

Recent anthropological research reveals that many aspects of the traditional beliefs and practices of aboriginal cultures are consistent with modern principles of conservation. This is not surprising. These societies are acutely aware of their dependence upon the environment. There are strong cultural sanctions against taking too many animals or wasting animal gifts (e.g., allowing meat to spoil). Taking more animals than one needs or failing to carry out traditional ritual acts of respect may result in animals refusing to renew their gifts in the future. Hunting cultures, we should remember, may be as valid today as any other way of living. As Alan Cooke points out, native people in northern Canada "gather harvests from land and seas that, through time, will be richer than any oil field."

At a time when radioactive dust circles the planet and cadmium and dioxins have been found in the organs of game animals in the far north, we need all the insight of modern science.

The modern fur trade is based on principles which accord the values now held by the majority of society. A high quality product and responsible conservation are no longer enough. An integral component of any responsible wildlife-use policy must be to ensure that the public is kept well-informed, on an ongoing basis.

THE ROLE OF BIOSPHERE RESERVES AT A TIME OF INCREASING GLOBALIZATION

Bernd von Droste

In the coming years we will most likely see an unparalleled expansion of ecological research at the local, regional and biospheric scales. At the planetary level this is due to the fact that humanity is now perceiving and experiencing a phase of ever-widening globalization—a time of chronic, large-scale, and extremely complex syndromes of interdependence between the global economy and the world environment. What were strictly local problems of air pollution or desertification are now elevated to the scale of entire continents, such as acid precipitation, or to the scale of the globe itself, such as in climatic change.

This trend toward globalization must be seen as a central issue. On one hand it is evidence of concentration of wealth and power within the global exchange economy which gets its impulses from a few centers of increasing influence. On the other hand it reflects a vast international grass-roots effort seeking new forms of self-help and cross-national cooperation which, by their very nature, are decentralized, citizen-oriented and fueled by NGO movements. Globalization is also the key to our current understanding of environmental processes, where we realize more and more that local phenomena are determined by global interactions. In socioeconomics too, we see that changes in the world market price system may have large-scale impacts on land use and resource management, which in turn may have positive or destructive effects on local environments.

There is a need to radically reform ecological research and conservation to reflect this globalization, since the environmental and resource management issues of today cut across traditional ecosystem boundaries, across social and economic systems and across political frontiers.

In the field of conservation and science is the multifunctional system of biosphere reserves. These are an international system of protected areas which are included in the Man and the Biosphere Program (MAB) both for their value in conservation and for providing the scientific knowledge to support sustainable development. The network of biosphere reserves is the foundation of a worldwide system of macroscale conservation and global scientific research. With the advent of globalization, biosphere reserves take on a new dimension which is complementary to their important task of resolving local problems.

Indeed, the International Biosphere Reserve Network deals with man/environment interactions at the micro, meso, and macrolevels. The individual biosphere reserve relates with its local community at the local scale; the biogeographical cluster biosphere reserve has a regional dimension, and finally the international biosphere reserve network as a whole has significance for global science, for the conservation of global biological diversity and for helping to improve human welfare.

The discrete building block of the international biosphere reserve network is the individual biosphere reserve site, which protects within its core zones a minimally disturbed ecosystem—hopefully allowing species to continue their evolution. The reserve zone also consists of a buffer zone where selected, controlled uses such as traditional land use, recreation and research can take place and human settlement may occur. The transition area—or zone of cooperation—which adjoins the buffer zone is used for demonstrating the application of ecological sciences to sustainable development, which is a top priority for the MAB Program.

The biosphere reserve concept can be adapted to specific cultural and socio-economic environments. The flexibility of the concept is increasingly attractive to policy makers and planners who wish to accommodate conflicting interests of conservation and development, to ensure relevant scientific progress and to develop efficient and cooperative relations with local people.

One major task of biosphere reserves is to stem the loss of biological and genetic diversity. Biosphere reserves should be located and managed in a manner which will help to prevent insularity and fragmentation of individual populations, which increases the probability of species extinction and accelerates the process of ecosystem decay, which in turn can precipitate biotic collapse.

A key subject for conservation research is how to manage the entire global system of biosphere reserves to maintain biological diversity while promoting the cultural identity of local people and safeguarding natural integrity to allow ecological processes to continue. There is a strong relation between sustainable development and conservation of biological diversity, but massive scientific research is required to understand it completely. Such research could focus on how much can we disturb closed canopy forests without upsetting the microclimate, or what determines the presence or absence of a given species. These are, among others, pertinent scientific questions for investigations in biosphere reserves.

Biosphere reserve managers should be concerned with maintaining biological diversity for two reasons: to preserve a unique set of genetic information and to maintain the integrity of a given ecosystem in the longer term. As biological diversity is lost at different levels of biological organization—species, population, communities or ecosystems—there is a decline in resilience and in the possibility for an ecosystem to recuperate from stress. Hence the need to maintain the integrity of entire ecosystems.

Biotic resource management in biosphere reserves requires a comprehensive knowledge of its biological resources. Biological inventories are presently carried out in several biosphere reserves in South America, such as Beni (Bolivia) and Manu (Peru), within the MAB/Smithsonian Biological Diversity Program. This program also gives priority to training. This year about 40 specialists will receive field training in biosphere reserves at the Smithsonian Institute in Washington. Another of the objectives of this program is to screen biological resources in the tropics for potential economic use.

Biosphere reserves work most successfully when they obtain the full support of local people who participate in their planning and management. Environmental awareness and education programs are key elements in this process. A recent survey of the 266 biosphere reserves which now exist in 70 countries shows that most of them have environmental education programs. Good examples are found at Tayrona (Columbia) and Pilis (Hungary). Furthermore, almost all biosphere reserves have facilities, such as at Berezinsky Zapovednik (Byleorussian SSR), Mt. St. Hilaire (Canada) and Montseny (Spain). However, a similar survey for research programs shows that only a small fraction of these programs correspond to the criteria established for MAB interdisciplinary research. Examples for successful research projects demonstrating sustainable development and cooperation with local people are found, for example, at the Trebon Biosphere Reserve in Czechoslovakia, at the Omayed Biosphere Reserve in Egypt, in the Cevennes Biosphere Reserve in France, at the Mount Kulal Biosphere Reserve in Kenya and in the Sian Ka'an and Mapimi Biosphere Reserves of Mexico. It is important to share this experience throughout the biosphere reserve network.

There are still many tasks ahead for most biosphere reserves. These include:
• Undertaking inventories of biological resources and of forms of traditional uses and technologies;
• Preparation of management plans which reflect the combined objectives of the Action Plan for Biosphere Reserves;
• Training of biosphere reserve managers who need to be "master integrators and motors" of the various cooperative functions of biosphere reserves, which have to be fulfilled locally and internationally;
• Establishment of long-term ecological research (LTER) projects in biosphere reserves. In the US, seven of the NSF-funded LTER sites are already included in the biosphere reserve network;
• Establishment of MAB pilot projects for sustainable development in and around biosphere reserves and,
• Establishment of mechanisms for cooperation with and participation of local people.

The mesoscale of biosphere reserves can be demonstrated by the example of the Carolinian–South Atlantic Biosphere Reserve in the USA, which is a biogeographical cluster biosphere reserve. This type of biosphere reserve is innovative in that it sets up a regional system which groups together disjunct conservation areas and major experimental strategy for a distinct biogeographical province within one biosphere reserve.

The cluster biosphere reserves are established to cover ecological gradients within a given biogeographical province and constitute major interfaces between ecosystems and other zones of high biological diversity. From the conservation biology point of view, biogeographical cluster biosphere reserves can be considered as the best possible insurance against uncertainty and surprise in a time of possible global change. This is because large, disjunct and diverse conservation areas are protected under coordinated management at strategic locations. These different elements of a cluster biosphere reserve should be linked to the extent possible through corridors permitting the movement of biota. Obviously, the management of biogeographical cluster biosphere reserves requires an innovative organizational framework allowing the close cooperation of different landowners and agencies. Such cooperation can greatly improve the quality of conservation and science at the regional level through increased interaction between those who would otherwise work separately.

The macroscale is the highest level of organization for biosphere reserves. Biosphere reserves will ideally cover all 193 terrestrial biogeographical provinces of the world. Today, we are 65 percent of the way in meeting this goal. In their final form they will constitute an unmatched system of macroconservation and global science.

Such a planetary network will be more than just an assembly of individual sites. Indeed, already today we anticipate that biosphere reserves will play a decisive role in global science in the 1990s as a planetary network for observation of global change, and more particularly, for the interpretation of its causes and prediction of its effects. This has particular reference to ICSU's emerging International Biosphere-Geosphere Program, a main objective of which is to understand the processes which govern the evolution of planet Earth on the time scale of years, decades and centuries.

The principal source of data for a study of this macrodimension will be the Earth satellites. The international network of biosphere reserves can provide key locations for research and monitoring, and as validation sites for modelling and remote sensing. Thus, a number of biosphere reserves can provide global observatories in critical, indicator biogeographical zones, such as the limits of northern forests with tundra, the alpine timberlines, the savanna/desert edges and flooded lowlands.

A number of biosphere reserves such as Lugillo in Puerto Rico (which in 1989 will celebrate 100 years of tropical-forest research), Bialowieza in Poland or Repetek in the USSR have some of the longest research records available. They provide excellent potential for long-term monitoring since this research has revealed the "background" fluctuations and ecological cycles upon which the more recent global changes are grafted.

The global network of biosphere reserves constitutes a vast laboratory for ecologists and other scientists. This potential is hardly exploited. The network lends itself to international comparative studies, in biosphere reserves having similar characteristics, to test hypotheses in ecological sciences and to develop a better theoretical basis for understanding the repeatability and comparability of ecological information. Such studies help to make ecology a more predictable—hence a more credible—science.

Four such worldwide comparative studies are under way jointly between MAB and NGO partners, particularly the International Union of Biological Sciences (IUBS). These include:
- Tropical forest biology as a basis of tropical soil fertility;
- Responses of savannas to stress and disturbance;
- Forest regeneration and ecosystem rehabilitation; and,
- The role of ecotones in landscape management.

A fifth theme, on human investment and resource use, will be examined by MAB in more detail as a special effort toward linking ecology and economy.

There is a need to study ecosystems both for comparative research purposes and to exchange experiences on basic biological research and technologies for the preservation of ecological diversity. For example, areas of study may include the design and management of core areas, the compatibility of specific uses in buffer zones and the overall question of how sustainable development relates to biological diversity conservation.

Increasing globalization of ecological and socioeconomic problems suggests that ecological studies and conservation efforts should be looked at and organized at different scales across—and beyond—ecosystems and with more orientation toward societal needs. Both conservation and ecological sciences have to move up in scale without neglecting crucial local tasks and integrate biological diversity conservation in a harmonious way with sustainable development.

The Biosphere Reserve Concept is pioneering such a harmonious approach. It is advocating an ecological ethic of cooperation, and more importantly, of man's partnership with nature.

TROPICAL FORESTS

TROPICAL RAIN FORESTS— GLOBAL RESOURCE OR NATIONAL RESPONSIBILITY?

Alan Grainger

INTRODUCTION

There is widespread concern about the future of the tropical rain forests, but considerable disagreement and uncertainty about how to resolve the problems that face them. This paper suggests ways in which scientific research could help us learn more about this important natural resource and manage it wisely. The central theme is the contrast, conflict and complimentarity between the national and international aspects of the tropical rain forests. Is it possible to safeguard these forests and if so, how? Who has the responsibility of doing this— the world, or the countries in which the forests are located? What is the most appropriate international role for tropical rain forest activities, and how does this relate to the individual national roles?

GLOBAL CONCERN AND NATIONAL NEEDS

Forests in the humid tropics are of global importance because of their sheer size. They cover over one billion hectares and account for two-fifths of all the closed forests in the world. Every year about 6 million hectares are cleared for agriculture and a similar area is selectively logged for timber. The tropical rain forests have an ecological importance because they form the habitat for 2 to 5 million species of plants and animals and have an as yet undefined role in the workings of the global ecosystem which we call the biosphere. They also have an economic importance as the source of 38 percent of all log exports, 14 percent of all sawn wood exports and 61 percent of all plywood exports.

Yet tropical rain forest resources are also very important to the countries in which they are located. Deforestation occurs mainly because people need to clear forest to grow crops in order to feed themselves. Logging is usually not a direct cause of deforestation. Because it is mainly selective and only removes a few trees per hectare, it does not normally remove the forest canopy. Although deforestation is caused directly by the expansion of cultivation, the primary underlying causes are population and economic growth. More people need more land to grow food.

How do we balance our international concern with the national needs of tropical countries? Didn't people in temperate countries clear their own forests in large measure for farmlands? Should we deny those living in the tropics the same right to choose how to use their lands? For that is what we do when we call for a halt to the clearance of forests to protect these marvelous ecosystems for all time; to conserve the gene banks of species of animals and plants which are good for their own sake and have important economic benefits; and to prevent the climate of the world from changing. These are all good reasons in themselves, but they are derived from our own perspective and not from the point of view of those who actually live in these countries, however much we claim to represent the world.

However, there is another kind of concern about these forests and the lands that they cover which may be slightly more justified. This arises out of an understanding that the soils underneath the tropical rain forests are for the most part poor in quality, so that when the forest is cleared and cropped for more than a few years at a time, the soil fertility is depleted and the land exhausted. The real problem of the tropical rain forests is that large areas of forest are being cleared for uses which are not sustainable. Magnificent ecosystems are lost for the sake of a few years of cropping or grazing, after which the lands are often abandoned so that yet more forest has to be cleared to provide more farmland. The way in which these forests and lands are being wasted benefits neither the tropical countries themselves nor the wider global community.

PRIORITIES FOR SCIENTIFIC RESEARCH

Since the loss of tropical rain forests is therefore often in conflict with national needs, one of the main concerns of the international community should be to help tropical countries to study their ecosystems so that they can decide which areas to conserve and to develop land uses which are appropriate in intensity to the capabilities of these ecosystems and the needs of their peoples. Otherwise, the forests and the lands beneath them will continue to wash away.

There are three main priorities for research: investigating the ecosystems themselves and the plants and animals which they contain; studying the human processes involved as a basis for modelling likely trends in forest cover; improving land-use planning; and mapping the extent of the tropical forests and monitoring the rates of deforestation. The next part of this paper outlines ways by which pure and applied research programmes can be expanded in each of these priority areas.

The main aim of science is to dispel our ignorance about the world in which we live. At the moment, ignorance is the best word which can be used to describe our level of knowledge of the tropical rain forests. We know so little about the species of plants and animals that live in these forests, the way in which ecosystems function and how to manage the forests for timber production in a sustainable way. Only recently has there appeared a glimmer of interest in developing cropping systems which are appropriate to the ecosystems of the humid tropics instead of merely being adapted from temperate agriculture.

The international community must provide far more support for both pure scientific research on tropical ecosystems and applied research to develop sustainable cropping systems for the humid tropics. Because it will take some time to establish sustainable agriculture, unless we expand our pure scientific studies now, much valuable fauna and flora will be lost before we have a chance to study it. All such research must be seen as a partnership between scientists from tropical and temperate countries and have a vigorous training component so that local scientists can grow as rapidly as possible in numbers and skills.

THE STUDY OF HUMAN PROCESSES

A considerable amount of ecological, zoological and botanical research is already being conducted in the tropical rain forests. However, the human processes which lead to deforestation and logging and which directly affect the future of these forests are hardly being investigated at all. What is happening in the humid tropics is probably the greatest land-use transition this century, yet we know very little about what is happening or the scale upon which it is occurring. This is a subject just as deserving of scientific study as the spatial distribution of a plant genus.

The study of the human impact on the tropical rain forests has been the focus of my own research since 1981. Research in Borneo and elsewhere indicates that action in the agricultural sector rather than the forest sector could well be the main factor that will influence future rates of deforestation. On the basis of this research, I developed a computer model to project future trends in deforestation for 43 countries, covering the major part of the humid tropics. Two scenarios were simulated, and they suggest that deforestation rates could fall to between a quarter and a half of their present levels by the year 2020, from 4.4 million to 6.6 million ha per annum respectively in 1980 to 0.9 million to 3.7 million ha per annum in 2020. This assumes that reasonable rates of improvement in agricultural productivity can be attained. These scenarios would lead to a reduction of between 10 and 20 percent in total forest area over that period.

Deforestation is but one of the two major impacts on the tropical rain forests. I therefore built a much larger computer model which includes both deforestation and logging. Simulations with this model show that the tropical rain forests are not inexhaustible sources of wood. Timber exports should peak before the year 2010, and by 2020, commercial timber reserves could be only a quarter of what they are today. Exports from Asia, which now supplies 80 percent of all tropical hardwood exports, should decline in the next ten years and by the end of the century will be only a small proportion of current levels. This means that logging will probably become much more extensive in Africa and Latin America. We should therefore begin planning today to anticipate future land-use problems and the need for improved forestry training if an uncontrolled plunder of forests is to be prevented in these two regions.

The model also predicts that intensive forest plantations in the humid tropics, which many thought would take over the timber production burden from the natural forests, will in fact only make a negligible contribution in the foreseeable future. So managing and protecting natural forests is especially important and will require a new programme of both silvicultural research and training so that countries in the humid tropics have sufficient techniques and skilled personnel for the future.

AN EARTH OBSERVATORY

The third research priority is to dispel our ignorance about the global extent of the tropical rain forests and rates of deforestation. There is still considerable uncertainty about the total area of these forests since only about half of it has been surveyed by any form of remote sensing since 1970. Tropical rain forests are but one of two major types of forest in the humid tropics (the other type is the seasonal, tropical, moist, deciduous forest) and we do not even have sufficient information to specify their separate areas. Similarly, current estimates of the annual rate of deforestation are based on actual measurements of deforestation rates for only six out of more than 60 countries in the humid tropics. Without better data it will continue to be difficult for us to convince decision makers of the importance of improving forest management and conservation and developing sustainable agricultures in the tropics.

This year marks the 15th anniversary of the UN Conference on the Environment at Stockholm, which urged that a continuous monitoring system be established to use the best satellite and other remote sensing technology to monitor the tropical forests. This vision has been lost and must be restored. We need a fully equipped Earth Observatory, preferably with its own remote sensing satellite, to continually monitor rates of deforestation and to tell us exactly how much tropical rain forest there is. It will also help us to gain more data about the other major environmental problem affecting our planet: the scourge of desertification which is rampant throughout the drylands of the world. What good is it to observe the other planets if we are content to remain so ignorant about our own?

PUTTING RESEARCH INTO ACTION

The final part of this paper considers how the results of the research proposed above could be put into action to achieve more appropriate and more sustainable uses for these forests.

Biodiversity and Conservation: Biodiversity, which describes the importance of conserving the tropical rain forests for their huge wealth of animal and plant species, is an admirable concept but of very little use until we can map tropical forests by ecological type and species composition. To do that will require the results of detailed ecological, botanical and zoological research together with the detailed maps of the tropical rain forests which would come from the Earth Observatory.

How do we assess our conservation priorities? The most logical approach would be to start with the most valuable areas of rain forest, identified by the research just mentioned, and then estimate which areas would be the most threatened within the next five years. This is where the study and modelling of human processes would come in, for by using appropriate modelling techniques and the data on the current distribution of forest and other land uses on a national, regional or global scale, we could project the likely future trends in forest clearance and therefore find the forests most likely to be under threat and in need of urgent conservation attention.

Once national parks or biosphere reserves have been established, it is then necessary to ensure that there is sufficient staff available to protect and manage them. To make maximum use of the limited personnel we do have, data obtained from the satellite linked to the Earth Observatory would allow local conservation officers to continually monitor the boundaries of national parks and reserves and take quick and effective action when incursions take place.

Controlling Deforestation: How can we bring deforestation under control? Because the tropical rain forests are situated on the sovereign territory of independent nations, it is their responsibility to control the way in which their land use develops. The fact that very often they do not exert this control is not because they do not want to but because they usually lack sufficient skilled personnel and technical knowledge.

The first step toward improving land-use planning will involve much closer cooperation between agriculture and forestry departments in tropical countries. Deforestation is not a forestry problem or an agriculture problem. It is a land-use problem and its ultimate solution depends upon a joint approach by agriculture and forestry departments to improve land-use planning and the sustainability of both forestry and agriculture.

However, land-use planning in the humid tropics is a little different from that in the temperate world, where an area of land can simply be designated for a certain purpose after due consideration of its various capabilities. In the humid tropics, shifting cultivation practices which move in space and time are already widespread, while supposedly permanent agricultures are in fact unstable and therefore also spread out over time to consume more forest. So even when sustainable intensive cropping systems are developed, it will still be necessary to blend these with existing practices. Change will not occur overnight. That is why we need a new form of dynamic land-use planning that will enable land managers in tropical countries to gain more control over land use and thereby over deforestation also. To develop these new techniques will depend heavily upon the results of the research into human processes mentioned above.

Climatic Change: There is already major international concern about future trends in global climates. Tropical forests are involved because the increase in carbon dioxide which results from their clearance and burning contributes to global warming. Other impacts result from effects on the water cycle and changes in the earth's albedo (or reflectivity) due to deforestation. At the moment, world climatic models have to depend upon very poor data on trends in tropical forest biomass and area. Obtaining more accurate estimates of deforestation rates, even in gross terms, would help to improve the quality of that input. However, we can also look forward to a time when we shall be able to combine our land-use models and the results from our observation with the Earth Observatory to create a fully spatial model of this portion of the earth's albedo and so improve the accuracy of our predictions about future climatic change.

CONCLUSION

It is possible for us to reconcile our global concern about the tropical rain forests with national needs if we can devise international research programmes that are complementary to national action but yet greatly increase our knowledge about these forests and the human impacts upon them. Such global concern should not, however, be aggressive, as is so often the case in the activities of some environmentalist groups, but neither should it be passive. We do not have any right to tell governments of foreign countries how to look after their forests, but we have every right to engage in scientific studies of large area change from outer space and a duty, if requested, to assist the scientists of tropical countries to learn more about their wonderful forests.

There is, however, a need for a new sense of urgency. Dramatic changes are taking place in the tropical rain forests now, and they need to be studied now. Some encouraging events have happened since the last Congress. For example, the International Tropical Timber Organization was established with a mandate to support research to develop sustainable management techniques for the tropical rain forests. However, we badly need a new initiative. The Earth Observatory, which would not only give us valuable new data but also make deforestation visible to millions of people all over the world, could be just such a thing. Time is passing, and for the tropical rain forests the future is closer than we would like to think. We need to act quickly to ensure that these forests have a future at all.

THE FAILURE OF CONSERVATION

F. William Burley

A World Wilderness Congress is supposed to be a happy event, a celebration of life and wild areas and our oneness with nature and a time to review our accomplishments in conserving the wonders of the natural world. So I ask for your indulgence for the next few minutes while I address what I feel has been a failure of conservation in the 1980s. The blame for this failure is on all of us, collectively. Most of my own professional life has been in conservation work, so I'll be the first one to claim at least part of the responsibility for it.

I see three areas in which those of us working in conservation and environmental protection have not done our job very well:

The first area in which we have generally failed is in identifying and agreeing on the most fundamental conservation priorities. Today there are no fewer than 40 groups worldwide who claim to be actively working on identifying priorities either globally or in the major geographic regions. When you also include other efforts focusing on the national or local scale, the number is well over 100. Many who are working on these priorities are here today.

But try to find some consensus among us on how to determine those priorities. The bird conservation people are working hard to determine their top priorities in conserving bird species and threatened populations. The primate specialists are doing likewise. The parks and protected areas specialists have their own lists and methods. We all speak of the importance of centers of endemism and areas of high species diversity, but in the end each group goes its own way. A report is produced, large maps are covered with colorful markers and formal presentations are made to governments and to development agencies.

But those who are making the real land-use decisions and who have the power to designate conservation areas or to move money into other conservation activities are deluged with recommendations—many of which are contradictory.

I can't blame them for being turned off and not taking action, because we conservationists do not yet have our act together. Some of us say training is the answer. Others say institution building is the key. Many of us worry that there is not enough time left—species and forests are being lost too fast—and we had better establish as many parks and other conservation units as possible, right away.

The final answer, of course, is that all these approaches are necessary and integral parts of conservation work on a global scale. But it is no wonder that the bureaucrats do not take action when we cannot agree among ourselves on which approaches are most important, where to apply them and in what order. For example, the recent U.S. Strategy on Biological Diversity Conservation contains no fewer than 67 recommendations for action and financial support by the U.S. Government. Yet for various political reasons, no real attempt was made to rank those 67 recommendations or even to make general statements about their relative priorities. So today it is more or less a free-for-all in Washington to capture small parts of the minuscule amount of government funding available for conservation work.

A second area in which we have failed is in making the case for conservation and the importance of conserving tropical forests and biological diversity. Despite all the publicity in the press about the loss of tropical forests and species, most people still do not believe that wildlife and forests are all that important.

This is even more true in developing countries than here or in Europe. We tell people about the origins of food plants, and about the role of wild plants in modern medicine and the importance of managing forests to preserve soils and water supplies. Major research volumes appear, like the impressive one recently by the Prescott-Allens on the use of wildlife and plants in the United States, but apparently all these arguments still are not very convincing to most people.

Only when we try to put dollar figures to some of these issues do people begin to listen. But even then, few government officials can look beyond their present terms of office—they have to see the prospect for immediate payoffs before they will support conservation projects.

A classic example of this failure to make the case for conserving species was a short piece I heard on public radio last Thursday. A physics professor from a university in my home state of Virginia was saying we do not need to worry about all this extinction of wildlife. The biologists tell us that extinction is a normal part of evolution and most species are doomed to extinction anyway. Besides, this professor said, most of the species going extinct today in the tropical forests are only insects, so why worry about them?

When you consider this failure to create public awareness of the issue and our own lack of agreement on how to determine conservation priorities, then it's not at all surprising that the current U.S. legislative earmark of $2.5 million per year for biological diversity conservation is so small. To keep it in perspective, $2.5 million is about 1 percent of the amount we Americans spend each year on our dogs and cats.

A third failure we must admit is our inability to clearly make the link between conservation and development. Despite the good efforts of IUCN, World Wildlife Fund and others in developing National Conservation Strategies, despite a week-long conference in Ottawa last year on this very topic, the conservation and development concept has been much more rhetoric than real action.

We must continue to build the system of parks and protected areas as an essential part of conservation, but we will fail miserably in this business if we think primarily in terms of parks and wilderness areas. We are all fond of saying that we must link conservation with development. But nobody knows how to do this very well yet, and we do not have very many good examples.

The whole arsenal of conservation techniques used in this country, Great Britain and Australia has hardly been used at all in the tropical developing countries. Many of them are not useful or applicable outside of temperate zone countries. I am speaking about methods other than land acquisition, such as leases, conservation easements, and a wide range of management agreements that can help achieve our conservation objectives without always having to buy land or lock it up in a park or strict nature reserve.

So far the conservation and development idea is mostly words. It is difficult to find five good conservation and development examples that are working today and have been working for at least five years, in each of the three major geographic regions. Rarely do we have a case in which a major conservation objective has been served, including perhaps the establishment of a core conservation area, while at the same time there being significant local economic development.

The best examples may be some of the MAB Biosphere Reserves. But in my opinion, even the MAB system needs to be broadened considerably and it suffers badly from the image of preservationism in the minds of many government officials. How many examples can we point to where timber harvesting has been planned or coordinated along with, or perish the thought, inside a "conservation" area?

Until we routinely think of doing conservation work in concert with—and as a component of—development, our conservation projects will simply be add-ons, and the conservation community will continue to be looked upon as just another special interest group fighting for a tiny share of the public treasury.

I agree very much with the comments of banker Michael Sweatman that we in the North do not really appreciate the development problems of the Third World. For this reason, we must be very careful with the concept of wilderness itself and with our advocacy of it around the world. To a very real extent, wilderness is a luxury we can afford here in the United States and in a few other countries. But it is anathema and an offensive concept to many persons in the developing countries—persons who must live day to day by exploiting the local forests and who may have no options other than destroying the local resource base.

As the Minister of Public Lands from Botswana asserted earlier at this very conference, if we expect to conserve forests and establish conservation areas in many of these countries, then not only must we help pay for it directly, but we must find new jobs and other sources of income and food for the people who may be displaced.

There is cause, however, for some optimism about conservation. There are three recent developments that, in my opinion, will bring about major changes over the next few years.

One example is the Tropical Forestry Action Plan (TFAP) that is being coordinated by FAO in close cooperation with developing country governments, the development assistance agencies, and a few non-governmental organizations. The TFAP grew out of the Global Possible Conference in Washington in 1984 and out of the work of FAO's Committee on Forest Development in the Tropics.

The Global Action Plan calls for major expenditures of at least $8 billion over five years to conserve and develop tropical forests. Major emphasis is placed on sustainable exploitation of the forests, on research and on conservation of tropical forest ecosystems.

The work so far has concentrated on outlining global priorities in forestry, on calling attention to the urgency and disastrous consequences of continued forest loss and on mobilizing action at the national level. Over 30 nations are now in the process of reviewing their forest sector, and they are developing national action plans to manage their remaining forests and to replenish or restore much of the forest already lost. Attempts are being made specifically to ensure that the forestry sector is being examined in relation to agriculture and national economic development more generally.

However, the Global Action Plan and the national plans following from it need improvement in several respects. There has not been enough emphasis on involving non-governmental organizations in the process, but steps are being taken now to correct this. The World Resources Institute cosponsored three regional NGO workshops this past year to try to get more national and local NGOs directly involved in the action plan process. Other NGOs are working at the national level in several countries to also ensure local participation in the process.

Further, forest ecosystem conservation needs more emphasis and monitoring in the action plan. However, if all the recommendations in the action plan about managing forests on a truly sustainable basis were to be carried out, many of the remaining tropical forests would be conserved and the biological diversity found in these forests would be less threatened.

The plight of indigenous peoples living in tropical forests is another area that needs more attention in the tropical forestry action plan process. I do not think that anyone knows the best answer on this difficult issue. It is far more complex than simply leaving these people alone—something that will not happen anyway.

Despite these weaknesses, the action plan process has so much potential to slow or stop deforestation that, in my opinion, we should give it our full support. There is no doubt that more funding already is being allocated to forestry by the development assistance agencies—in fact the doubling of development assistance in forestry called for in the action plan will happen in only three years, rather than five as we had expected. The development agencies are coordinating their development assistance better than before, although there still is much room for improvement. Financing continues to flow into some questionable development projects, but that too is changing. The question that remains to haunt many of us, however, is whether all of this response will be commensurate with the scale of the problem.

For that reason, another very encouraging prospect is the whole area of international financing for conservation. Debt forgiveness or debt swapping is only one part of a whole menu of possibilities. Several years ago, Ira Rubinoff and Nicholas Guppy separately proposed saving tropical forests by using innovative financing schemes to allocate much of the cost of forest conservation to the developed countries. Both of their proposals seemed to the economists to be unrealistic—but perhaps they were only a few years too early with their ideas.

Lastly, another recent development that promises to bring major changes is the crisis that is developing on the international conservation scene—a crisis of organizations—in modern jargon, a real "turf" battle. It revolves around the issues of conservation data and funding for conservation activities. I see this crisis as something positive that will force us all to reexamine our priorities and in some cases, our enormous organizational arrogance. In the process we may just happen to agree on the real conservation priorities and how to go about getting the job done. The identity of the major actors by the time of the next World Wilderness Congress is anyone's guess.

We had better enjoy wilderness, the tropical forests and biological diversity while we can, because clearly we are losing all of them. Regardless of our heroic actions to change this, it is inevitable that most of the tropical forests as we know them today and much of the world's biological diversity will be lost in the next 100 years. This fact will not change even if the most optimistic predictions of population growth and habitat loss turn out to be true.

In conclusion, I believe there must be changes in the scale of some of our expenditures. I have already mentioned the amount spent each year on our dogs and cats—it is more than we spend on biological diversity conservation projects. But the comparisons are endless. For example, the states of Texas and Florida together recently spent about $12 million to officially receive the Pope. Now I am not against the Pope's travels, but that amount is more than twice the ambitious fund-raising target that was achieved in the recent Costa Rica Parks and Conservation Campaign.

In America especially, I think we need to get our priorities straight. Thanks to our tax laws, we Americans give away more than $80 billion each year to our favorite charities. About half this amount goes to our churches—more money than goes into all foreign aid or development assistance each year worldwide. It is not surprising that far less than 1 percent of the $80 billion each year goes into conservation work in the broadest sense. This shows that those of us who are working in conservation simply are not working hard enough.

NATIONAL CASE STUDIES

"It is impossible to successfully resolve environmental problems in one country, no matter how large or advanced it is, without solving the problem in the whole world."
—Dr. Roman I. Zlotin
USSR Academy of Sciences

AFRICA

BOTSWANA—STRATEGIES FOR PROGRESS

Patrick K. Balopi

As a matter of priority, Botswana is currently preparing a National Conservation Strategy to deal with all the country's problems of environmental deterioration. Specific proposals which relate to the livestock, wildlife and other sectors will include:

• Range management techniques for farmers on the communal areas and on leasehold and freehold farms;
• Improvement of marketing facilities through which it is hoped distribution will be increased and thus the range be conserved;
• The implementation of relevant sections of the Agricultural Resources Conservation Act;
• Improved infrastructural provision for wildlife in the form of more water sources in their habitat, improved cordon fence alignments and others;
• Better marketing and sustained utilization of wildlife to generate employment in the rural areas;
• Better water-development planning, which is crucial to the survival of livestock, wildlife and man;
• Improved institutional arrangements to facilitate the formulation and implementation of appropriate conservation policies and projects;
• Improved systems of environmental education to enhance community policing of natural resources; and,
• Generation of alternative employment opportunities.

While the Strategy clearly seeks to address a wide range of natural resource management concerns, it also deals specifically with aspects of special environmental interest. Perhaps our most serious problem is that of overgrazing.

This has been a concern which we have tried to address almost since independence 21 years ago. Consequently, our first livestock development project was started in 1973, and the lessons learned from that contributed to the launching of the Tribal Grazing Land Policy in 1975. This policy was a positive attempt on government's part to encourage both individuals and groups with large cattle numbers to move from the communal areas in order to reduce grazing pressures and social inequality. Presently over 48 percent of the 300 or so allocated ranches are in the hands of these groups. However, this program has resulted in the "dual rights" issue, whereby the ranchers continue to have access to the communal areas, particularly after they have overgrazed their ranches. While government is aware of the need for change, it is also aware that this issue affects the constitutional rights of every Motswana regarding access to land. This matter is now under active government consideration.

Reverting to the wider issue of communal area grazing problems, the government of Botswana has recently introduced the National Land Management and Livestock Project. Government monitoring of the Tribal Grazing Land Policy has revealed that assumptions regarding availability of spare land, improvement of productivity and relief in the communal areas were overly optimistic. The National Land Management and Livestock Project has therefore not emphasized the development of new ranches, but has shifted the whole emphasis to management. One of the complaints from ranchers, however, is that lack of financial credit is hampering ranch development and better management which has led to a component being built into the project. These ranches occupy only 4 percent of our land area, nevertheless government has a responsibility toward seeking their proper management.

Though the credit component is large, in reality the main component of the National Land Management and Livestock Project is an attempt to address the communal area grazing problems where 80 percent of the national herd is located. Although this component looks very small in the project document, the people living in these communal areas have to be involved and therefore government has to go through a consultation process. The initial intention is to locate six or seven pilot areas in which the communities involved are prepared to commit themselves to managing their own grazing resources. If this program is to be successful, further consultation will be necessary. We believe this demonstrates a bottom-up approach to planning. In addition, government has commissioned an incentive/disincentive study under the National Land Management and Livestock Project so that it can create a framework for assisting all farmers, especially the communal farmers, to move toward better animal and range productivity.

There are other important thrusts to limit overgrazing that the government has undertaken. The national herd has grown primarily as a result of population growth and wage employment, and not because of outside interventions. In trying to promote distribution so that we can reduce stocking rates to levels compatible with seasonal carrying capacities, we require more abattoir capacity.

It is for this reason that government hopes to build a third abattoir. It is regrettable that pressure is being mounted by our critics against the financing of this project by the African Development Bank on the grounds that the project is harmful to the environment. Government's position is that increased distribution will reduce the incidence of overgrazing, which is presumably also the concern of the critics of existing livestock policies. Secondly, recognizing that the national herd is dependent on the range and that the capability to quantify and monitor range quality is very weak, government under the National Land Management and Livestock Project has commissioned a study to determine how it can provide this capability.

Perhaps the second most important issue is the question of wildlife conservation. In July 1986, my government passed the Wildlife Conservation Policy. This policy recognizes that Botswana has a wildlife resource that has economic, ecological and aesthetic values. Managed properly, wildlife can enable all these qualities to be exploited for human benefit on a sustained yield basis. The size of the resource after the recent drought, as determined from repeated surveys, stands at between one and two million animals. This is substantial. Given the abundance of the resource it has become necessary to adopt a management approach that allows for sustained utilization. Thus the Wildlife Conservation Policy does stress sustained utilization.

The Wildlife Conservation Policy also recognizes the land-use requirements of wildlife. It thus stresses allocation and maintenance of land for either exclusive or dominant use by wildlife. The exclusive use of land by wildlife is in the form of National Parks and equivalent Game Reserves, while the dominant use of land is in the form of Wildlife Management Areas. National Parks and Game Reserves account for 17 percent (over 100,000 square kilometers) of the country and are entirely preservation areas. No consumptive form of wildlife utilization is practiced here. The Wildlife Management Area boundaries, as proposed, now account for approximately 20 percent of the country. Here both consumptive and nonconsumptive utilization of wildlife are accepted. Wildlife and its utilization are regarded in wildlife management areas as the primary forms of land use. Other land uses are only allowed if they cause minimum disturbance to wildlife. Settlements for Remote Area Dwellers, for example, are compatible with wildlife management areas' objectives, whereas large-scale cattle ranching is not.

Wildlife Management Area location has been determined to take into account animal migration routes as well as to act as buffer zones between national parks/game reserves and major settlements and cattle-holding areas. They also will provide extra protection to some habitats and ecosystems which do not fall inside National Parks and Game Reserves. Thus wildlife management areas are regarded as an important land-use form which not only protects the animals but their habitats, while allowing such animals to be utilized on a sustained basis.

The foregoing should not be interpreted to mean all problems facing wildlife conservation have been taken care of. In some cases, fences have been constructed cutting across migration routes and obstructing wild animal access to water sources. The Kuke fence, constructed in the 1950s, is one such example and there are others. Lessons learned from the mistakes made in alignment of these fences have been painful and costly, and we are learning constantly. Current land-use planning in Botswana now takes into consideration all aspects related to any proposed use, and these include adoption of mitigatory measures. All fences in wilderness areas now have to take into account the wildlife movement patterns. Where areas have already been cut off by previous fence alignments, water is being provided for wildlife. Most of the boreholes for this purpose are located in the Central Kalahari Game Reserve and it is hoped that they will alleviate the water stresses of animals in the area. It is realized that providing artificial water points for wild animals can also lead to concentration of such animals around such water points and lead to further overgrazing and degradation. Thus, monitoring becomes imperative. Two projects currently being implemented by the Botswana Department of Wildlife and National Parks and funded by the EEC address both aspects.

Drought is another major problem facing wildlife conservation. Prolonged periods of drought reduce food availability and quality. To compensate for this, animals have to roam far and wide and many die from the stresses. Government is currently studying ways and means of reducing such mortalities, and methods such as culling, cropping and increased hunting quotas are now being given serious consideration. Poachers have been apprehended and intensified anti-poaching operations have been mounted.

In regard to our Remote Area Dwellers, of whom the Basarwa constitute a large proportion, my government has recently reviewed the Remote Area Dweller Policy. We are committed to giving such people land rights together with social and political rights in order to remove inequalities. What we cannot do is to prevent these people from adopting a more modern culture.

A fundamental approach in addressing these environmental issues is through the mechanism of land-use planning. This is why the Livestock Project was expanded to include a National Land Management component. There has been criticism that, because it is this livestock-related project that has helped develop our land-use planning capability in the districts with better coordination at the center, we are going to favor livestock. In fact, the contrary has happened. Our land-use planning provides the framework for facilitating all of government's development policies whilst minimizing land-use conflicts. Such policies include Tribal Grazing Land Policy, Wildlife Conservation, Tourism, Arable Development, Remote Area Dweller Programme and the National Settlement Policy. Thus we are moving closer and closer to having our land zoned for specific purposes. We see this as a vital step in preventing encroachment by other users and in focusing people's attention on management by realizing that there is no more land available. The intention then in each zone is to produce a management plan. For example, the Okavango Delta is largely zoned as a Wildlife Management Area. The Ngamiland District Land-Use Planning Unit has therefore embarked on a Delta management plan. This plan is vital, not so much because we see cattle as a threat to the area, but because other uses such as uncontrolled tourism also pose a real risk to sustaining this unique ecological system.

There are two additional and pertinent points still to be considered. My government is often questioned as to why it does not "use the stick" through legislative regulations, despite the fact that on the whole we do have good and adequate legislation. Botswana is a democratic country and we have a tradition of overcoming problems through consultation. Rightly or wrongly, we have felt that we must try to win commitment to better resource management through education. However, we do realize that things are moving so fast that we are going to have to rethink this strategy and seek better methods of implementing our legislative provisions.

The second point is an underestimation by the international forum on the effects of drought. Such conditions make it difficult to persuade people, particularly at subsistence level, to be environmentally aware in a way that is demanded by the environmental lobby. It is also difficult to disentangle temporary drought effects from longer term desertification effects. Drought is not an excuse, it is simply a reality.

The Botswana government is aware of the criticisms that have been leveled at the World Bank in regard to our National Land Management and Livestock Project. The American government has cited its concerns about this in its efforts to call for improvements to World Bank environmental procedures. We do not wish to get caught up in the need to reform the World Bank. What we want to put on record, though is that through misunderstanding and misinformation, this Botswana project has been singled out quite erroneously as a justification for such reform.

The government of Botswana is and has been aware of its environmental problems well before the orchestration of these international concerns. Pre- and postindependence practices were conservationist in orientation. A series of measures and policies, which I have already mentioned, reflect our own concerns. Further evidence for our independent concern is provided by the growing use of environmental impact assessments that the Botswana government carries out for itself, prior to project development.

Botswana is a sovereign, independent state that is master of its own destiny. We are not being dictated to by the World Bank or any other institution. Government believes that the National Land Management and Livestock Project meets Botswana's requirements and is an environmentally sound project. The World Bank, in this instance, has been sensitive to these requirements. Even if the World Bank is forced to revise its own policies, and if this is done in a manner which does not cause difficulties in meeting the needs of countries such as Botswana, then we will all strive to achieve sustainable development for posterity. The policy proposals which are being made to the bank are policies that Botswana already practices.

Mr. Chairman, I have had to concentrate on our Livestock and Wildlife issues. There is much international concern. To the government of Botswana, the important issue is the development of our National Conservation Strategy, in which we address all the problems of natural resources degradation in Botswana. The problems that Botswana faces presently are exacerbated by rapid population growth and the continuous drought which we have suffered for the last six years. These problems include soil erosion, overgrazing, desertification, deforestation, water pollution, rural-urban migration, unemployment, inadequate environmental awareness, poor range management techniques and, of course, the problem of livestock and wildlife management. In our quest for the achievement of sustainable development, we have therefore decided on an integrated, holistic approach to dealing with these problems through the preparation of a National Conservation Strategy which is based on a widespread consultation process.

We would like to extend an invitation to those who believe that we are on the wrong track to come to Botswana and to deliberate with us, to look at the people of Botswana's problems, as was done by Senator Robert Kasten. You will find us a warm and open people who take kindly to criticism, but who also believe in fair play and consultation to hear both sides of the story. We have nothing to hide and stand firmly by our approach to conserve our resources. We also appreciate that in the Okavango and the Kalahari we have wilderness areas that are worth sustaining.

KWAZULU—CONSERVATION IN A THIRD WORLD ENVIRONMENT

Nick Steele

Man is no longer at peace with his environment. The symbiosis that once existed—when man was part of the ecological cycle—has broken down. This breach has resulted in an insidious conflict that is reaching frightening proportions. The conflict is most apparent—and most intractable—in the Third World, where a fierce struggle for human survival is being waged with increasing desperation because of rampant human population growth on the one hand and an unsustainable depletion of natural resources on the other.

Rapid population growth is considered the greatest obstacle to economic and social advancement in most countries. From a 1980 total of 4,433 million, the United Nations expects the world population to reach 6,113 million by the year 2000.

Because of the age structure of the world population, a high level of population growth will be sustained well into the next century. A population exceeding 9 billion by 2050 is possible. To put global population growth in perspective, consider the following. In 1980, 75 million people were added to the world's population. In 1990 the annual increase is expected to exceed 90 million, and in the year 2000 it is anticipated that the figure will be over 115 million.

This vast increase in population has already had a dramatic effect on the natural environment. It is an effect that will worsen as more food, shelter and room to live is required in order to meet the demands of the increasing population. The resulting stresses placed on the natural environment have caused the balance of nature to break down. We all witness typical consequences: accelerated soil erosion, aggravated flooding during the rainy season and the drying up of once perennial rivers during the dry season. Other consequences are: increased water and air pollution, loss of crop yield and the loss or even extinction of many wild species. A diminishing quality of life for all is the inevitable result.

This is the situation in KwaZulu. This fragmented region resulted from the defeat of the Zulu nation at the hands of the British in 1879 and the consequential dividing up of the once-mighty Zulu empire into 13 separate chiefdoms. It has all the characteristics and problems of a Third World country. It is over-crowded—at present a population of nearly four million have to eke out an existence in an area of less than 33,000 square kilometers, of which only 23 percent can be considered to be suitable for crop production. The population growth rate presently stands at 3.1 percent, which makes it one of the highest in Africa. Nearly 60 percent of its people are under 20 years of age and so the present population of four million is expected to rise to over six million by the turn of the century.

Against this backdrop is the grim reality that, in many places, the carrying capacity of the land has already been exceeded. This has resulted in increasing desertification and deforestation as populations increase, and as more and more unsuitable land, such as steep hillsides, has been cultivated, more livestock is being kept on the reduced uncultivated land and more forest and natural bush areas have been cleared to make way for cultivation. There has been no alternative but to take more and more from nature in order to survive. As the downward spiral of environmental degradation turns, so the grip of rural poverty tightens.

This is well illustrated at Dlebe in the Mahlabatini district where some women have to spend up to nine and one-half hours covering 19 kilometers in search of one head-load of firewood. This load, if used sparingly, may be enough wood to supply a family's domestic energy needs for four or five days. The alternative is burning precious manure, when it is available, leaving the already exhausted soil deprived of valuable nutrients.

In a situation of steadily decreasing soil fertility, crops become more and more stunted, and consequently, food resources steadily decrease. In areas where there is still some natural vegetation, greater dependence is placed on those few remaining natural resources until they too give way with the heavier demand. In the end, starvation or migration to towns to join the swelling ranks of the underemployed living in squatter areas that surround the cities are the stark alternatives that face many of the rural poor.

One might well ask: In this situation of apparent helplessness, what thoughts can the people of KwaZulu possibly have for conservation? Let the Chief Minister of KwaZulu, The Honourable M.G. Buthelezi, answer that question. When he addressed the World Wilderness Congress in October 1977, he emphasized the importance of wilderness areas and went on to say, "Once we stop being wilderness-oriented, we are likely to feel caged, with a resultant desperation that overcomes all caged animals even if they belong to the species *Homo sapiens.*"

The Zulu people have a tradition of understanding nature. Their conservation awareness goes back to the foundations of their society. Because they lived close to nature, they lived in harmony with it and a balance was maintained between man and his environment. But this balance was lost when the white man arrived with his guns, his need for trade and, eventually, his soldiers, farmers and city builders. A new way of life, new priorities and new issues have developed but, in the case of KwaZulu, not at the expense of totally forsaking the values of the past. This commitment to the environment was given tangible expression by the KwaZulu government when the chief minister established a Bureau of Natural Resources in 1981, which reports directly to him.

The necessity of establishing the bureau arose out of a growing awareness that the classical approaches to conservation in nations with Third World characteristics are incapable of achieving their aims. Establishing inviolate wildlife sanctuaries or game reserves in order to preserve animals which had almost become extinct (following the wholesale destruction and wanton slaughter that took place at the hands of professional hunters, farmers and adventurers in the last century and the early part of this one) has little relevance to poverty stricken people preoccupied with survival. Indeed, these island sanctuaries contain a conspicuous but inaccessible wealth of natural resources and they are resented or are even a source of hostility among the people who live in poverty along their borders. Therefore, in order to make conservation relevant to people who have to live at the fragile interface between survival and starvation, the Bureau of Natural Resources is pursuing a conservation philosophy that is centered around three basic principles which Dr. Buthelezi has termed the ABCs of conservation:

- A is for Alternatives;
- B is for Bottom Line; and,
- C is for Communication.

Since rural people usually have no real alternative but to degrade their environment in an attempt to survive, it follows that for conservation to be effective, another alternative must be created. For example, in order to protect forest habitats against the strong demand for firewood, alternative sources of firewood must be found. This can be done by establishing woodlots. In KwaZulu, the Department of Agriculture and Forestry has established more than 100 woodlots. Another example is the use of plants for medicinal purposes. Traditional medicine is based on the use of barks, bulbs, roots and certain animals and reptiles. However, with increasing demand, more and more stress is being placed on available resources. In order to conserve the little that remains, alternative sustainable sources must be found. This is being done by the bureau, in association with various other conservation bodies, by establishing medicinal plant nurseries where endangered plants are grown and from which Inyangas (medicine men) can be supplied and/or assisted in establishing nurseries of their own.

The provision of alternatives is based on the philosophy that when the basic needs of the people are met through the provision of alternative sources of supply, then the restrained use of the remaining natural resources will follow almost as an automatic by-product.

The second principle of conservation in a Third World environment is the Bottom Line. This principle states that conservation cannot be practiced in isolation from the economy of the region in which it is situated. In other words, for people to value conservation they must receive some tangible benefit from it. There must be a bottom-line profit for the local community, otherwise no long-term conservation effort will be sustained.

Pursuing the bottom-line principle, Chief Minister Inkosi Buthelezi proclaimed KwaZulu's first game reserve on 21 October 1983. It is the 29,000 hectare Tembe Elephant Park, situated in Maputaland along the northern boundary of KwaZulu with Mocambique. The park consists of a mosaic of sand forest, woodland, grassland and swampland. The reserve was proclaimed in order to protect the last remaining herds of free-ranging wild elephant in South Africa, the endangered Suni antelope and the unique sand-forest vegetation.

The major significance of the Tembe proclamation does not lie in the fact that endangered species and habitats are being protected, but rather in the reality that the needs of the local people have been considered in determining the objectives of the reserve. The local people have thus not been shut out of the reserve, but instead were guaranteed controlled access to those natural resources that they traditionally obtained from the reserve area. For example, the people are allowed to collect reeds in the reserve for building their houses, provided they obtain a permit and harvesting is done at the appropriate time of the year. A percentage of all revenue earned by the reserve, including that from tourism, will be paid directly into tribal coffers. Income generated in this way will be used to build schools, clinics and other community projects.

The Tembe Elephant Park serves as a model for all of KwaZulu's future conservation areas. As new reserves are proclaimed, so the bureau will concentrate on integrating them into the local economy so that people will see that there is a bottom-line profit in it for them.

The principle of communication suggests that the success or failure of conservation in a developing region ultimately depends on the degree of support for, and active participation by, the people of the region. It is therefore vital that efficient two-way communication links be established between those who plan and administer conservation programs and those who have to live with the consequences of that planning and administration. In KwaZulu, the philosophy of "conservation by consensus" is actively pursued through close liaison with the local communities and the tribal authorities. Many tribal authorities have appointed conservation liaison officers who act as a link between the Bureau of Natural Resources and the community they represent. These liaison officers attend all management meetings for game and nature reserves within their wards, where they represent the interests of the local people. In this way, no action that may affect the local community can be implemented without their being aware of it and having an opportunity to influence the decisions taken. In addition, through this communication procedure, the community is able to request assistance and advice on conservation-related matters.

Central to good communication is the creation of an efficient extension service. The Conservation Extension Officer's task is to communicate with local people on a daily basis, visiting schools, clinics and tribal authority offices. They offer in-service ecology courses for teachers, conservation-awareness tours for chiefs and community leaders and conservation outings for schoolchildren. The bureau's extension officers also teach local communities the best methods of protecting and harvesting scarce resources. The relevance of this education has been readily appreciated by many rural communities, so much so that a number of Amakhosi (tribal chiefs) have set aside areas of land as community conservation areas. These areas of land range from small patches of natural forest to large areas of mountain catchment. As the areas vary so do the resources harvested. Forest patches may only yield medicinal plants, while larger areas may yield meat from game animals. All are important to a people who are dependent upon their environment for survival. The community conservation areas, of which there are now eight in KwaZulu, are managed by the tribal authorities with advice and guidance from the Bureau of Natural Resources. The purpose underlying the establishment of these areas is to create an area that is managed according to sound conservation principles and which allows for the resources of the area to be utilized on a sustainable basis. The community conservation areas of KwaZulu bear testimony to the reality that, given the chance, the people of KwaZulu have a strong desire to protect and care for their environment and to live once again in harmony with nature's rules.

Another example of conservation by consensus is the recent move by some tribal authorities to establish tribal game reserves. These reserves will be proclaimed in law and therefore the use of the land for other purposes will not be permitted. The reserves will be run by a management committee, with representatives from the community, the tribal authorities and the Bureau of Natural Resources. Staff will be trained and supervised by the bureau and will be paid jointly by the bureau and the tribal authority. The proposed tribal game reserves will fulfill all the functions of a traditional game reserve including patrolling, tourism and conservation management.

The battle for survival makes conservation in a Third World environment seem a luxury. But where the leaders of a Third World region have been able to exercise the discipline of standing back in order to view the broader issues involved, there is a realization that sound conservation is an essential weapon in the fight for survival. This is the situation in KwaZulu, where a policy of conservation by consensus is being implemented by the Bureau of Natural Resources. Through this policy of involving the community and gaining their consensus and commitment, conservation is being seen more and more as something that has meaning and tangible benefits and therefore is of relevance and value to the people.

Understanding the relationship between conservation and survival is essential because symbiosis between man and his environment must ultimately be achieved. If not, an increasingly bleak future, especially in the Third World, is the only realistic and infinitely tragic prospect.

Despite the omnipresent depressing realities facing KwaZulu, the underlying message that emerges is one of hope. Adopting a pragmatic approach, coupled with a genuine desire to help people attain their legitimate needs and aspirations, has minimized conflict between environmentalists and local communities. The resulting cooperative effort augurs well for long-term ecological stability in the region.

Wider application of the principles being developed in KwaZulu can help to ensure the survival of the world's remaining wild places and wilderness. After all, wilderness is really a by-product of a healthy environment.

EGYPT—THE RAS MOHAMED— CONSERVATION AND DEVELOPMENT

Hind Sadek

In August 1987, President Hosni Mubarak officially declared Ras Mohamed a National Environmental Park.

Ras Mohamed is located at the southernmost tip of Sinai, with which it shares a rich and varied wilderness of great beauty. The land bridge between Africa and Asia, Sinai was an important trade route throughout history and a crossroad that witnessed endless processions of armies from the times of the great Pharaohs of Egypt to Bonaparte and Allenby. We are told that Allenby himself found time, while battling the Turks during World War I, for bird-watching in the Sinai.

The land itself is barren desert in the north, with majestic mountains in the south and small towns and villages dotting the coastal areas, subsisting primarily on fishing and on trade. The mountains are rich in minerals, especially copper and turquoise, which although never exploited on a large scale, were known and mined since ancient Egyptian times. More recently, of course, oil is being extracted along the western shore of Sinai.

The climate is dry, with occasional low-pressure systems that bring rain from the Mediterranean to the northern parts; dry, easterly storms from the Sahara; and tropical storms from the Red Sea to the south. Daytime temperatures vary between 60 and 120 degrees Fahrenheit in the interior. In the winter, spring and fall a pleasant climate prevails.

Plant life is sparse, a result of both climate and over grazing. In the oases there are both the dome and date palm trees, and in the wadis, acacia trees grow. After the rains, annual plants cover the peninsula with beautiful and delicate flowers that survive during the dry seasons through their deep root system. This flowering of the Sinai desert usually occurs during the months of February and March.

Insects and other invertebrates are common in large numbers, especially after the rains. Butterflies visit the flowering bushes and plants, and beetles lay their eggs in camel dung balls on which the larvae feed—as did the famed scarab of Ancient Egypt.

The reptiles are well represented by the lizard, whose numbers include the desert monitor, agama and gecko. Snakes are also present, but rare.

Several species of mammal inhabit the Sinai, most of them nocturnal. In the past, excessive hunting unfortunately decimated their numbers, and despite bans on hunting some species such as the Sinai Leopard, they could not be saved from extinction. In the mountains, however, the ibex have escaped by being agile climbers, and in the wadis the elegant Dorcas gazelle survives and is increasing, thanks to hunting bans. Rodents include the desert hare and the hedgehog, both nocturnal, and a smaller rodent, the gerbil. Carnivores include the wolf, red fox, sand cat, striped hyena and the caracal or desert lynx. None are really dangerous to humans and all are now protected by law.

Birds are prominent in the Sinai, both migratory and resident. Among the resident species are desert, mountain and coast varieties such as the lark (desert), the partridge, eagle owl, raven and rosefinch (mountain), the grey shrike and babbler (wadis), Kentish plovers (coasts), and in the mangroves, important colonies of osprey, reef heron, spoonbill, tern and gull. Birds of prey are everywhere, the most common being the long-legged buzzard, short-toed eagle, Egyptian vulture, griffon vulture and falcon.

Far more numerous are the transient birds, who pass the Sinai by the millions on their way to and from the more hospitable climates of Africa. Herons, egrets and flamingos visit the northern shores and lagoons and sometimes stay to breed. Nearly 500,000 white storks and more than 200,000 eagles pass through every year. Many succumb to exhaustion and dehydration. Quail cross the Mediterranean by the hundreds of thousands.

By far the most numerous inhabitants of the Sinai are the songbirds, which occur there in great numbers and are present most of the year. Among them are wagtails, warblers, larks, shrikes and swallows, for whom Sinai offers a resting place. It is said that to witness the passage of these millions upon millions of birds is one of the most magnificent sights of the natural world.

The peninsula of Ras Mohamed is joined to Sinai by a land bridge of no more than 700 meters. It is surrounded by the waters of the Gulf of Aqaba, the Gulf of Suez and the Red Sea. Its coasts vary between beaches and precipitous, rocky cliffs. The latter, in the east, have acted as natural barriers so that corals and fish have been well protected there from human interference; in the south and west, on the other hand, the coast is more accessible and lends itself to development and to tourism. A shallow, protected gulf in midsection is also teeming with marine life. The Western coast faces the island of Ba'ira, with its vegetation cover of mangrove. Here again, marine life is protected from currents and offers tremendous varieties.

The geomorphological makeup of Ras Mohamed is the result of three geological events of almost equal magnitude: the first shaped its eastern shore, the second created the gulf of water mentioned above and the third caused the separation of Ba'ira from Ras Mohamed by a distance of only 70 meters, which could be joined by a bridge. These events have, of course, greatly influenced the composition and evolution of marine life, as have earthquakes, which are responsible for the formation of water caves in the lowest part of the peninsula.

Ras Mohamed falls within the southeast coast of Egypt and is characterized by a mild climate in the winter, spring and fall, with warm days and cool nights;

the summers, however, enjoy clear blue skies and hot direct sun rays. These sun rays exceed 450 watts from March to September and can be utilized for solar electricity projects. The coasts are exposed to the sea and land breezes. Depressions in the topography offer no obstruction to the northwest winds, which are therefore common to the region. Here, wind velocities, calculated at 3 to 8.5 miles per second, indicate another renewable energy source.

Based on the above, recommendations have been made by the Egyptian government to establish energy-oriented projects there, create a research center for wildlife (possibly on Ba'ira Island) and increase the scenic areas in Ras Mohamed. Outlines have already been drawn up to define the natural, legal and economic guidelines of the Ras Mohamed project, and are aimed at environmental protection and at the maintenance of the existing ecological balance.

SUSTAINABLE DEVELOPMENT: TOURISM

Ras Mohamed and the entire region of South Sinai enjoy natural resources that are rarely combined in any one area, making it a desirable spot for tourism. Controlled and well-managed tourism would create an important economic resource for the nation. Conversely, if not approached correctly the project would yield revenue for a short period of time, until unplanned tourist sprawl begins to pollute and visually diminish its natural beauty, as has happened all too many times before in many parts of the world.

Because of its location and environmental condition, Ras Mohamed offers a variety of interests and activities to tourists, ranging from cultural, historical, scientific, recreational and sporting, among others. Tourism, one of the sustainable development aims of this project, is based primarily on the diversity, beauty and pristine condition of the Ras Mohamed coral reef, one of the most beautiful and probably the richest in the world.

Coral reefs are formed over millennia by living animals—hollow-bodied, flower-like animals, with tentacles crowning the mouth that serve to trap tiny food particles suspended in the water. Corals can only survive close to the surface, as they depend upon algae for their growth. They usually form colonies of thousands of individuals. To form a coral reef takes thousands of years, to destroy it, considerably less. A coral reef broken down below a certain level will regenerate. Tourism, therefore, would be very clear on one point: No removal of corals!

THE REEF AND ITS INHABITANTS

With its intricate pattern of caves, nooks and crannies, the coral reef is the home of a multitude of animals. Undisturbed, it is teeming with life. At Ras Mohamed more that 100 species of coral have been identified, not all of them stony corals. There are also sponges, sea anemones, countless varieties of mollusks, snails, clams, crabs, shrimps, spiny lobster and other crustaceans, as well as the octopuses that lodge in caves.

But of all the inhabitants of the reef, the most spectacular of all sea life are the fish. The richness of the reef offers a home for many different fish, most of them quite colorful. The most beautiful among them is probably the angel fish, the most common and obvious is the sea goldfish. Other inhabitants of the reef are anemone fish, parrotfish, brick-colored big eye, streaked sea slug, and in the fore reef, the slingjaw or telescope wrasse, grey butterfly fish and the peacock cod (which lives in the coral), the starry moray (a nocturnal dweller) and the hairy scorpion fish (a bottom dweller). Stingrays, sharks and barracudas are also common to these waters, but are not nearly as dangerous as the hammerhead shark, who is most frequently found off Ras Mohamed.

A coral reef is a very specialized and fragile environment. Its destruction by man would be unfortunate, as the reef requires so long to develop. The many life forms inhabiting the reef should all be protected, since each plays its own role in the balance of nature. The removal of one would cause an imbalance in the entire reef ecosystem. A more recent danger to the reef and its inhabitants is major oil spills, which probably represent the greatest threat to this very unique life zone.

The government of Egypt is well aware of the potential of the Ras Mohamed project. The government is also aware that, from the outset, the project has great and immediate earning potential, and that with a sound plan for both tourism and sustainable development, it could assure the nation of a long-lasting and expansive source of income.

The Ras Mohamed project is more than a source of income, however, for it can be a sterling example of international cooperation and progressive nature conservation policy. In order to make this a true transnational park with Egypt leading the partnership and concerned nations participating, the project needs a special initiative which goes beyond basic conservation. Keepers of the unrivaled treasures of human cultural achievement, Egyptians are also the keepers of this most beautiful and unparalleled natural treasure. Indeed, the entire area of Ras Mohamed, Sinai, the Gulfs and the Red Sea should become an environmental park that illustrates one of the world's most exciting and innovative approaches to development and to conservation.

Dr. Atef Ebeid, Minister of Cabinet Affairs and Minister of State for Development of Egypt, has noted the special aspects of Ras Mohamed:

1. It is truly an international natural resource demanding immediate protection and preservation.

2. Throughout its history, Ras Mohamed was protected because it was isolated. This is no longer the case. Oil spills and other debris from the sea are threats to the coral reef that makes Ras Mohamed the magnificent park that it is. Recommendations have been made, therefore, that a park and wildlife refuge be established, with expert and complete management.

3. Construction for visitors within the park should be carefully planned, with minimal on-site facilities to accommodate wildlife observation, swimming, scuba diving, snorkeling and so on. Research will also be considered. All these must be part of a comprehensive master plan.

4. The clean-up of all coastal and upland areas, removal of all trash,

especially in the mangrove channel, will receive the earliest possible attention.

5. Ras Mohamed, the Gulfs and the Red Sea offer some of the best opportunities for ecological, biological and marine research. Considerations, therefore, will be given to the establishment of a marine research center, an aquarium and a field school to be located in South Sinai rather than on the peninsula of Ras Mohamed itself.

6. Ras Mohamed should be viewed as only part of the overall picture of potential development and conservation. Already, visitors are attracted and the establishment of properly regulated tourism and management of parks for the whole area is one of the most important projects of Egypt today.

The Ras Mohamed Environmental Park of Egypt is such an initiative and is a note of hope for conservation and development—perhaps the first of many more.

A new potential project is an environmental education project involving the future citizens of Egypt: its children. The Natural History Museum for Children in Egypt is being established under the chairmanship of Suzanne Mubarak, Egypt's First Lady, and aims to introduce children to the beauty of Egypt's natural world and to the need of protecting it.

Situated in a 14-acre park in Cairo's northeastern suburb, Heliopolis, the museum will invite children to visit integrated environments of Egypt's deserts, seas and its great river. They will examine Egypt's floral, faunal and mineral compositions through a discovery room, hands-on approach, a technique successful in the United States. Visitors to the Natural History Museum for Children in Egypt will explore varieties that are familiar and unfamiliar elements of the natural world, both indoors and outdoors. From the stuffed birds in the museum, to the aviary in the park, to bird-watching in nature, Egyptian children will observe, learn and acquire a more intimate understanding of the natural world. From that understanding will develop, *must* develop, a love of nature and a desire to protect and preserve it. I, for one, know no better way of teaching children to love and protect than by teaching them to know and understand.

Another long-term solution? Perhaps, but we trust that it will work.

EURO-ASIA

SOVIET UNION—NATURE CONSERVATION IN THE USSR

Roman I. Zlotin

Nowadays, the entire world follows the events that are taking place in the Soviet Union. The essence of these events may be expressed in three words: democratization, publicity and *perestroika*—economic restructuring. There is no need to translate them or to explain. Let me hope that there is also a growing interest in my country's vast area, which occupies one-sixth of the world's inhabited lands.

The state of land use in the USSR, with its diverse landscapes and long tradition in the field of conservation, problems and achievements, includes prospects in the matter of conservation of environment and wilderness. The report is based on analysis of the Soviet experience and published materials on regional and global problems of nature conservation, taking into account a number of overseas concepts.

In the USSR there is abundant scientific literature on different aspects of nature conservation. Unfortunately, it is of little use to many of our foreign colleagues as it is published in Russian. Equally, a wide range of Soviet readers, who are interested in nature conservation, are not acquainted with the broad flow of nature conservation information in Western countries. These circumstances, together with problems of a political nature, slow down the exchange of our achievements and the working out of the World Strategy of Nature Conservation. I believe that the future of the worldwide movement for the preservation of the biosphere is in an open exchange of information.

Before turning to the Soviet approaches to nature conservation, I would like to dwell briefly on our fundamental concepts of the ecological situation in the world. The problem of protecting wilderness has become part of a more general problem of environmental conservation. The protection and improvement of the environment should be provided for by the totality of international, national and public measures. It should be directed by rational use, renewal and protection of

124

natural resources. It should provide for the optimal living conditions of people and it should be able to satisfy the material and spiritual needs of the present and future generations of people. The concept of nature conservation in the process of a rational use of natural resources has become the core of the contemporary attitude to the environment.

Many Soviet scientists believe that the modern world is characterized by a drastic deterioration of the environment as a result of uncontrolled population growth, aggravation of socioeconomic relations and as a result, profound deformations in the nature-society system. We are not yet fully aware of the true scales of nature transformation, but with the continuation of current trends in population growth and in economic production, the pollution of the environment will lead to irreversible transformations of the biosphere and to an ecological global catastrophe.

Estimations of academician I.V. Petryanov-Sokolov show that with the current rates of economic development, the volume of industrial production in the USSR doubles every eight years. With the existing technologies and the rates of growth of the industrial production, its wastes will lead to a catastrophic pollution of the environment and to a regional ecological crisis within several decades—during the life of one generation of people.

Similar problems are also characteristic of many other industrially advanced countries. The problems of loss and pollution of fertile lands in the countries of predominantly agricultural orientation are as acute.

The pollution and destruction of the environment cease to be just a regional problem; it now goes beyond the boundaries of individual states and becomes global. A sad example in this respect is the problem of acid rains, which cross the boundaries of many states. And a sad proof of it is also the tragic accident at the Chernobyl Nuclear Power Plant.

Only One Earth, what Barbara Ward and Rene Dubois called their widely known book, was prepared on the basis of the materials of the UN Conference in 1972. In our days, it is impossible to successfully resolve environmental problems in one country separately, no matter how large or advanced it is, without solving this problem in the whole world. Professor A.V. Yablokov, a Soviet specialist on nature conservation, believes that "the modern world is in greater danger of perishing because of global pollution than because of intensification of class struggle."

In recent decades, different natural hazards have become more pronounced—droughts, floods, earthquakes and others. It is more and more often the case that they happen in those seasons of the year and in those places where they have never been observed before. The intensity and the frequency of such phenomena increase persistently. We are getting used to hearing the phrase, from weather forecasters: "Old-timers do not remember such hot weather and such rains."

We all remember such tragic events of the current year as the catastrophic flood in West Georgia, which has taken many lives, destructive mudflows in Kirgizea and Tajikistan, the unbearable heat in Greece killing thousands of people and the unprecedented summer floods in Iran with many human casualties. For many years now there is the tragedy of the Sahel desertification that has embraced an extensive area.

The processes of desertification have expanded around the planet, not only in Africa and the Near East. Desertification manifests itself in south Europe and in the southern regions of the USSR. Some frightening trends are under way. In the USSR, between the tenth and eighteenth centuries, an average of five droughts a century were registered. In the nineteenth century there were 10 of them, and at the present time in the desert-steppe zone of the USSR, droughts happen every three or four years.

The cause of these catastrophes is the growing impact of man on the natural environment. So far most natural hazards have been of local character, triggered by the transformation of those regions where they form and from which they spread. But the frequency and the growing area subject to them make us consider them to be the heralds of global catastrophic changes in the state of the biosphere.

The awareness of this danger is rapidly spreading among the Soviet public and is at the center of the Soviet government's attention. An ecological policy is becoming an important component of government activity. Approaches to the state ecological policy are found in the materials in the 27th CPSU Congress, in the June Plenary Session of the Party's Central Committee and in many current publications of the Soviet press. At present, practically every newspaper and every journal publishes materials on nature conservation daily.

Our science is called upon to play an important role in the solution of the urgent problems of environmental conservation. The Academy of Sciences of the USSR is working on two large programs devoted to environmental problems, the national section of the International Geosphere-Biosphere Program, the "Study of Global Change," and the National Program on Biosphere and Ecological Research in the USSR. The president of the academy, academician G.I. Marchuk, heads these programs.

What does the USSR represent in the socioeconomic map of the world and what is its contribution to the world community? I would like to present here some indices (as of the late 1970s) using data given in the Soviet press. The great dimensions of the country determine the proportional distribution of natural resources as compared to their worldwide occurrence.

In the past, the USSR was predominantly a forested country with a predominance of coniferous forests with nearly equal proportions of tundra and desert-steppe ecosystems. Economic utilization of natural resources has caused the ecosystems' cover to undergo great changes. Nowadays, the impact of man is found everywhere. For the most part there are no virgin ecosystems left within the USSR territory. In most biomes no less than one-third of the area is under anthropogenic stress. Only on 25 percent of the territory have natural balances been replaced by anthropogenic ecological complexes. In the main part of the country's area, rather stable, natural and seminatural ecosystems have been preserved in which the composition of plants and animals is close to the original.

Most transformed are the biomes of the south-taiga and broadleaved forests, as well as forest-steppe, steppe and desert biomes in particular. Here the natural ecosystem cover has been replaced by a type of anthropogenic field. In this natural anthropogenic field there arises different man-caused ecological problems and necessary environmental conservation measures are introduced.

The protection of nature in Russia has long-standing traditions. The first legislative acts on nature protection were adopted as far back as the eleventh century in the time of Yaroslav the Wise. In the thirteenth century, Prince Vladimir Volynsky decreed to preserve the territory of Byelovezhskaya Tushcha, which is now a State Reserve. In the fourteenth through seventeenth centuries in the southern borderland of Russia, there existed wide belts of reserved forests (the so-called zaseki) for protecting the southern tribes against nomads. In the same period, in accordance with the decrees of Tsars, populations of game animals such as beaver and sable were protected.

The nature protection decrees of Peter I played an important role in nature preservation. They were of an all-state character and primarily concerned the protection of riverside forests, where felling was prohibited. In the areas of felling timber for industrial purposes, reforestation was carried out. The water of large rivers, especially within city boundaries, was kept pure. The terms of hunting and fishing were strictly observed.

With growth of populations and development of capitalist relations in Russia as well as in other countries, a major attack upon nature began, characterized by a mass felling of forests, plowing of lands, and for the most part, uncontrolled destruction of animal resources. This process brought a wide movement of the Russian intelligentsia to life for nature protection.

Early in the twentieth century, the first societies of nature protection appeared in Petersburg and Kharkov. Reserves began to be created for protecting rare species of plants and animals, first by private capital and then as state establishments. Such were the Kronotsky Reserve (1882) in Kamchatka, Askania-Nova (1898) in Ukraine, and Lagodekh (1903) in the Caucasus. In 1916 the efforts of the Russian scientific community bore fruit and the first governmental act was approved. It accorded the organization of reserves for the purpose of conserving samples of nature. With the act, representatives of fauna and flora became an important national concern. The first state reserves established were the Lagodekh in 1912 in East Georgia and the Barguzin in the Baikal Region in 1916.

In the years of Soviet power, the ideas of nature conservation have further developed. The Soviet Government under the leadership of V.I. Lenin worked out about 100 documents on the rational use of natural resources and nature conservation. The decrees "About Land," "About Forests," "About Hunting" and "About Protection of Nature Monuments" were adopted in 1917 to 1921. Each laid down the socialist principles of nature protection. The All-Russian Committee on the Protection of Nature was established, which worked out a strict regime for the reserved areas' protection and delineated the first reserve areas.

The public has always played a significant role in the field of nature conservation in the USSR. In 1924 the All-Russian Society of Nature Protection was created, which is the largest public organization in our country dealing with conservation. In 1955, the Academy of Sciences of the USSR set up the Commission on Nature Conservation. It worked out comprehensive methods and measures for the protection of nature, coordinated the activity of scientists and established contacts with international organizations.

The USSR takes part in international cooperation in the field of nature conservation primarily through the International Union for the Conservation of Nature (IUCN), as well as in special commissions of the United Nations. A number of bilateral agreements on the protection of wilderness also have been made with the USA, Japan and other countries. A special environmental program was created, which unites the efforts of the countries—members of the CMEA.

In the USSR all natural resources are owned by the State, which helps apply legislative standards in the matters of the use of natural resources and preservation of environmental quality. The Soviet Constitution defines the duties of the State and of every citizen in the area of nature conservation. From 1968 to 1980 the Supreme Council of the USSR approved fundamentals of the legislation on land resources, forests, animals and the atmosphere. Corresponding laws were also passed in all the Union Republics of the USSR.

Working out the main orientation of the economic and social development of the country, the CPSU Central Committee and the Council of Ministers of the USSR constantly pay attention to the improvement, rational use and conservation of the earth and its resources—air, water basins, the plant and animal worlds. The possibilities presented by the state centralization in respect to nature conservation are so far not fully used. About 2 percent of the gross national product is assigned for the preservation of the environmental quality. This is not a small amount, but the several billion rubles allotted for this purpose is not highly effective. The reason is the dispersion of the state authorities concerned with the conservation and control of nature. Nine State Committees and seven ministries are responsible for the conservation of individual kinds of natural resources. They are, at the same time, the consumers of these resources.

Restructuring the management of nature conservation and the use of natural resources is being considered. The Soviet Government soon will make a decision about the creation of the All-Union and of Republican State Committees on the Conservation of Nature and Rational Use of Natural Resources. This will give a new impetus to the matter of nature conservation in the USSR. The great dimensions of the country, the diversity of landscapes and natural resources, as well as their irregular distribution create a complex nature conservation situation with many problems in the USSR. In the attempt to overcome these problems, about which our mass media speak much and openly, the state is taking many practical steps.

In the field of science, principles of economic and extraeconomic evaluation of natural resources are being worked out. On this basis, approaches are created and priorities set for the optimization of the use of natural resources. An obligatory consideration is the local account of natural conditions and natural resources. Much attention is being paid to the monitoring of a network of ecosystems and protected areas to determine effects of an intensive economic use. An important aspect is the determination of the factors and mechanisms influencing sustainability of ecosystems and particular elements of the environment under anthropogenic pressure.

An integrated geo-ecological prediction of possible consequences is the basis upon which we create a choice of optimal strategies to balance the use of natural resources with the need to preserve the quality of the environment and gene pool. In organizing the use of nature, scientific principles are introduced into the design of economic activity. The interests of different economic sectors are coordinated with the need to protect the health of people and wilderness. Here I would like to dwell, in short, on the organization of protected areas, since only this form of conservation provides for the saving of all the diversity of living nature and wilderness.

Between 30 and 40 percent of the area of our country has ecosystems whose state is close to the natural one. In the opinion of Professor A.V. Yablokov, which I fully share, about one-third of the area of all large physiographical regions should be preserved in a natural state. This is an indispensible condition for the preservation of the gene pool and is necessary for the living matter to be able to maintain its functions which regulate planetary homeostasis.

Here I mean not only nature reserves, in which any economic or recreational activity is prohibited, but all the other catagories of protected areas as well. In the USSR, there are also preserves and protected forests (where some kinds of economic activity are allowed), national parks and nature monuments. At present, all these catagories of lands occupy approximately 8 percent of the country's area; their area and the number are increasing.

There are more than 140 reserves in the USSR, occupying about 0.5 percent of the total area. It is in reserves alone that about half of all species of vertebrates and higher plants are protected. The entire system of protected areas provides for the preservation of the gene pool of the greater part of biota, including many rare species listed in the Red Book of the USSR.

In the field of technology, introduction and application of ecologically pure and economically profitable industrial and agricultural technologies are the main problems facing nature conservation. Waste-free technologies should become an imperative of industrial production, while in agriculture these must be ecological forms of the production of biomass.

There are four necessary conditions that determine the potential of rational use of natural resources, conservation of environmental quality and preservation of wilderness in the USSR:

1. To plan the national strategy for preserving the environment and wilderness, on the basis of an ecological theory which accounts for the dynamics of socioeconomic development of natural-economic regions and new technologies in the utilization of natural resources.

2. To see that all the existing rules and standards of nature use are observed.

3. To train all members of the society to be ecologically conscious.

4. To broaden the scientifically substantiated network of protected natural areas in order to preserve the entire diversity of ecosystems and their gene pools.

These tasks seem to be quite realistic, but are reliant on the condition that the development of our society and of the whole of mankind is peaceful, that the universal disarmament is successfully implemented and that the huge capital used for covering military expenses is diverted to the conservation of the environment.

USSR

Total area, % to the world land	16%
Population, % to the world population	6%
Closed forests, % to world area	31%
Woodstock in forests, % to the world stock	26%
Surface of forest cover, % to the total area	33%
Woodstock per person, cubic meters/person	310
Agricultural land, % to the world	14%
Agricultural land, % to the total area of the USSR	27%
Arable land	38%
Meadows and pasture	55%
Haying land	7%
Areas of irrigated lands, % to the world	6%
Mineral fertilizers, kg/ha	78%
Arable land per person, ha/person	0.86%
Cattle, % to the world	9%
Annual river runoff, % to the world	6%
Runoff used in economy, % to the world	12%
Unrecoverable water resources, % to the world losses	9%
Water reservoirs area, % to the world	20%
Total area of nature conservation territories in USSR	57%
The same, % to the world	14%
Number of species of vascular plants, % number of species in world	20%
Species of mammals	7%
Species of birds	8%
Species of reptiles	2%
Species of amphibians	2%

ITALY—THE VAL GRANDE— A WILDERNESS AREA

Bianca Vetrino

At the close of the 3rd World Wilderness Congress in 1983, a motion was approved inviting the Italian government and the government of the Piedmont Region to class the district of Val Grande, along with its minor valleys, as a "Wilderness Area."

Ever since, the Piedmont Regional Government has endeavored to achieve the longed-for result of complete protection of the Val Grande. To be able to understand the procedure adopted, it is necessary to offer a brief explanation of Italy's administrative structure and particularly the role of regions with regard to the central government.

The Piedmont region is one of the 20 Italian Regions. This type of territory is an administrative structure with a limited legislative power, as provided for by our Constitution. Every regional law must be submitted to governmental control and must conform to and be coordinated with the state's general laws.

The Piedmont Region is located in the northwestern part of the Italian peninsula and covers an overall surface of 2,538,000 hectares (25,380 sq. km). The region's capital, Turin, with its 1,100,000 inhabitants, has an economy based chiefly on industrial activities and is the site of the largest car manufacturer in Italy, the Fiat Co. From a morphological and environmental standpoint, the Piedmont Region is marked by three different characters: a mountain area (the Alps Chain), the hills and the plain. Thanks to these features, Piedmont is not only an important industrial district, but also an economically prominent agricultural region, especially in rice-growing and wine production. As to its more specific natural aspects, Piedmont is gifted with a great variety of environments, from glaciers to mountain forests, from woods of broad-leafed trees to lakes and water courses coming down from the Alps.

Because of this variety of environments, it has been possible in Piedmont to establish a system of protected areas of widely diverse and different dimensions, from the few hectares of some natural reserves to the 70,000 hectares of the Gran Paradiso National Park. I realize that such surfaces may appear trifling in a country like the United States of America, rich in great natural spaces. It is important to notice, however, that in a situation like Italy's or in Europe at large, the intense demography and the high population substantially modify the frame of reference, so any environmental defense policy must aim at the preservation of those limited but still natural spaces located among areas of high human concentration and activities.

In 1975, the regional government approved a special law and launched policy for the protection of the natural environments still present in its territory.

Twelve years after the introduction of this policy, 33 parks and natural reserves have been founded in aggregate. The program of the regional government is to establish, by 1990, 15 other protected areas. These areas, because of the environmental and territorial variety I have previously mentioned, have quite variable features (such as mountain areas, marshes, archaeological sites, natural monuments, rivers, historical and artistic areas). The zones deserving great attention from the administrators include chiefly that of Val Grande which, of all the possible districts to be protected, is the only one that possesses the features of wilderness.

The regional government, taking into account the pressures from the participants in the 3rd World Wilderness Congress as well as from the national naturalistic associations, has endeavored to protect completely the Val Grande area. It is an area that some people define as a "return-wilderness" area because in fact, this district has been inhabited and used for agricultural activities and was the scene of an intense deforestation in the nineteenth century. The increasing abandonment of the zone by the shepherds and the lower economic benefit of shepherding in comparison with other activities, has made the Val Grande slowly assume the characteristics of a wilderness area.

The procedure established to activate protection had to take into account a particular situation of both judicial and land-use concern in the district. In fact, the heart of the Val Grande is already now constituted as a natural reserve for a park and an oriented natural reserve for another classification. These forms of protection have been in force since 1971 and were provided for by the national government. Bordering these two natural reserves is an area owned by the Piedmont Region and therefore a public property. This is an exceptional fact in Italy, for about 95 percent of the territories designed for parks or natural reserves are privately owned. This seemingly favorable situation represents, however, a limit to the possibilities of intervention by the regional government. In fact, thanks to the definite provision of a national law, the responsibility for the natural reserves rests with the state, and the Piedmont Region cannot make any decision on the matter or legislate to impose safeguard rules. For the region-owned portion, on the other hand, the responsibility can be both of the state and the region, and national government is always entitled to intervene with its own regulations.

In order to overcome juridical difficulties, the Piedmont Region's government has proposed to the national government—namely the Environment Department—to establish a national park in the Val Grande, thereby taking a substantial first step toward the realization of the first wilderness area in Italy. Submitted April 8, 1987 the proposal located the borders of the area to be protected, covering a surface area of approximately 7,000 hectares. Though not very wide, the zone would have the characteristics of wilderness, making up a territorial whole we could define as complete and not directly influenced by man and his activities. It is possible to think of enlarging this proposed National Park by adding surrounding land, although this land could not be considered wilderness.

The proposal of the regional government discourages the construction of new hydroelectric power plants and has started a process with the national government that we hope may rapidly lead to the foundation of the National Park. This represents a full answer to all of those who have fought and still fight for the fullest protection of the Val Grande.

ASIA

NEPAL—THE
ANNAPURNA PROJECT

Hemanta R. Mishra

It is an unfortunate paradox that in the past, development planners of protected areas have often ignored the crucial link between nature conservation and economic development. Developers, too, viewed nature conservation as a hindrance to socioeconomic growth. But with increase in the rate of deforestation, soil erosion, and loss of productivity in the Himalayas, it has now been realized that the relationship between nature conservation and economic development is not antagonistic but symbiotic. Poverty and lack of appropriate technology have been identified as the root cause of environmental woes in the Himalayas.

The Annapurna Conservation Area Project (ACAP) is Nepal's latest innovation, integrating ecology with economics to halt the slide of environmental deterioration. It is governed by the needs for an ecosystem approach to maintain long-term integrity of the natural system while accommodating increased human usage including the tourism phenomenon. The important mission of the project, ventured jointly by the King Mahendra Trust for Nature Conservation and the World Wildlife Fund, is aimed at striking a balance between nature conservation, tourism and human needs.

In the center of the capital city of Kathmandu, there is an ancient man-made monument, the temple of the Goddess Annapurna, which in the local vernacular means "The Provider of Grains." Almost 100 kilometers northwest as the crow flies, in the heart of the Kingdom of Nepal, lies yet another edifice with the same name, created not by man but God—the Annapurna mountains. These mountains with snow-clad peaks that feed the river systems provide food grains and are a perennial source of water. Without water the civilization and agricultural development in river valleys, particularly the Indo-Gangetic plain, would not have been possible. These water resources also have led to much-needed electric plants and irrigation facilities for economic development in the latter half of the twentieth century. Similar to the American Thanksgiving, every year after harvest thousands of Nepalese pilgrims pay homage in Kathmandu to Goddess Annapurna. They offer rice, wheat, corn and other cereals as a Nepalese way of paying homage to the Provider.

In contrast to this man-made temple, the natural monuments of Annapurna attract a new breed of pilgrims: the twentieth century tourists armed with American dollars, British pounds, German marks and Japanese yen. While the temple has been sustaining the worshippers for more than four centuries, it is uncertain if the mountains can sustain another decade of human intrusion. The Annapurna range is a part of the fragile Himalayan Mountains, an ecosystem with its self-defense mechanism developed through the evolutionary process spread over millions of years. Patches of dense forest protected the steep slopes from direct impact of torrential rain. Rich and mushy green cover facilitated the absorption and delayed discharge in the form of springs and streams. Fresh soil and water resources of the Himalayas have acted as a nutrient bank for basic economic activities of agriculture and animal husbandry. Agriculture, trade and commerce flourished in the Annapurna basin for hundreds of years as human population density remained stable, with a minimum impact on the natural system as a whole.

The advent of tourism and the so-called rural development schemes, coupled with the increase in human population, triggered a process of environmental deterioration. An area that has remained virtually untouched and unchanged for centuries is now faced with a plethora of ecological hazards created by human interference in the last two decades. The pressure on nature in the Annapurna region is more profound than in other areas, such as Langtang and Sagarmatha (Everest). Each year more than 25,000 tourists—nearly five times more than those that visit the Everest region—spend an average of 10 days in the area. There are more than 130 trekking lodges and tea shops along the Annapurna trail alone. This has resulted in destruction of forest land creating a shortage of fuelwood and fodder. Tourism has become a major economic factor in Nepal and is deeply embedded in the overall socioeconomic development strategy. It is Nepal's biggest industry and the topmost spinner of foreign exchange, as far as the government is concerned. While the villagers of the area are worried about the loss of forest land, they do not refrain from demanding more roads, better housing facilities, drinking water, electricity and other paraphernalia of the modern age. Roads, agriculture and horticulture extension programs have been introduced.

Elementary human concerns for maximizing economic returns are not only restricted to the people of the Annapurna region. Yet, there are few regions where nature conservation is more vital to sustain the economic gains. The harsh realities in Nepal illustrate that it would be naive to assume that the issues of conservation can be isolated from the issues of economic development. Conservation essentially means creating an environment wherein wisdom is applied in order to create change for the benefit of humankind. It calls for an approach that regards man as a focal point for any conservation endeavor, right from the initial stages of planning.

It was precisely for this reason that after a tour of the area in the spring of 1985, His Majesty King Birendra Bir Bikram Shah Dev issued directives for the implementation of meaningful conservation measures. The royal directives clearly stipulate the need to strike a realistic balance between tourism, economic development and nature conservation in the Annapurna region. In essence, the Nepal Sovereign said that in the long run, tourism cannot survive without nature conservation. The trampling of the environment is like killing the goose that lays golden eggs.

In May 1985, the newly established King Mahendra Trust for Nature Conservation (KMTNC), took on the challenging task of implementing the directives of the nature-loving King of Nepal. The directors, under the stewardship of His Royal Highness Prince Gyanendra Bir Bikram Shah, decided to look for new and practical ways to integrate sustainable use of resources by the local populace, recreational trekking by outsiders and the national imperative to preserve the outstanding ecosystem of the Annapurna area.

By June 1985, with financial assistance from the World Wildlife Fund, a feasibility study was launched. The findings of this nine-month-long study germinated the Annapurna Conservation Area Project, which is an experimental model that involves public and private sectors—international, regional and local—centering on the theme "Conservation for Development."

THE SETTING

The natural systems in the Kingdom of Nepal range from the dense and steaming tropical monsoon forests in the southern terai, to subtropical and temperate forests in the midland regions, to the alpine pastures and forests in the high Himalayas, to the tundra-type temperature and barren land mass in the trans-Himalayan region. The biological diversities are best reflected in a wide variety of flora and fauna found in Nepal. To date, over 5,400 species of vascular plants (including 240 endemic to Nepal), 130 species of mammals, over 800 species of birds, 117 species of fish and innumerable varieties of other lesser creatures have been recorded here. A majority of these species and land types are found in the Annapurna Conservation Area.

Geography has dictated the presence in the conservation area of both the Oriental species of southern Asia and the Paleoarctic type of the Northern hemisphere. Wild animals of the area include some of the world's rare and endangered species such as the snow leopard, the musk deer, the red panda and many of Nepal's brilliantly plumed pheasants. In the botanical world, it supports lush patches of rhododendron and coniferous forests that contain several species of orchids and many of Nepal's 700 medicinal plants.

The area is internationally well known for its formidable peaks—a mountaineer's dream come true. In addition to some of the world's tallest mountains, the area also features the earth's deepest valley, between the Kali Gandaki, that lies in Dhaulagiri, and the Annapurna ranges. The Kali Gandaki meanders through these narrow gorges, forming rich river valleys that contain fossil ammonites dating to the valley's geologic origins in the Tethys Sea, 60 million years ago.

The United Nations has classified Nepal as one of the least developed countries. The population is currently 16.6 million and is increasing at an alarming rate of 2.6 percent. Thus, the population which had taken 60 years to double may now take less than 27 years to redouble. Nearly 40 percent of the population is less than 15 years of age. The density is 472 persons per square kilometer of cultivable land. More than 90 percent of the people are subsistence farmers who depend on depleted forest for fuel, fodder and water.

The fertility rate is one of the highest in the world, as it is most common for women to have five to seven children. Family-planning programs have been quite useful, yet only 17 percent of families practice birth control. Infant mortality is 133 per 1,000 live births and life expectancy is 44 years. Adequate health care is unavailable for most Nepalese—there is one doctor for every 32,000 persons and one hospital bed for every 5,000.

Despite government efforts to provide free education to all children, the literacy rate is a mere 23 percent. Only half of the eligible primary school-aged children enroll, even though education is free.

With the exception of tourism, industries are underdeveloped. They employ about 60,000 people and contribute only 4 percent of the Gross Domestic Product. Government has laid heavy emphasis on cottage industries, yet their average turnover is merely $150 per annum. The per capita income of $160 per annum is one of the lowest in the world. Nearly 65 percent of the 1.3 million rural labor force is either unemployed or underemployed.

In spite of these hardships, outsiders regard the people of Nepal as hardworking, friendly and tolerant. The Kingdom's Tibeto-Burman and Indo-Aryan ethnic groups form a mosaic of rich and diverse cultures that flourish to this day.

The Annapurna Conservation Area encompasses 2,600 sq. km. of undulating mountainous terrain. It harbors permanent human settlement with a population of more than 40,000 stretched over five administrative districts. Although all ethnic groups are found in the area, Gurungs, Magars and the Thakalis are dominant. Traditionally, men from the former two have served in the British and Indian Army. In contrast, the Thakalis have been traders, operating border business in Tibet and India. Incomes, levels of education and other socioeconomic indicators in the Annapurna region are slightly higher than the national average. Nevertheless, most of the people, who are poor rural farmers, depend entirely upon the land and upon nature for their livelihood.

THE SITUATION

Ecological issues in the Annapurna are not much different from those in other Himalayan and Hindu-Kush regions. The exception perhaps lies in magnitude of the problem. No other area is subjected to such a tremendous direct influx or impact of overseas visitors. Twenty years ago there was not a single tourist lodge along the Annapurna Trail. Now there are over 130 such lodges. Areas that contained patches of untouched virgin forest have been cleared within the last 10 years. New settlements to service tourists have cropped up along the trail right up to the Annapurna base camp.

Deforestation has increased with the increase in use of fuel-wood by tourist lodges. Selling wood has become a lucrative income generator. Deforested areas abound even in remote and core parts of the area. Toilet paper and litter are common sights even in spots of religious and cultural importance.

Because of public demand and lobbying by the elected lawmakers, a motorable road is being built along the southern periphery of the Conservation Area. A jeepable road has been completed through part of the once remote and enchanting Manang Valley which shelters cave-dwelling saints and sages.

Large hydroelectric plants are planned for the Kali-Gandaki river. Foreign-aided rural development projects have recommended introduction of exotic livestock with no consideration for the carrying capacity of pasture land. Rational forest management on a sustained yield basis is nonexistent. Poaching as a way to make cash has also been reported.

A lack of conservation awareness and conservation education programs have also contributed to the plight of natural systems. But it is clear that people will not want to preserve and protect an environment they do not appreciate or understand. Furthermore, it is doubtful if the poor rural population, preoccupied as it is with the problem of immediate needs for food, fuel and fodder, would care about intellectual discourses that proclaim long-term benefits from nature conservation. It has also often been emphasized that no conservation program can succeed without active involvement of the local people and without implementing programs that bring direct benefit to them.

In the past, few attempts have been made to integrate economic and social development activities for communities as part of conservation techniques. Conservation programs in the Himalayas have often failed because they focused mainly on an arbitrary enforcement of regulation. Efforts have not been targeted at the grass root economic and social factors that cause the villagers to illegally collect products from protected areas. Experiences have shown that income-generating alternatives must be provided to the villagers if we have to eliminate the need for them to engage in activities that adversely affect the environment. In short, the task is to strike a balance between the immediate requirements of the rural population and the long-term needs for nature conservation.

THE ANNAPURNA CONSERVATION AREA CONCEPT

The ideals of the ACAP are reflected in the statement of His Royal Highness Prince Gyanendra, the Chairman of the King Mahendra Trust, to mark the 25th anniversary of the World Wildlife Fund. He declared that the project "departs from the conventional approach and envisages a multi-dimensional strategy and maximum people participation, which stresses conservation for people and conservation to improve the quality of human life." Basically, ACAP recognizes the following concepts.

In the past, designations such as National Parks to National Recreational Areas had been proposed for the Annapurna region. In view of the complexities of issues involved, particularly the high human density and usage, a nine-month field study was authorized to find out what would be the most appropriate designation for the area. Without in any way diminishing the concepts and needs for national parks and wildlife reserves, the "Conservation Area" concept is an innovative exercise that will link conservation directly with human needs.

More flexible than a national park, it allows local villagers to continue to gather wood, graze animals and even hunt. The project design is based on multiple land-use concepts and the traditional methods of resource utilization. Programs include the formation of an effective system of zoning, with each zone having its own sets of management prescriptions.

ROLE OF NON-GOVERNMENTAL ORGANIZATIONS

Management of protected areas traditionally falls under the purview of government departments. But the question is can the governments in poor, developing countries with limited financial resources continue doing so? Even in the economically developed countries with large government budgets, non-governmental organizations represent a parallel alternative for implementing nature conservation programs. Unrestricted by cumbersome bureaucratic procedures, private institutions have the advantage to experiment with new ideas. On the other hand, non-government institutions cannot match the long-term commitments and legislative power of government institutions. Recognizing this fact, the Annapurna Conservation Area seeks the assistance of both the government and non-government institutions. A proposal designed to amend the existing National Parks and Wildlife Conservation Act is paving the way for declaration of "Conservation Areas." This new proposal to amend the ACT of 1973 provides for new incentives to institutions like the King Mahendra Trust to manage such conservation areas through active participation of the people.

THE KING MAHENDRA TRUST
FOR NATURE CONSERVATION

Fifteen years of experience in the field of National Parks and Wildlife Conservation in Nepal have revealed that efforts of government alone are not enough in an impoverished country like Nepal. The realization sparked the idea of a conservation trust. A number of experts were consulted, from organizations such as the Smithsonian Institution, World Wildlife Fund, IUCN and the International Institute for Environment and Development (IIED). By the end of 1982 the seeds finally germinated when the elected legislature passed the King Mahendra Trust for Nature Conservation Act. The trust is named after the late, revered monarch of Nepal, without whose foresight areas such as the Royal Chitwan National Park and the Sukla Phanta Wildlife Reserve would have been converted into agricultural land 20 years ago.

The trust is an autonomous, nonprofit institution established for the solepurpose of conserving natural resources to improve human life. It is an action-oriented organization that aims at achieving a balance between basic human needs and the needs of conservation.

A unique feature of the trust is that the governing board of trustees comprises not only Nepalese, but personalities of note from abroad. It is Nepal's only non-government organization to have been created by a special and separate act of the Rastriya Panchayat (National Assembly). The gracious consent of His Majesty King Birendra Bir Bikram Shah Dev to be its patron, and the nomination of His Royal Highness Gyanendra Bir Bikram Shah as the first chairman, has been a source of great encouragement to all of us who believe firmly and irrevocably in conservation for development.

The goals of the trust have been broadly defined in the act. This includes bringing about attitudinal changes in the masses through conservation education and by implementing programs that involve participation of the local people. It works in close collaboration with His Majesty's Government and foreign donor agencies. The trust supports field projects that the government or others are unable to finance or execute, including research and development of alternative sources of energy besides fuelwood, implementation of an effective conservation education and publicity campaign, applied ecological research and captive propagation of endangered species. Above all, its target is to launch programs that support the ethics of conservation for sustainable development as outlined in the World Conservation Strategy.

The King Mahendra Trust is a novel concept for a developing country like Nepal. Its success has an immense demonstration value for other Third World nations. As a body adhering to the basic principles of an NGO, some of its characteristics are bound to be unorthodox. However, the motive behind the creation of the Trust is to ensure that conservation programs are pragmatic and in harmony with Nepal's overall development aspirations.

Despite increasing conservation consciousness, no non-governmental organization has undertaken responsibility to manage protected areas of such global implications as the Annapurna Basin. Thus, the incentives for the King Mahendra Trust are not only to set a pilot project for Nepal, but also to set an example for the rest of the Third World.

MAXIMIZE BENEFITS TO THE LOCAL PEOPLE

Pragmatists have often remarked that money and personal benefits constitute the best motivations for humans. ACAP, for example, insists that the local inhabitants must reap maximum benefits from tourism.

Tourism surveys conducted by the King Mahendra Trust indicated that less than 10 cents of each tourist dollar is spent in the area. Most of it is not even retained in Nepal. Visitors on luxurious trips using high-tariff trekking agencies contribute less to the local economy than individual travellers who use the local lodges and tea shops. Of the 130 trekking lodges, 96 percent are operated by owners themselves who have, in most cases, merely expanded their homes to accommodate tourists. Interestingly, 82 percent of these people say they are planning more to improve their facilities—a clear indication of their faith in the burgeoning trekking tourism. As evidence of the tremendous growth in lodge construction, 68 percent of the owners say they built their lodges in the last five years.

Almost all of the lodges use firewood for cooking and a significant 48 percent of them say they bought their firewood. This demonstrates an improvement in the spending power of the local people. Significantly, 60 percent say they would be willing to cook on kerosene or other alternative energy if it is available and cheaper than firewood.

Easy accessibility is an attraction of the Annapurna region for trekkers and mountaineers. It is, therefore, clear that firewood consumption and impact on nature will continue until alternatives are provided.

One of the mandated responsibilities of ACAP has been to advise the local people to improve the quality of lodges and to help them standardize the pricing pattern. In addition, it has proposed a user fee that would be ploughed back to the area for conservation and development. His Majesty's government charges fees for trekking permits. But like most government agencies, the revenue goes to the central government treasury. This system discourages any entrepreneurial local management. A questionnaire survey of visitors indicated that 61 percent would be willing to pay between (U.S.) $5 to $10 more, on top of the government fees, if the money would be ploughed back to the area for protection and improvement of the environment.

A modest increase in the quality of facilities and services of lodges and consequent price rise may meet with little resistance. It can be assumed that low-budget trekking lodges will continue to thrive regardless of improvement and in spite of the not uncommon fear that this place will turn into the Alps.

The money raised will be pumped back to the Annapurna Conservation Area. This in itself is a radical and novel concept—non-governmental agencies with ability to apply funds from entry fees to a reserve toward conservation development of the area.

PEOPLE PARTICIPATION

One of the important aims of the Annapurna Conservation Area Project is to incorporate the local people's participation in the development and management of the area. If living resource conservation for sustainable development as outlined in the World Conservation Strategy is to be achieved, it must involve the local people, along with their traditional values, as an integral part of any conservation strategy.

Historical evidence testifies to the fact that the administration and protection of the forests in the mountains of Nepal proved effective wherever local control existed, because the interests of the villagers were clearly tied to schemes of rational and sustainable use of forest resources. The Forest Nationalization Act of 1957 brought major changes as centralized government control was exerted in forest protection and management. Consequently, the sense of belonging between the people and forest resources that had developed over generations was eventually lost. This triggered heavy damages by a free-for-all exploitation of the forests of Nepal. Even stricter forestry laws introduced in the 1960s and the 1970s had no effect as the local communities lost a sense of affiliation and involvement in forest management plans.

Ironically, by the 1980s, the government realized the need to revert back to the traditional system. Community forestry programs were again recognized as an effective means of protecting and managing forest resources. The ACAP recognizes the importance of traditional conservation practices. By setting up a chain of Panchayat (village) Conservation Committees, the ACAP aims to empower and involve the local communities in protection, law enforcement, management and use of forest resources on a sustainable yield basis, in addition to other nature conservation activities in the Annapurna region.

PROJECT ACTIVITIES
ESTABLISHMENT OF FIELD HEADQUARTERS

The size of the Annapurna Conservation Area, with its high human population, dictates a phase-by-phase approach. The first phase of the activities has been concentrated in one district and in an area where conservation action programs are deemed urgent.

Following a nine-month, in-depth survey, implementation schemes commenced in December 1986. Headquarters were set up at Ghandruk village, en route to the highly disturbed Annapurna Sanctuary. The core area of the Ghandruk basin is considered the "nerve center" of the first phase of operation. It is located along the popular and most disturbed trekking route. A day's walk to the east is the village of Ghorepani, a typical tourist village, along the old trade route to Tibet. Two days to the south is Pokhara, the administrative headquarters of the Western Development Region of Nepal. Located at an altitude of 1,950 meters, the population of Ghandruk village is about 4,000. The activities described below represent pilot efforts to integrate conservation with human needs.

FUELWOOD CONSERVATION

Water Heaters: Tourism being a major factor contributing to high consumption of fuelwood, with their demands for cooking, hot showers and campfires, it was decided to introduce energy efficient wood-burning technologies as one way to minimize wood consumption. Field tests were conducted for displacement water heaters with circulation coils. This system heats water while preparing a normal meal. It would make better utilization of cooking fires, as heating water alone consumes an excessive amount of firewood. A staff of the ACAP and two local tradesmen were engaged full time in installing these systems. Presently, eight prototype water heaters have been installed and are being monitored. Lodge owners and villagers have shown keen interest in these systems. This system is expected to generate additional income by charging tourists extra for hot baths.

Kerosene Depot: A kerosene depot has been set up at Chhomrong, the last permanent village before the Annapurna Sanctuary. A local management committee has been formed and a concessionaire has been selling kerosene since March 1987. Provisions have been made for renting stoves and containers at the site. A depot management committee has fixed the price of kerosene at Rs. 11.00 (50 cents U.S.) per litre. Presently all trekking groups and 12 lodges beyond Kinko Cave cook with kerosene and the scheme is expected to save over 1,600 kgs of wood per day.

SOLAR TECHNOLOGY

A prototype model of a low-cost solar water heater was designed and is in the process of being installed in Ghandruk. The conventional solar water heaters produced in Kathmandu are found to be too expensive and inappropriate as they were designed for a mild climate. This prototype was built using much of local materials and improvisation. This prototype can be built and installed by the local tradesmen themselves.

FOREST MANAGEMENT

Forest Management Committee: The Project recognizes the knowledge of the local people and their views on methods of resource utilization. Before the Forest Nationalization Act (1957), Ghandruk Panchayat had a very effective rotational system for woodcutting and livestock grazing. They had developed and formulated their own regulations that enabled them to appoint a number of forest guards to penalize offenders. Revenues collected were spent on community programs such as trail construction or even religious festivities.

In the beginning of March 1987, ACAP organized a public meeting in Ghandruk, where the concepts and planned activities of the project were explained. The local people were in favor of reestablishing forest management committees similar to the ones they had. A 23-member forest management committee was formed with at least two representatives from each of the nine villages. This committee has formulated a set of rules to define where, when and what species of firewood to collect. It is active and has already penalized seven people for cutting excessive amounts of wood. Once this type of local committee is fully operative, ACAP will supplement their traditional wisdom with technical advice, and financial and legal support.

Four nurseries have been established in Ghandruk and Chhomrong, and 70,000 seedlings were distributed during this monsoon. A third forest nursery for raising high-altitude species has been established in Ghorepani.

Near Ghandruk, an area has been fenced and planted with more than 7,000 fodder and firewood saplings. The plantation on six hectares has been chosen as a demonstration plot for raising both fodder and firewood trees.

CONSERVATION EDUCATION AND PUBLIC AWARENESS

The heart of the program is to enhance environmental consciousness through conservation education and public awareness campaigns. In order to avoid misunderstandings and injudicious expectation, public meetings in the villages were held to explain the aims and objectives of ACAP. The most promising development has been the formation of the Forest Management Committee, described above, and a Lodge Management Committee, which consists of selected lodge owners and an ACAP staff person who also oversees the use of kerosene.

At the behest of the ACAP, the lodge owners agreed to form a cartel. At a public meeting held in Chhomrong, 47 owners gathered to form a Lodge Management Committee. This committee has fixed a standard for ervices and prices for food and board in the area. Most of the lodges in the core area are temporary in nature, with bamboo structures. They decided to improve the existing structure to offer better facilities for visitors. ACAP outlined the basic necessities for a lodge in order to qualify for cartel membership. The cartel has the authority to penalize or dismantle lodges not complying with the basic standards. Lodge owners can apply to the ACAP for loans up to NC Rs. 5,000 (approximately U.S. $250) for improvement of lodges, and particularly to build latrines and rubbish pits.

Environmental education is an important component of ACAP. The extension unit has developed courses in environmental education for the Ghandruk High School and the children have begun course work on practical aspects of environmental conservation.

Presently, activities include examples of vegetable plots, forest nurseries, latrine construction and drawing and organizing essay competitions. ACAP staff imparts environmental instruction once a week to the eighth-, ninth- and tenth-grade classes.

On the occasion of Nepali New Year 2044 (April 14, 1987), the ACAP launched a campaign to clean up the villages. The teachers and students of the high school, ACAP staff and others, including village leaders, took part in this campaign.

A slide program has been put together and presented in the open school ground in the evenings. This has proven to be a popular and an effective means of conveying conservation messages. So far this program has been organized in four of the villages, but plans to show it to other villages are under way.

The importance of the women's role in the development process is universally acknowledged. However, village women in general do not participate in the decision-making process. A female extension worker has been hired to develop suitable programs to involve women in project activities. She undertakes home visits as part of the informal community programs to create environmental awareness. One of her tasks is to develop a mechanism for women to participate in reforestation, agriculture, sanitation and other activities of the project.

In collaboration with Tribhuvan University, renovation is under way of the Prithvi Narayan Campus Museum to house the new ACAP Information Centre. This will house a photographic display on natural and cultural features of the area. Three foreign volunteers have contributed their expertise in setting up exhibits of birds and butterflies found in the area. Minor repair work on the museum and construction of facilities for visitors is being undertaken.

The village around Ghandruk, where the project headquarters are situated, has a population of approximately 7,000 and receives an average of 15,000 tourists each year. The nearest hospital is in Pokhara, about two days' walk away. Villagers have repeatedly requested the government authorities for a health clinic. ACAP has proposed the establishment of a community-supported health centre in Ghandruk. One health instructor has been hired for one and a half years to train local health workers and to run the clinic until the trainees themselves can handle it. After this period, the clinic will be run totally by the village health workers under the guidance of a Village Health Committee. The villagers have raised an endowment fund of RS 100,000 (U.S. $5,000). ACAP will provide matching funds at a ratio of 2.1 rupee for every rupee the villagers collect. It is expected that the clinic will operate from the interest accrued on the endowment fund.

At the request of some of the villagers of Ghandruk, ACAP initiated a drinking-water project. A local committee was formed to carry out the construction work. The villagers provided labor for half the total cost of the project. ACAP provided funds to purchase pipes, cement and other materials. Successful completion of this project has inspired requests for similar support from other villages.

Sanitation problems are encountered along all popular tourist trails. Ranging from indiscriminate disposal of waste to crude toilets located directly over rivers and streams. ACAP has initiated sanitation programs by constructing two vent-dry pits and two composting toilets.

Over 60 percent of the households in Ghandruk do not have a toilet. A survey carried out by the ACAP extension unit showed that the majority of the residents expressed a desire to install appropriate sanitation systems in their homes. This project, it is hoped, will continue to encourage and assist in toilet building in the project area. Local tradesmen were trained in constructing composting and dry-vent toilets in the village. This project has proven to be particularly popular with lodge owners.

At the request of the village Panchayat, ACAP oversaw the repair and maintenance of suspension and wooden bridges. The local people provided free unskilled labor, while the ACAP paid for the services of skilled technicians.

RESEARCH AND SURVEYS

The study of wildlife habitat in the Nar Phu Valley in the Manang district is being continued by a zoologist from Tribhuvan University. These areas are included in the second phase of the Annapurna Conservation Project. Findings indicate that the Nar Phu Valley has a good population of blue sheep and snow leopard. However, wildlife is being threatened by overgrazing by livestock and hunting by people from outside the valley, although tourists are not yet permitted to visit this area. The Ministry of Agriculture has a pasture development project and the Livestock Development Board is considering setting up a yak farm in the area. The study will provide baseline data to integrate wildlife management with other development activities.

Feasibility studies of three rivulets for micro-hydro projects have been complete with assistance from Butwal Technical Institute. The findings indicate power generation from several sites in the ACAP area is possible. Site survey for a headquarters building at Ghandruk has been prepared.

Soil surveys have been conducted at several locations for plantation and nursery development at Ghandruk and Chhomrong in collaboration with soil scientists from the Research and Survey wing of the Department of Forestry. A report on soil conditions and choice of species for reforestation programs has been prepared. Two British ornithologists conducted a bird survey of the Modi Khola, a major river valley in the special management zone of ACAP. Arrangements are being made to publish their findings as a guide to birds and mammals of the Annapurna Conservation Area.

Multilanguage posters in English, Nepali, Japanese and French were designed and posted at strategic places for the benefit of tourists. The posters outlined some of the environmental pressure on the Annapurna area and how the visitors can help reduce them. ACAP has also produced an informative brochure for distribution and sale to tourists. It explains the uniqueness of the aims and objectives of resource conservation in Annapurna and includes guidelines on how to minimize the damage on nature.

TRAINING

Four persons from the project area received two months' practical training in nursery management at the British-aided Agricultural Centre at Lumle. One trainee from Ghandruk spent two months at the Department of Watershed Management and Soil Conservation of His Majesty's Government while four local semiskilled tradesmen received on-the-job training to improve their skills in plumbing, carpentry and masonry works. Two of the project staff recruited from the region will attend a degree course in protected area management in New Zealand. The Overseas Development Agency of the British Government has provided ACAP with one fellowship for practical course work in conservation education in the United Kingdom.

A training program specially designed for lodge operators was held in Chhomrong in July this year. There were 65 participants from 47 lodges in the week-long program conducted jointly by the Department of Tourism and the ACAP. This training was the first of its kind to be held outside Kathmandu and has proven to be effective, as indicated by the lodge owners' reactions.

At first it was difficult to convince the local people that ACAP is an integrated development project. They feared that the area will turn into another national park with restrictive government regulations. Villagers demanded ultimate benefits from the project. But as the pilot projects described above commenced, they began to show interest in conservation. By necessity, the project activities are kept flexible to allow individuals and communities to adapt to new ideas. The effectiveness of the programs is being monitored in consultation with the local people. Some changes and adjustments in the priorities as set forth originally have been necessary.

PARTNERS IN CONSERVATION

The World Wildlife Fund–USA has been Nepal's key partner in the conservation of the Annapurna area. A preliminary study and surveys financed through a grant from the WWF were conducted by Nepali and American experts. The chairman of the World Wildlife Fund/Conservation Foundation, Russell Train, is also a member of the Governing Board of Trustees of the King Mahendra Trust for Nature Conservation. The bulk of the financial resources required by the King Mahendra Trust for the Annapurna has been provided by the World Wildlife Fund. In addition, a number of experts from the WWF have visited the area and provided technical advice. Besides the WWF, the ACAP has received supports from a few other resources both local and international.

The King Mahendra United Kingdom Trust for Nature Conservation has provided funds and expertise for the conservation education programs. The British government has provided grants for training ACAP staff. Similarly, the idea and funds to operate the kerosene depot have been provided by the German Alpine Club. An Australian NGO, AREA, in collaboration with the ACAP, has undertaken reforestation projects in Ghorepani and helped in the production of water heaters. The government of New Zealand has provided training and fellowships to develop a cadre of managerial manpower. The government of the People's Republic of China has provided two micro-generators for electricity.

Within Nepal, the Tribhuvan University provided facilities for an information centre in Pokhara. Various agencies of His Majesty's Government have provided support. The Ministry of Tourism has given the ACAP a building at Kuldighar.

In addition to these, various individuals, both Nepali and non-Nepalis, including a Japanese taxi driver, have donated their time and expertise. The support-mobilizing efforts have been quite useful in getting new ideas on ways and means of generating international support. At times it fitted the predictions made by the Brundtland Commission that international assistance has not only been inadequate, but too often reflects the priorities of the donor rather than the needs of the receiver. Nevertheless, the ACAP has also been an experience in the integration of different kinds of international cooperation for the attainment of a specific goal in a specific area.

CONCLUSION

It has been recognized that large-scale poverty coupled with lack of technology is the root cause of environmental problems in the Himalayas. Thus, conservation programs should not be dictated by actions that discard economic growth, but by plans that are capable of diverting attention toward rational use of nature resources. In the past, international organizations with nature protection bias have often ignored this fact, as they have isolated the issues of economic development from those of environmental conservation. Recently, the World Conservation Strategy and the Brundtland Commission have recognized that it is impossible to separate these issues.

The harrowing account of happenings in Africa has tragically illustrated how ecology and economics are interlinked. The Annapurna Conservation Area Project is an experiment of a concept that seeks to demonstrate that good ecology is good economics, and vice versa. If over-development, over-consumption and waste are the problems of developed countries, then poverty, hunger, apathy and lack of economic infrastructures are the seeds that breed environmental woes in the underdeveloped nations. It has been pointed out that people who are ill-fed, in ill-health and have no shelter or jobs cannot understand paternalistic concerns for conservation of their environment. When the source of their next meal is a major worry, lofty principles of nature conservation for sustainable development have little relevance to them. The programs of the Annapurna Conservation Area are governed by the needs for an ecosystem approach to maintain long-term integrity of the natural systems, while accommodating increased human usage, including tourism.

Today, most conservation programs in the Third World are financed by either tax payers or tax-free money. While the former comes in the form of government inputs (either national or through bilateral foreign aid), the latter has been funnelled through numerous NGOs in Europe and North America, which receive tax deductible donations from concerned citizens.

But neither bilateral aid through governments, nor private contributions through non-governmental organizations, have attempted to ensure that nature conservation programs are self-supportive and economically viable for poor, developing countries. To the contrary, in the last two decades, these contributions have made Third World nations become not less, but more dependent upon international charity—a fact implied in the report of the World Commission on Environment and Development. The ACAP incentive of the King Mahendra Trust is an exercise that seeks to demonstrate how a nationally-established protected area serves as a catalyst for socioeconomic development through a system of imposing and recycling a user fee for visitors from the rich and developed countries.

Half a century ago, Aldo Leopold stressed the need to understand the relationship between the human environment and wilderness areas within the context of ecosystem interdependence. Though Leopold's ideas were concerned with wildlife conservation in the United States, his wise words have universal application even five decades later in the Annapurna region of Nepal. As the catchment of one of the major river systems in the Himalayas, the Annapurna basin is not only of aesthetic value for foreign tourists, but it is vital to the conservation of soil, water and resources for the people of Nepal. Thus, as has been emphasized by others, there is a clearer need to understand the human dimension of conservation programs, particularly the human and nonhuman dichotomy. It calls for recognition and understanding of the interaction between nature and humans who use and exploit natural resources. Problems once perceived as biological in nature are now known to be economic, social and cultural in nature as well as in implications. Conservation issues in the Annapurna area tend to verify these predictions. Thus the ACAP is an endeavor to bring about awareness through people's participation. It is an exercise that attempts to ensure that the fruits of conservation go directly to the local inhabitants. No program, however ambitious or well planned, can succeed unless it identifies with and seeks the support and cooperation of those who are to be the real beneficiaries.

The Annapurna Conservation Area Project addresses the problem of maintaining a crucial link between economic development and environmental conservation. It recognizes that protection of critical habitat and sustenance of species diversity cannot be achieved without the betterment of economic conditions of the poor villagers who inhabit the mountains of the Third World countries. Unlike the national parks and wildlife reserves, the ACAP regards humans (rather than any particular species of wild animals or plants) as the focal point of every conservation effort right from the beginning. After all, as aptly stated by the Chairman of the King Mahendra Trust for Nature Conservation, His Royal Highness Prince Gyanendra Bir Bikram Shah, "What is conservation—if not for people? It must be viewed only as a means, the end being the improvement of the quality of our very existence."

ACKNOWLEDGMENT

It would not have been possible for us to attend the 4th World Wilderness Congress without the gracious consent and encouragement from His Royal Highness Prince Gyanendra Bir Bikram Shah, Chairman of the King Mahendra Trust for Nature Conservation.

INDIA—THE CONSERVATION MOVEMENT

Dilnavaz Variava

Respect for nature—and the active protection of the environment—have ancient roots in India. The royal edicts of the emperor Ashoka, dating back to the third century B.C., provide lists of wild species to be strictly preserved and injunctions on the protection of forests. They are often quoted as one of the earliest known examples of wildlife protection legislation. The Mogul Emperors—kings and nobles of more recent centuries—protected areas primarily for their personal sport and pleasure, and some of these are amongst our richest wildlife refuges today.

Religious scriptures of Hindus, Buddhists and Jains enjoin respect for all forms of life. In practical terms, religious sentiments have resulted in specific cases of protection through community efforts throughout the length and breadth of the country, for which this generation must be deeply grateful. Sacred forests which were set aside for various deities preserve small islands of rich genetic diversity in areas that are otherwise barren or cultivated. Even when no trees remained in the areas surrounding such sacred forests, their sanctity remained inviolate. The Bisnois of Rajasthan, whose religion is based on 29 principles for the conservation of animals and plants, once sacrificed their lives to protect their trees from the axemen of their king. Even in times of drought, blackbuck have been known to feed undisturbed on their standing crop. The rich bird sanctuaries of Ranganthitoo Vedanthangal and Kokkerebellur in south India owe their survival to the strict protection afforded them by local populations. Tribals in every part of the country have lived in harmony with nature, strictly regulating the exploitation of forests through elaborate social and political systems.

In the past century there has been a systematic breaking down of traditional norms of environmental protection. This has been partly due to the increasing pressures of an exploding population and the breaking down of religious and social taboos. The real root of today's problems, however, goes back to British rule when forests were taken away from the village communities, who used and protected them, to be systematically exploited for commercial purposes to meet imperial needs. Unfortunately, the postindependence government in India continued to treat forests primarily as a source of state income. Village communities stood by helplessly as the resources of their well-being slipped away.

Occasionally, in the face of some cataclysmic policy or project such as a dam, which would destroy the very foundations of their sustenance by uprooting prosperous village communities from river valleys and casting them onto barren hillsides, local resistance would develop but would usually be crushed through state action. In rare cases, without being able to halt such projects, large-scale agitations by affected populations forced concessions from the government. A case in point is the widespread agitation by farmers in the state of Maharashtra against successive dams which resulted in this being the only state government to concede, through legislation, to the demand that displaced persons be allotted land in the areas benefited by the projects. All these agitations were on economic rather than environmental grounds.

An environmental, or rather wildlife, conservation movement of the type known in the western world was first launched in India by the Bombay Natural History Society at its Golden Jubilee in 1933. This organization, founded in 1883 by sportsmen and naturalists, contributed a great deal to the initial documentation of India's flora and fauna. In later years, it played a quiet but useful role in protecting endangered species of wildlife, lobbying for the creation of sanctuaries and in framing wildlife protection legislation. The World Wildlife Fund, launched in 1970, played an important role in publicizing wildlife conservation, primarily among the educated elite. Both these organizations could occasionally obtain governmental action largely because of the personal interest and commitment to conservation of two of India's prime ministers who held office for 34 out of the 40 years of India's independence—Pandit Jawaharlal Nehru and Indira Gandhi. In the absence of any grass-roots contacts, however, both these organizations and many other local environmental groups which sprang up in different parts of the country were forced to restrict their interventions to appeals to the central and state governments, and were helpless when such appeals were ineffective.

From the mid-1970s a truly exciting trend has emerged with the explicit and successful linkage of environmental, social and economic perspectives. This has sprung from groups engaged in local development and economic issues which have perceived and integrated environmental imperatives in their campaigns. A landmark was the Chipko Andolan—the now-famous Hug-the-Trees movement—born in the foothills of the Himalayas in 1973. An unprecedented flood of the Alaknanda River in 1970 left a trail of death and destruction among the peaceful inhabitants of the valley. It also left, however, a new awareness of the tragic consequences of the past deforestation of their hillslopes, primarily by government-approved contractors. In March 1973, when representatives of a sports factory reached Gopeshwar village to cut 10 ash trees, the villagers courteously asked them not to do so. But, when they persisted, the villagers went to the forests and hugged the trees, forcing the axemen to retreat empty-handed. A few days later they went to another village, 80 kilometers away—and the men from Gopeshwar travelled those 80 kilometers to again foil their attempt. Finally, the contractors chose a day when they knew that the men were away to cut trees at the village Reni. Another landmark in the conservation movement occurred when the village women stood in the path of the contractors, singing that the forest was their mother's home, which they would protect with all their might.

Women bear the heaviest burden of environmental degradation in India, often walking many wearying miles to fetch fuelwood and fodder. They have traditionally borne this ever-increasing burden helplessly. Traditionally, they have no say in community matters. Now, in a few cases, women have come to the forefront in a movement that concerns them deeply. In village after village in the Gathwal area, women were pleading for Chandi Prasad Bhatt to visit them and help them reforest their lands. Bhatt is the father of the Chipko movement, who, with young volunteers, has been spreading awareness of forest conservation and organizing ecodevelopment and reforestation camps. The women then set up regulatory mechanisms for equitable and ecologically sound use of the firewood and fodder that becomes available.

Like their Chipko sisters of Reni village, the women of Khirakot also found the courage to face a powerful mining contractor who was making their land barren through soapstone mining. The women of Khirakot caught hold of the implements of the miners and would not let them dig. They raised money from every household and sent their men off to file a court case. Finally the lease was cancelled. The women of Khirakot are also from a hill district not far from where the Chipko movement started. It should be noted that the proportion of women on the work force is particularly high in mountainous regions and in some tribal regions. This has perhaps given them the confidence to take initiatives that the more economically oppressed women of the plains have not yet been able to take. It is, however, a significant beginning and a possible new direction for the environmental conservation movement in India.

Elsewhere, though women have not played a leading role, the Chipko movement has inspired similar conservation action. In Karnataka State in southern India, the Appiko movement is successfully challenging unscientific felling by the forest department. Throughout the country, groups which once confined their tasks to rural upliftment of health, education, or economic development are turning toward the issues of protecting existing forests and affirmative reforestation of barren areas. The survival rate of trees in community reforestation programs has been as high as 90 to 95 percent, whereas in government sponsored projects they are generally much lower—sometimes as low as 10 percent.

Another important factor from the environmental perspective is that community movements often underscore the need for preserving the natural diversity upon which the community depends for a variety of its needs. Government programs are often only too willing to promote high-yielding monocultures of eucalyptus, teak and other commercial species for meeting urban and industrial needs, regardless of either ecological imperatives or the welfare of local communities.

If the Chipko movement is a pointer to the new and most welcome direction of integrating environmental and economic issues through grass-roots movement by affected communities, the Silent Valley campaign provides a landmark of a new awareness among intellectuals of the dangers of blind allegiance to models of development based on large, high-technology projects.

India has made amazing strides in self-sufficiency in food grains in the last two decades. It has also been one of the world's leading builders of dams in its postindependence era. Pandit Jawaharlal Nehru, free India's first prime minister, called these large projects the "temples of modern India." Although there were agitations for better rehabilitation terms for affected populations, or occasional protests by wildlifers when they were likely to submerge a national park or sanctuary, their sanctity remained unquestioned in the public mind until the Silent Valley controversy rocked the foundation of a proposed hydroelectric dam in the state of Kerala. In my involvement in Bombay as Honorable Coordinator of the Save the Silent Valley Committee, I was able to gain a unique understanding of this important campaign.

THE SILENT VALLEY CASE STUDY

Protected over millennia by its virtual inaccessibility, this 8,950 hectare valley of tropical, wet evergreen forests forms part of a magnificent block of almost 40,000 hectares of contiguous forest. The Silent Valley itself is one of the few areas in India to have been almost free of human habitation and intervention. It provides a home for endangered species like the tiger, the niligiri langur, the giant squirrel and for one of the only two viable populations of the lion-tailed macaque—one of the world's most endangered primates. In its dense vegetation are found wild relatives of pepper, cardamon, tobacco, black gram and other commercially valuable species. It is a genetic resource essential for the survival and development of their cultivated counterparts and many medicinal plants are found there which could provide the basis for modern life-saving drugs.

Unfortunately, it was identified as far back as 1929 as an ideal, almost textbook, location for a dam site. As so often happens, environmentalists woke up to the existence of this area—and to the devastating effects of the proposed hydroelectric project—at a stage when the project had already been cleared by the Planning Commission for implementation. In fact, preliminary work on the project had already started in 1973, but in 1976 to 1977, a government-sponsored task force for the Protection of the Western Ghats, headed by Mr. Zafar Futehally, recommended that the project be dropped. Fearing, however, that the odds against this happening were too great, it added a series of safeguards if the project were to be implemented.

Ironically it was the Kerala State Electricity Board, concerned by the contents of this report, which drew the attention of environmentalists by lobbying public opinion through the press. It gave this logic in the intense campaigning that followed:

1. That the hydroelectric project, situated in one of Kerala's poorest regions, was an economic necessity for Kerala. It would generate 500 million units of energy, irrigate 10,000 hectares of land and provide employment for 3,000 people during its construction phase.

2. That the Kerala State would have a power deficit by 1985 without it.

3. That every single political party in Kerala had joined forces to demand

from the then Prime Minister Shri Mararji Desai the implementation of the hydroelectric project. (In fact, no political party in Kerala dared ask for the abandonment of this avidly awaited project!)

4. That the project had been cleared by Prime Minister, Shri Morarji Desai, on the state government enacting legislation for implementing the safeguards listed in the Task Force report.

5. That the ecological damage by the project was negligible—and the area itself was of little ecological interest.

6. That the Kerala High Court had cleared the project for implementation.

"MAN VERSUS MONKEY"—
THE ELECTRICITY BOARD'S CASE

With many lucrative contracts for timber felling and construction at stake, the Kerala State Electricity Board (KSEB) and its unions mounted an "environmental education" campaign of its own by:

1. Projecting unknown college professors as "eminent scientists" and getting them to produce a number of books and scores of articles for the local press denigrating the ecological value of the Silent Valley. The objective was to create an impression that "scientific opinion was divided" on the value of this forest.

2. Taking legislators and journalists to the dam site, already denuded of trees, to show them how ecologically poor the Silent Valley was.

3. Dubbing eminent scientists and environmentalists who called for the dropping of the project as stooges of the developed countries, or cranks who were more concerned about the welfare of monkeys than of men.

4. Assiduously lobbying officials, especially Keralites, who occupied key positions in the central government (including the chairman of the Central Water Commission, an authority concerned with the implementation of hydroelectric projects throughout the country) and providing them with distorted information about the biological wealth of the area and the ecological impact of the dam.

5. Whipping up the sentiments of the local population so that environmentalists who went there ran the risk of physical assault if they advocated dropping the project.

"MAN AND MONKEY"—THE ENVIRONMENTALISTS' CASE

Environmentalists, on their part, mounted an unprecedented national campaign to create public pressure to stop the project. Starting in 1977, when a few naturalists in Kerala visited the area after reading the KSEB-sponsored barrage in the newspaper, the campaign gained national momentum by 1979 with "Save the Silent Valley" groups springing up in different parts of the country. The key elements of this campaign were the following:

1. The seeds of public debate on the wisdom of the project were planted by a group of intellectuals in Kerala through newspaper articles and speeches. Among these were scientists, poets, economists, and political activists opposed to the project.

2. The executive committee of the Kerala Shastra Sahitya Parishad (KSSP)—an organization committed to taking scientific and socially relevant concepts to the people of Kerala—was inspired, primarily by the persuasions of one of its members, Professor M.K. Prasad, to undertake a technoeconomic, sociopolitical assessment of the implications of the Silent Valley project. The report, produced by its multidisciplinary task force consisting of a biologist, an electrical engineer, an economist and an agricultural scientist-cum-economist, provided a turning point in the Silent Valley campaign and a landmark in inter-disciplinary cooperation on environmental issues.

3. The cogent analysis in the KSSP report provided environmental activists with important data, namely that: the energy contribution of the Silent Valley project was really marginal in the context of Kerala's power requirements; alternative sources for augmenting power existed; ground water provided an effective and economical source for irrigation; and, far more employment could be generated in this economically backward region through medium- and small-scale industries than through this one major hydroelectric project. More importantly, it convinced the 60-member executive committee of the KSSP to take up the fight to save the Silent Valley.

4. The KSSP's 7,000 members—teachers, doctors, engineers, lawyers, scientists, agriculturists, trade union workers and others—fostered public debate on the Silent Valley issue throughout Kerala. The youth, especially the college-going youth, were convinced. KSSP members focused on the effects of deforestation through their unique annual *Jatha*. This is a 37-day marathon march from one end of Kerala to the other using traditional cultural media such as dance, drama, poetry and music. The *Jatha* covers 300 to 400 villages along its 6,000 kilometer route.

5. A court case, though eventually lost, brought an invaluable stay on KSEB operations, thereby providing time for the educational campaign to have full effect.

6. International and national organizations like the IUCN, WWF, Bombay Natural History Society, Indian National Science Academy, Friends of the Trees and other organizations throughout the country adopted resolutions and lobbied through letters to the central and state governments.

7. Save Silent Valley committees, which sprang up in different parts of the country, lent considerable support to the movement in Kerala. One of the most active was the Save Silent Valley Committee in Bombay which worked closely with groups in Kerala. Some of the tasks it undertook were:

• Persuading eminent scientists and environmentalists to make public statements regarding the importance of preserving the Silent Valley;
• Persuading members of the government-sponsored task force on the Western Ghats to publicly state that they had been mistaken in recommending the so-called "safeguards" which had been misused by the protagonists of the project;
• Feeding the national press with information against the dam, which was

particularly important once the local press in Kerala was muzzled by vested interests;
• Working jointly with activists in Kerala to get the most eminent scientists like Dr. Salim Ali and others to persuade key decision makers to save Silent Valley— or at least to keep options open until all other power generating alternatives in Kerala had been exhausted.

Key decision makers became one of the most valuable forces in dropping the project. Dr. M.S. Swaminathan, who was then Secretary of Agriculture, prepared a report highlighting the genetic wealth of the area and the desirability of postponing the project until this resource could be studied and tapped. E.M.S. Namboodripad, secretary of the powerful (especially in Kerala) Communist Party of India, left the matter open for debate within the party, having been convinced that the proposed hydroelectric project was not an unmitigated blessing for the people of the area.

India's foremost naturalist, Dr. Salim Ali, played a major role in convincing Indira Gandhi, who again became prime minister in 1980, to ask the state government to halt further work until the central and state governments could explore the implications of the proposed hydroelectric projects and the alternatives that were available. A committee with representatives of the state and central governments was set up by her, under the chairmanship of Professor M.G.K. Menon (then Secretary of the Department of Science and Technology) to look into the ecological implications of the project.

THE OUTCOME

In November 1983 the Silent Valley hydroelectric project was officially declared to have been shelved. Steps have been initiated since then to create the Silent Valley National Park. In the conservation field, no battle is ever final. The Silent Valley may again one day resound with controversy. A campaign involving three successive prime ministers (Morarji Desai, Charan Singh and Indira Gandhi) led to the most heated public conservation debate among intellectuals throughout the country. Perhaps the most heartening indicator that the environment education campaign had succeeded was the absence of public outcry when the project was dropped. In the Palghat district, where the project was to have been located and where environmental activists once faced the possibility of physical assault, the people asked KSSP activists to organize a felicitation for the prime minister for her wise decision to drop the project.

LESSONS OF THE SILENT VALLEY CAMPAIGN

While it is difficult, even at this stage, to precisely pinpoint all the factors which contributed to the shelving of the Silent Valley hydroelectric project at the eleventh hour and in the face of formidable odds, some factors may bear consideration in similar campaigns elsewhere:

THE CAMPAIGN THEME

A major requirement of such a campaign is a constant sensitivity to what is the most appropriate message, to whom it should be addressed and by whom. Lion-tailed macaques were useful in obtaining support from international and national conservation bodies, but counterproductive at the local level. The genetic treasure house concept was effective for both decision makers and the general public. The Silent Valley name was deeply evocative, and if such an advantage does not exist in other cases, it would be useful to search for some element that could create it.

Above all, however, the environmental education effort must start with an effort to understand the needs of the local people and project how the proposed conservation movement is directly beneficial to them.

THE MEDIUM

Since the dropping of the project involved convincing many different levels in the decision-making process, different media had to be used:

At the prime minister's level, letters from such an eminent naturalist as Dr. Salim Ali, a report prepared by Dr. M.S. Swaminathan and representations from reputed international conservation bodies carried weight.

At the popular level, the use of the press created national interest in the fate of the Silent Valley and the KSSP's annual *Jatha* took the issue of deforestation to the countryside. During an unprecedented drought in 1983, the KSSP organized a special 12-day *Jatha* covering all districts in Kerala which still had forests. Signatures were collected from 200,000 people asking the government of Kerala to have a moratorium an all development projects in forested areas and to stop all clear felling, especially on steep slopes.

The decision not to use a particular medium is often as important as the decision to use it. At the state level, representation from international conservation bodies, with headquarters in Western countries, would have been counterproductive and were not used because of the prevailing communist ethos in this state.

A 35-mm film, on which much labor was expended, was never released for screening to millions of people through the film division because, by the time it was ready, the campaign had moved into a phase of behind-the-scenes diplomacy rather than public outcry.

In the final stages of the campaign, when key officials in the central government were looking into alternatives and trying to find a possible solution, I had a four-hour discussion with the initially hostile chairman of the Central Water Commission, himself a Keralite. It was agreed that the best strategy would be to call a halt to the public controversy so that positions would not harden further and so that the central and state governments could work on resolving the problem in the right atmosphere. There was accordingly an immediate de-escalation of the press campaign by both sides.

METHODS AND STRATEGIES

Some of the following strategies paid dividends and may be useful elsewhere:

Have a multidisciplinary report so that the benefits of the project itself can be questioned on economic grounds;

Lead the supposed beneficiaries of development projects to look at and question the benefits which the project promises to bestow. Without this, it is difficult for economically deprived people to sympathize with environmental positions which require them to sacrifice even small short-term gains in the interest of sustainable development;

Ask for a postponement of the project until other alternatives have been explored, rather than demand a dropping of the project. This can generate public support and provide a face-saving escape from the project;

Expend the necessary time and energy to muster data in order to convince key decision makers. Government officials who do not have a vested interest in a project, either in potential income or prestige, can be most helpful. Those who have open minds should not be blamed if the pro-project lobby does a better job of communicating with them than environmentalists do;

Have maximum organizational flexibility in campaigning. The established conservation bodies, with their multitiered organizational structures, were less effective in responding to the demands of rapidly evolving situations. An ad-hoc group, like the Save Silent Valley Committee (Bombay), strongly focused on a single environmental issue. With no hierarchical structure and no requirement to perpetuate itself once the campaign was over, it could draw together interested members from various organizations and pool their valuable contacts and expertise;

Coordinate strategy formulation and decentralization in action for powerful campaigning. Although Silent Valley groups had sprung up spontaneously and independently in different parts of the country, a division of functions emerged. Groups in Kerala created public awareness in their respective areas, the Friends of Trees unit in Kerala pursued the court case, the Society for Environmental Education in Kerala worked largely with children's groups. The Save Silent Valley committee in Trivandrum, capital city of Kerala, provided a meeting point for important activists from different walks of life and from different political parties;

Undertake public education—through the press and through direct contact with organizations and the activists in whom they have confidence—to make decisions politically acceptable. Though the prime minister's personal interest is invaluable, it does not provide a simple solution for a politically complex or sensitive issue.

The ability of public opinion to stop a dam and the protracted public debate on the merits of implementing major projects at the cost of environmental factors have provided an impetus to anti-dam campaigns in other parts of the country.

The Bedthi project in Karnataka was dropped when rich local farmers, supported by economists and intellectuals, successfully sought and argued the case in a public debate sponsored by the state government. In other cases, the struggles against major dams are continuing.

The destruction of valuable ecosystems and the displacement of thousands of people, many of whom live in tribes whose culture, religion and very survival is closely interwoven with the forests, have formed the focus of these debates. Interestingly, it is once again not the national environmental groups like the World Wildlife Fund and the Bombay Natural History Society that are in the forefront of raising public awareness. It is local leaders who have worked for many years on the development issues connected with these communities who are now combining environmental, economic, and humanitarian arguments in the struggle to ensure that local communities are not destroyed by projects which will benefit distant urban groups. Thus, Mr. Chandi Prasad Bhatt of the Chipko movement is campaigning against the Vishnuprayag dam which will submerge the Valley of the Flowers. Dr. Baba Amte, who has worked on health and leprosy issues amongst the tribals of Gadchirolli district in Mahatashtra, is leading them in the struggle against the proposed Bhopalpatnam and Imchampalli dams. The Koel Karl Jana Sangathan, consisting of the headmen of all the affected villages, is fighting to secure suitable rehabilitation schemes that will look after the needs—economic, social, and cultural—of the tribals of Koel Karl. And, four social service organizations in Gujarat are in the forefront of the struggle against the mammoth Narmada project being implemented without sensitive, egalitarian and comprehensive handling of the rehabilitation of oustees!

The message of hope that the 1970s and 1980s have provided to the conservation movement on India is that grassroots organizations in many parts of the country, without even having heard of the World Conservation Strategy, are affirming the tenets of sustainable development and forging crucial links between development and environment issues.

The dissemination and sharing of experience are vital for this movement to gain strength. A significant contribution in this direction has been made by the two citizens' reports on the state of India's environment, published by the Center for Science and Environment.

THE INDIAN ELEPHANT

R. Sukumar

Worshipped and hunted, carrier of human burdens and killer of human life, companions of kings and commons, war machine and peace ambassador, the sheer contrast and splendor of the association between elephants and people in Asia is unequalled by any other interaction between animal and man in the world.

During prehistoric times the elephant was viewed by hunter-gatherers probably only as a source of meat, ivory, hide and bones. But this perception must have changed once man realized the potential of using such a large and powerful beast as his servant. The earliest records of domestication are engravings on seals during the Indus valley civilization, from the third millenium B.C. This ancient relationship between elephant and man provided a strong motivation for the development of a science of elephants.

Ancient literature such as the *Rig-Veda* (twentieth to fifteenth century B.C.), the *Upanishads* (ninth to sixth century B.C.), the *Gaja-sastra* (sixth to fifth century B.C.), and the *Tamil Sangam* literature record details of elephant distribution, life and habits, (though mixed with mythology, imagination, and exaggeration) with instructions on their capture and training, maintenance and treatment of diseases. The *Gaja-sastra* is probably the world's first such monograph on the elephant and its author, Papakapya, the first elephant scientist.

The domestication of elephants certainly meant their reduction in the wild but there seems to have been knowledge of prudent capture even in early times. Kautilya's *Arthasastra* (circa 300 B.C.), a treatise on state administration, urged setting apart tracts of forest on the periphery of the kingdom as elephant sanctuaries. These sanctuaries were to be patrolled by guards and anyone who killed an elephant there was to be given the death penalty. Among the instructions given for capture of elephants, the treatise prohibited the capture of elephant calves, elephants with small tusks, tuskless males, diseased elephants and female elephants with young or suckling calves. It further recommended that a 20-year-old elephant should be caught. This practically meant that only adult male elephants with tusks could be captured. This was the most scientific and prudent way of harvesting the wild elephant population given the fact that domestication was inevitable.

The period after Christ saw a steady decline in elephant numbers over the Indian subcontinent. We know that elephant captures were not always prudent. Entire herds were often captured in stockades by the keddah method. With the enormous pressure on elephants and their habitats over many centuries from the human population, it is perhaps surprising that the elephant has survived to this day. The cultural and religious traditions certainly played some part in their conservation. The elephant is worshipped in the form of Ganesha, the God of Learning. Religious taboos against the killing of elephants is widespread over most of the Indian subcontinent, except in parts of the northeast. Sport hunting of the elephant was not known until the eighteenth century of British India. By contrast, another large mammal, the American bison, was almost completely wiped out within a century due to hunting.

Today, elephants survive in four major regions of the Indian subcontinent— about 500 of them in the northwest, 9,000 to 12,000 in the northeast, 1,600 in central and 6,000 to 7,000 in south India. We face the challenge of conserving elephants scattered in numerous populations, small and large, surrounded by human societies whose traditions are changing with the assault of modern civilization. To me, the elephant in India symbolizes a conservation culture which represents the meeting point of rich traditional values, evolved over centuries, and modern conservation needs responded to with scientific good sense. I shall now refer to a study I carried out on the ecology of the wild elephant and its interaction with people in southern India with a view to providing a scientific basis for their conservation. The study was sponsored by the World Wide Fund for Nature, through the Asian Elephant specialist group of the IUCN.

In southern India the elephant is found in a wide variety of habitats ranging from dry thorn jungle through deciduous forest to wet evergreen forest. The 1,000-square kilometer area in which I studied elephants had a good representation of this diversity. One of the basic questions on elephant ecology I studied was how elephants utilized this diversity of habitats to obtain their food requirements on a seasonal time scale. Elephants were identified based on morphological characteristics. Data from resightings of such elephants indicated minimum home range sizes of 100 to 300 square kilometers for elephant family herds and adult bulls. The seasonal spatial distribution patterns and observations of feeding demonstrate that elephants utilize different habitat types with a view to optimizing their consumption of food and water. During the dry season (January to April), elephants typically congregated at high densities of up to five elephants per square kilometer in river valleys or swampy grasslands. With the onset of rains (May to August), they dispersed over a wider area, mainly into deciduous forests with tall grass. Later, during the second rainy season (September to December), they moved out of tall-grass hill forests into lower elevation short - grass open jungle.

Elephants are both grazers and browsers. Though they consumed a large number of plant species, more than 80 percent of their diet consisted of only 25 species from the botanical taxa *Gramineae* (grasses), *Cyperaceae* (sedges), *Leguminosae*, *Palmae* and *Malvales*. Feeding was predominantly on browse (69 percent) during the dry season while grazing on tall grasses (54 percent) increased with the onset of rains. Consumption of tall grasses again decreased during the second wet season. The movement pattern and feeding preferences were related to the changing nutritive content, particularly protein, in food plants. During the dry season the protein content of tall grasses is less than 4 percent, which is insufficient for maintenance. Hence, elephants clearly prefer browse plants which have 8 to 20 percent protein. The new flush promoted by the rains has 8 to 10 percent protein; hence its increased consumption during this season. When the grasses mature they become fibrous and unpalatable, with a drop in protein value, and elephants now switch over from tall grasses to short grasses and browse.

The lesson for conservation is that elephants need a diversity of habitats to optimally satisfy their food and other requirements. During the dry season they need habitats with browse forage, such as leguminous plants of tall grasses in swampy grasslands. They need river valleys for water. Riparian forests and evergreen forests also afford them shelter from fires which are frequent in the dry forests. Deciduous forests are utilized for their tall grasses mainly during the rainy season. Thus, the highest densities of elephants under natural conditions can be maintained in regions with a mosaic of habitats. Human use of the habitat through selective timber felling or extraction of certain forest produce need not be incompatible with the elephant's use of the habitat, since elephants adapt well to secondary vegetation. However, the systematic destruction of certain habitats such as river valleys for dams or for cultivation does not augur well for the elephant.

Elephants may encounter cultivation in the course of their natural seasonal movements. Since many cultivated crops—cereals, millet, oil palm, coconut— are analogous to the wild grasses and palms, elephants are likely to consume these crops as any other wild plant. Crop raiding by elephants is a serious conservation problem. A detailed monitoring of crop damage in several villages revealed some interesting implications for controlling this problem.

Crop raiding was most frequent during the second wet season, when a large proportion of land was cultivated for the staple crop finger millet (*Eleusine coracana*). During this period there was also abundant forage in the natural habitat. There was no correlation between the frequency of raiding in villages with the quality of the natural habitat around them. These observations suggest that elephants would raid crops irrespective of the availability of sufficient food in the wild. The ultimate cause of crop raiding is the higher palatability and nutritive value, in particular protein, sodium and calcium, of cultivated crops compared to the analogous wild plants.

One significant observation was that adult male elephants showed a far higher propensity to raid crops than did the female-led family herds. An adult bull raided crops on average of six times more frequently than did an elephant belonging to a family group. Consequently, adult bulls derived about 9 percent of their quantitative food requirement from cultivation compared to less than 2 percent for family herds. Male elephants also joined together to form larger "bachelor bull groups" in order to raid crops more effectively. Not only did an adult bull raid more frequently, it also damaged more quantity of crops per raid (being larger in body size) and also the more economically valuable crops such as coconut than did an elephant belonging to a family herd. The cumulative effect of this meant that the average annual damage to crops was about $500 per bull and only $25 per elephant belonging to a family herd.

Another unfortunate consequence of the interaction between elephants and people is the killing of people by elephants. In southern India about 30 to 50 people are killed each year, while in other regions of India another 70 to 100 people fall victim to elephants. Records of manslaughter showed that a significant 45 percent of instances occurred within cultivation areas and the rest within the forest. Adult male elephants were responsible for almost all killings within cultivation areas and for 80 percent of overall killings. I must add here that 77 percent of people killed were adult men. The tendency for male elephants to show more aggressive behavior leading to manslaughter could have its origin in their more intensive interaction with people within cultivation. This behavioral difference between male and female elephants in raiding crops and in killing people has important implications for management.

Elephants are also at the receiving end, since between 100 and 150 male tuskers are shot every year in southern India by poachers for their valuable ivory. Unlike the African elephant, female Asian elephants do not possess tusks.

This human/elephant interaction has direct consequences for the elephant population. To understand the dynamics of the population, I obtained its age structure by aging elephants from their shoulder heights measured by a photographic method, estimated its fertility and mortality rates, and incorporated these into a matrix model to simulate demographic trends using a computer. The age structure shows a strongly female-based sex ratio; the adult ratio was one male for every five females. Female elephants first give birth at 17 to 18 years and continue to do so every 4.7 years on average until about 60 years. Three sets of mortality rated for male and female elephants were considered—a low mortality schedule representing the minimum rates expected, a medium mortality schedule incorporating the rates estimated to be currently operating in the population and a high mortality schedule which could be reached during periods of stress such as drought or increased poaching.

Computer simulations revealed the following trends: The elephant population seemed relatively stable at present. It had the potential to increase at not more than 2 percent per year in the long term. However, the disparate sex ratio would further widen due to the high male mortality from poaching. To a certain extent a disparate sex ratio would not affect the fertility of the population in a polygamous society, since an adult male can mate with many females. At some value of a disparate ratio there would certainly, however, be a decline in fertility. Too few males also means a reduction in genetic diversity and problems associated with inbreeding, especially in small elephant populations. It has been suggested by conservation geneticists that a minimum population size of 500 breeding or adult individuals is necessary to maintain the long-term evolutionary potential of the population. This may mean a total population of about 1,500 to 2,000 elephants. If elephants exist at an average density of 0.5 elephants per square kilometer this also means that the minimum viable area is 3,000 to 4,000

,square kilometers. This study certainly suggests that an adult ratio of one male to five female elephants in a large population can still maintain a relatively high birth rate, and hence, demographic vigor of the population. At present no clear answer is available to determine a safe level of a skewed sex ratio in elephant populations.

In managing elephant populations, advantage can be taken of the fact that some males can be harvested, especially from a large population, without any detriment to the population's demographic vigour. This would substantially reduce damage to crops and save human lives. This should not be taken as a justification for poaching; there are legal and ethical issues involved in the wasteful slaughter for ivory. However, since there is a tradition in Asia of capturing elephants for domestication, selective captures of notorious crop-raiding bulls could be permitted.

The elephants' depredations will have to be minimized if its conservation is to be accepted by people in modern rural society. Trenching around cultivation has largely failed to keep away elephants. One product of technology, the high-voltage electric fence, holds promise of containing elephants. A typical design used against elephants gives a 5,000-volt current in pulses of very short duration, say 1/3,000 second every second, and is not harmful to animals. Intelligent elephants have, however, used their tusks, nonconductors, to break an electrified wire and enter cultivation!

The grand symbols of Indian culture are derived from nature—mountains (the Himalayas), rivers (the Ganga), trees (the peepal or fig), animals (the elephant) and only an occasional human edifice (the Taj Mahal). Sages retired to the solitude of the Himalayas in order to promote lofty ideas. Bathing in the Ganga symbolized a spiritual cleansing. The modern protest by peasants against deforestation in the Himalayas or the physical cleaning of the polluted Ganga are manifestations of these deep-rooted traditions. The Buddha attained enlightenment under the peepal tree; today, we still find a revered peepal in every village. In many regions the only remnants of undisturbed forests are the sacred groves dedicated to deities. The elephant has shared with people war and peace, joys and tribulations, pomp and neglect. It is still a powerful symbol around which the conservation of India's natural heritage can be organized.

© Fiona Silver

CHINA—WILDLIFE CONSERVATION

Liu Guangyun

Upon receiving the Worldwide Conservation Leadership Award on behalf of the Ministry of Forestry, People's Republic of China:

China, with vast area, complicated topography and varied climate, is rich in wild fauna and flora. Some of them, such as giant pandas, golden monkeys, white-lipped deer, brown-eyed pheasants, black-necked cranes, Chinese alligators, dawn redwood and *Cathsya argyrophylla* can only be found in China. In order to protect and reasonably use the resources of these wild fauna and flora, the Chinese government has done a lot of work, establishing management organizations at different levels, making laws and regulations, providing lists of wild fauna and flora to be protected and strengthening scientific research.

Saving endangered species is one of our important works. In 1981 we found seven crested ibises still surviving in the wild. After several years of strict protection, its population has been increased to more than thirty. With artificial breeding, we have bred more than 1,000 Chinese alligators. In 1983, the bamboo died on a large scale in areas where giant pandas live. In order to save giant pandas, our government allocated special funds. Altogether we took 86 dying giant pandas, of which 62 survived, thus decreasing the loss and achieving good results. We are now working with the World Wildlife Fund (WWF) to make a comprehensive inventory for the giant pandas and make protection and management plans for the future. We have introduced Pere David deer and wild horses, which were extinct in the wild in China. We have established a breeding center in Jiangsu Province and Beijing for the deer and Xinjiang Autonomous Region for the horses. We hope to recover their wild populations in China.

Nature reserves are our important base for protecting the natural environment and wild fauna and flora. By the end of 1986, we established 333 different types of nature reserves with a total area of 19,330,000 hectares, amounting to 2 percent of our land. Facts show that our nature reserves have played an important role in protecting the natural environment and resources, especially in protecting and saving endangered species.

It is imperative to have international cooperation to protect wild fauna and flora. We have joined cities, signed treaties to protect migratory birds with Japan and Australia, and have nature conservation protocol with the United States. We work closely with the WWF, the International Union for the Conservation of Nature and Natural Resources (IUCN) and the International Crane Foundation. Many foreign scientists have come to China to work for the protection of wildlife and scientific research on wildlife resources and make contributions to our work. I would like to take this opportunity to express to them our sincere thanks.

China is a developing country. Although we have made some achievements in nature conservation, there is a long way to go. We want to cooperate closely with other countries, organizations and individuals and to make greater contributions to world nature conservation.

The Worldwide Conservation Leadership Award
presented to
the Ministry of Forestry, People's Republic of China

for excellence and international leadership in:

- efforts to preserve the panda and its wilderness habitat
- establishing national forestry education and research system
- conservation of natural resources through population planning
- implementing creative solutions such as the use of birds for the control of damaging insects

presented this 12 day of September, 1987, on the occasion of the 4 World Wilderness Congress, by the International Wilderness Leadership Foundation

Dr. John Hendee
Dean, College of Forestry
Wildlife and Range Sciences
University of Idaho

Dr. Ian C. Player
Vice Chairman
Wilderness Leadership School

Vance G. Martin
President
International Wilderness Leadership Foundation

AUSTRALIA

THE AUSTRALIAN GOVERNMENT AND CONSERVATION

Patrick J. Galvin

Australia has been involved in earlier World Wilderness Congresses and is proud to have hosted the 2nd Congress at Cairns and to have participated actively in Inverness and Findhorn.

At the time of the 3rd World Wilderness Congress in Scotland, the Hawke Labor Government had been in office only seven months. The government's election platform included a strong commitment to conservation and environment protection. The then Federal Minister for the Environment, the Honorable Barry Cohen, in addressing the congress, described the steps the government had followed to prevent the building of a dam in the Western Tasmania World Heritage Area. He reminded the congress that the first legislative action of the new government, on its election, was to introduce to the Parliament a bill to make provision for "the protection and conservation of those places . . . that are of such outstanding universal value that they are recognized as part of the cultural or natural heritage of the world." That legislation, calling up the World Heritage Convention, stopped the building of the Franklin Dam.

Four-and-a-half years later the Hawke government has been reelected for its third term. Throughout this recent election campaign the government's commitment to conservation and to the protection of the environment was a significant issue.

Following are some remarks of the prime minister in opening the election campaign:

"The task of protecting the environment imposes a heavy responsibility on the whole community. For Australians, that responsibility is a particularly important one since we have the good fortune to live in a country of unsurpassed environmental magnificence.

"However, protecting the environment also requires us to find a delicate balance with legitimate economic interests. The Hawke government can point with pride to the progress Australia has made in recent years in striking that balance and in securing our environmental heritage.

"The matchless beauty of our land has a value beyond dollars and cents. That's why we stopped the Franklin Dam. That's why we have made mining illegal in Kakadu. It's why we are protecting the special forests in Tasmania. And that's why we will save the Daintree."

It is this recognition of the responsibility of the present generation of Australians for the welfare and quality of life of our successors, and of the world at large, that forms the basis for all the federal government's policies and actions on conservation. This approach, of course, is in line with the philosophy of the World Conservation Strategy. Australia was one of the first countries to accept the World Conservation Strategy and to develop a National Conservation Strategy.

Yet the Australian Constitution makes no mention of environment or conservation. It was drafted in the 1890s and reflects the perspectives of those times. Decisions on land use, forest management, wildlife conservation and pollution control are primarily the responsibility of each state.

Wherever possible, the federal government has sought to cooperate with state and territorial governments in developing conservation policies and addressing priority conservation issues. However, there have been issues of national and international concern where the federal government has found it necessary to intervene and to use the powers granted to it by the Constitution. These include: trade and commerce, external affairs and the power to legislate in its own territories. In this action it has had the support of the courts.

Australia has a land area of about 7.7 million square kilometers (roughly the same area as mainland United States, excepting Alaska). It spans more than 30 degrees of latitude, from the tropics to the edge of the Southern Ocean. It is, for the most part, a flat, arid continent—one-third of the total land mass has a mean annual rainfall below 250 mm (10 inches). The human population is about 16 million (less than that of New York State). More than 85 percent of Australians live in about 10 cities on the coastal fringe of the continent, leaving the inland very sparsely inhabited, though by no means unaffected by human habitation.

Australia has the distinction of being the only country in the world to occupy a whole continent. It contains a great variety of environments, ranging from a vast arid inland to complex rain forests, large sand islands, ancient coastal landforms, enormous coral reefs, and small areas of Alpine heaths and snow-fields.

The scientific importance of the Australian landscape and its flora and fauna is well recognized. The Australian government accepts the obligation to conserve this natural heritage.

During the more than 40,000 years of Aboriginal occupation, human activities established an equilibrium with the environment. While Aboriginal land-use practices left their mark on the vegetation—especially through the use of fire—there is no doubt that these practices were sustainable in the long term. The same cannot be said for those who followed.

In 1988 Australia will celebrate 200 years of European settlement. It is an important time to reflect not only on our achievements but also on our mistakes. Massive forest clearing, overgrazing, introduction of weeds and pests, poor irrigation practices and the overuse of artificial fertilizers have occurred. All seemed good ways of maximizing yields and profits at the time, but the consequences have been devastating.

At the time of European settlement about 10 percent of the continent was covered with closed forest. This area has been progressively reduced to about half that amount. It has been estimated that three-quarters of the rain forest has disappeared.

The conservation of Australia's remaining native forests is the major issue of serious conflict between conservation and development interests in Australia today.

The responsibility for use and management of forests in Australia rests with the state governments. However, international trade and commerce are matters for the federal government. A federal decision, for example, whether to issue a license for the export of wood chips may well be the determining factor in the development of the timber industry at regional or local levels. There is obvious potential here for conflict.

In the past few years there has been a succession of widely publicized conflicts—at both government and community levels—over the clearfelling of native hardwood forests to produce wood chips for overseas markets. Clearfelling, especially when followed by burning, is hardly consistent with conservation of natural communities, especially that of native fauna.

The most significant of these events has occurred recently in Tasmania. The federal government had made clear its opposition to forestry operations in areas containing nationally and internationally important conservation values. In December 1986, it indicated its intention to stop logging in parts of the Lemonthyme and Southern Forests adjacent to the Tasmanian World Heritage Area and consequently initiated legislation to establish a Commission of Inquiry to examine whether the values in the Lemonthyme and Southern Forests are themselves of World Heritage Value.

On September 3, 1987 the government was successful in obtaining a temporary High Court injunction to prevent logging in these forests pending hearing of a High Court challenge by the Tasmanian government to the legislation establishing the inquiry. The Tasmanian government, which initially refused to appear before the inquiry, has now agreed to do so.

Only a small proportion of Australia's remaining forests are rain forests. Australia's rain forests are relics of an ancient environment which is believed to have once covered most of the supercontinent of Gondwanaland. The tropical rain forests of northern Queensland are of particular scientific interest. Conservationists and the federal government are determined that logging in these rain forests must cease if destruction of their scientific values is to be avoided. The decline of rain forests throughout the world adds to the urgency.

In recognition of the importance of Australian rain forests, the federal government last year established a National Rain Forest Conservation Program and agreed to provide funding of $22.25 million over three financial years. The program is being implemented in cooperation with the states and the territories. It includes survey and research, the acquisition of privately owned rain forests for inclusion in parks, plantation establishment to provide alternative sources of timber and studies of the tourism potential of rain forests. Components of the program are already being successfully undertaken.

A major objective of the program was to establish cooperative arrangements with the Queensland government for the conservation of tropical rain forests in Northern Queensland. Unfortunately, that state government did not choose to enter into acceptable arrangements. In particular it refused to cease logging.

In June 1987 the prime minister announced the federal government's determination to protect the outstanding values of this region. He said, "The Queensland Government must be made to recognize the need to change its management practices with regard to irreplaceable environmental heritage." He announced that the federal government had decided to proceed immediately toward nomination of the wet tropics of North-East Queensland to the World Heritage list.

World Heritage listing will enable the government to prevent further rain forest logging in the wet tropics. Recognizing that this action will affect the livelihood of timber workers—at least in the short term—the government has agreed to make substantial funding available for industry readjustment.

In determining the boundaries of the area to be nominated, the government has undertaken an extensive program of community participation and consultation. During this consultation, the minister has visited most areas in the region. Of course the reaction of those who clearly will lose their present employment is not a particularly happy one. The most recent visit to a town called Ravenshoe resulted in some violence. Nevertheless, the government is determined to go ahead.

Neither in the case of logging in the Lemonthyme, nor in conservation of the wet tropics, has the federal government been able to achieve its objectives with state government cooperation. However, we have now come to a good working arrangement with Tasmania to manage the Western Tasmania World Heritage Area.

In the years since the last Congress, the federal government has cooperated with the Tasmanian government to restructure parts of the Tasmanian economy affected by the loss of the dam project and to develop management arrangements for the Tasmanian World Heritage Area. In January 1985 agreement was reached between the federal and state governments on the establishment of a ministerial council to advise on policy, management and financial matters relating to the area. The council itself is advised by a consultative committee which includes representatives of tourism, research, conservation, bushwalking and local government to enable the users of the area to have a say in the decision-making process. Once virtually unknown outside Tasmania, the Franklin River and the Tasmanian World Heritage Area are now popular destinations for conservationists, scientists, wilderness adventurers and tourists from all over the world.

Despite the differences over the North Queensland Rain Forests, good cooperation has been achieved with the Queensland government in the management of the Great Barrier Reef. Legislation to establish the Great Barrier Reef Marine Park was enacted in 1975. In 1979 a ministerial council was established to coordinate the policies of the federal and Queensland governments in relation to the Marine Park. Formal arrangements have been made for public involvement in its management, and a Great Barrier Reef Consultative Committee provides advice to the government and to the management authority.

The scientific and recreational qualities of Marine Park are well known, and in recognition of these qualities the whole area, comprising federal waters and some Queensland Islands, has been inscribed on the World Heritage List.

One of Australia's most serious national conservation problems—the environmental degradation of Australia's largest and most important river catchment, the Murray-Darling Basin—has evolved slowly over many years and involves four states.

The Murray River forms the border between New South Wales and Victoria and flows into the sea in South Australia. The Darling River flows from southern Queensland to join the Murray near the South Australian border. These two rivers and their tributaries have a combined length of 3,780 km (one-and-a-half times the length of the Colorado River). The basin covers nearly one million square kilometers (about 15 percent of the continent) and has a population of 1.6 million people. Throughout much of Australia's history, the Murray-Darling Basin has been one of its most important agricultural and pastoral areas. Although it still produces over half the nation's agricultural output, much of the area is now severely degraded by soil erosion, dry-land salinization, poor river-water quality and rising groundwater tables.

In November 1985, the federal government and the governments of New South Wales, Victoria, and South Australia agreed to cooperate in planning and management for the use of water, land, and environmental resources in the Basin. A strategy for integrated management of these resources is being prepared and a Murray-Darling Basin Commission, representing the four governments, is to be established by legislation of all four parliaments involved, and will oversee future management of the Basin.

The federal government recognizes the special relationship between the Aboriginal people and their land. Large tracts of Australia, especially in the Northern Territory, are owned by Aborigines. The federal government has successfully sought the cooperation of Aboriginal people in conserving and managing lands which contain some of Australia's most outstanding natural environments. Uluru National Park in central Australia, which contains the world famous Ayers Rock (or Uluru) and the Olgas (Katatjuta), has enormous religious and cultural significance for the traditional inhabitants. In October 1985, the Aboriginal people's traditional ownership of Uluru was legally confirmed in a ceremony at the Rock in which the governor-general handed over a deed of title to the Katatjuta Aboriginal Land Trust. On the same day, the Katatjuta Trust leased the area back to the director of the Australian National Parks and Wildlife Service for management as a national park.

Kakadu National Park, established in the magnificent tropical floodplain and escarpment country of the Alligator Rivers Region in the Northern Territory and featured in the film *Crocodile Dundee*, is also partly owned by Aboriginal traditional owners. In 1975, following discoveries of uranium deposits in the area, a government inquiry was set up to consider the future of the entire region, including the ecological and wilderness values, traditional ownership claims, commercial fishing, mining, pastoral activities and interests of the Northern Territory government. The inquiry recommended the establishment of a major national park in the region to include the entire catchment area of the South Alligator River. The federal government intends that Kakadu National Park will eventually meet that specification.

The original Kakadu National Park was proclaimed in 1979 and inscribed on the World Heritage List two years later. An adjacent area (Stage Two) was proclaimed in 1984. In September 1986, the government decided to acquire the Gimbat and Goodparla pastoral leases, which contain the headwaters of the South Alligator River, for further extension of the park.

Last year the government nominated Kakadu Stage Two for the World Heritage List. The World Heritage Committee deferred consideration of the nomination, at the request of the Australian government, after a legal challenge was initiated by mining interests. The case was decided in the government's favor by the Full Bench of the Federal Court earlier this week, enabling the government to proceed with the nomination.

Land rights over substantial areas of Kakadu National Park have been granted to an Aboriginal Land Trust and leased back to the director of the Australian National Parks and Wildlife Service on the condition that the Aboriginal people be trained, employed, and otherwise involved in management, development and planning of the park. The government has pursued this policy actively and with considerable success.

The choice of priority between conservation of living natural resources and exploitation of rich mineral deposits in the Kakadu region has been an important political issue in Australia. There are proven uranium deposits in addition to the present Ranger and Nabalark mines, and much of the region is said to be highly prospective for gold, platinum, and other metals. The federal government's uranium policy precludes further uranium mines, but there are strong economic pressures to extract other mineral resources.

The government decided in December 1986 to declare as a Conservation

Zone one-third of the Gimbat and Goodparla pastoral leases and to allow mineral exploration, in that zone only, under strict environmental guidelines for a period of five years. The act provides for a conservation zone to be declared for the protection and conservation of wildlife and natural features of the area until a decision is made whether or not to declare the area a park or reserve. The government's intention is that ultimately as much of the conservation zone as possible will be incorporated in the park. Only mining prospects of major economic significance—not merely economic viability—will be allowed to proceed, and then only provided that strict environmental guidelines are met.

The government is determined that the wilderness value of Kakadu will be protected against the effects of minerals activity and maintained for nature conservation and for the large number of tourists from all over the world who visit the Northern Territory. In May 1987, the Parliament enacted legislation to prohibit exploration and mining in the area declared as Kakadu National Park.

Protection of wilderness has been a significant part of almost all of the federal government initiatives. By wilderness, I mean loosely those areas of substantially unmodified native plant and animal communities and the landscapes they inhabit that are sufficiently large to make it practicable to maintain them in their natural condition in perpetuity.

The Tasmanian World Heritage Area, Kakadu National Park, and the Wet Tropics of North-East Queensland contain major wilderness areas, by any definition. Some attention is being given to better defining wilderness values and identifying areas suitable for wilderness preservation. The Australian Labor Party, which holds government in Canberra and in four of the six states, is committed to encourage and promote the preservation of Australia's wilderness areas under appropriate legislation.

Bearing that in mind, and with the constant prodding from the community and especially the conservation movement, I believe that the future for wilderness conservation in Australia looks very bright.

Action to protect forests, the Wet Tropics, World Heritage Areas and the important Murray-Darling Basin are major and significant political issues. The government's conservation agenda also includes a National Soil Conservation Program, a National Tree Program, protection and management of native fauna and flora, measures to combat environmental contamination and, of course, public education and awareness programs.

The government values the international aspects of its conservation and environment protection policies. Its participation in UNEP, IUCN, CITES, the South Pacific Regional Environment Program and other international activities is active and interested. We have shown special interest in the support and promotion of the World Heritage Convention. So far, some six sites are included on the World Heritage List. The government has nominated Uluru and is moving to nominate the Queensland Wet Tropics Region.

Much of this has been achieved through a growing acceptance by Australian citizens of conservation values. There can now be no doubt that environmental awareness and concern have reached a high level.Recent surveys and analysis of election results demonstrate this clearly.

Recognizing that conservation is a matter for the whole community, the government has made considerable efforts to involve community interests and to strengthen the voluntary conservation movement.

Federal government grants are made to these bodies in recognition of their important role in raising environmental awareness in the community and contributing to the development of effective environmental policies.

During a record four years as environment minister, Barry Cohen met with the 20 or 30 representatives of the major federal and state conservation groups two or three times a year to discuss with them whatever matters they wished to raise and to inform them of government thinking on conservation issues. The prime minister has met with representatives of conservation groups to discuss contentious issues. The newly-appointed minister, Senator Graham Richardson, has already gone out into the community to meet and listen to many groups of people affected by government policies. He intends to continue the regular process of consultation with the voluntary conservation movement. Government conservation and environmental protection policy has been enriched and certainly better informed by the process of community involvement and participation.

At the 1986 IUCN conference on implementing the World Conservation Strategy in Ottawa, it was clear the Australia had made comparatively good progress in implementing the strategy. I do not believe we could have achieved this without the very positive contribution of the conservation movement.

There is now considerable intellectual support for the view that Australia's economic development should be pursued through careful integration of development and conservation policies. Among the public at large there is increasing commitment to ensure that no development takes place without its environmental implications being thoroughly understood and weighed against its economic benefits. A network of legislative and administrative environmental impact assessment processes is well developed.

Despite this, I would not wish to leave you with the impression that in Australia we have found it easy to put into practice the principle of conserving living natural resources for sustainable development. In our experience this has been, and will continue to be, a difficult and challenging assignment.

I fail to be convinced that development and conservation are natural bedfellows. They can be brought together in appropriate circumstances with deliberate effort, but we have found that it is not always possible to accommodate environment and conservation in the same place. In some cases the conservation stakes are so high that economic development cannot be permitted. The government took that view when it decided to stop the Franklin Dam, when it legislated to ban mining in the Kakadu National Park and when it moved to preserve the Wet Tropics of Queensland.

In many cases we do not fully understand what constitutes a sustainable level of use of our living natural resources. How many trees can be safely removed without destroying a forest? How much vegetation can be cleared without causing the soil to blow away? The dilemma of governments is that they cannot afford—economically or politically—to suspend all development until they have the final answers to these questions. But nor can they afford to ignore long-term conservation needs simply because Australia is not—at this time—a major environmental disaster area.

Although the Australian environment may be unique, most of our conservation problems—both in their technical and political dimensions—are also found elsewhere. Therefore, we must also attempt to contribute to conservation on a wider scale. We can share the lessons we have learned from our own experience concerning two essentials for progress: positive leadership from a committed government, and the support and participation of an environmentally conscious public. Through our participation in the World Wilderness Congress and at other international venues I hope we can both share and learn.

Secondly, like any country, we can apply sound principles of conservation to the management of the part of the world's living natural resources with which we have been entrusted. In our case it is quite a large part. I hope I have emphasized the seriousness with which we accept this responsibility.

We in Australia are lucky to have a large, well-informed and committed conservation movement which, in cooperation with government, has been successful in raising the level of public awareness and understanding of conservation issues. We are also lucky to have governments prepared to adopt policies which will preserve resources for long-term survival, even at the expense of short-term wealth. Prime Minister Hawke has said, "We have never believed that the only values in life—in the life of our nation, in the life of our families—are the ones with the dollar tag upon them.

"The environment can only be destroyed once. But when it is protected and preserved, the benefits are permanent and will be appreciated for generations to come."

© Australian Government

THE
AMERICAS

BRAZIL—
CONSERVATION POLICY

José Pedro de Oliveira Costa

To describe Brazilian conservation is a difficult task, as there are an enormous amount of problems. I will try to give you a slight idea of what the country and our 8.5 million square kilometers of territory was like before the arrival of the Europeans.

We're more or less divided into two deep tropical forests: the Amazon forest, which takes half of the Brazilian territory and is shared with other South American countries, and on the eastern border of Brazil we had what we call the Atlantic forest, mostly on Brazilian territory, with a little bit of it in Paraguay and Argentina close to the Iguacu Falls border. Between these two forests there was an area covered with two types of savanna vegetation: one called caatinga, which is very dry and almost unfit for human habitation; and another called cerrado, which receives more rainfall and is better suited for habitation.

The caatinga would originally represent 15 percent of the Brazilian territory, and the cerrado savannas would correspond to 20 percent of the territory, the Atlantic forest 10 percent and the Amazon 50 percent of the Brazilian territory. The last 5 percent would correspond to the Pantanal zone, a freshwater marsh in the middle of the South American continent between Brazil, Bolivia and Paraguay. The Pantanal area has the largest concentration of wild fauna of all South America. It is a very important place for wilderness conservation, having a high concentration of birds, mammals, and reptiles, and an enormous population of crocodiles.

In early years we also had a huge Indian population. Some experts estimate a population of over a million, while others speak of around five million Indians in the Brazilian territory at the beginning of our colonization. They lived there for at least 30,000 years with a balanced way of life. They did use nature and they cut forests, but in such a way and with such a technology that they did not damage the environmental equilibrium. They produced wonderful pottery and superb feathered artifacts that are still considered the greatest expression of Brazilian art. It's said that when Columbus arrived in America he was so impressed by the tropical forests that he thought he had reached paradise. Columbus left us several writings about the everlasting summer of the tropical forests, the perfumed flowers and the wonderful birds of the Garden of Paradise. Amerigo Vespucci, when he passed by the Brazilian coast, also described this region as a paradise. Even the name Amazon comes from the medieval myth of the women warriors who protected the sacred garden.

The first Christian name of Brazil was The Land of Saint Cross, but with the rise of mercantilism during the Renaissance, the name was soon changed to Brazil, the name of the wood which was exploited in our country. Brazilwood was used as a red dye for clothing and was the first product to be exploited in our country.

After almost 500 years of colonization in Brazil the Atlantic forest has been reduced from covering 10 percent of our original territory to covering 0.2 percent. It is the area where the most of our endangered species are found. We have at least six species of primates in danger in the remainder of the Atlantic forest, among them the Muriqui, the largest monkey in the Americas. We have two wonderful species of parrots and dozens of other species ranging from mammals to butterflies, all of them endangered. Guaira Falls, as magnificent as the Iguacu Falls on the Paraguayan border, was transformed into an enormous dam for electrical energy during the military regime. Our mangroves, which are responsible for the production of the marine life in the tropical region, have been mostly destroyed for the construction of ports and cities and by oil spills. The Caatinga region is undergoing fast and thorough desertification. The Pantanal area, where the greatest portion of fauna exist, has been assaulted by people hunting crocodiles for their skins. We know that at least one million crocodiles are killed each year. Although the greatest portion of the Amazon has been destroyed, it has still been better preserved than any other ecosystem in Brazil. Currently, around one million hectares of the Amazon forest are being destroyed each year. Mercury is being used by gold miners in the Amazon and in the Pantanal to separate gold from sand in the riverbeds. With the uncontrolled contamination of the Pantanal and the Amazon, the Indian population is being decimated. We are living in the Wild West of the nineteenth-century United States, and the only difference is that this time the filmmakers are on the side of the Indians and are making films to try and protect them.

The current social and economic situation in Brazil is that half of our population of 140 million live in a reasonable condition, some of them in a very privileged condition even compared to those living in the developed nations. The other half, however, are living a subhuman, subsistence lifestyle. They are not eating enough, they do not consume enough calories. They are not receiving enough education, when they are educated at all. The political decision of the government is that we need to develop in order to feed all these people. Development means that we need exportation, we need dollars, we need industrialization, we need to modernize the country. At the moment, Brazil is a food-exporting country especially of soya beans, meat and several other goods. The decision has been made to put more land in production to feed the people and to export. Brazil has a $120 billion debt which was not assured through a decision of the people, but mostly by a military government that was not elected. More than $10 billion of this debt is to be paid as interest per year to the international monetary system. The problems are huge and the solution so far has been to occupy more areas, to destroy more of the Amazon forest and to sell whatever products of the forest could be sold, regardless of the serious possibility of desertification and all of the problems that come with it.

At the time the debt was made, the World Bank was financing development based on a Western definition of progress. Roads were being built and destruction was taking place. Now we are trying to find solutions to all of these problems and discussing what we should do about our $120 billion debt. There's a possibility of negotiating that and transforming part of the debt to conservation, as recently happened in Bolivia, which is a very welcome thought. Population control will be necessary in order to stabilize the economy, but this has still not been completely adopted by our government as policy. We need to preserve the productivity of our soil, we need to prevent desertification, we need to preserve our endangered species and those traditional people will be endangered if we continue this way. The kind of development that Brazil needs is not the kind that can be translated into numbers on a piece of paper. We are not interested in this kind of development. The type of development we need is food for the people, education and medical care for our population. Destruction that appears as numbers on a sheet of paper is different from the concept I have of development. We have already destroyed a lot of the Atlantic forest to plant coffee in the last century. We sterilized great parts of the soil of our country and we are still destroying and sterilizing a great part of the Amazon forest. We need a kind of sustained development, as do other underdeveloped countries, to develop in such a way that the country will maintain the capacity of production.

To illustrate my story I will relate my own experience when I got back to Brazil after living in Berkeley, California for two years. I was in charge of implementing an ecological reserve in the Atlantic Forest, in a place called Juriea that still has a large amount of primitive forest and other associated ecosystems. I went there in 1979 when the biggest challenge we faced was land speculation. We were trying to preserve a beautiful place that real estate companies wanted to turn into a beach resort. We found several endangered species in the area, and we also found that the people who lived in the poor soil areas were feeding on the rare animals. How could we deal with an endangered species that people were still eating? One of these animals is the Murigin, a slow monkey that's very easy to catch. These people needed to eat, they needed to feed their children, and they didn't know anything about endangered species and were just using all of their available resources to feed themselves. So we have to find alternative ways to approach endangered species preservation, get information to the people and give them an alternative to feed their families. This we did with reasonable success.

One year later, the federal government decided that this area was one of the least populated areas of Brazil and decided that two atomic plants should be built there. So we had to deal with the idea of having two atomic plants within the boundaries of our ecological station, and in spite of all these problems we have just decided to stay there. After five years of economic problems and other set-backs, the government has decided not to build the atomic plants after all. Last year our ecological station was made official. A bill was signed and 82,000 hectares of the Atlantic Forest have been officially designated as an ecological station. That doesn't mean that the fight is over. We still have to get the money to buy the land for the government. We still have to make improvements, we need guards to protect the area, but we are creating a reserve. We have already established an NGO that's in charge of taking care of the area.

The current situation is still tenuous. The military wanted to build the atomic plant to have control of the atomic system. All countries in South America wish to have such power and control. This is where all the money is being spent. We need a democratic government, we need to get rid of the dictatorship. I believe that the only way to prevent destruction is to have the people making the decisions. I do believe that the conservation of nature is the way of doing what is necessary for the people now and in the future.

I apologize for all of this bad news. Help and support is needed for the conservation of the land of Brazil, and to reinforce our hope for our fight. I also have some good news. We are having great support from the press in Brazil, which is very important for nature conservation. The other news I have for you is that we have created two new private foundations for environmental conservation in the past two years. These new foundations will support and contribute to the work being done by our other foundation which is now 20 years old. More than 100 NGOs are being created every three to four years, and at the moment I would say that there are about 400 NGOs in Brazil. We are having big demonstrations in our cities. I live in Sao Paulo, a metropolitan area of around 15 million people who are becoming concerned about the environment. Last year a representative of NGOs was elected to the national congress. This congress is responsible for writing our new constitution and there is a proposal for a whole chapter on the environment. In this chapter it is stated that the government is responsible for the preservation of all the species of animals native to Brazil.

Throughout South America the story is the same: destruction of our forests, destruction of our ecosystems. We need to face this reality so that we may find a strategy: we need plans, we need scientific effort. The tropical climate and environment calls for a different approach and different technology from the temperate climates. We need the help of anyone who can support us technically, financially, or politically. Any kind of support will be important. We already have very good help from the World Wildlife Fund and it is very important that we have the support of the American public. For example, the World Bank has, due to different pressures, offered several hundred million dollars for the preservation of nature in Brazil and we are going to take it. That will change our possibilities of treating our problems. We need environmental education, we need to reinforce the protection of our national parks and we need to create new national parks. We also need a good use for developed areas. We believe we are entering a new era of treating the conservation problems of the world. It is a long and hard fight but we will succeed by all working together.

ECUADOR—
THE PROMISE AND PROBLEMS
OF WILDERNESS IN THE THIRD
WORLD

Yolanda Kakabadse

A couple of months ago a tribal group of the Amazonian region of Ecuador killed a priest and a nun who intended to land in their territory on a friendly mission. The news of this episode was spread all over the world and became an important topic of discussion. We all speculated on the motives.

What led this tribe of only 50 or less individuals to kill two innocent people? Among the many answers, we can be certain that one of them was the defense of their territory, their integrity, their wilderness.

Those indigenous peoples that still remain within the wild lands of South America are slowly but aggressively being pushed away from their lands. The reasons? Mainly economic ones. As long as the exploitation of the natural resources within wild areas means business, there will be little that we can do to stop the process.

International commerce between developed and developing nations has no pity on local resources. There is a foreign debt and local economic pressures that have to be met, and decision makers from the public and the private sectors fall into the vicious circle of intensifying the exploitation of natural resources to increase the national income.

Such is the case in Ecuador and its neighbor countries when we talk about shrimp production for the international market, versus the conservation of the mangroves; or timber, versus tropical forests that are being destroyed at an incredible speed; or flower plantations that have put aside local agricultural products and practices.

I believe it is important to emphasize that there is a definite relationship between a country's financial obligations—foreign debt—and its capacity to preserve its natural resources and wild lands. More so, when we consider the lack of awareness on the part of the majority of the population about the advantages or disadvantages of conservation.

What does conservation really mean in most of our countries? Let's go back a couple of decades. Conservation programs and national parks systems were created as a result of well-planned and successful international lobbying originated in the North. It started in the North, and rightly so, because most of its wild lands had been destroyed by human action and many species had already disappeared. The sense of loss and the sense of responsibility for the future made the Northern countries design and implement conservation programs and transfer them to the Southern countries that still had abundant wild areas at hand. Third World countries felt that there was no problem in introducing these conservation programs in their development plans, but felt no urgency to implement them. We still don't. The reasons? On the one hand we haven't suffered the absence of resources; on the other hand there are other national priorities.

The budget assigned for these departments are usually too low. Motivated personnel soon feel defeated and the local population does not understand their goals.

Decision makers consider wild areas as potential alternatives for large investments if natural resources are abundant, or for colonization programs if they aren't.

The general public does not have a definite attitude toward those areas as long as their personal or group interests are not affected. Some groups of the population consider that the benefits of the wild areas are a luxury for the privileged classes who, in addition to what they already have, want to own large territories for their personal enjoyment.

Indigenous people do not believe in conservation programs, whether they be presented by national or foreign organizations, official or private. In the last centuries and in the name of progress, their natural areas and resources have been taken from their hands and have been unmercifully disposed of.

Then, there is the smallest group: the NGOs, formed by environmentalists, scientists and common people, young and old, poor and rich, men and women, who are striving to put things right by:

• Working on legislation to update obsolete laws and regulations;

• Working on pesticides to stop—at least in Ecuador—the corruption of some industries that produce only for export to the Third World;
• Working with the conservation authorities so as not to let them be defeated by the influence of decision makers;
• Promoting applied research among scientists and scientific institutions to identify local alternatives;
• Dealing with indigenous groups that lose faith and hope as the years pass by;
• Negotiating with individuals of the industrial sector to have them change their attitudes toward society;
• Implementing public awareness and educational programs to modify our behavior before it is too late;
• Dealing with officials of bilateral and multilateral agencies, proving that we can do it ourselves; and,
• Promoting institutional building among the other countries of the region so as to strengthen our work.

It is not easy. All these efforts require faith, time, effort, money and international support. Conservation programs, though, have some exceptions, for example those in the Caribbean region and the Galapagos Islands, which are highly profitable largely due to high visibility and tourism. This evidence forces us to conclude that unless conservation projects turn out to be financially successful, they will not be seriously considered by Third World authorities at the moment.

Our actions in conservation must consider the following challenges and meet them effectively with action:

• There is an urgent need to educate and raise awareness among all sectors: decision makers, children, university students and the general public;
• We must look for economically sound alternatives for the people who are presently depending on an irrational use of the natural resources;
• The current situation of the tropical rain forests of the world is a global problem, therefore solutions must also be global;
• The debtor-lender relationship, when focusing on conservation, has proven to be ineffective. We must start or continue to look for solutions that invoke North and South, specifically through NGO cooperation; and,
• Proposals and their implementation will only be feasible if they become an authentic and global partnership.

There are only two paths for the near future. Total destruction of the remaining resources—basically the tropical forests—implies a massive loss of biological and genetic diversity and endangers the survival of the human species. More difficult, but of critical importance is an intensive and immediate action to prevent this destruction.

CONSERVATION BY TRADITIONAL CULTURES IN THE TROPICS

Arturo Gómez-Pompa and Andrea Kaus

It has been said that the main problem in conservation in the tropics has been the activities of native people whose populations have grown to such high density that they have destroyed their soil resources, deforested their lands, overgrazed their pastures and overused their agricultural lands. It is not uncommon to read and hear that shifting agriculture is the main problem for biological conservation in the tropics, a claim made by a few speakers even at the World Wilderness Congress.

The wrong but pervasive concept that the tropical forests represent a poor and difficult environment for the development of complex human societies has been used as a basis for denying the high degree of sociopolitical complexity reached by civilizations in the tropics. This denial led to the acceptance of such sites as merely ritual centers of shifting cultivators coexisting with magnificent forests. The same superficial concept asserted the emptiness of the tropical regions, the low value of their forest resources and the low agricultural potential of the tropical soils. One well-known example of this view is the common belief that the old and magnificent Classic Maya civilization had a major collapse because of a failure in the proper management of the environment.

This conception of tropical forest environments has strongly colored modern approaches to their use by directing attention away from their potential as any kind of renewable, sustainable resource and promoting instead a troubled and erroneous dichotomization between pristine conservation on the one hand and totally unthought-out use on the other. The result has been the over-exploitation of the forest resources, mismanagement of soils and neglect of the human groups who have lived there in the past and live there presently.

Under this belief our society has directed its efforts to preserve pieces of "wild lands" without people and without the influence of people in parks and related protected areas. This approach has been followed by many temperate countries with some success, but the same approach in the tropics has been difficult to implement.

The common conceptual framework behind these efforts lies in the belief that preservation of pristine environments without human interference is the best way to preserve biological diversity, and also helps to reconstruct environments similar to those before the impact of humans. This concept is heavily charged with emotion and its followers are mainly urbanites educated in modern universities, who lack a link with the land and its resources or consideration of the traditional cultures which inhabited the land before them. Such modern perceptions of preservation forget our past and jump over a long history of human occupancy back into prehuman "pristine" lands.

In contrast with this, there is the need to promote economic development. The "unused" pristine areas often provide the only unreclaimed space (agricultural frontier) available to accommodate landless farmers and open new agricultural and pasture lands. The dilemma of conservation versus development is one of the most important problems facing the underdeveloped world today. It seems to us that these opposing views toward resource management have been overstressed and misunderstood from a historical perspective.

HUMAN IMPACT ON "PRISTINE" ENVIRONMENTS

What we want to preserve today is the result of a complex set of changes that have occurred through time. Climates have changed drastically in the last 20,000 years, as have soils and the biological diversity of ecosystems. Humans especially have had a strong impact in many ecosystems far beyond our present understanding. Fires, deforestation and agriculture have occurred all over the world through historical times. The fact that history is better known outside the tropics does not necessarily mean that equivalent changes have not occurred in the tropics.

Human impact in the tropical areas needs to be studied from an objective approach to understand past and present influences on the structure and composition of tropical ecosystems, and consequently, the human role in the conservation of biological diversity. In order to do that, more knowledge of present-day ancient cultures that subsist in the tropical world is needed to learn their successes and failures, thereby increasing our understanding of the failures and successes of their ancestors.

In the Americas during pre-Hispanic times many cultures lived in the diverse environments of the continent from Canada to Tierra del Fuego. These indigenous groups lived efficiently from the land and its resources in various ways. They were efficient hunters, gatherers, fishermen, agriculturalists and forest managers. They practiced shifting as well as sedentary agriculture, and they managed their wildlife and fisheries. The "pristine" unused environments of the conquerors were the subsistence fields of the natives.

In the tropics we have the longest history of sedentary human occupancy. Very few places in the tropics exist where it can be assured that there are no evidences of human occupancy or human influence in the past. The recently discovered stone-walled forest gardens in the Maya area, the pet kot, were previously confused with climax forests.

Many of the tropical "pristine" forests of today are the result of the last cycle of abandonment by humans. In the history of humankind there have been many cycles of occupancy and use-perturbation, with corresponding cycles of abandonment. Some abandonment cycles are planned and others are unplanned. The best-known planned cycle is that of shifting agriculture, varying from two to five years of use and from three to 20 or more years of fallow. One very well-known cycle of unplanned abandonment occurred during the European conquest of the Americas, when war and disease reduced the population in some areas down to 20 percent of previous levels.

Many tropical "pristine" forests in America are remnants of managed forests abandoned for nearly 500 years with scattered periodical perturbations, both natural (cyclones, fires) and human (timber mining). In the last 20 to 40 years the greatest known disturbance of the tropical forests of Mexico has occurred. The reasons for this frightening perturbation of today's tropical forests are well known, and with the advent of machines and chemicals, the rate of deforestation has increased immensely. As a result, the forests are entering into a very dangerous stage of perturbation (for its extension and intensity) without anyone's knowledge of when the next abandonment will occur. It is of utmost importance, then, to try to understand what the minimum requirements in ecological and biological diversity are at the present time that may ensure a good recovery in the future, or which may be used if our society decides wisely to restore the lost forest ecosystems.

MAYA SILVICULTURE

In order to answer that question it is necessary to understand what the Maya culture did in order to maintain a high population density in the lowland tropics without diminishing the biological diversity potential of the area. This particular ancient culture, which is a case study on this subject, is suitable for this purpose because there exists very good evidence of the management techniques used in the past that enabled the Maya to conserve the biological diversity we are unsuccessfully trying to preserve today.

In contrast with what is commonly believed, the Maya had a very complex system of natural resource management in which conservation of biological diversity seemed to be a common denominator.

Table 1
Maya Subsistence Systems

Present-Day Maya	Ancient Maya
Milpa	Raised Fields
Kitchen Gardens	Terraces
Ka'aanche'	Silviculture
Orchards	Milpa Forest Gardens (Pet Kotoob)
Plantations	Wildlife Management
Hunting and Gathering	Aquaculture
Livestock/Small Animal Husbandry	Water Management
Irrigation Agriculture	Intensive Animal Husbandry
Forest Mining	Biological Conservation
Fishing	

These complex systems allowed them to attain population densities of 500 people per square kilometer in contrast with present densities of five people per square kilometer. A great variety of subsistence systems available to the Old Maya have been discovered rather recently and include a great diversity of agricultural systems and silvicultural techniques. Several books and articles have been written on this subject and new information is continuously appearing in the literature.

From the biological conservation point of view, the most important subsistence system is the one related to the management of forests and trees. The Old Maya have been blamed for the deforestation of their lands that triggered an ecological disaster, a theory which has then been used as an explanation for the Classic Maya collapse in the ninth century. Recent evidence challenges this assertion.

The concept of "virgin" forest has been challenged for a long time, as several scientists in the past have noted the impact of humans on the vegetation of the tropics. It has been mentioned that the abundance of palms, fruit and other trees in the native vegetation is evidence of past human intervention. In 1937 the American botanist Lundell explored the vegetation of the Peten in Guatemala and found a great abundance of fruit trees in the Maya ruins, which suggested that they may have been planted by the Old Maya. In addition, he later pointed out in 1939 that tree species of economic importance found on the ruins were also species commonly planted by the modern Maya.

More recently, Puleston suggested that the "ramon" tree, *Brosimum alicastrum*, with its edible seeds, may have played a role in the subsistence of the Old Maya. Today these seeds are still used as a substitute for corn or are mixed with it. An important controversy is currently going on over the role of this species in Maya subsistence. The fact is that the present-day Maya, as well as other cultures such as the Huastec and Totonac, still protect and cultivate this tree in their home gardens and have many uses for it.

In addition to this species, the present-day Maya have a great variety of trees that they plant and protect for their own use in kitchen gardens and other similar agroforestry systems. Some of the important species used by the Maya for their tropical fruit and other products include *Artocarous, Bactris gasipaes, Diospryros digyna* and others. All of these species are assumed to have been present in the native flora, and the most important species were selected through time for different purposes. Such is the case of the ciruelos (*Spondias spp.* and *Ziziphus sp.*), from which the Maya of one locality recognize 22 varieties. For a complete reference of species use and management in tropical areas write the Fund for Conservation Projects of Young Scientists and Students in Developing Countries, UC Mexus, University of California, Riverside, CA, USA 92521.

What is most intriguing is the fact that many of these species are very abundant in different natural ecosystems of the region and other tropical lowland regions of Mexico and Central America. Many of them are dominant in a number of communities. This extraordinary coincidence of abundance of useful trees in mature ecosystems is a central question in the understanding of the success or failure of the Maya through time. In addition, these facts may be of great importance in the design of strategies for the conservation of biological diversity in regions with high population densities. The problem, then, is how can the abundance of useful, dominant trees in the old, mature forests of the Maya area be explained? Five different hypotheses can be formulated:

1. Deforestation hypothesis—The Old Maya destroyed most of their forests and thereby caused their own collapse. The natural regeneration process occurred after their collapse in all the deforested areas. In this regeneration process some useful species that were scattered in the area gained an advantage and have dominated the vegetation until the present.

2. Natural hypothesis—The trees were abundant in the area before any human occupancy and the Maya and their predecessors were lucky to find such a rich environment.

3. Accident hypothesis—The trees were there before human arrival but were not necessarily abundant nor dominant, and through their activities humans have by accident created ecological niches (such as those of the archaeological sites) that favor these species.

4. Man-made hypothesis—The species were present in the area but were not necessarily abundant nor dominant, and humans over time selected, protected and cultivated the most useful ones. These actions explain their abundance and dominance in the forest today.

5. Mixed hypothesis—The species were there in the area in some abundance, and humans improved and maintained that abundance and by accident created niches that favored the useful species.

From the available evidences we have found sufficient data in the present-day activities of the modern Maya to support the man-made and mixed hypotheses. From these a silvicultural system for the Old Maya based on the knowledge and techniques used by the present-day Maya has been proposed.

Table 2
Silvicultural Techniques of the Maya
(Gómez-Pompa 1987:6)

Cenotes
     Introduction of useful trees
Dooryard Gardens
     Germination of seeds in *caanches*
     Tree planting
     Selection of wild useful trees at beginning
"Natural" Forest Ecosystems
     Conservation of forest patches
     Selection of useful trees
     Introduction of useful trees

Pet Kot
        Selection of forested sites
        Selection and protection of useful wild trees
        Introduction of useful trees
Raised Fields
        Trees in borders of fields
        Tree plantations (cacao?)
Shifting Agriculture
        Selection and protection of trees
        Coppice of selected species in slash
        Tree planting before fallow
Tolche
        Different sizes and forms of forested belt
Tree Plantations
        Fruit trees
        Cacao plantations with legume trees
Other
        Living fences
        Trees in urban and religious centers
        Sacred groves
        Trees in terraces?

These techniques that integrate the Maya silviculture are not all practiced in any one area by the present-day Maya, but all occur in the region. Given past internal communication, political complexity and general levels of empirical knowledge in the Maya area, these techniques were likely to have been integrated at times in the past. They help to explain the presence of useful "natural" forests (forest gardens) in the zone and their possible role in Maya subsistence.

In order to accomplish this hypothetical system of silviculture, there must have been a good biological diversity conservation strategy involving a plan of resource management that ranged from intensive crop cultivation in the ancient irrigated chinampa fields to the creation of artificial forests and with less use the conservation of "pristine" ecosystems. In between, they had many agricultural, agro-silvicultural and silvicultural systems in which the maintenance of biological diversity was the rule. This is probably why, in spite of the fact that the Maya area was densely populated and intensively used in the past, there is no evidence of mass extinctions of species, nor any evidence that species diversity or richness was diminished by the actions of the inhabitants. The proof of this can be found in the richly endemic flora of the Maya area. The secondary succession forest composition, as well, provides evidence of tree species manipulation which maintains a high degree of diversity and usefulness. The regeneration of the ecosystems of the Maya area after successive abandonments was possible only because of the existence of insitu seed banks in managed and "natural" ecosystems, and because of land uses that did not cause irreversible damage to the soils.

In an ongoing literature survey we have been doing in other tropical regions of the world, we have found several examples of similar situations to that of the Maya area. Many communities of the mature primary vegetation are dominated by species of trees that are well known to the local people for their uses. Examples of conscious manipulation of these tree species exists as does evidence of inadvertent manipulation through the combination of cultural practices with ecologically sound measures. For example, trees protected for religious reasons and taboos are unconsciously given competitive advantage in the forest. Other tree species, such as some fire-resistant palms, are better able to survive or coexist with human activities. Even negative manipulation by avoidance of certain toxic tree species (such as *Rhus*) may explain their abundance.

To illustrate what has been found, we have produced a list of some of the tree species reported as dominant in the natural communities of different areas of the tropics which are also reported to be useful or managed by the local cultures. The results so far have been very encouraging, as a strong association exists between the abundance of trees and the uses and management practices such as planting, protecting, and sparing (during forest clearing) of these tree species. Cultural groups which report using and managing these species include: Ashanti, Bokata, Bora, Boruca, Enga, Guaymi, Huastec, Ibo, Jicaque, Kayapo, Maring, Nuaulu, Maya, Talamanca, Terraba, Totonacan, Waika and Zenu.

It is clear that the conservation of the biological diversity of the tropics should have the highest priority. It is also clear that a great many of the areas occupied by the tropical forest ecosystems of today were occupied by traditional cultures for millennia. Many tropical forests are, in fact, managed forests by local cultures, both past and present, and it is to everyone's advantage to learn more about the forests and the people who inhabit them.

Even though the number of managed tree species known by modern science is very low if compared with the tree flora of the region, we have to understand that each culture has its own interests and its own uses for the trees. The more we know about cultures, the more we learn about their value to the trees. As a result, the of managed trees is longer. This important issue has been overlooked by the majority of researchers, modern resource managers and conservationists.

The biological diversity we want to conserve today has been influenced by generations of inhabitants. Even with our modern scientific knowledge, we should be humble enough to learn from the knowledge developed over these many generations by traditional cultures in the tropics. Research on this subject has implications for formulating alternative conservation plans in development schemes. Man-made forests with high diversity can play an important role in the conservation of biological diversity. They offer niches for a great diversity of plant and animal life and also act as biological buffers between the agroecosystems and the natural "pristine" ecosystems, while still providing tangible benefits for local people. We must then realize the importance of human experience in the design of the ecosystems of the past, learning from their successes and failures in order to design the ecosystems of the future.

CANADA—THE NEW FRONTIER IN CONSERVATION

Thomas McMillan

The challenge for humankind is to ensure that we heed the wise counsel of Madame Gro Harlem Brundtland and the World Commission on Environment and Development toward "our common future." Otherwise, the world itself will be history. Certainly, what future we and our children might be able to look forward to will be as grim as it will be short.

Fortunately, the WCED is already having an impact on world thinking and, even more important, on our actions. The choice of themes for the 4th World Wilderness Congress—conservation, the need for a global inventory of wilderness areas, the development of conservation strategies and international banking and the debt crisis in the Third World—reflects the growing recognition that environmental and economic decisions must be integrated if the human family is to survive beyond the twentieth century.

The subject of Third World debt might, even a few years ago, have seemed an unlikely subject for environmentalists. Now, however, it is automatically considered as legitimate a topic as the plight of tropical rain forests. Indeed, the world is beginning to recognize that the latter cannot be adequately considered without the former. As the Nobel laureate Dr. George Wald has said, the current state of the Third World debt load is equivalent to modern-day "peonage." The abject poverty and the heavy debt load it breeds drives Third World nations into environmentally disastrous decisions that compound the economic crisis in which they find themselves. If the vicious circle is not cut, neither their economy nor their environment will last. For the Third World, poverty is pollution and pollution is poverty.

But we in the industrialized nations have no cause for feeling superior. We are not only destroying the environment in which we live, we are, wittingly or unwittingly, encouraging others to destroy theirs as well. Only recently, for example, has Canada's multimillion dollar foreign assistance program required environmental assessments for development projects it funds in the Third World. In the past, we have been a party to some of the most obscene violations of the environment ever committed in that part of the planet—all in the name of altruism. We have helped give the Good Samaritan a bad name! If, in the words of the late Richard St. Barbe Baker, the planet is being "skinned alive," we, like other industrialized countries, are largely responsible for the offense.

It is as though humankind's ultimate purpose in life is to exploit every natural resource until nothing remains of it. Having decimated one species, the object is to line up the next victim for slaughter. Isn't it ironic that, throughout the course of history, the very resources that humankind has extinguished have been renewable? One wonders whether we are driven by some kind of death wish that challenges us to test the outer limits of our capacity to destroy everything we touch, including ourselves. Perhaps Bertrand Russell was right when he observed, "Ever since Adam ate the apple, man has never refrained from any folly of which he was capable."

It requires a special kind of arrogance, I think, to assume that we *Homo sapiens* are the lords of creation and that it is there to serve only us. That kind of pride is not just one of the seven deadly sins, it borders on pathological stupidity. In our headlong selfishness we forget that, in destroying what we deem nature has put there to serve us, we increase the likelihood of our own extinction.

We must realize there is nothing intrinsically hospitable about planet Earth. Our planet does not support a rich and complex way of life because it is ideally suited for that purpose. It is ideally suited to support life because of the rich and diverse ecological systems. Without the moderating effects of vegetation, of gas exchange and of the recycling of materials conducted by billions of invertebrates—the unsung heroes of planetary survival—the planet Earth would be as unlikely a site for the Garden of Eden as Mars or Venus.

The message and challenge of the Brundtland Commission has come none too soon. Canada is committed to meeting that challenge.

In October 1987, as Canada's spokesperson in the special UN debate on the Brundtland Report, I will respond formally to the Commission. A major portion of our response will be based on a Canada-wide task force on environment and economy established last year in anticipation of the Brundtland Commission's report. It has drawn on the skills of six federal and provincial environment ministers, industrial leaders, environmentalists and academics.

The task force will be issuing its plan next week in Quebec City. The plan underscores the need for fundamental changes in the way environmental and economic decisions are made. And it will call, in particular, for the development of conservation strategies—an approach already taken in my home province of Prince Edward Island and begun in Canada's north by the Inuit and territorial governments.

Reflecting an awareness that conservation must be woven into the very fabric of the economy, Canada is attempting to practice the Brundtland ethic. On the international front, the Canadian International Development Agency—the federal government's principle arm for foreign aid—has adopted a radically different policy to avoid the kind of misguided altruism in the Third World to which I referred earlier.

In the same vein, Canada's minister of external affairs announced earlier this month that the country is forgiving almost a billion dollars of debt owed by African nations to Canada. Many more millions will be forgiven by Canada in the future. We believe it is insane, if not criminal, for the poorest nations on earth to pay more money to wealthy nations like Canada than they receive in aid from those same countries.

Canada has just hosted arguably the most important international diplomatic conference on the environment and economy ever held. At that conference, nations around the world agreed to an historic protocol: to slash in half by 1999 the production of chemicals that destroy the stratospheric ozone (that layer of gases around the earth that protects the human race and all other life forms from the most lethal of the sun's rays). The Montreal Protocol constitutes the first-ever global treaty on the atmosphere—in effect, a law of the air.

Scientists confirm that since 1970, the earth's sun shield has been weakened by some 3 percent. It is projected that, without the Montreal Protocol, the ozone layer would be depleted by 15 percent in the next 45 years. With each 1 percent decrease in ozone, the incidence of cancer would increase by 4 percent, not to mention increases in eye disease and in injury to the human body's immune system. The same chemicals risk devastating the world's capacity to feed itself. Grains and fish are especially vulnerable.

Indeed, at the current rate of destruction, the ozone layer is thought to have a life span of no more than 100 years—a period that scarcely extends beyond that of our generation's grandchildren. One does not need to be a prophet of doom to recognize that a planetary time bomb is ticking away and that the pace is accelerating. The Montreal Protocol imposes tough restrictions on governments, on industry and on consumers around the world. The Protocol contains provisions for tough trade sanctions against violators. Every country contributed to the success of the Montreal conference.

To my mind, the ability of the human family to forge a genuinely useful global law on such a contentious set of issues demonstrates that when the political will is mustered, it is possible to improve the odds in the risky game the world has been playing with its own future.

Surely, the Montreal Protocol and the way in which it was forged should serve as a model for the world community in addressing other transboundary environmental problems.

Of particular concern to Canada are sulphur dioxide emissions that travel long distances, even countries away, from their origins. Acid rain is devastating the natural environment of my country. Some 14,000 lakes have been acidified, 150,000 others are in the process of acidification and another 150,000 are vulnerable. Nowhere else is the environment-economy link more obvious than in the area of acid rain. Just ask the hundreds of tourist operators whose lodges face closure as the lakes die, the fish disappear and the sports fishermen no longer come. Acid rain is now one of the government of Canada's two or three major policy priorities. And it is the number one Canada-U.S. issue with the Canadian public.

Within Canada itself, strict controls have been imposed on industry through legally binding federal-provincial accords, supported by a $3 billion government-industry program designed to slash total acid rain-causing emissions in half by 1994, based on 1980 levels. But our program, strong as it is, deals with only half the problem, because the United States exports to us 50 percent of the total emissions that destroy our crops, retard our forestry, kill our lakes, destroy our built heritage and compromise our health. When our prime minister said he wanted free trade with the United States, acid rain was not what he had in mind!

The acid-rain issue is not just an environmental or economic issue to Canadians. We see it as a litmus test of whether Canadian-U.S. relations are merely an accident of geography or an exercise in genuine cooperation in areas of common concern. The chilling fact is that if two countries with such close historic ties cannot make progress on an issue like acid rain, with its terrible consequences for both countries, what hope is there for progress on environmental issues among nations less bound by links of friendship? Is the Montreal Protocol, however important, to be merely an aberration in world affairs?

Just when one is tempted to despair, something miraculous occurs to give all of us reason for hope. One such miracle occurred in my country. And because of the worldwide salience of the issue, that miracle should inspire us all.

At stake was a remote and magnificent archipelago, an area that many of you know as South Moresby. It has been described as the Canadian Galapagos, harboring, as it does, species of flora and fauna unique in the world. It also contains some of the last virgin rain forests in this continent, with Sitka spruce and cedar over 1,000 years old and as large as any in the world. Just as it is home to bald eagles, sea lions, the world's biggest black bear and streams rich with salmon, so also it is the ancestral home of the Haida. That great nation flourished in the area 5,000 years before Christ. While their numbers in the last century were decimated by white man's disease, the Haida did survive and their rich cultural heritage is as much a part of what makes South Moresby unique as the wilderness itself.

But all of the natural and cultural splendor was nearly lost to the world in a classic struggle. The Haida, allied with dedicated environmentalists, fought to save their ancestral homeland as a powerful but troubled forest industry set its sights on the trees that rise so tall their lowest branches are like the vaulted ceilings of the great cathedrals of Europe.

Most of you are familiar with the happy outcome. Instead of clashing fatally, the environmental and economic goals were reconciled. Following an eleventh-hour intervention by the Canadian prime minister, the government of Canada and the relevant provincial government agreed on a multimillion dollar package—$106 million from the federal government alone—to create in South Moresby a national park as part of a total economic development strategy for the area. The Haida themselves will play a leading role in that connection.

The great Haida artist and carver, Bill Reid, wrote during the height of the battle to save South Moresby, "These shining islands may be the signposts that point the way to a renewed, harmonious relationship with this, the only world we're ever going to have."

For Canada, South Moresby was a watershed. Thousands of Canadians who had not before seen themselves as environmentalists were galvanized in a great national cause to save what they instinctively recognized as part of themselves.

No other issue had so illuminated the fundamental importance Canadians attach to environmental values. I am convinced that, appearances and Lord Russell to the contrary, we humans have it in us to save ourselves from ourselves.

An ancient Chinese proverb goes something like this: "If we don't change our course, we will end up where we are headed." I assert that we don't want to be where we are headed.

The World Commission on Environment and Development provides a new path. Let us follow it and, in doing so, ensure that we end up where we and our children and, indeed, the generations yet unborn, would want to be.

THE UNITED STATES— WHY WILDERNESS?

Roderick Frazier Nash

This is a time of irreversible decision for wilderness on earth. As a species, our kind has followed with a vengeance the advice of the Old Testament prophet and "made the crooked straight and the rough places plain." The transformation of wilderness into civilization has taken on aspects of a religion and crusade and nowhere is this more than in the United States. Presently in the 48 continuous states, excluding Alaska, the amount of protected wilderness is approximately equal to the amount of pavement: about 2 percent of the total land mass is in each category. Michael McCloskey's world inventory of wilderness (also included in these proceedings) makes the point another way. Wilderness is indeed an endangered geographical species.

Today, not 1890, is the effectual end of the American frontier. Our generation is making the final decisions about the continuing presence of wildness in the environment. The limits of the earth are rapidly being reached, and what this means is that wilderness will no longer exist as left-over or forgotten land that nobody knows. It will either be consciously and deliberately preserved by policy and law or it will vanish. The future will hold us accountable for the quality of environment it inherits. Will we pass on an enduring legacy of wilderness or will we bequeath a totally-modified earth?

Pioneering in the past involved the destruction of wilderness, and it has almost completely succeeded. Future pioneering should emphasize preservation. The mission of the new frontiersmen should be centered on restraining, not extending, civilization. The point is that we have conquered the wilderness; now we need to conquer ourselves and our appetite for growth and development. Axes and rifles, barbed wire and bulldozers were useful in a time when civilization was struggling for a foothold in the wild world. But now it is wilderness that is struggling for existence, and the need is for new tools. Research into and education about the value of wilderness are the appropriate tools for the new frontiersmen. So are institutions such as the proposed World Conservation Bank. A congress like this one gives promise of a new perspective.

There is substantial wilderness left on parts of the planet. The polar regions are largely wild, as the McCloskey inventory suggests, so is the floor of the ocean and the moon. But for most of us these are not "meaningful" wildernesses. Like heaven, it is nice to know it exists, but most of us are never going to get there! More specifically, in the tropical and temperate latitudes, where most humans live, wilderness is melting away, as Bob Marshall liked to say, like a snowbank in the August sun. Extrapolating from the recent growth of science and technology, can we be certain that we will not have within our power in a few decades the ability to civilize the poles, the oceans and even the stars? The necessity, again, is for restraint. We need to understand that on a limited planet everything must have limits. This includes our numbers and our impact. It is time to understand that civilization can be ironic: some is undeniably good, but in excess it can destroy itself by its own "too much." Balance is the key. Wilderness should no longer be seen as a threat to civilization, but rather as a valuable part of a rich and full civilization—an asset and not an adversary. In time we might discover something the old-style pioneers could not have been expected to know: Wilderness is not the enemy of civilization, but a necessity if that civilization is to live up to its potential as a human habitat.

Just a century and a half ago, on the great plains of Colorado, buffalo thundered, wolves howled and grizzly roamed the creek bottoms. Humans living then were wilderness people. We called them Indians. In 1837 another kind of people, the mountain men, were entering Colorado, and the last thing on their minds was the preservation of wilderness. What concerned them, understandably, was the preservation and extension of the civilization of which they were vanguards. Yet ironically, these frontiersmen sowed the seeds of wilderness appreciation. Their success in extending civilization made wilderness rare and, according to the scarcity theory of value, appreciated. Whereas a century and a half ago it could be said that there was too much wilderness, now, as we look around Denver's smog-fouled air basin, there is too much civilization. We have come full circle from the plains where deer, antelope and buffalo played to a metropolis where we plan strategy for finding places for the buffalo to roam again.

Edward Abbey, the writer, says that wilderness needs no defense, only more defenders. Respectfully, I disagree. There is a pressing need for elucidation of the underlying principles and values upon which an effective defense of wilderness can be built. Such a philosophy of wilderness has been notable for its absence in the U.S. preservation movement.

We have, rather, witnessed a series of frantic, subjective and highly-emotional defenses of particular places. "Save the grizzly!" or "Save Grand Canyon!" we cry. If anyone asked, "Why?" there was a sharp intake of breath, a scowl and the reply that it was the *Grand Canyon*. But that is not enough. The questions remain: *Why* save a place like the Grand Canyon, *why* keep it wild?

The point is that wilderness appreciation has been a creed, a faith, something you felt in your bones, something that was almost sullied by analysis and explication. But that is not good enough, especially when the world's wild places are increasingly hard-pressed by demands for the expansion of civilization. There is a need for an articulation of wilderness values based on historical fact, contemporary experience and the projected future needs of human life and of all life. This is the vital philosophy of wilderness. It must lie behind the defense of particular wild places like the philosophy of human dignity lies behind defenses of human freedom. Philosophers have spent 2,500 years setting forth the liberal philosophy. So, when Thomas Jefferson wrote his famous Declaration, when Lincoln emancipated the slaves or when more recent protests of discrimination occurred, few needed to ask, "Why?" The value of liberty and equality is well defined. Not so with the value of wilderness. The appreciation of wild places and wild creatures is, after all, barely a century old.

We should pause for a moment to consider several ways *not* to defend wilderness, ways that do not make the best case for preservation. The first is *scenery*. The problem here is that wilderness is not about scenery; it is about the absence of technological civilization and its controlling influence. Now some people do find the absence of civilization "scenic," but many others find it strange, weird, harsh, frightening and decidedly unlovely. They value it not because it is beautiful but because it is wild. Basing a defense of this kind of country on scenic beauty is to leave the case open to all sorts of logical pitfalls. How, for instance, is fire to be justified as a natural part of a wilderness ecosystem? Using beauty to defend wilderness, in sum, is like saying that only beautiful people are to be accorded rights to exist. We abandoned that tactic long ago in defending human rights, and it is time to question its validity in making a case for wilderness.

Recreation is another sandy foundation for wild country because it is not wilderness dependent, to use a concept developed by John Hendee, Robert Lucas and George Stankey. People can and do recreate and generally have fun outdoors in very nonwilderness settings. Camping can be had in KOA campgrounds, and excellent hunting and fishing is available in fenced and stocked compounds. We need to investigate what it is about *wilderness* recreation that is different and valuable.

A third way not to defend wilderness is *economics*, and I say this with the full realization that cost-benefit analyses and the expenditures of tourists have been used repeatedly to justify the existence of wildness. Generally, proponents of the economic argument are interested in offering a countervailing argument to the developers' calculations of the cash value of natural resources present in wilderness. The problem is that wilderness almost always loses in such figuring. Its "benefits" are invariably less than, say, that which timber or mineral extraction, or condominium building, would provide. And tourists utilizing hotels and restaurants always spend more than backpackers. Economic arguments are thus a dead end for wilderness. Moreover, there is the point that wilderness should be measured on a different scale of value, like the Parthenon or Chartres Cathedral or a beloved person. I am reminded here of an exchange I once had with a distinguished resource economist who was using the cost-benefit technique to evaluate wilderness. At the conclusion of his remarks, I simply asked him, "What's the cost-benefit ratio of your 87-year-old mother?" Affronted, the economist blustered, "Well, that's different." So, I submit, is wilderness. It's our biological and cultural mother. The point is that wilderness defenders should have the courage to not go to the economic mat with their opponents. They should remember that economists are sometimes accused of knowing the price of everything and the value of nothing.

A corollary to this reasoning is that the wilderness we have protected around the world is generally worthless land. There are few designated wildernesses in Iowa or France. We have saved places that are high, dry, cold and remote. When an economic use is found for such a place, more likely than not, its wilderness value is forgotten. The classic instance in U.S. history is Yosemite National Park's once-spectacular Hetch Hetchy Valley. In 1913 San Francisco convinced Congress that the highest value of the region was as a municipal water reservoir and hydropower facility. It was removed from the national park and flooded, a reminder to our foreign guests that the U.S. example can demonstrate how not to care for wilderness as well as how to preserve it. The lesson is that those who lean too heavily on economic arguments for wilderness run the risk of having their leaning posts cut off at the roots.

Reviewing the liabilities of scenery, recreation and economics as defenses of wilderness, and thinking about the reasons why we love it, I thought about an analogy. May I address the men in the audience for a moment? Isn't it true, gentlemen, that we have all been asked by a woman at one time or another (usually, it seems, late at night), "Why do you love me?" I suggest that three reasons that won't be satisfactory are scenery, recreation and economics!

So how are we to answer the question, "Why do we love wilderness?" I will sketch, briefly, seven reasons that are wilderness-dependent, historically valid and shaped by an understanding of both the realities of wilderness and the needs of civilization. They have been refined by our best wilderness philosophers and they constitute the granite philosophical bedrock in which the case for wilderness should rest.

1. The first might be called the *scientific value*. It rests on the idea that wilderness is a reservoir of normal ecological and evolutionary processes as well as a kind of biological safe-deposit box for the many forms of life. One variation of this value is quite utilitarian and might be called the "cure-for-cancer" argument. The wild places of the world harbor species presently and potentially

important to human welfare and even survival. As David Brower is fond of saying, "Wilderness holds the answers to questions we do not yet know how to ask." Norman Myers prefers the metaphor of an ark: those who protect wilderness are like Noah. They make sure that nothing is lost from the full complement of genetic raw material evolved on earth. But on a less instrumental plane, the scientific argument suggests that humans have no right to disturb the evolutionary process. We have already modified the planet enough. When it comes to the existence of species, we should be careful about playing God in Yellowstone or anywhere else. Perhaps Aldo Leopold put it best when he observed that the first law on successful tinkering is to save all the parts. Our own survival, and that of many other creatures, depends on wilderness environments far more than we think. And mistakes in this area are generally final. Extinction, as the Nature Conservancy likes to point out, is forever.

2. *Spiritual values* are the second important pillar in support of wilderness. For many people wilderness is as important as temple or church. We might start with the American Indians and other aboriginal people who regarded places, not just buildings with steeples, as sacred. Commonly, these sacred spaces were in the wilderness where the messages of divine powers seemed the clearest. Later generations, pursuing answers to the weightier problems in human existence, found wilderness to have religious significance. Some worshipped nature outright, some found evidence of God in the natural world and some simply turned to wilderness as an appropriate place to pray and reflect. Henry David Thoreau and Ralph Waldo Emerson, the American Transcendentalists, certainly believed that nature was the symbol of the spiritual world. And John Muir regarded Hetch Hetchy Valley as a temple. Even Colorado's own John Denver sings about cathedral mountains. Around the world we find that the deserts and open spaces have been the source of many of the world's great faiths. Jesus was not the only religious leader to commune with deity in the wilderness.

The religious significance many find in wilderness raises the possibility of defending it on the grounds of freedom of worship. This is a basic right in U.S. culture and in many others. Even if wilderness is a church for a minority, do not they have a right to worship as they choose? Indians have been accorded this right under the Native American Religious Freedom Act of 1978. Although hitherto neglected, it could become a bulwark of non-Indian defense of wilderness.

3. Earlier I dismissed scenery as a basis for a wilderness philosophy, but there is an *aesthetic value* dependent on wild settings. The Romantic movement of the seventeeth and eighteenth centuries had a word for it: "sublimity." It involved awe in the face of large, unmodified natural forces and places such as storms, waterfalls, mountains and deserts. Some people find a beauty here that cannot be replicated in pastoral settings, cities or art museums. If the destruction of beauty is to be avoided, then wilderness should be preserved.

4. The *heritage value* of wilderness is grounded on the fact that wild country has been a major force in the shaping of character and culture. As a species, we have lived in the wilderness a thousand times longer than in civilization. In

nations like the United States, Canada and Australia, wilderness has had a very recent and very strong formative influence. The U.S. historian Frederick Jackson Turner pointed to one form when he argued in 1893 that the frontier experience built respect for the individual and, later, for democratic institutions. We need wilderness, Turner implied, if we are to understand the source of freedom. Wilderness nourishes it by permitting people to be different, to escape the controlling force of established institutions. The Puritans in Massachusetts Bay and the Mormons in Utah understood this association. So do contemporary freedom fighters who take to the hills to continue their rebellion if the hills exist. Parenthetically, the totalitarian regime that George Orwell described in his novel, *1984,* made its first concern the elimination of wilderness. Big Brother could not control thought in wild country.

Wilderness is also an historical document just as much as a collection of manuscripts or a bill of rights. Losing wilderness means losing the ability to understand our past; it is comparable to tearing pages from a book in the library. Could we go even further and say that people have a right to their heritage, their history? If so, the preservation of wilderness is incumbent on our generation.

5. Physical health is not wilderness-dependent. You can become very fit at an urban health club. But wilderness has *psychological value* based on the contrast it offers to the environments which most people occupy most of the time. When these civilized environments become repressive, to use a concept the psychologist Sigmund Freud popularized, wilderness offers a unique opportunity for psychological renewal—literally recreation. The reason is that our minds developed under wilderness conditions for millions of years. Suddenly in the last few hundred we have been propelled into a world of bewildering speed and complexity. For some people occasional relief is a vital mental necessity. They covet the chance to drop back into the older and more comfortable channels. Isn't this what Grey Owl, whose statement graces the program of this Congress, meant by offering distraught civilized humans a green leaf? He is not alone in holding that idea. Primitivists from Jean-Jacques Rousseau with his "noble savage" to Edgar Rice Burroughs and Tarzan have argued that the wild world produces a superior human being. Overcivilization is a real and growing danger. Contemporary therapy programs, such as those of Outward Bound, use the challenges of wilderness to build self-reliance and self-respect. A wilderness area may well have more psychological importance than hundreds of beds in a mental hospital.

6. Wilderness has *cultural value,* because in the words of Ralph Waldo Emerson, it permits an opportunity for an original relationship to the universe. The wild world is cultural raw material. Artists, musicians, poets and writers have turned to it repeatedly in their quest to shape a distinctive and distinguished culture. In the United States, cultural independence from the Old World did not come until writers such as James Fenimore Cooper and painters such as Thomas Cole began to use wilderness as a setting for their work. This has been true around the world. If we preserve it, wilderness can continue to inspire cul-

tural creativity. Without it we will be reduced to making ever-fainter copies of copies, like a Xerox machine. Indeed, wilderness seems to be associated with the very roots of the creative process. It is no accident that artists and scholars use adjectives such as "pathbreaking" and "pioneering" to describe fresh work. They speak of the "frontiers" of knowledge. The unknown is the primary goal to discovery, and classic wilderness is the unknown. Its presence invigorates a culture, in Henry David Thoreau's terms, as fertilizer does a barren, sandy field. Perhaps this is what Thoreau had in mind when he wrote in 1851 that in wilderness is the preservation of the world.

7. The last and least anthropocentric wilderness benefit derives from the very recent idea that nonhuman life and even wild ecosystems themselves have *intrinsic value* and the right to exist. From this perspective wilderness is not *for* humans at all, and wilderness preservation testifies to the human capacity for restraint. A designated wilderness, in this sense, is a gesture of planetary modesty and a way of demonstrating that humans are members, not masters, of the community of life. In the last decade, environmental ethics and deep ecology have called attention to the idea that rights, and ethical obligations, do not end with human-to-human relationships but extend to the farthest limits of nature. Americans, especially, should not find this concept strange because the history of liberalism in the United States has been one of a selected group of white males; we now find the limits of liberalism extended to the rights of nature. In the course of this progression slavery disappeared and now the more radical environmentalists are calling for the end of *land* slavery. Wilderness is the best place to learn humility, dependency and reverence for all life.

From this nonanthropocentric point of view wilderness preservation is truly a radical act. It is indeed subversive to the forces that have accelerated modern civilization to power but now threaten its continuation: materialism, utilitarianism, growth, domination, hierarchy, exploitation. Development and the preservation of wilderness are *not* compatible. If we are going to really have enduring wilderness on earth, we must challenge the growth ethic. In a limited world everything must have limits including human population and civilization. Only cancer cells respect no limits, and in doing so they destroy their habitat and perish. Civilization has cancerous tendencies; wilderness protection is an antidote. Growth, it increasingly appears, is like a drug that can destroy the user. The antidrug slogan on the streets is, "Just say NO." It is time to apply the same logic to growth. The existence of wilderness is the surest sign that mankind has understood this truth and that he is prepared to put his own legitimate demands into ecological balance with those of his fellow travelers on spaceship earth.

In conclusion, let me return to the analogy of the woman who asks, "Why do you love me?" Thinking about the values of wilderness outlined above, try telling her that you worship her, that you cherish the life you have lived together, that she is necessary for your mental welfare, that her presence in your life makes you different, that in her own special way she is beautiful, that she inspires you to be creative, and that she challenges you and offers you an alternative to the way most other women are in the world. Finally tell her your love is totally disinterested, that you love and value and respect her just because she exists and not for anything she does for you. You love her like the climbers say, "because she is there." You want to protect and nurture her because she has a right to exist. I believe, gentlemen, that this will be a successful response. In the 1980s I think it is called "being sensitive about relationships."

Wilderness appreciation is very new under the sun. The World Wilderness Congress would have been inconceivable a century ago or even 70 years ago when Gifford Pinchot and Theodore Roosevelt called governors together at the White House to discuss the importance of conservation. They meant *utilitarian* conservation and the sustaining of growth and greatness. John Muir, who loved wilderness, was pointedly excluded from the 1907 gathering. Today wilderness has a major place in the world's conservation agenda and Muir's memory is honored, but we still have miles to go before wilderness has a secure, permanent place in all the representative latitudes of this planet. The final fruits of our efforts may not be harvested quickly, and in this connection it is well to recall a story that John F. Kennedy liked to tell when he was president of the United States. It concerned an ancient Chinese monarch who was planning an orchard. Informed that a particular tree would not bear fruit for a century, the wise monarch responded, "In that case, let us plant it this morning!"

In protecting wilderness we are also planting ideas and policies that will be slow in maturing. We should do well, then, to start the process immediately.

SELECTED BIBLIOGRAPHY

For further discussion of the meaning and value of wilderness in contemporary civilization: Nash, Roderick. *Wilderness and the American Mind.* New Haven, CT, Yale University Press, 1982; Driver B.L., Roderick Nash and Glenn Haas. "Wilderness Benefits: A State-of-Knowledge Review." In Robert C. Lucas, ed. *Proceedings—National Wilderness Research Conference,* "Intermountain Research Station General Technical Report" INT-220. Ogden, UT, U.S. Forest Service, 1987, pp. 294-319; and Ralston Holmes. *Philosophy Gone Wild: Essays in Environmental Ethics.* Buffalo, NY, Prometheus, 1986.

THE AMERICAN STORY

Douglas Scott

The history and organization of the conservation movement in the United States holds lessons and suggestions for similar groups contending with similar issues in other lands.

The origins of the conservation movement in the United States go back a long way. The organizational development of the environmental movement began in the latter part of the last century. The Sierra Club, for example, was organized in 1892 and is now busily planning its centennial. The movement to conserve our environment sprang from nature appreciation, from the movement for scientific resource management. It was inherently elitist, small and primitive. In those early days it neither intended to have mass membership nor was it a political movement. Less than 100 years later, we have an enormously popular movement for the environment in the United States. This movement is aligned with overwhelming public support and public opinion. We enjoy public confidence and we represent and work with literally millions of members from many national and local organizations. We work with a diversity of styles and we have achieved great political and social power in our society.

We are near the end of the Reagan Administration in the United States. In these Reagan years, we have seen proposals for the drilling of oil and gas in our preserved wilderness areas. We have seen proposals for stopping completely the acquisition of additional lands for national parks and wildlife refuges, and the actual cessation of the designation of additional areas of wilderness in this country. We have seen an eager industry lobby, with its friends in the White House, which was confident that it could cut the Clean Air Act and weaken all of its provisions in the Congress. We saw an administration that was intent on blocking toxic substances controls, we saw an administration that had an enormous lack of sense and vetoed the Clean Water Act, which this country needed so badly. We also saw a Congress that overrode that veto with bipartisan enthusiasm in January 1987. This is an administration that would drill for oil on the distant coastal plain of the Arctic National Wildlife Refuge, the largest nature preserve in the circumpolar arctic that remains pristine. Our environmental movement has stopped these initiatives and will stop the drilling proposal in the arctic as well.

The attributes and characteristics of the environmental movement we have in this country derive from our history. We have woven together different issues which a variety of people felt were important.

One is the wise use of resources started by the scientific forestry movement in the last half of the last century. It stopped the exploitation and depletion of our natural resources and stressed management of those natural resources under such concepts as multiple use.

The second is the nature preservation movement. The national parks movement began with the establishment of Yellowstone National Park in 1872 and continued with the designation of wilderness areas and strict nature preserves on our federal lands all across this country. This has been a movement not so scientifically oriented, but instead, prepared to speak with emotion about the value of the land and the wilderness and the wildlife.

A third great theme is the quality of life, which has emerged more in this century, particularly in the post-World War II era. The focus of attention has been pollution control because of the adverse impacts of technology run amok, purely for the sake of industrial development.

All of these approaches brought us to the fourth great theme of our movement, the twentieth-century theme of ecology. This has united all of the approaches under the ideas of limits, choices and self-control in a society clearly prepared and equipped to destroy the entire earth. The movement against nuclear war is a part of the environmental cause.

The development of citizen action in the United States on each of these four separate themes was very similar. Each began with small numbers of people, bold leaders and visionaries who saw the problem and projected it to a larger audience. It takes someone to see the vision and to see the value of the wilderness, as did John Muir, Emerson, Thoreau, the poets and the artists of our nation, to bring the value of what would be lost to the public's attention.

Seeing the problem, we needed to translate it into political action. Leaders such as John Muir, Aldo Leopold and Rachel Carson stepped across that brink to say, "We must act for change." They were evangelists who, along with many others, mobilized public attention to these problems as a way of stimulating political action. We must help educate, train and organize the mass public to affect the decisions of our government and of our other social institutions.

The history of the wilderness designation process in our country is notable as an example of public action. Until 1924, there was no formal designation of wilderness areas. Even through World War II the designation was a matter entirely at the discretion of agency administrators who could change their own minds just as new presidents and new political currents change the administrators. The wilderness areas that were preserved in those early years were exceedingly fragile and endangered.

After World War II, the huge economic machine of this country turned inward to development and to exploitation of resources. The defense of even those few wilderness places that were preserved by action in the 1920s and 1930s became foremost. Dams were proposed all across the great wilderness landscapes of this country, roads punched further up the valleys and into the mountains, and timber cutting and clear-cutting moved higher and higher on the slopes into precious natural areas.

It was clear to the leaders of that era that, although they could fight to stop each dam proposal and to stop each timber sale, they needed a positive weapon. They had the vision to see that they needed to equip society as a whole with tools that people could use to protect their wilderness areas, whether government would do so or not. That tool was the Wilderness Act. It was not conceived by the bureaucracies of the National Parks Service or the forest service, but by the conservation leaders of the 1940s and 1950s. It took eight long years and an intense battle, the likes of which we had not yet experienced in our movement, to get that simple law passed in the Congress.

When the Wilderness Act was enacted in 1964, it protected nine million acres of land. It was a tool, forged to help all of us to ensure future generations of the ability to take the concept of wilderness and the specific policies for its protection and apply them to additional areas. The time for implementation began in the late 1960s and continues to this day. As of 1987 there are 91 million acres of federally designated wilderness areas in our system; each area is protected by an act of Congress and by an extraordinary exercise of political will by the majority in our country.

Behind each of those wilderness areas is a story of individual people. They did not wait to be rallied by some organization or wait for a call from Washington or San Francisco, but instead sensed that a place they cared about was in danger. These people knew that they were going to have to rise to its defense, mobilize public opinion and use the Wilderness Act to directly pressure Congress to see their area saved. There are ranchers, housewives, teachers, doctors, lawyers, druggists, hardware-store owners and others across this country who know in their hearts that theirs was the voice that saved one of those places that make up the 91 million acres that are protected by law. There are hundreds of thousands of similar people working this very day to continue that fight for the protection of additional wilderness.

The Wilderness Act was a tool because it gave people access. It required something simple but profound—a local, public hearing, the record of which would not stop with the local forest supervisor or the local park superintendent, but would travel to Washington, D.C. and through the maze of the bureaucracy and into the White House itself. Ultimately the record would find its way to Capitol Hill. It did not matter whether or not the agency and the president in power at that time would recommend that area for wilderness or recommend an area large enough. The voice of the people organized in those hearings continued to be used to bring pressure to influence their own congressmen, reaching over the bureaucracy and the politicians in order to say, "We love this place, we know what is best, we know where the lines should be, and we ask you, our elected officials in the Congress, to be responsive to the public opinion."

That is the vision, and it's true in pollution fights or energy fights or the anti-war fight in this country as well. Find tools that give access for ordinary people to influence the processes and decisions of government that otherwise would not be adequate to the challenge we face. We have opened up the U.S. Congress as literally a citizens' hearing board to listen to the complaints of concerned people. We have utilized the courts to great significance and we've created new laws in our society to give citizens a greater handle in court.

For example, the Clean Water Act provides for legal redress. If the law isn't being enforced, anyone can walk into any court in this land and demand that it be enforced. The National Environmental Policy Act forces decision makers to cast up the alternatives and give those alternatives serious public scrutiny. The Right-to-Know provisions in our toxic control laws insist that local communities which will feel the effect of hazardous waste, chemicals and air pollutants be made aware of the chemical soup around them. Awareness is the first step to mobilization.

Americans have learned not to wait for Washington to act. We have developed a system to empower, structure and organize at the grass roots so that people can act. This is a hallmark of the modern environmental movement in this country, not in offices in Washington, D.C. or San Francisco, or a small staff of professional environmentalists, lawyers, scientists and agitators. We have passed that power across our society, organizing networks and communications to people affiliated with each national organization and to the many more people who are not affiliated to the local citizens' group and to the people gathered around a kitchen table, frightened because they've heard the Forest Service is going to allow the cutting of timber just up the valley from their homes. This is the heart and soul of our environmental movement.

The obligation of national organizations and mobilization centers is to organize that power, to train those people to develop their knowledge of the issues and to develop their understanding of our political processes. The skills to influence decisions are not readily available in this society or in many others. What we learned in high school civics is largely irrelevant to the real world of power in Washington and our state capitols. The key element is access to knowledge. Once informed and trained, simple people can affect the decisions that are made.

There are nine lessons which can be summarized from the history of the American conservation movement.

1. Deliberate action is necessary. Government will not act alone, and if it will, it will act too late and not strongly enough. If wild places are to be protected, we must take the initiative. If pollution is to be regulated, we must take control of that process.

2. It is important for groups to specialize, but all must work for the big picture. National park groups must work for clean air. Clean air groups must work to stop the drilling in the arctic.

3. Fit your political action to your society and your system. As a loyal and patriotic member of my own society, I have learned that one must work in the system until its inability to respond has been proven. This has a better payoff, because the system, if you can move it, will move in the direction that you want it to go.

4. Ally yourself with the culture and the literacy of your country. The Sierra Club and other groups, by using all forms of media, have done a great deal to build public support by showing people pictures of the beautiful places at stake and pictures of the ugly things that are being done to them.

5. Avoid elitism and don't get too excited about professionalism. The volunteer, grassroots, ordinary citizen center of our movement is its heart and soul. Be independent. Tie yourself to no political party, ally yourself with no temporary social movement. Work on government rather than in government.

6. Build policies that give tools to the public. Remember the example of the Wilderness Act—empower people by making it easier for them to get the information they need.

7. Avoid the propensity of government to give you false action. Advisory committees are usually made up of one environmentalist, one grazer, three loggers, two miners and you know the rest. That's one way to do things, but it's better when everyone sits down to plot your strategy.

8. Trust decentralization. Beware of your own bureaucracy and your central office, because it kills personal involvement.

9. Organize and train. Share the skills you have. No fight is really worth winning if we've won it by ourselves without bringing more into the fold by spreading the knowledge and sharing the skills. Build coalitions, train for real political skills and empower people.

In brief, this is the story of how, for the last 100 years (and most particularly the last seven under Ronald Reagan) the conservation movement in the United States has reached right over the heads of politicians who could not see our vision and could not grasp the public cry for a clean and safe environment, for wilderness and wild places.

John Muir was not one for meetings or bureaucracy. We should act upon his advice when he said, "Let's sit down and do something that will make the mountains glad."

LESSONS IN CONSERVATION AND DEVELOPMENT— MOVING INTO THE 1990s

William K. Reilly

Two hundred years ago the Constitution of the United States was ratified and the Northwest Ordinance was enacted. The Ordinance provided for the mapping, marking, subdivision and settlement of the Northwest Territory, the frontier beyond the Appalachians that was to become the American Midwest.

This year a new constitution is being drafted in Brazil. This constitution may contain an article dealing with conservation. Whether Brazil's constitution will also attempt to chart a course for the future settlement of the world's richest biological wilderness remains to be seen.

A high drama is unfolding in Brazil. This vigorous and capable nation, a country of boundless resources and millions of idle hands, hungry mouths and "empty" land, a place full of promise and debt, is poised in a pivotal position between conservation and development. Will they save the Amazon? That is what we conservationists want Brazil to do. That is what we want Mexico and Indonesia, Zaire, and Madagascar and Nepal and Peru, and so many other poor nations of the biologically rich tropics to do: Save their forests and spare their habitat of countless species of wildlife. Convincing them to do it and helping them to do it in ways that further their national development and enrich their people are the premier challenges to conservation in our time.

The Conservation Foundation has been involved in the developing world, since its founding in the late 1940s. The Foundation began work on soil conservation projects, especially in Latin America, in the 1940s and 1950s. We have been active in park planning and wildlife conservation, beginning in Africa in the 1950s. We began almost 40 years ago at the foundation to assess the relationship between population growth, resource use, and living standards in the developing countries.

World Wildlife Fund has worked in developing countries since its start in 1961. Likewise the World Wildlife Fund has worked for 26 years helping our colleagues in Costa Rica develop their national park system. In the process, we have learned that preserving the parks depends as much on influencing the human activities taking place outside park boundaries as it does on managing wildlife and wild lands within.

World Wildlife Fund is one of 23 national organizations in the WWF family. With more than two million members worldwide, it has shaped, supported and managed programs around the world that put theory into practice. WWF-US has supported 1,100 field projects in 96 countries to preserve natural areas, study ecosystems, educate local people, strengthen local organizations and, most importantly, to provide alternatives to short-term plunder of natural resources.

Some current World Wildlife Fund projects might surprise you: We are financing a kerosene fuel business in the Annapurna Conservation Area in Nepal. We are supporting 26 tree nurseries in Costa Rica. We are helping fishermen increase their catch in Africa's Lake Malawi. We are supporting a new timber and Christmas tree industry in Michoacan, Mexico. We also are experimenting with new forestry techniques in Mexico. We are helping local people exploit the tourism potential of mountain gorillas in Rwanda, of parks in Colombia, and we are paying for cadastral surveys and land titling in Central America.

Each of these efforts has a long story. Each grows out of indigenous needs and responds to local wishes. None seems on first inspection to have very much to do with wildlife. But they do. They represent tenuous yet promising steps toward coexistence, the survival together of plants and animals and people. I believe these projects point to the future of conservation in the developing world. And I believe they have some lessons for us today.

First, these projects depend very little on accepted theories of economic development. In fact, economic development theory has never had much to say about conservation of natural resources. Development economists have taken natural resources pretty much for granted and many large development projects have wrought havoc and destruction on a scale as large as the grand construction schemes themselves. They have been disappointing economically as well.

Now there is a welcome reassessment under way within the community of development economists. New environmental requirements are being imposed. New attention is given to the secondary effects of big dams, of road development schemes, of rangeland projects and cattle ranches.

This reassessment comes at a time when public interest from the United States in the wildlife and forests of the developing world is growing dramatically. World Wildlife Fund's membership has increased 50 percent to 320,000, during the past year alone. World Wildlife Fund is exclusively oriented to international conservation, and our membership growth is a measure of the U.S. public's increasing awareness of these issues. So, too, growing congressional interest and new federal laws affecting the conservation activities of development assistance agencies is a measure of changing public attitudes in this country.

The second lesson our projects underscore is the increasing significance of natural resources in the development of the Third World. World Wildlife Fund's efforts are aimed at saving forests and wildlife by finding a means for local people to improve their material well-being. To a very large extent the economies of developing countries depend on renewable natural resources, on agriculture, forestry and fisheries. This has been true for hundreds, even thousands, of years and in many of these places continuing harvests have not impeded natural productivity. Yet it is not clear that modern economic livelihoods can be sustained for large numbers of people in rain forests and savannas. That is the experiment under way.

As a joint undertaking of both World Wildlife Fund and The Conservation Foundation, we have recently established a major new enterprise, The Osborn Center for Economic Development. This center will inject us directly into the debate about economic development. The center draws on the natural scientists and field projects of World Wildlife Fund, and the social scientists and research skills of The Conservation Foundation. Its research, field projects, experiments and communications will, we intend, inject a powerful new voice for conservation into the economic development debate, as we bring a greater awareness of economic realities to conservation action.

The urgency of these efforts was brought home starkly to me during a visit to several of the magnificent national parks of Costa Rica. Costa Rica is justly regarded as the most successful of developing countries at creating parks, building a professional park service and enlisting widespread public support for conservation. Yet around many of these parks, farmers without land are clearing forests to establish ownership claims. The forests are falling at a rate expected within 10 years to leave Costa Rica a net importer of timber, which historically has been a major export. The handwriting is plain to see. Many of Costa Rica's parks are not secure, as growing incidents of poaching, squatting and mining have demonstrated. In the simplest sense, World Wildlife Fund's long and substantial investments in 16 of Costa Rica's 22 national parks and reserves are not secure. There is little time to find economic solutions that will save the tropical forests of Costa Rica. In many other developing countries there is even less time.

A third lesson from our experience is the value of involving local people. In the search for conservation methods that work, we have learned to rely on the locals. Local people operating through indigenous organizations are involved in virtually all our activities. We are giving the highest priority to fostering indigenous leadership and building enduring institutions.

Last year World Wildlife Fund held a conference on conservation in Latin America to celebrate our 25th anniversary. The sophistication represented in the leaders of Latin American nongovernmental organizations was impressive. My reaction to them was to begin an assessment of the degree to which we can increase our support to them while cutting the strings on our assistance. Particularly in Latin America, where many private conservation groups now have 10 or more years experience, they are coming of age. They often need help with organizational issues such as fund raising, relating to Boards of Directors and managing contacts with a variety of constituencies. But they are also increasingly professional, stable and effective. They are finding their own voice and charting their own course. Our job is to help them find a conservation strategy suitable to their own culture, its politics and economics.

Working through indigenous organizations helps keep outsiders like us honest. It makes for a modesty in our operating style that is consistent with trying to influence the policies of countries other than our own.

We have learned something else about these groups: They are becoming critical agents of initiative and change, even in societies that don't permit or have a tradition favorable to much activism outside of government. In Brazil, even under the generals, scores of neighborhood groups were formed and tolerated to effect environmental improvements. Today they are flourishing. In Chile, environmental action at the neighborhood level and in the universities has provided experience in democratic organization to a cadre of potential future leaders. In Mexico, private organizations have entered into unprecedented partnerships with government to establish wildlife reserves, promote water conservation and change policies on hazardous waste management. The experience of these groups is valuable to their countries, even beyond what they achieve for the environment. They are pointing the way to greater democratization in the conduct of public life.

A fourth lesson from our experience speaks to wilderness. Wilderness, as Rod Nash has written, occupies a special place in the American mind. People in this country in the 1980s have an idea of wilderness as being "forever wild," a place where humans enter as visitors, but neither stay nor leave any mark.

The American idea of wilderness is not easily exported to the developing world. There the challenge is to look for sustainable uses and compatible economic activities. An economic justification to create a park or reserve must often be found in the first place.

There is nothing surprising about this. A 1985 report of The Conservation Foundation, "National Parks for A New Generation," recounted the history of some U. S. parks. A good many of them owe their existence to local chambers of commerce whose members saw a national park as a means of bringing tourists and their dollars to remote mountain wilds. Railroads, realtors, public-relations experts and promoters of all sorts played central roles in winning park designation for early U.S. national parks. And so, too, economic arguments will matter when park proposals are advanced in the Third World countries.

A fifth lesson from our experience has to do with something we are not doing, but something I wish we were doing: rehabilitating degraded lands. There is an understandable tendency for international conservation groups to concentrate their energies on the very richest and most biologically diverse habitat. We do it. It is written into the criteria we at World Wildlife Fund apply when judging the suitability of a project proposal of a country where we might work: How important is the place biologically? How rich is it in terms of flora and fauna? How many of its species are endemic, that is, found nowhere else?

We will continue to apply these criteria, yet the march of deforestation and desertification have proved formidable in many countries. Degraded lands are expanding far faster than parks.

We conservationists are fond of final warnings. Our nightmares are of irremediable change. Truly, extinction is forever. The Amazon, once stripped of its forest cover, is mostly unproductive—of cattle and crops as well as of wildlife. Yet the day will arrive when we will become actively engaged in the search to return much of the deforested Amazon to productivity. The day has already come when we need to apply our energies to rehabilitating degraded lands. Virtually every country has an abundance of them. We cannot write these areas off because their trees and wildlife are gone. These vast, eroding, played-out wastelands can often be reclaimed. Huge tracts of clear-cut hill country in the Appalachians and Alleghenys were once the cause of heavy flooding and loss of life in Pittsburgh and other eastern U.S. cities. The federal government bought these lands for 50 cents an acre, beginning early in this century and continuing into the 1930s. The lands nobody wanted are now home to a rich variety of wildlife, and they contain a huge stock of hardwood timber. Benign management by the U.S. Forest Service of its acquired eastern forests brought them back. This is more difficult in many parts of the tropics but also more urgent. For conservationists, rehabilitation of degraded lands has not really been on the agenda. It needs to be there.

In the United States the Northwest Ordinance played an essential role in settling the continent. It unleashed the energies of countless people who moved westward in search of opportunity. Yet, consistent with the spirit of the newly emerging United States, the surveys commissioned by this historic document imposed an egalitarian grid system on the landscape, laying the basis for land ownership and land-use patterns that are with us today. The survey lines cut indiscriminately across wetlands, watersheds and other natural features that we now know have important functions in keeping the land healthy and productive. After the Northwest Ordinance, environmentally sensitive lands opened to settlement. Settlers were encouraged to farm in places where the lack of rain all but assured failure. Native Americans were driven from lands they had inhabited for generations in some sort of harmony with the natural world. This, too, is the legacy of the Northwest Ordinance.

Imagine for a moment the difficulties and tensions that would arise today if, as a society, we were faced with establishing parameters for settling our frontier. Would our leaders draft a Northwest Ordinance in 1987 that respected what we know about the land and natural systems? Would they instead emphasize the economic opportunities or security aspects of settling the continent?

This is the dilemma currently faced by the people in developing countries rich in biological resources. We conservationists in the United States hope that as they settle the Amazon region and other frontiers they will take advantage of 200 years' experience in settling our continent not all to the good. A difficult battle lies ahead simply to provide in a useful and constructive way the benefits of our successes and our failures. We in the developed world are support troops who must above all keep the ammunition flowing to our friends on the front lines in the developing world. Sometimes I think the marvel of it all is that we are, from time to time, even winning some battles. But the outcome of the war is by no means certain. What is certain is that to win the war for conservation we must also win the war against poverty.

INTERNATIONAL PROGRAM INITIATIVES

Jay D. Hair

The scientific and conservation communities are only too aware of the serious global environmental problems that we humans have produced in the last few decades. Just consider some of the major environmental disasters of the last three years.

Worldwide, an estimated 60 million people have died of diseases related to unsafe drinking water and malnutrition. Most of the victims were children.

In Africa, environmental neglect and misguided development created a crisis, triggered by a drought, that put 35 million people at risk. It may have killed as many as one million human beings.

In Bhopal, India, a pesticide leak killed more than 2,000 people and blinded or injured more than 200,000 others. In the USSR, the Chernobyl accident sent nuclear fallout across Europe, increasing the risk of future human cancers. In Europe, mercury-based agricultural chemicals and solvents accidently flowed into the Rhine River, killing millions of fish and threatening drinking water in West Germany and the Netherlands.

In the United States, acid rain alone is causing profound damage to natural resources, leaving thousands of lakes and streams devoid of any life, devastating forests and perhaps causing as many as 50,000 premature human deaths each year.

But perhaps the worst environmental assault mounted by humankind in recent years is the mass extinction of wild species. The global rate of species extinction is greater than any we have seen since the age of the dinosaurs. Although we can only tentatively predict the full global impact of these extinctions, we do know the impact will be profound.

While I have recited a familiar litany of environmental disasters, I do not intend to leave you with a bleak picture of a world descending into ruin, devoid of hope. There are solutions to our environmental problems. Humankind, after all, has the capacity to abandon old patterns of thought and action. We have the capacity to create new approaches, but only if we acknowledge some essential facts and act on them.

First, we must understand—really understand—that the earth is seamless. Environmental degradation recognizes no geopolitical boundaries. Extinction of a wild species indigenous to one hemisphere is really a loss affecting all of the earth's living resources.

Second, we must acknowledge that human health as well as the health of wild species are directly dependent on the health of our global environment. We must help the world's policymakers devise strategies that will enable countries to escape the various cycle of overpopulation, resources depletion, environmental degradation and human misery.

Third, we must recognize that environmental protection and economic development are not arch rivals. They are not mutually exclusive. Indeed, they are mutually dependent.

No nation, whether developing or developed, can hope to attain or sustain economic progress while sacrificing environmental quality. Instead, we must pursue economic development which respects both the environment as well as the cultures of native peoples. I believe the U.S. conservation community is determined to do just that around the world.

Certainly, the National Wildlife Federation is committed to these dual and compatible goals. Let me briefly outline our current international program initiatives.

In 1980, our Board of Directors authorized the formation of an International Wildlife Federation. Our international program was initiated in 1982 by Barbara Bramble, who still serves as the program director. The federation, through Barbara and her staff, has been working closely with the local non-governmental organizations to help Third World people maintain their cultures, their homes and their environments.

Indeed, we have been pressing the world's multilateral development banks to assess the environmental impacts of projects before they approve funding.

Our efforts and those of other conservation groups have begun to pay dividends. The World Bank has announced the formation of an environmental department. It is beginning to deny loans to projects whose by-products include environmental degradation. That is not the only innovation in the international financial picture.

The National Wildlife Federation participated in and endorsed a second, major step—the first implementation of the debt-for-nature concept—as government agreed to set aside nearly four million acres of rain forest in exchange for retirement of $650,000 of debt. Moreover, the federation fully supports Congressional legislation to encourage the World Bank to suspend loan payments for countries that protect tropical forests. Debt for nature swaps are golden opportunities to save critical wildlife habitats while paying off a portion of the Third World's $1 trillion debt. They are dramatic events on the global stage.

Yet, the federation's international environmental programs go far beyond the financial arena. Following are examples of how our educational and research efforts have touched citizens in every part of the world.

International Wildlife, spotlighting nature's wonders, is one of our four major publications. Published bimonthly since 1970, it appears as *Biosphere* in Canada, available in both English and French. For many, years we published it in Japanese. In 1972, it was the only non-governmental report officially distributed to the delegates at the United National Conference on Human Environment.

Our educational efforts have gone far beyond *International Wildlife* magazine. We are working with the government of India to adapt our 50-year-old National Wildlife Week campaign to its culture and needs. The federation is also working to adapt our premier teaching guide, *NatureScope*, for use by school teachers in India.

With funding from the U.S. Agency for International Development, the federation has mounted a traveling show called, "Our Threatened Heritage." The program illustrates how birds of prey represent the need for international conservation efforts.

The federation's Institute for Wildlife Research has been pivotal in our international conservation initiatives. Our Feline Research Center has been active in research on ocelots and margays in the nation of Belize. With funding from the World Wildlife Fund, we have translated the Wildlife Society's *Wildlife Techniques Manual* into Spanish.

In the near future, we will sponsor the publication of (in English and Chinese), the proceedings of the First International Conference on Wildlife Conservation in China.

Four years ago, the federation brought together scores of researchers from around the world for a unique International Cat Symposium. Written proceedings from that symposium are now available in a single volume, perhaps the richest collection of ideas on the subject.

For many years, our Conservation Fellowships have offered research funds to students at schools across North America. This year, for the first time, a Chinese student will receive one of the fellowships.

We also supported travel of conservationists from other countries to participate in conferences and training sessions in the United States. We sponsored the travel of several delegates to this World Wilderness Congress. In the spring of 1988, we will sponsor four Chinese wildlife researchers for the training sessions at the International Crane Foundation in Baraboo, Wisconsin.

As you can see, the National Wildlife Federation's international efforts have not been limited to one focus nor even to the organizational confines of one office. Yet, as fruitful as our efforts and those of other organizations have been, the world's environmental problems, and especially those of the Third World, demand more attention.

In the face of overwhelming Third World poverty, traditional environmental solutions may simply not be enough. They may not be enough to designate a park or a biosphere as critical habitat. They may simply not be enough to declare another species as endangered.

Many of the Third World's environmental problems are caused by poverty itself, then exacerbated by misguided development proposals that ignore local cultures and native needs. New ideas and new approaches are desperately needed if conservationists hope to assist the Third World in recovering its economic stability without sacrificing its unique natural resources.

In 1981, Norman Myers, an outstanding British scientist who was completing 20 years of work in Africa, presented a thought-provoking idea. If wildlife is not economically self-sufficient, he wrote in *International Wildlife*, there is little point in saving its living space. If it pays its own way, some of it will survive. If it can't, it won't.

He went on in the article to call for the commercialization of wildlife in many parts of Africa. In certain key ecological areas, he called for total protection. Elsewhere, he said, "The sooner Africans can enjoy gazelle goulash and wildebeest casserole, and the sooner the trade in zebra skins is regulated and expanded, the sooner a more hopeful era will dawn for African animals."

Not only did Norman Myers advocate tourist lodges in African park ecosystems, he suggested canning factories to package meat from excess wild game, a practice that was already going on in South Africa's Kruger Park. He advocated conservation planning that would accommodate, not exclude, human communities.

In 1981, Norman Myer's article caused a furor. Outrage was voiced far and wide. In the next issue of *International Wildlife*, the federation published two pages of letters to the editor.

Indeed, economic exploitation to conserve wildlife appears, on its face, to be a contradiction in philosophy. In fact, it is not.

A survey of international conservation leaders, conducted by *International Wildlife* just about two years ago, indicated the same belief: That wildlife and wilderness ecosystems must be given an economic value or we stand in danger of losing them to the poverty and hunger of the Third World.

Economic value can, of course, mean tourism, if the tourist dollars go into the pockets of natives who may lose their livelihoods in the wake of environmental protection. A story from Mexico will illustrate my point.

Eight years ago, a television reporter traveled 80 miles outside Mexico City to do a story on the winter hideaway of more than 100 million monarch butterflies. At the time, the area was a hotbed of logging and agriculture. But each winter, the fir trees became golden with the color of thousands of monarchs nestled in the branches.

The reporter came across a native ready to cut down one of these fir trees. She asked, "Why chop down this tree? Aren't the butterflies in danger?"

The native pointed to the village, where his family waited for the money he earned by logging, and said simply, "I do it for my children."

Last year the television reporter returned to the monarch's winter kingdom. This time, a roped-off walkway wound through the trees. Signposts along the way explained how the forest acts as a watershed. How it prevents soil erosion, protects scores of animals and plants and shelters the wintering monarchs.

The Mexican government had, of course, declared the area an ecological preserve. It had placed stringent restrictions on logging. This time, the same native who had met the television reporter years earlier was not a logger, but a tourist guide in the preserve.

Naturally, the reporter had to ask, "Why are you working here as a guide?" As he had the last time, the native pointed to the village where his family waited for his paycheck, and he answered, "I do it for my children."

Indeed, he was earning a living for his children. But in the process, he was also saving wildlife and habitat for generations yet to be born. His work on behalf of conservation was finally putting food on his family table and guaranteeing a future for wild species.

Few stories in the Third World end so happily. Indeed, the verdict is still out on the monarch butterfly's preserve area. Only with time will the Mexican government and the natives who depend on the area be able to tell if tourism will provide an adequate livelihood. But it is an experiment worth emulating around the world.

Conservation can best succeed if it pays its own way. That is not a theory of exploitation, but a fact of life. The sooner experienced wildlife scientists help developing countries devise profitable conservation plans, the sooner wildlife and the habitats on which it depends will be protected for the benefit of future generations.

The writer John Hersey, in his new book entitled *Blues*, writes of humankind's environmental abuses, "If these follies continue to go unchecked, they are liable to break forever—irreparably—the delicate laws of balance. If that happens, links of life on earth—the fragile chain—will part and will never be able to be mended. We'd better marvel while we can."

I'd like to amend that last line. I believe it should read: "We'd better mend while we can." For ours may well be the last generation given the opportunity to protect the final critical vestiges of environmental quality.

The National Wildlife Federation is planning to expand significantly its international program initiatives in response to the growing global need for conservation programs. Today and in the future, we look forward to working with you in building a world that lives at peace with itself and in harmony with its natural resources and environment.

GLOBAL CHALLENGES

Peter A.A. Berle

Virtually anywhere one might choose to look in the world—from the population crush in Mexico and Egypt to the deforestation of Indonesia and Central America—nations of strategic importance are suffering from environmental and population problems that have frightful potential to destabilize their governments and the regions in which they are located.

Those of us in the U.S. sustainable development around the world have a unique opportunity now and over the next few years. This is our "window of opportunity" to establish in the public mind and in U.S. policy the strong link between the environment and security.

The report of the World Commission on Environment and Development has given us a powerful tool—a tool that is most useful to us right now.

Environmental and conservation organizations in the United States—both large and small—have not only an opportunity, but a responsibility, to advance the cause of environmentally sustainable development. The enormous scope of the global conservation and population problems confronting us calls for a comprehensive approach, which from the standpoint of a nationwide grass roots organization like the National Audubon Society, has several major components.

1. Reevaluate "National Security." We, as citizens of the globe, must bring about a reevaluation of the concept of national security by all nations. Historically, national security has been closely related to the development of sufficient military strength to defend against aggression, or to protect national interests around the globe. This notion also has driven efforts to protect industries from foreign competition, or to encourage industrial establishment.

We must keep upper most in the minds of the public and our leadership that environmental protection and sound resource use is at least as important. This includes environmental protection within every nation-state and outside its borders as well. Internally, environmental protection ensures the public health, food supply and sound resource use, without which no nation can survive. Yet maintaining a sound environment at home is not sufficient to protect any nation-state. The events at Chernobyl just over a year ago and the contamination of the Rhine by a chemical fire in Switzerland remind us that an environmental disaster in one country can put a neighboring country at risk.

In effect, the national security of all of us depends to some degree on the effectiveness of environmental protection within neighboring states.

Furthermore, in a world economy, everyone depends on products from somewhere else. That supply can only be assured in the long run if the supplier follows sound environmental protection practices.

National security also is dependent on mutual and collective efforts among nation-states to protect the global environment. Depletion of the ozone layer, the greenhouse effect and resultant global warming, the spread of toxins in food chains which know no national boundaries: These are all phenomena that a great many nations are contributing to and, in varying degrees, each threatens the safety and the national security of us all.

The challenge for all of us is to persuade governments and policy makers that, by ignoring environmental protection and conservation, they put their own nations at risk.

2. Building a Domestic Constituency. Another important component of our strategy for meeting the global challenge involves public education and grass roots activism through which the U.S. conservation community should be working to build a strong constituency for supporting environmentally sustainable development as an integral part of U.S. policy. This has been and will continue to be hard work. But it can be done—both through vehicles of mass communication and on a local level. We at Audubon see public education as a key to the success of any popular campaign on behalf of sustainable growth. These educational efforts can take many other forms, such as classroom education and leadership training of local activists, to name two important ones. At Audubon we recently completed production on a 23-minute video production designed to build local support for population programs. This is not something we expect to see broadcast nationally. We are working with local Audubon

chapters in many states where this program will be shown in places like local activist meetings and on community access cable television channels. The success of this particular project, it should be emphasized, will depend on countless hours of work by our staff and volunteers to ensure that the message of this video gets out.

3. Reforming U.S. Policy. A third part of our strategy focuses on ensuring as much as possible that the concept of sustainable growth runs through every aspect of U.S. foreign assistance, both directly through U.S. assistance programs and indirectly through international organizations that the United States helps to fund. This means we must work toward a comprehensive redefinition of both U.S. foreign assistance and foreign policy objectives. This will be no small task. But we have nothing to lose by aiming high. The place to start is with the environmental and population programs of the U.S. Foreign Assistance Act. We need to tell skeptical policymakers that these programs need major strengthening and that environmental destruction in the Third World poses extraordinary threats to international stability. Both elected and appointed government officials in Washington must hear again and again that a U.S. foreign policy which encourages sustainable development will, in the long run, do more to promote stability and security than our current overriding emphasis on weapons programs and military strategies.

Equally important, however, is that we must focus on the "sustainable" part of our message. We must be sure to make the point that all our efforts—from family planning to forest conservation—will be truly effective among Third World peoples only if we tie these programs to the believable promise of a better life. That is the uplifting vision we must offer.

4. Practicing What We Preach. The fourth and final component of our campaign to encourage environmentally sustainable growth is based on the belief that we must practice what we preach. As watchdogs over U.S. policies, U.S. environmental organizations must work to ensure that the United States is not asking the people of Mexico City or Lagos or Calcutta to do something that people in New York or St. Louis or Denver won't do. Let us note, for example, that in some areas of the United States, groundwater which cannot be replenished is nonetheless being "mined" both for agricultural and municipal uses.

We also should note that the United States in some ways encourages developing nations to diminish their natural resources. Throughout the Third World, toxic chemical contamination threatens water quality. This is largely because industrial nations have left vast loopholes in their laws which permit banned or restricted products and processes to be exported to developing nations. These nations usually lack the regulatory mechanisms necessary to protect themselves.

In some parts of the United States, our government pursues a so-called "forest management" policy for national forests which encourages harvesting of old growth forests at an unprecedented rate. We are changing the face of the forest for hundreds of years before we fully understand the biological value of these ancient forests. Practiced elsewhere, we call this deforestation, while here we call it "management." We also must note that in other areas of the United States—some not very far from where we sit today—hundreds of thousands of acres of fragile land are being overgrazed as a result of crazy-quilt government policies that actually subsidize this environmental destruction.

In the American west there is a river called the South Platte. By the time its waters join in Nebraska with the North Platte, they form a place of worldwide environmental significance. The story of the Platte, I believe, epitomizes America's wasteful use of natural resources. Each spring in March and April, a half-million sandhill cranes—80 percent of the world's population of this species—gather on the Platte as a staging area for their northward migration to the Arctic and Siberia. During their stay of several weeks on the Platte, the birds gain critical food reserves. We cannot overemphasize the importance of the Platte as nature's fueling station for these cranes. To help understand this, paint a picture in your mind of an hourglass superimposed on a map of North America. The wide segments are to the south around the Gulf Coast, Texas and Mexico, and to the north in the Canadian Arctic and parts of Siberia. In between those wintering and summering grounds is the narrowest part of that hourglass—along a small section of the Platte in central Nebraska. At times each spring, it is possible to view tens of thousands of cranes on and around the Platte. This makes for one of nature's true wonders of the world.

Yet the Platte is a river under siege. A series of dams and reservoirs now diverts surface water and groundwater for irrigation, electricity and municipal water supplies. A total of 70 percent of the river's historic flow is gone. But this is not the most significant threat to the river and its wildlife. The river is under siege because of a single-purpose push for total development of its water resources. The most immediate threat comes from Denver, with a project called Two Forks Dam being pushed by the Denver Water Board. If this Denver water project, with all the environmental havoc it will wreak, were being sponsored by the World Bank in a developing nation, there would be a hue and cry from people both in the United States and elsewhere about wasteful environmental destruction sponsored by foreign assistance. But we all know that this kind of environmental waste—and destruction—is much too common in the United States. That is why, in our enthusiasm for sustainable growth policies, we must not forget that promoting sustainable growth starts at home.

Looking to the future, let me reiterate that conservation and environmental organizations—whether they are local, regional or national in scope—have a particular responsibility. We must raise public awareness of the principle that the human race is the steward of the earth's environmental health and vitality. As a start, we must work to make the public and our leaders understand that for the first time in history, we face a situation in which unprecedented numbers of people are using and misusing their natural heritage in ways that cannot be sustained. The solution to this enormous challenge is found in a myriad of policies that will slowly turn this situation around to one of sustainable growth.

BEYOND OUR BORDERS

Michael Fischer and Michael McCloskey

While the Sierra Club is best known for its work on U.S. environmental issues and campaigns, we have had an active international program since 1971. Sierra Club participated in many of the international conferences that have been held over the last 15 years where vital environmental issues were debated. We were active in the development of the United Nations' Charter for Nature. We worked actively in developing the environmental components of the Law of the Sea Treaty, though unfortunately, the United States has not chosen to ratify this critical agreement. We were active in the process of developing the Camilar Treaty, dealing with the Antarctic and Southern oceans. We worked under a United Nations Environment Program grant with the government of Venezuela to survey its forests, and that survey helped them to set aside some 22 new national parks in the mid-1970s. Not too long ago we undertook a study of Mangrove forests in the Caribbean.

However, in 1985 we chose to change the focus of our programs somewhat, when we moved from being close to the United Nations in New York to Washington, D.C. We now have two thrusts to our program. The first draws upon our active membership base in the United States to influence the U.S. government to be as environmentally responsive as possible. We put special emphasis on lobbying the U.S. Congress to, in turn, induce the executive branch to improve its performance.

The second thrust of our program involves reaching out to like-minded environmental groups around the world, particularly in developing countries, to encourage them to proceed with their efforts to press for environmental reforms in their own countries and develop the political will to act.

Given these two aspects to our program, we are now focusing strong efforts, with a coalition of groups in Washington, D.C. and in other countries, on reforming the lending practices of the multilateral development banks, particularly the World Bank. We're working closely with the U.S. Treasury Department as they try to induce the World Bank to adopt the 19-point program which the U.S. Congress has asked the bank to pursue. We published a major brochure, entitled *Bankrolling Disasters,* on the problems posed by the insensitive practices of the lending institutions. It has been widely distributed throughout the world and is designed to develop the constituency for that reform and to document the need for those changes.

Among the critical changes for which we and this coalition are pressing is the enlargement of the environmentally trained staff of World Bank. The president, Barber Conable, has recently promised to do that, although a controversy rages over the degree to which that will actually happen. We are trying to get World Bank to actually follow through and implement its many policies which sound good, but which in practice are often ignored. We also want the World Bank to avoid projects that would encroach on wilderness, to enforce its policies for the protection of wilderness and to withhold funding if its policies are violated as a project proceeds. The U.S. executive director of the bank has begun to vote no on bad projects. We welcome Treasury Secretary Baker's leadership in this regard, particularly his efforts to press for even better bank policies on such matters as grasslands, and his ideas concerning debt relief projects that would provide new advances for conservation in return.

We're working to persuade other countries to also vote no, when appropriate, at the World Bank. This past year a number of projects have been suspended as a result of such votes, so progress is being made. We are reaching out to NGOs in other countries to get them to persuade their governments to join this effort. When the World Bank meets in Washington, D.C. in a few weeks, we, as part of that coalition, will be working to get the bank to take the coalition's concerns more seriously. For the first time NGOs are being admitted as observers at World Bank meetings.

We're also working to persuade the regional development banks to follow suit. We brought 15 Latin American NGOs into the May 1987 meetings of the Inter-American Development Bank to observe the proceedings. We were among those encouraging the IADB to bring in the environmental ministers from the participating countries to create a dialogue with the finance ministers. It is vitally important that the ministers involved with finance and development hear that the concerns which the NGOs have voiced are also shared by these government officials from the environmental ministries in their own countries. They are discovering that it is not just the NGOs from developed countries that are voicing criticism.

In June 1987, we were invited to make a presentation to the African Development Bank in Cairo on how it might give greater regard to the environment in its work. We have now been invited to advise them in setting up a meeting similar to that held by the Inter-American Development Bank.

Finally, we have been working to encourage the U.S. development assistance agency, AID, to move more aggressively in the environmental field. We worked with others to get the U.S. Congress to pass two landmark pieces of legislation in 1986 to direct AID to do more to protect tropical forests and promote biological diversity, and to spend greater sums toward those ends. We are working this year to increase the funds for that purpose. The legislation passed in 1986 also bars any U.S. funding for projects that would invade or significantly degrade protected areas such as wilderness areas and national parks. We are working now for legislation that would increase the funding for financial assistance in Africa and earmark specific sums for both environmental and population work on that continent. I should add that in the past we have worked very hard with others to sustain and increase the levels of funding for the United Nations Environment Programme.

Not only is our staff active, but our volunteers are active too. As is very much the pattern in the Sierra Club, we have volunteers who are working as part of the IUCN and who work with the World Wilderness Congress. We also have a volunteer who is working with environmentalists in Puerto Rico, building a cadre of citizen conservationists.

We feel it very important to enhance communication with environmentalists in other countries, which we do through our Earth Care Network. This is an informal network of like-minded groups who want to extend themselves to help each other whenever they are mounting major campaigns in their own countries. There are no dues or obligations of membership, but the network does operate in the spirit that we can all help each other in our moments of need. The Sierra Club donates its services as the secretariat. We spread the word when groups want world attention to their campaigns, when they want to show their governmental officials that the interest is not just local but widespread. We will attempt, with others, to generate publicity abroad on those issues and to spread word about international campaigns such as the efforts to reform the World Bank. We also try to encourage exchange between environmental groups and our chapters in this country with environmental groups abroad, so-called sister city-type relationships.

Finally, the World Wilderness Inventory has been a new, specific project which we developed especially on the request of the World Wilderness Congress. This pioneering project will continue to grow and expand in the years ahead. A great deal needs to be done in the years ahead, and we look forward to working with other groups to make conservation the priority item on the world's agenda for sustainable development.

PROTECTING LAND AND BIOLOGICAL DIVERSITY FOR THE FUTURE

Frank D. Boren

The threat to wilderness and the global environment is well documented, therefore I will not make mention of them. The flora and fauna of our planet are increasingly endangered and the Nature Conservancy is committed to respond to this critical issue. In doing so, we will make its resources available to work cooperatively with other groups that share our mission to preserve the earth's threatened natural heritage.

It is the Nature Conservancy's mission to preserve biological diversity. We do it domestically as well as beyond the borders of the United States. Domestically, through state natural-area inventory programs now operating in nearly 50 states, the conservancy identifies those areas and habitats that must be protected. We then move quickly to protect those sites, most often by purchasing them. Once the land is acquired, we bring in our stewardship program, which monitors the land to make sure the reasons for setting it aside are not lost through lack of tender loving care. We currently own and maintain over 1,000 preserves, the largest private preserve system in the world. We also assist government agencies in this country to do likewise.

We have been in the international conservation business for nearly a decade. It's a tough business. With other groups, we have set up seven Conservation Data Centers in Latin America, modeled after our domestic heritage programs. Although the diversity of habitats is much greater in Latin American countries, the data is becoming available to decision makers in these seven countries to enable them to determine preservation priorities.

The second part of the program is to support other nonprofit conservation organizations, initially in Latin America and later, elsewhere. They need to be self-sufficient in order to help influence their governments and citizens of the importance of setting aside preserves for natural diversity. With other conservation organizations, we are now working with non-governmental organizations in Costa Rica, Panama, Venezuela, Columbia, Ecuador, Peru, Paraguay and Brazil (just starting), and the Netherlands Antilles. We are beginning programs in the Caribbean and we are again active in Puerto Rico.

We train people here and abroad in how to run the data centers with basic Nature Conservancy software. This software is not proprietary, nor do we want it to be. We also train people in stewardship, the care of the land set aside for preservation and in how to raise operational funds.

We are trying to stay with what we already do well and can pass on: namely stewardship, scientific and protection expertise. We are not economic consultants. But we realize that the world needs sustainable growth and we welcome as partners in our mission those organizations that have the capacity to foster that sustainable growth through economic analysis and other means.

We are also not in the grant-making business. We will help an NGO get up and running, but then we will strive to make it self-sufficient. We have found in our limited experience that we do not gain the respect of our partners by simply passing out money. Our partners abroad are equals.

The conservancy offers many resources and assets for conservation projects:

1. *A businesslike approach to conservation*—The Nature Conservancy has been in existence for 36 years and it prides itself on achieving results. In the United States we are now saving 1,000 acres a day, every day. We want to help achieve similar records internationally.

2. *People*—The Conservancy now has 46 active chapters with more than 1,000 dedicated volunteer trustees leading them. These trustees and our members are good, intelligent, caring Americans who are knowledgeable and concerned about the international environmental situation. They understand the threat and they are willing to fight it with financial support.

3. *Financial resources*—The Conservancy is undercapitalized for its mission but compared with some other nonprofit organizations we're doing well. In the United States we can mobilize up to $60 million for a preservation project at any time. We are willing to use our resources for international conservation. But it has taken us 36 years to build our financial base; we will not jeopardize it by acting imprudently.

4. *A science-based program*—We believe good, objective data is critical in the international arena. But to ensure we're on the right track, we're having our science program reviewed by some of the most eminent people in the field. If it is confirmed that our software for data collecting and dissemination is as good as there exists in the world, we will accelerate our efforts to make it available to Latin America.

We feel that the loss of diversity on the planet is a threat to mankind. We consider it to be like a war. We feel that when the people on this earth regard the extinction of species as a threat equal to the threat of World War II or Adolf Hitler, we will then realize collectively that we don't have enough time to determine who is the leader of the allies. We'll realize that we must act together with anybody who brings competence and skill to attack the problem.

The Nature Conservancy does not have all the answers. We consider ourselves more in the trade-school production business than the think-tank business. We pride ourselves in our execution and delivery on the ground.

We look forward to working in a collective effort to make something happen.

CONSERVATION AND NATIONAL PARKS

Paul Pritchard

In our world, three distinct philosophical approaches to man's relationship with wildlife and wilderness have evolved. First, there are those who believe that man is the dominant animal, the controlling variable, the ultimate predator.

Second are those who believe that man is but a player in a broader system. And third, there are those who follow the Gaia philosophy—that man is a part of this organism called Earth.

Three different angles. Yet each must inevitably lead to the same conclusion. Man the dominant must assume the responsibility of his role as steward or threaten his own survival. Man the player must realize that, as in the game of chess, each piece, king and pawn, is necessary to play the game. Man the earthling must assure the health of the whole organism, Earth, in order to secure his own place on it.

I think we can all agree that mankind's existence is only as rich and diverse as the richness and diversity of a healthy planet. In light of recent world economic development and demographic trends, the next 10 years are being looked upon as the ultimate opportunity for U.S. conservation organizations to assess mankind's impact on his environment and shape a positive plan for a sustainable future.

AN AMERICAN DREAM

In 1916, the U. S. Congress established the National Park Service to regulate the use of federal parklands, "to conserve the scenery and the natural and historic objects and the wildlife therein and to provide for the enjoyment of the same in such a manner and by such means as will leave them unimpaired for the enjoyment of future generations."

The U.S. National Park System is held in high regard by park professionals and citizen conservationists throughout the world. Since the establishment of Yellowstone National Park as the world's first national park in 1872, U.S. national parks and their administrations have been and continue to be the stimuli for similar conservation efforts by other nations.

But, sadly, public funds and political wills do not always stretch far enough to provide the care and protection that our 340 national park units need. To give an independent voice to the national parks, Stephen Mather, the first director of the U.S. National Park Service, took measures that led to the founding of the National Parks and Conservation Association (NPCA) in 1919. Since that time, NPCA has been the only national, nonprofit, membership organization in the United States whose mission is to protect and improve the quality of our personal commitment to national parklands on the part of the American people. We continue today as a constructive critic of and advocate for the national park system.

SHIFTING TO A GLOBAL PERSPECTIVE

While the National Parks and Conservation Association's focus is the U.S. National Park System, it has recognized in recent years a need for participation in the international park movement. As an expert on our national parks, NPCA has supported and advised other countries as they develop their own park systems. The primary thrust of NPCA's efforts is to assist in the establishment of non-governmental organizations similar to NPCA to develop and protect parks in their respective countries.

NPCA provides support for the preservation of significant international resources through its participation in world park conferences, authorship of international parks' publications and sponsorship of specific international conservation issues.

NPCA's most recent involvement on the international level included participating in the Bali World Parks Congress in Indonesia and hosting a working conference on new directions for parks and equivalent preserves held in the Federal Republic of Germany in 1983, as well as cosponsorsing a voluntary-organizations workshop on the occasion of Canada's National Parks Centennial held in Banff in 1985.

In recognition of its efforts to advance the cause of parkland conservation in the United States and other nations, NPCA was the first recipient of the Albert Schweitzer Prize in 1986.

At the request of concerned citizens of British Columbia, NPCA spear-headed efforts to establish the International Coalition to Save South Moresby, which led to the establishment of the South Moresby National Park Reserve in British Columbia's Queen Charlotte Islands.

THE NEED FOR NGOS

In light of the emerging international conservation movement and the growing existence of important cooperative ties between NGOs and national park agencies, there is both a need and an opportunity to assist local and national initiatives with appropriate international cooperative assistance.

Just as the time is ripe for adding to the world's network of protected areas, so is it time to aid conservation consciousness among citizens and local officials in these nations confronted with threats to existing parklands. NGO groups are in the best position to enlist public support for this purpose as well as to give an independent voice for park-management problems caused by budgetary and personnel constraints, encroachments, pollution and other issues.

A FORUM FOR ACTION

NPCA, with the Canadian Parks and Wilderness Society and the National Parks and Environment Foundation of Panama, has initiated an International Parks Forum of the Americas and the Caribbean. We were pleased to launch this new effort in Pan-American environmental cooperation in conjunction with the 4th World Wilderness Congress.

The forum seeks to promote the exchange of information and technical expertise between participating NGOs and individuals; communication and action on common problems, transnational park issues and issues of broad international concern; and the strengthening of voluntary heritage organizations established to promote and protect national parks and protected areas.

Fifty-three participants from 17 countries attended the forum's first session, which was organized by NPCA and chaired by Dr. Felix Nunez, President of the National Parks and Environment Foundation of Panama.

CARRYING ON THE DREAM

Park lands and park resources are only secure when they are understood, appreciated and personally committed to by local officials and institutions. The important and legitimate role that U.S. NGOs can play in assisting the conservation affairs of developed and developing nations should not be underestimated. The National Parks and Conservation Association will continue its involvement in advancing the world parks and protected areas movement. Whether predator, player or earthling, mankind has the opportunity now to decide his role on our spaceship Earth.

CONSERVATION BEGINS AT HOME

George T. Frampton, Jr.

It's interesting to recall that the reports brought back in the late 1860s by the first white explorers in Yellowstone of bubbling geyser pools and jagged peaks, waterfalls, bison and grizzly bears thick across the plain, were widely dismissed in the East as lies and fabrications. It only took a few years for Congress to be sufficiently convinced to set aside two million acres of the Yellowstone Region as our first national park.

In the ensuing decades, many of the crown jewels of our natural landscape were included in the park system. When you consider that our forefathers in this country viewed wilderness primarily as something to be conquered, tamed, colonized and above all, used, the creation of our National Parks System was really an act of extraordinary foresight. The same foresight was present when a group of conservation professionals concerned about the loss of wild lands in this country, largely outside the parks system and in our national forests, banded together in 1935 to found the Wilderness Society. It took Bob Marshall, Aldo Leopold, Aldous Murray and Benton McHigh (who invented the idea of the Appalachian Trail) nearly 30 years to persuade Congress to enact into legislation the National Wilderness Preservation System.

In the years since the Wilderness Act of 1964 we have succeeded beyond their wildest dreams, including almost 90 million acres in the wilderness system of this country. It is because of these acts of foresight that my generation of Americans has inherited a unique legacy. A small but significant percentage of the original wild nature of this country, millions of years of nature's evolving hand substantially untouched by human development, was passed on to us by our forefathers in trust and as William Mott states, to be passed on by us to our children and grandchildren, unimpaired for the enjoyment of future generations. It is going to take at least that kind of foresight to protect what we have received in trust and to live up to the trust that's been placed in us.

The American experience with Yellowstone Park illustrates two principal threats or problems through which this foresight can be experienced:

Population—We are truly in danger of loving some of our most important parks to death. It is interesting that, in 1872 when Congress created Yellowstone, the only real opposition came from people who said that it was unnecessary to make it a park because the area was too remote and nobody would ever go there. This summer, well over 1 million people visited Yellowstone, resulting in many cars, plastic cups, plastic bags and, in some cases, too many campsites in prime habitat areas. Excessive concessions, airplane flights, helicopter flights and all of those things not only stand to ruin a visitor's experience today, but to ruin the park tomorrow. We are going to have to learn how to manage the use of our parks and wilderness. We were the pioneers in this country in setting aside and designating this legacy for future generations, and if we expect other countries to manage what they have, we are going to have to take the lead in managing our own resources.

Development of adjacent lands—We have in the last 10 or 15 years begun to realize that our parks and wilderness areas are not islands. Yellowstone is more than the sum of its parts. Yellowstone National Park and Grand Teton National Park are far less than 50 percent of the region. These parks are surrounded by national forests, two wildlife refuges and a great deal of state and private land. The U.S. Forest Service has permitted clear-cutting up to the boundary of the park. If you look at a map of the Yellowstone region, with the national forest areas colored which have already been leased for oil and gas development, you'll see that between 70 percent and 80 percent of the region around both parks has already been leased. Only $18 per-barrel oil is saving us from substantial development threats to the parks. In this country we must begin to figure out how the different agencies of the federal government can begin to plan to protect our parks and wilderness areas.

If we're not able to ensure that the agencies of our own federal government can protect park wilderness, do ecosystem planning and begin to plan for buffer zones that are necessary to protect our existing parks and wildernesses, how can we ask other countries to do it? It seems as if we are unable to understand and then implement the Biosphere Concept in Yellowstone, Glacier, Everglades, Southern Appalachian Highlands, the California Desert and the big natural areas in this country which have national parks at their core but are surrounded by federal land managed by other federal agencies. Therefore, when we do analyses of the national park in Honduras to demonstrate that the park is an integral natural resource for that country because of the water supply that it provides for the capitol, how can we expect the government of Honduras to take seriously our representations to it about this concept?

Yellowstone Park also provides a significant opportunity to make progress in restoring natural areas. Most environmental groups in this country are accused of just being *against* things. I think it's very important that private and non-governmental organizations in the United States demonstrate that we can be affirmative. We need not only to be in a position of simply stopping the destruction of wild lands, wildlife and other natural resources, but to have a program for expanding this resource. Yellowstone gives us an opportunity to do that.

The Greater Yellowstone Ecosystem has been substantially fragmented in some places by roads, clear-cutting and other types of development. These are areas that can be restored. The opportunity exists in Yellowstone to reconnect the park and two or three large wilderness areas that have been separated over the last 30 or 40 years. The areas through which development has occurred may never become wilderness again, at least in the strict context of U.S. law in the Wilderness Act of 1964. However, by closing roads, zoning and planning to limit certain kinds of development, thereby allowing those areas to restore themselves, it is possible in Yellowstone to create what we've begun to call at the Wilderness Society, "Phoenix Areas." This would not only be a resource area, but by the year 2000 a much larger natural area would exist than we have now, creating new wildlife corridors and a larger reservoir for biodiversity.

This is going to take land-use planning among federal agencies in the Yellowstone region and elsewhere. This is going to take the kind of land-use planning that we are urging upon other countries. If we can't do it, we're in no position to ask others to do it.

© Geoff Tischbein

THE IMPORTANCE OF RESOURCE MANAGEMENT

George M. Leonard

In the United States, we've had an abundance of resources to work with. We've used them—not always well—and, hindsight being better, not always wisely. There was a time when, as a nation, we faced a new land and the continent laid out before us was wilderness—3.6 million square miles, plus or minus a few. And out of those miles of wilderness we've drawn our resources and carved our nation.

We settled the land, broke sod, and plowed and planted the soil. We cut timber from our forests, mined minerals from our mountains, grazed cattle and sheep over our rangelands, and took game from our forests and fish from our rivers and lakes. We've used the land and its resources to meet our needs and build our nation.

We made mistakes along the way. We sometimes plowed where we ought not have, sprayed when we shouldn't have, and sometimes we grazed more live-stock on the land than we should have. We overcut some of our forests, drained some of our wetlands, and polluted our air and water. We turned some of our best farmland into subdivisions, and pushed some of our wildlife species into extinction.

We eroded some of our soils. It was little more than 50 years ago that "black blizzards" of dust were lifting topsoil from the plains of Colorado and carrying it across the continent and out over the Atlantic Ocean. We have made mistakes with our resources and suffered the consequences.

But we learned from our mistakes and stepped in to correct them. We learned conservation tillage and other soil-saving methods, planted shelter belts and established conservation reserves. We learned forest regulation from Germany, and applied sustained yield forestry. We applied safer methods of pest manage-ment, protected endangered wildlife and fish species, and developed a Smokey the Bear fire prevention program.

We built federal and state conservation programs and established national forests, national parks, and national wildlife refuges. We preserved some areas as wilderness and set aside others for science. We've protected, preserved, reserved, restored, and maintained our resources.

One of the things we've learned is that, with good management, the land and its resources can recover. In the southern part of the United States, where 156 million acres of forest had been overcut by the 1920s, the forests have been restored to productivity. On many of those lands we are now planting the south's fourth forest. In the east, lands that had been overcut and abandoned—that nobody wanted—under federal management have become shining gemstones of multiple-use management. Streams that once ran dirty now run cleaner. Good habitat management has begun to move Kirtland's warbler, the bald eagle and peregrine falcon, the Lahontan cutthroat trout, and other species back from the brink of extinction. And on the Great Plains, the soils of the "dust bowl" have been restored to productivity.

In the United States, we have had the advantage of an abundance of resources to work with, and this has shaped our progress. Our people have basic needs— food to eat, homes and jobs—and we have used and managed our natural resources to meet those needs and build a strong and robust economy. The strength of that economy has caused demands on our resources to continually grow and multiply, and to embrace new needs and wants such as recreation, spiritual growth, wilderness, and a clean, healthy environment.

Our history in the United States has been one of continuing expanding cycles of resource exploration, development, and use, interspersed with progressive cycles of conservation, scientific resource management, and environmental protection. Each of these cycles has presented us with a more complex mix of wants and needs to meet, and more sophisticated means of managing our resources to meet them.

As I've traveled in North America and abroad, in Europe and Asia, I've thought about how our experience with resource management in the United States compares with the experiences of other nations. One of the factors which has made our experience so different has been the sheer extent and variety— capacity—of our natural resources.

We have 2.3 billion acres of land and 107 million acres of water. We have 737 million acres of forest, 820 million acres of rangelands, and 421 million acres of croplands. We have 70 million acres of wetlands. These lands embrace resource conditions ranging from "used up" to untouched. They provide habitat for about 200 species of amphibians, 900 bird species, 1,100 fish species, 400 species of mammal, 350 species of reptile, and countless invertebrate species. They involve environments ranging from polar to tropical, and support an equally broad range of plant life. They contain large quantities of coal, oil, natural gas, and minerals. The commercial forest lands are among the most productive in the world.

This wealth of resources has permitted us to grow as a nation despite mistakes made with our resources which might have ruined nations less richly endowed. Of course, we are still struggling to find an acceptable balance among commodity uses and amenity uses for these lands, and I expect this struggle will continue. In effect, this struggle represents the continuing evolution of our economic and social systems.

There has been some question about the utility of the U.S. experience to other nations which have not shared it, especially to those seeking to become established and to develop their resources.

Our experience encompasses a great deal—what we've done well in managing our resources, and things we've done wrong. The sum offers several basic lessons which may apply elsewhere:

—One basic lesson is that it is appropriate for a nation to use its resources to meet its peoples' needs. We were in a new land once. We explored and settled the wilderness, and we used our resources to build our cities, feed our families and keep our factories running. It is a basic responsibility of any nation to meet its peoples' needs.

—A second lesson is that it's necessary for a nation to manage its resources to sustain its peoples' needs from one generation to the next. We have learned at least part of this lesson the hard way.

We cleared the land and neglected our forests. We saw the consequences of overcutting and wildfire, saw the milltowns close, and heard predictions of timber famines. We plowed the land and neglected our soils and erosion turned the Great Plains into a dust bowl. We saw farmland lost, farms abandoned and the cars of the displaced people on the road to California.

But we found that sound, scientific resource management can protect and sustain the forests, that it can stabilize and rebuild the soils. And we found that scientific resource management can expand resource capacities, increase per-acre yields and improve resource utilization. We put policies in place and practices to work to sustain our resource needs. It is a basic responsibility of any nation to protect and manage its resources in a socially responsible manner.

—A third lesson is that a nation's needs change, and it is necessary for the focus and purpose of resource management to change as well.

When we were a new nation with the wilderness before us, we were two million Americans with a toehold on the continent. We needed to multiply and develop the land, and we did. We tapped the wilderness for its resources, passed a billion acres of public land into private ownership, and plowed the hillsides to plant our crops.

Now we are settled. There are 240 million of us spanning the continent and then some. We have a robust economy, a surplus of several agricultural crops and products, and we import and export more than any nation.

Our needs have changed and multiplied—evolved—and so, too, has the focus of our resource management programs.

We are setting aside wilderness—over 89 million acres in the total system so far, with more to come, to ensure the survival of our natural heritage. In the past 40 years we have tripled the area of federal land devoted to national parks. We have broadened management of the national forests to address a wider variety of uses and values—for recreation, wildlife habitat, aesthetic values, biological diversity and other purposes in addition to timber production, mining and grazing. And through the Conservation Reserve, we are paying thousands of farmers to convert millions of acres from agricultural crops to trees or grass.

In developing our resources, the United States has also developed a great deal of scientific and technical expertise in resource management. We are leaders in multiple-use land management, tree genetics and improvement, fire management, watershed science and management, and the biological control of pests.

Within the structures of the United Nations, the U.S. Agency for International Development, the Peace Corps, and other cooperative and exchange programs available, we're proud to share what we know with others. We share our expertise so that other nations, operating within their own unique social and political systems, can meet the needs of their people for food and shelter while protecting the land's productivity for future generations.

But it should be pointed out that the United States also benefits from such programs. We have always borrowed a great deal from the professional expertise of other nations. Bernhard Fernow, our first trained forester in the United States, came from Germany. And Gifford Pinchot, who put forest conservation high on our nation's agenda in the early 1900s, was a forester trained in France and Germany.

We've borrowed genetic resources from other nations, as well—Scots pine, Norway spruce, and eucalyptus among them. And we look to other nations for other expertise—to Sweden and Norway for their timber harvesting and utilization technologies, to Germany for its experience with atmospheric deposition, to Venezuela and other nations for what they've done with urban forests, and to Japan for expertise in cultivating one of our more recent products of the forest, Shiitake mushrooms.

Yet I believe that one of the greatest benefits of international cooperation is to our own people—to the people we send abroad, the technical experts who work with other nations. They return to us with a renewed realization of the ultimate connection between a nation's resources and its people.

We live in a world increasingly pulled together by our resources or lack of them. And we need to understand much. We have shared resource problems and solutions. Acid rain, the protection of whales and migratory birds, population pressures and the effects of deforestation on the global climate are only part of the spectrum of natural resource subjects that increasingly bring together people of the world. And, as a result, I see the nations of the world working more closely together.

As the pressures rise and the problems emerge to bear more heavily on our resources, we need to expand international cooperation. I envision more exchanges of scientific and professional personnel among nations—exchanges of students or faculty between universities, and of research scientists and technical experts between institutions of science and management.

I envision a recognition by nations of their joint responsibility, in the larger world, to share resources and expertise in managing and protecting them, as well as other information. If we shirk such responsibility, then the abundant resources of many of our nations may make them rich oases in a world of need.

Developed nations with abundant resources must somehow resist the strong temptation to ignore the rest of the world's resource problems. For those are the nations with the strength, wealth, technology, and institutional skills needed to reduce the loss of the world's resources and to help ensure their continued sufficiency.

The first obvious step in this effort is to set the example of wise planning and proper stewardship of our own resources. But a necessary second step is to view scientific knowledge and technology as basic global resources and to share them as we are able, with other nations.

In the words of a former U.S. statesman at the United Nations, the late Adlai Stevenson:

"We travel together, passengers on a little spaceship, dependent on its vulnerable resources of air and soil; all committed for our safety to its security and peace; preserved from annihilation by the care, the work, and the love we give our fragile craft."

THE AMERICAN NATIONAL PARK SYSTEM —NEW CHALLENGES

William Penn Mott, Jr.

In 1870 a small party of campfire philosophers elected to seek preservation of Yellowstone's wonders for public use rather than for private development. In doing so, they sparked a world concept of national parks. They also recognized that some natural treasures deserve protection for the benefit of all rather than development for the enrichment of a few.

As is the case with many historical leaders of new concepts, these campfire philosophers likely had no idea their approach would extend into the future and become worldwide. Since that decision to seek public use, there has been a steady course toward preservation of special areas and unique resources for the use of all.

Two years after the Yellowstone decision, in March 1872, the Congress of the United States designated Yellowstone as a public pleasuring ground. In 1916 Congress established the National Parks Service with a mandate to "conserve the scenery and the natural and historic objects, and the wildlife therein, to provide for the enjoyment of the same in such manner and by such means as will leave them unimpaired for the enjoyment of future generations."

Then, in 1964, Congress enacted the Wilderness Act, specifying that designated areas "shall be administered for the use and enjoyment of the

American people in such manner as will leave them unimpaired for future use and enjoyment as wilderness. . . ." And, further, wilderness was defined as "an area of undeveloped federal land retaining its primeval character and influence, without permanent improvements or human habitation, which is protected and managed so as to preserve its natural conditions. . . ." Along the way there was enacted the Antiquities Act of 1906, the National Environment Policy Act, the Clean Air Act and the Endangered Species Act.

My premise today is that preservation of wilderness, natural areas, back country, wild areas, and scenic areas and their resources, has been an integral part of the management philosophy of the National Parks Service since its beginning. Its acceptance has been national. The statutory authority to do the job has been defended and broadened as the years passed.

Wilderness, as experienced in 1805-1806 by Lewis and Clark and later by John Muir and other U.S. forebears, is no more. Like our youth, it can never be completely recaptured. Nevertheless, we must preserve what is left and, to the best of our ability, restore what once was. This is a complex and never-ending task. The National Parks Service Management Program is designed to safeguard and preserve the quality of wilderness wherever it is assigned to our charge. We seek these goals in all backcountry, whether it is a part of the national park or is designated or proposed for wilderness classification. In those instances where our management fails, we invite all observers to report the failures to us. We have noticed no particular reticence in this regard.

I know of no better way to assure the general public and devoted wilderness advocates that our wilderness management is applied honestly, fairly, and in full measure than to present our management program for all to observe and to comment upon. Changes are taking place, some of which we have little or no control over. We must have the flexibility to change, always keeping in mind our basic mission which requires that, in our judgment, if we err it must be on the side of preservation.

The initial goal of natural resource management focuses on reserving unique areas and providing the recreating public access to them. There was a pressing need for access roads and comfortable accommodations. Early depredation of wildlife, timber cutting for buildings and fuels, and other uses made it apparent that a much more protective management program was necessary. Evolving preservation concepts first placed emphasis on protection of things such as geysers, trees, magnificent vistas, special historic sites, or routes of travel and wildlife. Some things were considered "bad," such as the predatory wolves, grizzlies, mountain lions and so forth. Others, such as elk, deer, and bison, were "good." Management sought to eliminate the so-called "bad" resources while increasing the "good" resources.

Changes became necessary after research evidence mounted, indicating that poor resource conservation, or lack of area-wide management, would not protect designated parks and preserves. The Secretary of the Interior's advisory board recommended in 1963 that the National Parks Service protect "vignettes" of primitive America. We soon found that we could not perpetuate vignettes because we manage changing, living systems. Gradually, we developed a philosophy of protecting the whole environment. Full stewardship preservation requires understanding of how these natural systems function. Further, management techniques need to be such that ecological systems are allowed to evolve as naturally as possible.

Population growth, a turning to the outdoors for recreation, modern technology and all the attendant impacts have created a climate which permits few mistakes. We must have adequate funding, sound information and organizations staffed by people who are qualified to make decisions that make preservation work. Further, our programs must be applied with the cooperation of adjoining land managers—federal, state, local and private. Increasingly, too, it becomes apparent that air quality, water quality and climate know no national borders and may, in fact, be global. So, what are the ingredients of our management program?

Management Policies, published by the National Parks Service in 1978, states the general national policies for the management of the National Park System areas. Each area manager is responsible for the preparation of a general management plan. This plan must state the park's purpose and management objectives. All land and water are classified into natural, historic, park development and special use zones. Resources in the natural zone—where wilderness and backcountry are located—are managed to ensure that natural resources and processes remain largely unaltered by human activity. The general management plans interrelate proposals for resource management, interpretation and visitor use, and permit general development. An assessment of alternates specifies the consequences to be expected under varying management approaches. These plans must be prepared with open, cooperative regional planning, public participation and review, and consultations with park advisory boards and regional advisory commissions.

We are currently revising our management policies, as a part of a 12-point plan and a 32-point action program, to guide and safeguard the National Parks System in the future. As a part of this effort, we seek to develop a nationwide, systematic resource strategy, improve wilderness management and pursue cooperative agreements with land managers, owners and communities near park units and particularly near wilderness areas. Further, we would increase public understanding and participation in the roles and functions of the National Parks Service. We will reemphasize that our "management policies" are the basis for all future decision making.

A Wilderness Task Force in 1986 recommended the existing "management policies" be changed little. The task force recommended that we make management of wilderness more systematic and consistent from area to area and nationwide. The group further recommended that we designate wilderness coordinators in the national office and in each of the 10 regional offices; perfect our wilderness management techniques; examine permissible carrying capacities;

increase education and training of our wilderness personnel; educate the public; and, coordinate management with other agencies. The latter would involve a National Wilderness Coordinating Group seeking cooperative activities with all land managers surrounding a wilderness area and developing interagency program teams.

Wilderness is thought of being from the surface land to the tops of the trees. We dared to suggest that at Mammoth Caves and other caves that are underground, we should develop in these areas underground wilderness areas. We should establish these as part of the responsibility of the National Park Service in developing wilderness concepts. So we will be developing underground wilderness areas to protect these underground resources that are our responsibility.

In addition, we have recently received legislation that indicates that both the Congress and the administration recognize that silence is an attribute of a national park unit. So, in the development of plans where we are having difficulty over flights by aircraft, we are proposing and suggesting that in making these areas flight-free zones we are also extending the wilderness concept upward above the tops of the trees. So, we believe that in following these two pieces of legislation, we will establish forever the fact that wilderness not only is from ground level to the tops of the trees but it extends underground, under the water and above the trees for an unlimited distance.

Management of parklands possessing significant natural features and values is concerned with ecological processes and the impacts of people upon these processes and resources. It is interesting to note that conflict develops around the question of long- versus short-range planning and management. The National Park Service's responsibility is the protection and conservation of the natural and cultural resources entrusted to it forever. So we must think in long terms while most people are thinking in short terms.

In the absence of adequate knowledge, operational programs are aimed at maintaining the status quo. We seek especially to avoid long-term or possible irreversible impacts upon priority areas and on our research that we are developing for these priority areas. For example, management policies which must be reflected in the natural resource management plans include:

—Agricultural uses are not permitted in natural zones.

—Commercial grazing is not permitted in any park where such use is detrimental to the primary purpose for which it was established. Grazing is permitted where authorized by law or where grazing rights have been granted for a term of years as a condition of land acquisition. Trail stock grazing is permitted where incidental to passage through natural areas, but under very careful management of each sight used.

—Native animal life shall be given protection against harvest, removal, destruction, harassment or harm through human action, except where: hunting and trapping are permitted by law; fishing is permitted by law or not specifically prohibited; control of specific populations of wildlife is required for maintaining a healthy park ecosystem; or, removal or control of animals is necessary for human safety and health. So hunting, trapping and other methods of harvest of native wildlife are not permitted by the public in natural zones except where specifically required by law.

—Fishery management shall be specifically aimed toward preserving or restoring the full spectrum of native species and regulated for native species so that mortality is compensated by natural reproduction.

—Threatened and endangered species and their critical habitat requirements are identified. Visitor use and access are controlled so as to perpetuate the natural distribution and abundance of threatened and endangered species and to protect the ecosystem on which they depend.

—Exotic plant and animal species are managed, up to total eradication, when they threaten protection or interpretation of resources being preserved.

—Native insects and diseases are allowed to function unimpeded except where they threaten to eliminate other native species; threaten to spread outside the area; threaten endangered species, unique plants or communities; or where they pose danger to public health and safety. Insect and disease control in wilderness areas is limited to the minimum necessary to prevent escape from the wilderness environment.

—Natural fires are recognized as natural phenomena and are permitted to influence the ecosystem so that truly natural systems will be perpetuated.

—Waters of the parks are a primary resource on par with wildlife, forest, geological and historic features. Emphasis is placed on conservation of water so as to meet the needs of visitation without the addition of water development.

—Terrain and vegetative cover are manipulated when necessary to restore natural conditions on lands altered by human activity. This includes removal of man-made features, restoration of natural gradients, revegetation with native species, restoration of natural appearance in areas disturbed by fires and control activities, and minor rehabilitation of visitor-impacted areas.

—Shoreline processes—erosion, deposition, dune formation, inlet formation and so on—are allowed to take place naturally except where life and property are threatened.

—The National Park Service is responsible now to try to eliminate many of the exotic plants and animals that exist in our National Park units. We are finding that we are getting good support in that program. For example, we have eliminated practically all of the burros in Death Valley. The few that are remaining will be shot on sight by our rangers. In spite of the emotional impact of that kind of a statement, I can tell you that the public is now supporting that concept wholeheartedly and so we are in the process now of a major job of trying to eliminate the wild pigs and the exotic plants from all of the units of the National Parks Service. It is not going to be an easy job. It is going to take a considerable amount of time to accomplish that objective, but we're bound by our mandates to accomplish that objective and we are working at it very, very hard.

Throughout the country we have about 20 cooperative park study units that carry out research and advise parks and regional chief scientists on specific resource management problems. These bring close interaction between the scientist and management staffs. Management planning occurs side by side with research, when required. These units serve as a catalyst for developing interagency agreements with the Forest Service, the universities and others interested in mutual problems. In one region alone, this arrangement was once compared to having a science staff of 200 available on call to park managers. And the benefits are similar in other regions. Under our current alignment, the Cooperative Park Study Units research projects and interaction with managers extend directly to the regional offices and the individual park units. I might say that the increased entrance fees will make it possible for us to spend something in excess of $76 million next year for research, interpretation and resource management.

Perhaps our major challenge today is the preservation of wilderness in the face of increasing public use. Backcountry use nationwide has grown. There is indication that this type of recreation is now leveling off. Migration of populations to the Western states is major factor. Our great Western natural parks are bound to be affected by proximity of increasingly larger populations.

It seems to me the National Park Service has a major problem in that we are going to be faced with ever-increasing pressures on the units of the National Park System which we once thought were islands secure in themselves. Through the increased research that we have been doing, we realize that this is not true, that the parks themselves are not islands and that they must be protected from within and on the outside. All of our managers now are being trained this way to protect the parks from within as well as to work with all of the agencies that surround the National Park system and protect those areas from the outside interest of development. They also try to mitigate any development in order to make it less difficult for us to manage the parks themselves. We are doing a great deal of work along these lines to make sure that the information is available to us to do a better job.

ECONOMICS, DEVELOPMENT

and

ENVIRONMENT

> *"Damage can result when people fail to recognize that the future of the human race depends to a large extent on a sensible compromise between economic and environmental considerations."*
> —David Rockefeller

FINANCING CONSERVATION AND SUSTAINABLE DEVELOPMENT

ECOCONVERGENCE— ECOLOGY AND ECONOMICS FOR PLANETARY SURVIVAL

Maurice Strong

Why does the World Wilderness Congress deal with such a broad range of issues? Why are we talking about the world economy, the debt and trade issues and the poverty issue, as well as moral and ethic guidelines, in a wilderness congress? Because we have learned that protection of the world's wilderness areas cannot be divorced from what is happening in the rest of our global environments.

More than ever before, we have come to understand that the world is no longer made up of individual governments, economic systems, national or ethnic groups. We've come to regard the world as a system, as a living organism. Just as a prick on your toe can infect your whole body, what we do in any part of the body of our planet affects all of it—and all of us.

We have also come to realize that our species is in a whole new situation. In this century alone, population has grown from 1.6 billion to 5 billion. By the end of the century, it will grow by another billion—and four out of five of the world's people will live in developing countries. Industrial production has also exploded, by a magnitude of 50, and fossil fuel use has increased by 30—most of this since 1950. More land has been cleared for cultivation in the last century than in all previous human history.

Overall, the condition of our environment and thus our natural resource base continues to deteriorate. Devastating droughts in Africa, acidification in the northern parts of the world, the disappearance of species, the destruction of the tropical rain forests, climate change, ozone depletion—these are all global issues. All of these ecological disasters have occurred at a level of population and human activity far lower than those that will exist in the next century. All of them are connected with human failure—ignorance, policy mismanagement and ecological insensitivity. And, more than anything else, all of these problems have been exacerbated by poverty, poverty which forces people to degrade their environment and to destroy the very resources upon which their future depends—in an intolerable, vicious circle.

The 4th World Wilderness Congress marks the emergence of a new alliance dedicated to finding new solutions to the problems of our earth. Not only environmentalists, but also scientists, politicians, financiers, businessmen, leaders of North American and African indigenous peoples, leaders of non-governmental organizations, development-assistance agencies and multilateral agencies—all these groups are combining forces, seeing themselves as allies in the search for an economically and environmentally secure future for humanity. The wisdom of indigenous and tribal people and the passion and expertise of environmentalists, combined with the business and scientific approaches, are forces that will develop the best, most holistic solutions.

What we are recognizing most clearly is that the only possible solution to our environmental dilemma is a new era of economic growth, an era of sustainable development for all countries. This is only possible if we change our ways. We must create a more positive synthesis between environment and economics, what I would call an ecoconvergence. Saying that this must occur doesn't make it happen, doesn't remove the conflicts and the difficulties, but it does provide the objective within the framework, within which we must all work. Clearly, there are cases where environment and conservation on the one hand will be in conflict with an immediate economic objective, but, broadly speaking, they are and must be compatible.

We must try to find ways for environmentally sound projects to pay for themselves. To do this, we will need innovative thinking and action, especially if we're to meet the financial needs of the developing countries. For one thing, we must improve cost-benefit analysis to take into account longer-term environmental benefits and costs. Many conservation projects do not show a good rate of return in conventional economic terms, of course, but we may be encouraged by the evidence that other such projects do, in many cases bringing a higher economic return than more conventional, infrastructural projects. For these profitable projects, we must develop new sources of finance from private investment.

We must also take a look at the role of development assistance and learn to make better use of existing funds. Aid is essential but it is not enough, as we learn from the World Commission on Environment and Development Report—a report that might well serve as a basic text for this new era, a guidebook for all. We also need to promote the synthesis of environment and economics through changes in the macroeconomic and policy structures. The developed nations must work in new ways with the developing world, toward the kinds of economic growth that will meet the legitimate aspirations of all nations for a fair share of the world economy. We need to provide markets for products of the developing countries and give them a fair deal in trade and for carrying the burden of their debts. Removal of agricultural subsidies is directly relevant to developing countries, since it would enable them to do what they can most competitively, and would stimulate them to sell their products to us. These debt and trade issues, the science and technology transfer issues, private investments, redistribution of global industrial capacity—all are absolutely germane to the central subject of environment. Developing countries must be full partners, not just marginal recipients of our bounty. We must understand that their economic and ecological health are intimately related to our own economic and environmental security. If they are going to share in the responsibility for our planet, they must be able to share the benefits.

The World Wilderness Congress presents some of the new ideas we'll need. The World Conservation Banking Program demonstrates how private funds can be mobilized to meet conservation-related development needs and still achieve an effective economic rate of return. The Tropical Forestry Action Plan is an excellent example set recently by a number of important non-governmental and intergovernmental organizations—the World Resources Institute, the World Bank, the FAO, the IUCN and others—of how to tackle the immense problem of the destruction of tropical forests. The idea of swapping debt for environmental action is another new idea with great potential. Those who make economic policy—leaders of business, ministers of industry, agriculture, forestry and transport, who also make environmental policy—must be accountable for their effects on the earth.

The future of the planet is everybody's responsibility and it involves everybody's future. No longer can we secure our individual futures and those of our children by our own individual activities and plans. If we do not join in ensuring planetary survival, we will be building our own individual houses on sand. Cooperation, caring for and sharing with each other are not just pious ideals but are imperative for economic and environmental survival. Most importantly, such attitudes also strengthen human morals and spirit, the most important values which undergird all economic and environmental factors.

It is sometimes said that conservationists are always "preaching to the converted." Yes, in a sense we are. But the circle of the converted has widened broadly in recent years, as the 4th World Wilderness Congress makes clear, and it is our job to widen it further, much further. We must make it clear that worldwide cooperation and caring for each other are essential. In many ways we are all parochial, but we can develop a global form of parochialism that will embody the truth of those words of Chief Seattle, "If we care for the earth, the earth will care for us."

ECONOMIC GROWTH AND CONSERVATION: PARTNERS, NOT ENEMIES

James A. Baker, III

Those who know some economics may have heard of something called the Phillip's Curve. This was the rather startling theory, popular in the 1960s, which stated that in order to reduce unemployment you had to tolerate higher inflation or vice versa, that to tame inflation you had to have high unemployment. This theory never did stand the test of time.

Yet I sometimes think a cousin of the Phillip's Curve survives in the way we often look at environmental policy. We seem to assume that to protect the environment, we must have slow economic growth. For if we desire fast growth, then inevitably we will degrade the environment.

I don't subscribe to this bleak choice any more than I believed in the Phillip's Curve. I think growth and conservation can coexist. Indeed, I'd go so far as to restate things in a much more positive way: that growth and development are essential for conservation, and conservation is essential for growth. Despite some assertions to the contrary, these concepts are not mutually exclusive. In fact, they should not necessarily be deemed mutually antagonistic.

I am not saying that growth and development do not put new and difficult strains on the natural environment. The lesson of centuries is that they often do—and with tragic results when men and women are careless.

Yet I also think we have to be realistic about those strains. They are going to continue because the drive for growth and development will inevitably continue. No U.S. political leader who wants to remain in office will endorse a slow-growth platform.

In the same way, no leader in the developing world is going to tell his countrymen they cannot aspire to the same standard of living as Americans simply because their ambition strains the ecology of the rain forest. Those of us who care about conservation will not persuade anyone with a "Limits to Growth" philosophy.

Instead, I think we have to pursue, both in the United States and abroad, a philosophy of growth combined with conservation. This philosophy has its roots in America's own conservation heritage. Gifford Pinchot, who headed America's Forest Service early in this century, believed in what he called "utilitarian conservation." At the risk of oversimplification, the concept is very much like a growth and conservation philosophy.

Pinchot's insight happened to fit beautifully with the mood of the times and with the views of his president, Theodore Roosevelt, and he was able to accomplish a great deal. Pinchot—with his political skills and practical vision— did more to preserve this nation's environment than did most of his more celebrated, and more purist, contemporaries.

Conservation, Pinchot once said, is "the greatest good for the greatest number over the longest time." It is a sensible definition and a catchy political slogan at the same time. Under Pinchot and Roosevelt, the amount of forest under control of the U.S. Forest Service tripled and our great national treasure, the National Parks System, was greatly enhanced. Pinchot and Roosevelt never lost sight of the fundamental importance of a growing economy, and so they never lost wide public support for their energetic conservation programs.

As important as these political realities are, we can also make a strong, practical, economic case for the benefits that growth can have on conservation, especially in the developing world.

At a basic level it is simple common sense. Expanding wealth eases the pressure that the poor feel to work constantly just to survive. In short, it creates opportunities for leisure. And when people have the luxury to take time off from the burdens of subsistence, they invariably turn their attention more to the condition of the environment and the quality of life. They begin to care more passionately about the cleanliness of rivers, or the preservation of wildlife.

We saw this in our own nation's history, as conservation became an important political movement only after the strong industrial growth of the late nineteenth century. And we saw it again in the 1960s after another run of industrial growth, rising incomes and expanding time for leisure.

The same holds true today in the developing world. Often the countries with the poorest conservation records are the poorest countries, those that consider clean rivers or the preservation of natural wildlife habitat something to care about only after their citizens have made a living or fed their children.

In some of the countries of Africa, for example, we've seen great pressure from farming put on the natural ranges of elephants and other wildlife. The populations of these countries have exploded and each family naturally wants its own plot of land. Tragically, these countries have often pursued mistaken policies that have damaged economic growth and denied their people opportunities other than farming, such as work in industry or in urban centers that might ease pressure on the land and on that continent's inspiring and irreplaceable wildlife.

The story is very different, however, in some of the more successful parts of east Asia. In Korea and Taiwan, industrial development has eased the pressure on the environment from farming by drawing workers into the cities, just as it did decades ago in our own country.

It's certainly true that industrial development has created new problems such as water and air pollution. But at least growth has helped these nations escape the environmental degradation of the poorest countries. As a by-product of their increased affluence, we've also seen growing public concern in Korea and Taiwan about the new problems of pollution. I'd submit that here is a clear case of growth aiding the cause of conservation.

I see a trend away from the idea that conservation is a luxury that wealthy countries can embrace while the developing world faces more pressing economic problems. The political leadership in the developing world is increasingly responsive to the underlying reality that sound conservation is good economics. It recognizes a direct correlation between wise use of natural resources and economic growth. The perceived tension between the need to create economic stability and the obligation to preserve resources for future generations may be easing.

I think we can make an even stronger case when we look at the new and advancing technologies that tend to accompany growth. Peter Drucker, the business and management expert, once said, "The only means of conservation is innovation." And he's probably right. We've seen technology help us better dispose of industrial waste. We've seen advances in biology help us restock rivers with fish and reforest our woodlands.

Perhaps most significantly, the industries that we consider high-tech—important growth industries of the future for America—are primarily less intrusive environmentally than the industries of the smokestack age. Simply compare the quality of the air and water around Pittsburgh or Chicago of 40 years ago with the air and water around Silicon Valley or Route 128 near Boston today.

I am not suggesting that new technologies will lead us inevitably into some brave new world of environmental safety. They clearly present their own dilemmas and challenges. But these technologies—and the economic growth that spurs and sustains them—can often help us to ease the environmental problems of the present if we apply them wisely.

CONSERVATION AT THE WORLD BANK:
A NEW EMPHASIS

General principles also have practical consequences. Perhaps I can give a better sense of that practical impact by telling how the Reagan Administration has been trying to encourage greater concern for the environment in the way the World Bank promotes economic development.

The World Bank and some of the other development banks have not always had the best conservation record. Indeed, I think even most bank officials will acknowledge this. They'll admit that in pursuing the very hard work of economic development, they may not always have given the environment enough attention.

We've all heard of the roads and other development projects in tropical regions, assisted by the World Bank, that have encouraged the uprooting of rain forests without regard for conservation or sustained use of this precious land. Because of the rain forest's delicate ecology, the result has too often been erosion, despoilment and ultimately disappointment, even for the once hopeful developers of this land.

Another example of environmental damage exists in the African nation of Botswana—a superb country with an outstanding record of political stability and democratic tradition. I couldn't help but admire the magnificent wildlife on that nation's splendid savanna. At the same time, however, I also couldn't help but notice the pressure on parts of that savanna from overgrazing by livestock.

As U.S. Treasury Secretary a few years later, I happened to see a report on a World Bank loan to support grasslands development in Botswana. I made sure that, in its role as a major contributor to the bank, the U.S. Government urged the bank to make concern for environmental management a central part of lending criteria for sub-Saharan Africa. Earlier this year, during the visit to Washington of Botswana's vice president, we discussed the importance of that issue. And the bank is, in fact, incorporating these concerns into its development lending.

What the Reagan Administration wants the World Bank and the other development banks to do is make environmental analysis, systematically and routinely, a central part of every loan proposal. We want the bank to draw on the expertise of trained environmental analysts—both from its staff and outside consultants—who know developing countries and can assess just what impacts any new project or policy will have on the ecology of those countries. It should then incorporate that analysis into its lending decisions and assistance from the very beginning of the lending process.

We have found a receptive audience at the development banks when we've made these points among bank officials, among other contributing countries and even among borrowing countries such as Botswana. We had a frank discussion of these issues at the meeting of the World Bank and IMF Development Committee in Washington last spring. And we expect to have a similar discussion and to make further progress on specific proposals at the next World Bank/IMF meeting.

It is my goal that by the end of this process the bank will have adopted specific procedures that make conservation and environment a centerpiece of its development program. All nations, rich and poor alike, can't afford to support development that does not also support the environment any longer.

In that spirit, we at the Treasury Department are looking closely at ideas that some of you here have brought to our attention that would convert some

LDC bank debt to local currency specifically earmarked for use for environmental activities and sound development projects. There is some question as to whether this would require legislation or might be done by interpretation of current rules. We still are working on the complicated technicalities, but I can tell you this: We believe in the concept and are working to produce results.

In our debates about the environment, we need voices of moderation and common sense. Voices like yours, that recognize the importance of preserving our environmental heritage, but that also understand that the importance of continued economic growth and progress are valuable contributions.

We cannot expect to conserve our environment if we preach a policy of limited growth and opportunity. We will not succeed in achieving our conservation goals if we deny to the citizens of the developing world the dream that built our own nation—the dream of economic opportunity and a better life. But I believe we can succeed in preserving that heritage if we make clear that the fulfillment of that dream depends upon conservation. Conservation should not be the enemy of prosperity; it should sustain and enrich our prosperity.

A NEW FRONTIER IN DEVELOPMENT AND THE ENVIRONMENT

Charles Lankester

I shall briefly describe the world economic scene as I see it, international aid flows in particular and how these have an impact on the environment; the distinctive characteristics and responsibilities of the United Nations Development Programme (UNDP); and illustrate how progress has been achieved in tropical forestry and energy and what lessons may be learned from these models.

Although official development aid to the developing countries rose to $37 billion in 1986, this amount represented a sharp decline over 1985 figures, as higher official aid failed to balance the continued net decline in export credits and commercial bank lending. It is noteworthy that agricultural aid, including land-use surveys, irrigation schemes, forestry and wildlife, and extension work, is estimated to constitute 26 percent of this aid, and that agriculture's share has increased by about 4 percent over the last eight years.

But I think the figures show us that we must reconcile ourselves to the fact that significant increases in such aid flows are unlikely to occur in the short term. Readjustments within the package will continue but are unlikely, in my opinion, to be significant. Consider two facts: firstly, that noble American initiative the Marshall Plan, initiated 40 years ago, channelled $3 billion into Europe each year for four years, or 1.3 percent of the gross national product (GNP) of this country. As the Administrator of AID recently noted, a comparable sacrifice today would correspond to a $50 billion program, or $13 billion more than the global aid flow I referred to a moment ago. Secondly, at the present time, only four Scandinavian countries amongst the entire donor community have reached the current UN target of 0.7 percent of their GNP for aid.

Against this background of resource availability, what other challenges have confronted decision makers in the developing countries? The three most commonly referred to are:

• Declining standards of living. In Africa today, for example, we have lower standards of living than we had ten years ago;
• Burgeoning debt-servicing schedules; and,
• Capricious and disastrous markets for the primary commodities exported from these nations.

The facts are well recorded and understood. I would ask you to just reflect that since the Special United Nations Session on Africa some 15 months ago, commodity earnings by these African nations have declined by $19 billion.

Confronted by an inability to service their debts, many countries turned to the IMF for advice. The prescriptions were almost unanimous—to restrain demand rather than to increase supply—and they were unpopular. Certainly they had certain desirable effects. Inefficient factories were closed down, unproductive jobs in the public sector were slashed and food subsidies were reduced. But we have all read of the consequences and the social unrest that these policies caused. These adjustments, then, were achieved at tremendous social cost. Expenditures on health, nutrition, education and housing have all been drastically slashed, just to cite some critical subsectors.

Against this background of draconian cuts, how did the environment fare? With few exceptions, it didn't. And it wasn't just the pure environmental projects, but even the environmental content and safeguards of many projects that went by the board. I well recall the cool efficiency with which environmental projects were withdrawn, postponed and canceled in the late 1970s and early 1980s. And when progress was achieved, it was often through the extraordinary energy, dedication and persuasiveness of the private sector, most notably the NGO community and its work in national parks and the wildlife fields.

Now, fortunately, a shift has occurred. The sharp focus on demand restraint that began in the late 1970s began to blur by 1984, and today it is increased economic growth (sustainable economic growth) that captures our attention.

UNDP believes that, on balance, a renewed emphasis on growth is appropriate, particularly when it is accompanied by a strengthening of basic human services. But we must at all costs avoid a repetition of those examples whereby growth was achieved at the expense of the natural resource base.

Confronted by this situation, the challenge facing the leaders of the developing countries and development agencies is quite daunting, particularly given the magnitude of the environmental degradation that has occurred since the Stockholm Conference under Maurice Strong's leadership in 1972. To what am I referring? You can take your choice. Environmental deterioration and loss of soil fertility have undermined the ability of many developing countries to feed their peoples. Projections indicate that unless trends are reversed by the end of this century, as many as 65 developing countries will be unable to feed their populations. Deforestation has reached 27 million acres a year. Eighteen and a half million square miles are threatened by desertification. And population—we cannot avoid the subject—must be discussed. In July 1987, the five billionth person joined our spaceship earth. Africa's population growth is three times that of its growth in food production. Unless Nigeria can hold its numbers down, its population by the year 2040 will exceed the population of the entire African continent today. By the year 2000, three of five cities with populations of five million or more will be in the developing world—a developing world with ten cities where over 30 million people will have to live.

The situation is bad. It demands our best skills and cooperation. We cannot afford to fail. In this climate of growth management, the imperative needs for sound environmental planning and management of our heritage must receive renewed attention.

Environmental management and sustained economic growth are global problems and global responsibilities. The life of everyone is threatened by deforestation, desertification, the pollution of our oceans and our atmosphere and other injustices. Sustained economic development will only be possible if decisive action is taken today.

Characteristic of many of these environmental problems is that they recognize no frontiers. Think of acid rain, or of dust in the Bahamas that originates from dust storms in Mauritania in western Africa. Think of the scourges of onco, or river blindness, and the problems of international trafficking in wildlife and the global imperative to conserve germ plasm.

Common interests require articulation through international cooperation, and UNDP is a global organization. It is the world's largest grant-assistance agency on a multilateral basis. It is multilateral because we receive voluntary—and I do emphasize voluntary— contributions from as many as 150 countries in the whole range of the development spectrum. We provide assistance through a global network of some 112 field offices to about 130 developing countries. To give you an order of magnitude, our 1986 expenditures were approximately $690 million. And our assistance is not tied to the provision of particular resources to particular countries. The technical assistance that we provide, whether it is experts or consultants, equipment or materials, is drawn from the best sources that we can identify: either from market, mixed or centrally planned economies. Our task is to provide unbiased, objective counsel to governments, to transcend political and economic tensions and the patterns of development. We have no ax to grind. And many governments specifically request our guidance on activities with subregional, regional and global ramification. Thus our involvement in these issues is substantial and it is hardly surprising that an in-house review we undertook two months ago showed that the contents of our portfolio pertaining to the environment has risen from some 10 to 20 percent since 1976 and that expenditures over the same period have tripled.

UNDP has also a special—and critical—aid coordinating responsibility with recipient governments. Experience has shown that separate inputs by a multiplicity of donors usually does not add up to a coherent program. Common sense dictates that we reduce the number of aid missions that: (1) collect data in a different format; (2) have varying procedures and regulations; and (3) which unbearably strain the human resources in ministries of planning, finance and natural resources.

Roundtable discussions between the donors and the recipients and national capacity surveys have become critical coordinating mechanisms and are especially important responsibilities for our organization. Please, then, do not see UNDP as just another source of funds for developing countries. Maintaining dialogue constantly in each country,(providing impartial advice on what may or may not work and why, why failures that have occurred should not be copied, why successes in some other countries should not be copied,) is our special responsibility. Only when our assistance fits into a sound development strategy is it provided.

Two recent initiatives in which UNDP was engaged with other development partners, including NGOs, illustrate important patterns that are emerging in development assistance.

During the late 1970s and early 1980s, the magnitude and impact of tropical deforestation really began to be realized by development planners. But there was no coherent global program and aid flows were actually slipping. It was as if we had given up on the problem. Where were the foresters? They were overburdened and struggling with technical problems and forwarding technical facts to budget committees and ministries of planning and finance. But seldom did their presentations achieve more support. Often the reverse occurred. So an international program, initially conceived in the minds of just three or four people, was conceived.

The impact of deforestation on agricultural trade, health, school attendance, the transportation and energy sectors, employment and the balance of payments was studied and articulated. The social and economic costs of inaction were measured. How many more children had to die because fuelwood was not available to sterilize water or to cook their cereals? How much grain production was foregone in the developing countries because crops and animal residues were being used as fuelwood substitutes? And how many environmental refugees had to be given basic services as they retreated to the cities after deforestation and desertification overtook their own villages? These numbers had an impact. The facts were laid out, key development officials and world leaders were advised, and the press was deliberately engaged as an ally. Political will and interest by donors and recipients gathered momentum. Success stories were collected, analyzed and information shared. Enthusiasm built up. And in this process not only was the top-down approach required with political and financial leaders but also the constituency of the people, the grass roots, had to be and is still being consulted.

Finally, attainable targets were set, consortia formed, coordinating mechanisms established and, not so surprisingly, there emerged a global Tropical Forestry Action Plan. It is a plan that still has many flaws and needs constant correction, but which in just two years has achieved its five-year target of doubling aid to the sector. With better knowledge of what our priorities are and with clear objectives, the entire development community is moving forward on this subject with renewed purpose.

The second example I take is the energy sector, to illustrate how the perceptions of development needs have evolved in the past decade and what the response by the international community has been. Earlier investments in this sector were heavily biased toward large-scale infrastructures, dams with hydro-electric and irrigation objectives. Some of these projects proved uneconomic, however, and they often failed to take into consideration the needs of the local population. All development agencies have a terrible responsibility to make sure that the real economic costs of such schemes are brought home and fully understood by the leaders of the developing countries before these projects are implemented. Typically in the case of dams, I am referring to the necessity for doing watershed management and reforestation upstream.

The energy management assistance program, called ESMAP, was launched in 1983 as a joint program between the World Bank and UNDP. It is directed at assisting the urban and rural poor to meet their energy requirements and to meet them in a manner which minimizes impact on the natural resource base. The focus is on the household and has necessitated combining again the top-down with the bottom-up approach. Other donors, finding a well-coordinated plan that corresponded to national priorities, quickly responded and within just two years became the major source of financing for the program. Already 10 other donors are involved with us in some 60 developing countries with special attention on sub-Sahelian Africa. It is noteworthy that virtually all of the recommendations of the Brundtland Commission which relate to the energy crisis in the developing countries are being systematically addressed by this ESMAP program.

Please note the common characteristics between these efforts:

- problem identification;
- gaining the help of the media to build awareness and political will;

- forming a consortium of donors;
- emphasis on social as well as economic benefits;
- engagement of the private sector, notably the NGO community, and involving women throughout the development process; and,
- how regular coordination and consultation was organized between the donors and the recipients.

Good projects do find adequate financing. The proposed World Conservation Banking Programme would provide a mechanism for any government, government agency, aid agency, multilateral development bank, corporations, foundations, NGOs and private citizens to join together in a communal response to finance and cofinance the necessary environmental projects that others have eloquently talked about and outlined. Pioneering and innovative thinking and consultation have been problems for over two years. Clearly there are very major headaches and problems to be resolved, but in UNDP we think it is time to take this idea out of the closet and have a far broader and more systematic consultation with donors and recipients, and I particularly emphasize participants because many of these countries are blocking the use of foreign currencies earned from development and private enterprise activities within their borders.

I can announce UNDP's intention to join as soon as possible with two or three other organizations, ideally a multilateral financing institution and a strong bilateral aid program, to finance an independent in-depth feasibility study of this proposed World Conservation Banking Programme. Collectively our organizations should risk some resources to determine whether this scheme will fly and if so, how to build and launch it properly. In conducting this study, I believe we must draw on a far wider circle of pragmatists, enlightened leaders and financiers—and please note I separated them out—than has been the case to date. And we should try to have a broader spectrum of support, for this will be absolutely essential before we can go any further with this proposal for a conservation facility. We must reach out beyond the advocates of the scheme so far.

The UNDP is in consultation with probable partners in this exciting investigation and will be very interested in the outcome of further deliberations on this subject.

ECONOMICS AND THE NATURAL ENVIRONMENT

D. Jane Pratt

There is an urgent need to defend earth's natural resources. The hour is late for action on the global environment, but not too late for effective, concerned, consistent measures of conservation.

It is my belief—and it is also the operating policy of the World Bank—that sustainable development and the nurture of human resources depend on a sustaining stock of natural resources. That statement is a truism, not a pietism, but it is only the beginning of wisdom. It establishes a sense of direction, but not a road map for environmental or economic progress. The World Bank is now engaged in charting such a course.

For 41 years the bank has been an international investor, first in the postwar reconstruction of industrialized nations, then in the development of Third World economies and societies. We provide investment financing and technical advice, primarily to governments, and, until a few years ago, primarily for large-scale projects in industry, agriculture, health, education, family planning, housing and, neither last nor least, conservation. The bank's central purpose is also its original one: to promote steady economic growth as the surest means of alleviating poverty in the world.

In 1970 the World Bank became the first multinational institution of its kind to formulate an environmental policy and establish a high-level adviser to assure its implementation. But until very recently the policy largely amounted to a developmental injunction, similar to that of the Hippocratic Oath: Do no harm. We have learned, however, that prevention is not just difficult to ensure, but often inadequate to the goal of resource preservation.

Thus, we have done what large institutions do as a first step toward reform: we have created an environment department. Its mandate is to reach into all phases of the bank's investment and technical operations and to develop a positive program both for reversing environmental degradation and for assuring that nature's wealth is used for sustainable development. In short, its mandate is to make sure that the bank unfailingly implements in practice what it has long embraced in principle and to harness the enormous financial and intellectual capital of our institution in the service of sustainable development.

Such development, as the World Bank's president, Barber Conable, declared, "depends on managing resources, not exhausting them. Economic growth based on any other premise is a costly illusion." That principle is the foundation of a genuinely new and exciting development discipline: the endeavor both to analyze the environmental consequences of economic policy and to harmonize long-term profitability and long-lasting protection. As Conable said, "Environmental action adds a new dimension to the fight against global poverty. It recognizes that sound ecology is good economics. . . ." Where short-term economic progress conflicts with natural resource preservation, and where conservation values are of paramount significance, we must endeavor to ensure that development defers to preservation. This is a monumental challenge where development is, as in much of the Third World, synonymous with simple survival.

The World Bank has long understood that poverty and overpopulation can do more environmental harm than industrial progress. That Malthusian reality is all too evident wherever too many poor farmers use too many poor farming practices. Slash-and-burn cultivation, overgrazing, and overplanting destroy the land and its capacity for renewal. It is not just logging and mining companies, after all, that assault the wilderness areas.

People who live in poverty on the edge of land that is—or should be—protected as wilderness, or reserves for tribal people or national parks can hardly be expected to respect those boundaries if the forbidden ground seems the only firm ground on which they can settle for survival. To protect against such encroachment, it is, of course, a great help to define boundaries. That is why the bank has been so glad to work with the Sierra Club and IUCN's Monitoring Center on initial efforts to digitize and map these sensitive areas. That initiative is a sound starting point.

Effective wilderness protection, however, requires more and more complex, environmentally sensitive development strategies. Among the solutions are intensified agricultural practices, land tenure adjustments, crop-pricing policies, industrial job creation and other actions by governments, local and international institutions to accelerate economic development in buffer zones, to manage the human pressure on the wilderness, and to manage, indeed, human pressures on our global biosphere.

Conservationists must help, not just to write laws and to draw demarcation lines, but to effect reforms in funding and manpower that can improve agriculture and stabilize population levels and thus relieve pressures on wilderness. Bank-supported programs that help reduce poverty by improving agricultural techniques, introducing new skills promoting energy conservation and controlling population growth are therefore not just developmental measures. They are also effective means of environmental protection.

The World Bank deserves the aid of environmental activists in promoting this patient, vital work throughout the developing world. We would be pursuing these antipoverty strategies even if they were not also investments in environmental protection. But in asking that they be recognized for their dual merit, I am not suggesting that the bank's role in defending natural resources ends with its offensive against Third World rural poverty and overpopulation.

Our commitment to sustainable development—to controlled, enduring economic growth—requires not just a sensitivity to limited natural resources but an emphasis on renewable resources and on renewing them. That priority defines the juncture between environmental and developmental concerns.

What sustainable development teaches is that we must treat natural resources as productive capital—not just when they are mined or harvested as commodities on their way to market, but as working stock that is critical to continued production. Conventional economics knows how to measure man-made assets. It can put a value on buildings, equipment, roads, dams and sewers. It can define them as productive capital to be written off through depreciation against the value of production.

Our scale for valuing natural resources has been less precise. For too long, owners tended to look at natural resources in terms of the short-term income generated and to celebrate the way that income rises even as the assets disappear. Environmental consciousness has exploded that method of accounting. It has shown the world that the bottom line of environmental abuse is a hideous deficit between what we use up today and what we need to live well with tomorrow.

Still, that discovery only directs investment away from the worst forms of pollution and environmental degradation. It writes a readable debit column in the ledgers of economic policy makers. But it does not give them the other tool that investors always need, a cost-benefit calculation of the return on sound natural-resource management. It is that economic instrument the World Bank is now working to sharpen and to apply. Some specific examples of this effort to set a realistic value on the environment and on measures to develop and protect it simultaneously follow.

The world's forests are among our most endangered life support systems. Tropical rain forests, as you know, are vanishing at the rate of 11 million hectares a year, and the World Bank, which has put over $1 billion into forestry projects over the last decade, is planning to raise its lending assistance in this area from $138 million in 1987 to $350 million in 1989.

We have never questioned the urgency or the value of such work. Conservationists long ago succeeded in demonstrating the wisdom of renewing woodlands as they were harvested. In 19 industrial forest-plantation projects the World Bank has supported since 1978, the return on capital ranged from 10 to 16 percent. That is a very credible performance, but it turns out that doing good in other forms of forestry does even better.

Social forestry—helping small farmers and producers to grow trees for fruit, for fuel, for soil protection—had its start in initiatives aimed more at rural poverty than environmental neglect. It is paying off, however, in showing the complementarity of the two concerns. The results are in and the payoff is handsome—first in terms of environmental protection, but in financial terms also.

The rates of return on 27 bank-financed social forestry projects between 1978 and 1986 ran twice as high as plantation forestry investments. And that 20 to 30 percent rate of return ran parallel to the performance, between 15 and 21 percent, of five watershed rehabilitation projects in such fragile environments as Nepal and parts of India.

Even in Rwanda, where dense population has severely degraded natural resources, farm-level agriforestry work has given the land more trees now than grew there 25 years ago.

What these examples show—indeed, prove—is that it makes sound financial sense to invest for both humanitarian and environmental profits in bettering the lives of the poorest of the poor.

Agriforestry can increase productivity and income in the countryside and also protect the farming ecosystem, especially soil and water. It is a convincing instance of the potential harmony between sustainable development and sustaining nature. It is not, however, the only marriage the Bank helps make between ecology and economics. The other unions we are working to establish are broader in scope but less immediately obvious in their impact.

The opportunity to promote such compacts arises, ironically, from economic failure rather than perceived environmental danger. More and more in the recent years of global economic stagnation—decline and depression in many Third World countries—the World Bank has been providing support for a process that the euphemism-coiners call by the name of adjustment.

That's a soft word for a hard reality, for a sometimes revolutionary and always painful combination of austerity and reform in social spending, pricing policies, public employment and other macro-economic policies. Heavy debt burdens and institutional inefficiencies have forced nation after nation to change old ways for new, state controls for market realities, mistaken subsidies for the risks and rewards of trade liberalization.

Environmentalists have worried, understandably, that programs of conservation will be among the "old" expenditures sacrificed to the "new" exigencies. But justified as that concern is, it should not blind us to the opportunities to build environmental protection into macro-economic adjustment.

Again, from the perspective of the World Bank, the broadest field for action is also the one most in need: agriculture and the rural destitution of the hundreds of millions who live off the land.

In fostering reforms that aim to better their lives, we believe economic advance can bring ecological savings as well. The body of knowledge and theory on this point, however, is still thin. I hope you, as environmental activists, can help fill in the many empty spaces.

One problem—and one area where some remedies are becoming clear—is the pricing and other incentives that lead farmers to behave as they do.

Fragile soil that does not feed a family with a single crop will inevitably be denied the fallow time that it needs to renew itself. Overvalued currencies that encourage imports will inevitably deny farmers access to their own domestic markets, hence adequate incomes, for the produce of a single planting and harvesting cycle. Spending too much on industrialization will crowd out investments in the basics of rural productivity—from appropriate technology to effective transportation networks. Subsidies for pesticides will encourage their misuse; subsidies for livestock raising will lead to the destruction of precious pasture; subsidies for irrigation can leave good land waterlogged and salt-poisoned.

And the contrary is true. Reformed agricultural-pricing policies can turn behavior around.

Increasingly, in what is called policy-based adjustment lending, and in the counseling that goes with its financial support, the World Bank is in a strong position to help developing nations join environmental and economic reform under a common policy umbrella. Our analysts understand the problems involved. No one fully understands the technical solutions.

Thus, it is here that I would urge environmental activists to turn some of their attention and energy. I hope you will become partners in the economic policy adjustment process. As the advocates of sustainable development look for new ways to protect and renew natural resources, the defenders of earth's ecology should join in that search with a fresh eye on the economics of environmental abuse and protection.

The governments, the organizations and the experts at the World Wilderness Congress have an unparalleled wealth of firsthand knowledge of the practices that threaten nature and endanger mankind. With hands-on, close-up expertise, the World Bank and its members can gain new insights on current and past policies. You have the power to advance conservation by helping to direct change.

I would ask you to look at your experience in a new light, to examine development not just for its attendant evils, but for the opportunities reformed growth policies are opening for redemptive, preservative treatment of natural resources. I would ask you to look at poverty, especially the rural poor and the population pressures they represent, as a danger to the environment every bit as grave as the waste products of the rich, the exploitative practices of the greedy and the indifference of industrial polluters. And I would ask you to regard the World Bank as your ally in a common cause, a common sense of economics and ecology as companion disciplines. Those in conservation have already helped by joining forces with those working inside to prod the bank to a new level of activism. We are grateful for that.

I said earlier that the World Bank provided its help in the past primarily to governments, primarily for large-scale projects. That practice is still what we are best equipped to conduct. But we are learning to appreciate small-scale possibilities as well as giant challenges. And we are relying on the help in the field of the army of non-governmental organizations that work, as we do, to combat poverty and despair. That army encompasses neighborhood associations in the cities of Venezuela and anti-Bwaki leagues fighting malnutrition in the villages of Zaire. It ranges from rural credit unions in Bangladesh to family-planning organizations in Turkey.

You are leaders in that campaign of conscience and consciousness-raising. If we are to overcome the global threats of pollution, deforestation, overpopulation, erosion, desertification and ozone depletion, we must clearly have a global force mobilized in concert for the survival of the planet.

The World Bank is working to be a potent force for sustaining that struggle as it works to sustain development. We all seek the same ends. We can work best by working together.

THE NEED FOR PARTNERSHIP

David Rockefeller

Damages result when people fail to recognize that the future of the human race depends, to a large extent, on a sensible compromise between economic and environmental considerations. Extreme positions at either end of the spectrum are dangerous. There is an urgent need for a majority consensus when it comes to matters affecting human survival.

I see two extreme positions that could threaten the future of our world. The first extreme is the one taken by those who helter-skelter pollute our environment and destroy the globe's seed corn, as it were, for our children and grandchildren. The second extreme that gives me concern is that of those who would place all environmental concerns before the economic well-being of the people living on this planet.

In the past, the two fundamental drives behind these extremes—namely, economic growth and environmental protection—have been viewed by many as basically antithetical.

Happily, however, there increasingly seems to be some meeting of the minds—some understanding that man and nature can, and indeed must, work together creatively.

One of the more rewarding experiences for me in preparing for this paper was reading the report of the World Commission on Environment and Development. The very fact that the environment and development are placed together is, in itself, encouraging. The emphasis in the report on "sustainable development" is especially encouraging if we are to escape the tyrannies which are the product of extremes and absolutes.

The first extreme I refer to—that of the ravagers of our natural resources— is in part rooted in the belief of some single-minded businessmen that it is acceptable to sacrifice the environment of the future for present profit. Alas, there have been too many examples of people in the industrialized world who, out of greed, ignore pollution standards, destroy the landscape, poison the waters and create such conditions as acid rain. There is no question but that blind pursuit of short-term economic gain can and has enacted its own form of tyranny on the rest of humankind.

To place all of the blame for unacceptable environmental behavior on industrialization or large corporations, however, is clearly grossly inaccurate. Much of the devastation of the world's environment, especially in today's world, is due to individuals who are without power and who are trapped in grinding poverty. Deforestation, for instance, is often more the product of actions taken out of desperation by the poor rather than through irresponsible exploitation by industrial giants. Some 70 percent of the world's rapidly growing population currently relies on wood for energy to cook and heat. The consequences of this fact are little short of disastrous.

A similar problem arises from overgrazing which leads, in arid areas such as the Sahel of Africa, to desertification. But for the individual farmer, over-grazing may be his only way to stave off immediate starvation. By the same token, it should not be surprising that for people in desperation it is more rational to slaughter rare wild animals for food or for sale to the affluent than it is to preserve these animals for their biological role in the world and for the enjoyment of future generations. A combination of ignorance and the desperate will to survive is at the root of a large part of the devastation of our natural resources which is taking place today.

Ecological damage, whether it is caused by the less affluent or the more affluent, has a cumulative effect which is far broader than the area of primary impact. Deforestation, for instance, not only causes floods and droughts in the nations where it takes place, it can also produce a change in the globe's climate and can further reduce the ability of the atmosphere to absorb the carbon dioxide created in increasing quantities by industry.

It is important to recognize, however, that in most cases there is a basic difference between factors contributing to ecological damage in the industrialized world as compared to the developing world. The industrialized nations have enough wealth and technological expertise to have options, even if some of these entail slower short-term growth rates, to preserve resources for the future. On the other hand, for many people living in developing nations located especially in Africa, Latin America and Asia, these options do not presently exist. People are simply too poor and their needs too pressing to allow them to take the necessary steps to preserve the environment on which they depend. Without prompt assistance from the outside, concern for the environment may literally be a luxury they cannot afford. For this reason the industrialized nations have a compelling obligation to help their less well off neighbors, in their own self-interest as well as for humanitarian reasons.

The fact that it is poverty which drives so many to ravage the land brings me to the second extreme: the attitude of those who would place ecology before humanity.

Life on this planet is an evolving ecosystem. Future generations of humans may well view us with as much curiosity as we now view our more remote ancestors. Resisting change, whether man-induced or otherwise, is as futile as it can be harmful. Perhaps what we can do is guide change in a manner which, as much as possible, will better protect the long-run interests of humankind.

Yet there are some who would fight even the smallest disruption of the environment. They seem to forget that the history of the world has always been one of evolution and that adaptability is one of the wonders of nature.

It is true that the potential forces of potential man-generated destruction are now greater than ever. But more and more people are recognizing and taking into account the importance of the earth's biological diversity to future important breakthroughs in the biological sciences which will support sustainable growth. Those solely concerned with preservation for preservation's sake, however, run the risk of going to extremes which lose sight of the urgent economic good of people at large. And, once people's economic welfare is adversely impacted, their concern for their environment can only decrease. The situation is obviously self-defeating if a too-narrow focus on ecology creates economic deprivation which in turn forces people to generate yet more environmental damage.

Getting past these opposing extremes—of greed or necessity on the one hand, and of dogmatic ecological and environmental purity on the other—may require more definitive steps along the lines of those suggested in the recent World Commission's Report which calls for the real integration of environmental concerns and economic needs.

Most people today recognize that the two must be viewed as equal partners, but this has not always been so. Too often in the past, environmentalists have pursued causes they believed in passionately with a certain arrogance and self-righteousness which many times actually hurt their cause. In some cases, they became spoilers—adept at stopping economic progress, but offering few constructive alternatives and basing their position on lopsided reasoning.

By the same token, many major economic players have tended to view environmentalists as wooly-headed tree-huggers. Those who focus solely on economic growth tend to scoff at what they see as the excesses of the environmental movement. At the same time they often ignore legitimate early warning signs of basic threats to future survival, for they themselves may be partly responsible.

Neither of these extreme positions is constructive and both ignore the deep interrelationship between our economic and environmental well-being. But fortunately, I believe we are seeing progress on both sides.

The question is, what more can be done to promote cooperation between those concerned with protecting the environment and those dedicated to promoting economic growth? I have three suggestions:

First, I suggest that environmental concerns be made integral—not add-on—priorities wherever economic decisions are made. It is encouraging that the World Bank, which had in the past been lax in this regard, now is taking environmental issues more seriously. But a systematic approach to this problem needs to be taken by all governments and all economic institutions in both the public and private sectors. There have been a number of interesting and constructive proposals along these lines, such as debt-equity swaps and the creation of a World Conservation Bank. I applaud these, but I also believe that the most far-reaching hope for significant progress is through concerted action by all our major institutions, economic and political.

Second, I believe that we should consider incorporating economic impact statements as an integral part of environmental impact statements. I am not suggesting more bureaucracy, but I am concerned that at present special interest groups are able to use environmental impact statements with great effectiveness to stop projects they do not like, but which have substantial economic and social importance. If economic considerations were examined concurrently with environmental impact, a more balanced result would be likely to emerge.

Third, and finally, I believe that we should look at new growth strategies for the developing nations which will help to alleviate the poverty which now makes the environment a second-class citizen.

Just last year, I was involved in an extensive study called "Toward Renewed Economic Growth in Latin America," which was jointly carried out by El Colegio de Mexico, the Fundacao Getalio Vargas and the Institute for International Economics. While the emphasis was on Latin America, I believe that many of the proposals that emerged from this study are valid more broadly.

Simply stated, this strategy has four parts—three for developing nations, and one for the developed world. The parts for the developing nations call for a more outward orientation with an emphasis on exports rather than import substitution. In addition, it calls for new efforts to induce savings and investment, and for a substantial reduction of the role of the state both in directing economic affairs and in the production of goods and services.

An underlying theme of the study is the promotion of greater entrepreneurship in the private sector and a stronger sense of ownership by people involved in the production process. It seems to me that, in addition to generating more economic growth, this sense of ownership will also foster more reliable protection of the environment.

If people do not feel a personal stake in their grazing land or farmland or forests or waters, it is doubtful that they will do much to protect them. Without a sense of ownership there is no incentive to preserve. Indeed, the opposite may be true. The natural tendency is just to leave matters to the state or to exploit resources as much as possible before someone else does.

On the other hand, a feeling of ownership, combined with appropriate technology and better education, can do miracles in terms of making people care about preserving their natural resources at the same time that they enjoy better standards of living. A farmer who is passing his land on to his children will think carefully before destroying it. Given greater knowledge and meaningful options, it is possible for more and more people to play constructive roles as guardians of global resources.

The developing world cannot, by itself, overcome economic stagnation and the resulting ecological myopia. The developed nations have a major role to play in providing markets as well as technical and financial assistance. In addition, there is a need for a combination of renewed economic growth, trade liberalization, cuts in budget deficits and real interest rates. The Third World needs substantial new funds from private sources and international agencies such as the World Bank.

These proposed strategies will be difficult for both the developing and the developed worlds to accept. Nevertheless, we must make every effort to adopt them, for I fear that the alternatives can only mean continued economic deterioration with consequent destruction of the environment.

We come now to a final point I would like to make. It is a point which was also stressed in the report of the World Commission on Environment and Development. This is that the environment should be everyone's concern and not just the province of a few, isolated specialists.

CONSERVATION AND SUSTAINABLE DEVELOPMENT: THE ROLE OF U.S. ASSISTANCE

Nyle C. Brady

The growing number of international and national meetings concerned with conservation issues attests to the global concerns for the protection of the earth's natural resources. I share this concern—personally as a scientist and officially as Senior Assistant for Science and Technology of the U.S. Agency for International Development (AID).

In terms of overall concepts and perceptions, there is a growing international consensus that:

—Environmental problems have no national boundaries;

—Human health depends on world environmental health;

—Environmental protection and economic development need not be in opposition, but can be mutually supportive;

—We must be concerned about our children's futures; and,

—If we are to win the conservation war, we must win the war on poverty.

Perhaps I can give another perspective to these concerns and the linkages between conservation and development, as an AID official concerned with science and technology; and, in addition, discuss the role my agency has played, and likely will play in the future, in the area of environment and natural resources.

First, it is important to understand the external political, social and intellectual context in which AID operates. As a scientist and administrator, new to government bureaucracy, I have been singularly impressed by the degree to which a bilateral donor such as AID must respond to influences external to the agency. The primary influence, of course, is and should be from the developing countries that we are supposed to help. As one of the most decentralized donor organizations, most of our program decisions are made by our 60-country missions in consultation with developing country counterparts.

Another external influence is the legislative branch and other executive agencies of the U.S. government. We are bound by bills passed by the Congress, which reflect differences of opinion among the branches that are ironed out by compromise during the legislative process.

The most complex of all these outside influences are the many non-governmental constituencies which support foreign assistance, each with very specific interests and ideas. They include the university community, the private voluntary organizations, commercial and business interests and non-governmental environmental and family-planning groups.

Their interest and support are critical but their views and interests can be conflicting in many areas such as agriculture, health and family planning. Common to them all, however, is the desire that their individual concerns receive equal treatment. Arriving at a fair balance among these important external interests can be a delicate and difficult task.

Second, it is useful to remember the historical context of U.S. foreign development assistance. The first "big project" phase (1949 to 1972) was patterned after the Marshall Plan for European recovery after World War II.

The emphasis was on short-term activities to support infrastructure construction and industry. Little or no attention was given to human resource development or institution problems. Environmental matters were largely ignored. The focus of the project was on rapid assessment of development needs, quick action on projected solutions and funding, withdrawal where appropriate, then movement on to the next project.

This approach was mutually agreed upon by the donor and recipient countries since the accepted perception of the road to success was to mimic the U.S. and other more developed countries. The underlying concept was that foreign aid should be both temporary and short term.

Though there were some notable successes, in most cases the results were, unfortunately, disappointing, primarily because the benefits of the investments did not reach the poor people who were most in need.

Since recognizing that support for industrial development as the sole engine to drive social and economic development was inappropriate, the next phase

(1973 to present) has been to focus development assistance on those who need it most—low-income citizens. Emphasis has been placed on agricultural improvement, rural development, better health and education and family planning. While the results have not been uniform, very significant progress has been made:

—The "green revolution" prevented the massive starvation predicted in the 1960s by the experts, notably in Asia and Latin America;

—Life expectancy has increased dramatically and infant and child mortality decreased, although it is still disgracefully high; and,

—The rate of population increase has been slowed significantly in some countries.

Unfortunately, environmental concerns and natural resource management were not given high priority.

The third phase, which is only now beginning, is emphasizing sustainable development as a primary goal. This does not require abandoning the fundamental focus on the needs of the people and the need for economic development. It does add a complementary concept that whatever we support must be sustainable over time by our developing country partners. It means that along with meeting the immediate human needs for food, fiber, health, energy and income, the equally important needs, particularly for children, of environmental quality, biological diversity and natural resource conservation must be attended to.

This new phase has been heavily influenced, as it should be, by private voluntary organizations. It has only begun and will likely last a long time.

AID has made significant progress relative to this third phase. In 1976, when the agency's environmental policy was adopted, it had three major objectives:

—To ensure the environmental soundness of all the projects we support;

—To help the developing countries with whom we work to build their institutional and scientific capacity to identify and solve their environmental and natural resource problems; and,

—To promote environmentally sound development by other donors.

To implement that policy, we conduct environmental assessments of projects that have the potential for negative impacts on the environment in our cooperating countries. We created a new Office of Forestry, Environment and Natural Resources and expanded our technical staff in these fields both in Washington and in our overseas missions. More importantly, we provide loan and grant funds to support programs that address environmental and natural resource management needs as identified by our host countries. These range from water-quality improvements to forest management and conservation. Our expenditure in this area in fiscal year 1987 was about $155 million.

We continue to refine our approaches to emerging international issues such as those on the agenda of this meeting. AID's concerns for conservation of biological resources led to our support for a U.S. Strategy Conference on Biological Diversity in 1981 in cooperation with the State Department, other U.S. federal agencies and the scientific community. One of the recommendations of that conference—the establishment of an Interagency Task Force on Biological Diversity—was translated by the U.S. Congress into an amendment to the Foreign Assistance Act of 1983. The amendment called for AID to take the lead in preparing a U.S. Strategy for Conservation of Biological Diversity in Developing Countries. Following the preparation of the strategy, Congress passed new legislation in 1986 setting aside approximately $2.5 million of the fiscal year 1987 AID budget for specific conservation activities.

Some of the specific actions under way include:

1. Identification of priority countries, ecosystems and programs in each of the three geographic regions in which AID works.

2. Investment in improving the present methods of economic analysis that better measure the real costs of natural resources depletion and the economic benefits of maintaining ecosystems processes and conserving wildlands.

3. Expansion of research efforts to help us better understand and maintain biological diversity. Biological and physical science studies will be complemented by social science research to reveal and modify how human activity impacts on biological resources and their loss.

4. Intensified efforts to develop alternatives to unsustainable agricultural practices, such as slash-and-burn agriculture, and to incorporate the use of multipurpose tree species in all agricultural projects to reduce pressure on natural habitats.

5. Use of our experience to encourage other public and private donor organizations to invest in conservation. To enhance collaboration in this area we helped initiate and are providing support for a Consultative Group on Biological Diversity. In addition to AID, the initial members of this group are a number of the major U.S. private foundations that support work in both conservation and development.

We have also recently redefined the agency's approach to agriculture and rural development, incorporating three equally important goals:

—Increasing the incomes of the poor majority;

—Increasing the availability and consumption of food; and,

—Conserving the natural resource base.

We are working with groups outside the agency to see how this new focus can be carried out. We will need help from these and many others as we move forward in implementation.

EXAMPLES OF PROGRESS

There are some good examples that combine these concerns for improved incomes, food consumption and conservation of natural resources. One example is the Central Selva Resource Management Project begun in 1982 in the Palcazu Valley of the high jungle in Peru. The project is jointly funded by AID and the government of Peru at a total of $30 million over six years. Its purpose is to test a methodology to promote sustained productivity in the Palcazu Valley and to institutionalize capability within the country to plan and implement integrated regional development. Covenants included in the project agreement required that the government of Peru designate a national park and a protected forest area in the watershed, and assign technical staff to the area. The project design was derived from an environmental and social assessment that analyzed land-use capability.

The assessment concluded that production forestry held the greatest potential for development, that previous plans for large resettlement of people to increase food production were not feasible and that major attention should be given to managing the area for existing inhabitants, many of whom were native peoples.

The project's goal is to develop sustainable production in the high jungle with systems less destructive than the traditional "exploit-and-move-on" methods. Major activities include agricultural development and integrated agro-silvi-pastoral livestock management, health and environmental sanitation, roads, communications, and two of particular interest: natural forest management for sustained yield and the establishment of protected areas.

The forest management plan is testing rotational, narrow clear-cuts based on new scientific knowledge about how plants recolonize cleared areas and the regeneration requirements of tropical forest canopy tree species. This technique will hopefully permit natural forest regeneration over 30-year cycles, and generate an adequate annual family income from 80-hectare holdings.

The park and forest reserve areas were selected because protection of upper watersheds helps maintain the economic returns from downstream production forestry and agriculture. They also provide a refuge for the unique flora and fauna of the area.

We hope that the Central Selva Project will demonstrate an ecologically sound and sustainable production methodology that, with adjustments, will apply to other high jungle areas in the Amazon as they are opened for development. However, it also raises the issue of what is the appropriate duration of projects that deal with environmental degradation and renewable natural resources.

The six-year time frame already appears too brief given the severity of the problems, the time required before returns on investments may be realized and the need to test new and sometimes risky technologies. Ten to twenty-year commitments may be necessary, requiring that governments and lending agencies rethink existing policies and approaches.

AID is now designing projects with longer time frames, which is a significant breakthrough and, in fact, is negotiating an extension of the Central Selva Project. Another example is a ten-year natural resources project for Panama which has four components: watershed management, natural forest management, private industrial plantations and farm woodlots. The project rationale is based on the need to protect the economic values of existing agriculture and commercial investments, including the Panama Canal, to maintain electricity and water supply to major urban areas, to reduce dependence on wood imports and to enhance employment.

FUTURE CONCERNS

I strongly believe that economic development and concern for environmental and natural resources provide the twin engines for sustainable improvements in the low-income countries of the world.

There is a growing recognition in developing and donor nations alike that economic development and the maintenance of environmental quality and biological diversity are not only compatible but can be mutually supportive. It is no longer viable to think in terms of economic development versus environmental quality. The two must work hand in hand for the betterment of human life around the world.

While governments must continue to be major players in sustainable development activities, they must have help from non-governmental organizations (NGOs) and private enterprise. NGOs from both the Third World and donor nations must help in conceptualizing what is needed and in planning its implementation. Private efforts will be the backbone of sustainable development implementation. Countries with successful economic growth have done so under the leadership and initiative of individuals and private enterprise. The second wave of countries accelerating their development has provided greater opportunity for individual effort. Their example could be followed.

While more financial resources are essential, another element must be considered. It is time for those concerned with the environment and natural resources to do a better job of coordination than has been evident in the past. This includes coordination among donors and coordination by the environmental community. The international agricultural research effort could be used as a model. It provides coordination without homogenization.

TOWARD SUSTAINABLE GROWTH: A NEW APPROACH TO WORLD ENVIRONMENTAL PROTECTION

William D. Ruckleshaus

If I had to sum up the recently released report of the World Commission on Environment and Development in a single phrase, it would be this:

That the survival of this planet as a decent home for all who share it depends on us making profound changes in the way we do business.

I have chosen the word business deliberately because few things affect the environment more directly than the way we extract material from nature, add value to it by industrial processes and bring it to market. In America we refer to these processes as "doing business."

Since what I have to say derives largely from the World Commission Report and from my personal experiences as a member of that commission, let me begin by setting out why I believe its findings demand the closest attention from the world's economic and political leaders, whatever their nation's stage of development or their economic or political system.

First, the World Commission has made a clear finding that for most of the developing world, mindless continuation of current practices will lead to descending spiral environmental degradation, increased poverty, desperate remedies inflicting further destruction of irreplaceable environmental assets, political disorder and even social chaos. The statistics on what conventional "development" has wrought in terms of desertification, soil erosion, impoverishment of rural people and the loss of tropical forests are by now depressingly familiar.

Second, the continued prosperity of the developed world is dependent on the accelerated prosperity of the developing nations in an environmentally responsible manner. The developed world is increasingly dependent on the developing countries for markets, and this dependency will increase. Even now, the developing nations represent a larger market for U.S. goods and services than all the developed nations combined, with the exception of Canada. Such markets will vanish if the developing economies do not resume their expansion. Most cannot resume if the present environmental warnings are ignored.

Think of this: We in America have always viewed environmental degradation as an unwanted side effect of industrialization. Today, in the developing world, just the opposite is true. Environmental degradation equals absence of development.

Third, it follows from this that economic development and environmental protection are complementary rather than opposing goals. They are two sides of the same coin. This, I believe, is the central—and jarring—finding of the World Commission's report. Nations that remain poor will not protect their environment; nations that do not protect their environment will either remain poor or gain poverty.

Finally, the World Commission proposes sustainable development as a new model for economic growth. Sustainable development means increasing prosperity without the destruction of the environment from which all prosperity ultimately derives. Twenty years ago, when the roots of the present environmental movement were being formed, such an idea would not have been welcomed or understood. Environmental protection was seen by most business and developmental interests as an overblown stumbling block. Most environmental interests saw development as the cause of environmental degradation. Many preached that the world economy had reached its limit and that redistributive policies leading to a static, universal human leavening were the only moral choice.

The commission saw both these views now as shortsighted. Our view was that environmental protection, far from hindering economic progress, is its irreplaceable partner; it is growth, not poverty, that will save the environment.

It is for the economic powers of the world to lead the way in the creation of this growth. Success in fighting environmental degradation depends on reinvigoration of the world economy, a task that lies largely within the power of the developed nations, their firms, their governments, their financial and human resources and the multilateral lending institutions they fund and control.

The developed nations have a special responsibility for another reason. Perhaps the greatest luxury of a certain level of prosperity is the freedom to plan beyond the immediate future. We can see, if we will, that unless the world economy moves in the direction of sustainable development, all nations will eventually be paupers, living in a tumbledown shack of a planet.

In recent times, the poorer nations have not had that luxury. At a certain level of desperation, tomorrow is swallowed up by the mouth of today. If you are worrying constantly about what your child will eat, it is impossible to be much concerned about what your grandchild will breathe. So we see nations beginning to act like starving people, eating their seed corn, boiling it on the fires of the last tree. The developed nations have too often contributed to such situations, without any excuse for doing so. Ravaging the environment in exchange for marginal increases in the bottom line was never an ethical choice: we now see it is stupid as well, when considered in anything but the shortest possible view.

Let me make two final points about the World Commission findings. The first is that it is not a prediction of doom. It is the most hopeful major environmental document to be published in the past twenty years. The trends which the commission notes are a warning but, as René Dubois has said, they are not our inevitable destiny. There is not much time to change, but there is time.

The other point concerns the practicality of instituting economic changes on the scale required to make sustainable development a reality. We should understand that these changes, while possible through execution, are by no means painless. Economic policy and strategies for promoting growth in both the developed and developing nations are products of power balances among various interests. Some of the interests adversely affected will surely have their oxen gored by the changes recommended by the World Commission and will resist them.

We dare not be put off by such resistance. The world requires an economic order that will realistically promise sustainable development and hence a livable future. Indeed, I detect hopeful signs that significant changes are already under way. I would like to touch on some of these in the context of the recommendations of the World Commission report.

First, there have been significant changes in the attitudes of many corporate leaders in the developed world toward environmental concerns. In the United States over the past 15 years, Americans have generally accepted that environmental protection is a necessary cost of doing business. Transnational corporations are a major influence on the environment throughout the developing world, and a major source of both pollution and the diffusion of environmentally sound technologies. The proportion of money flowing into developing countries from private sources is much greater than the total of official development aid. Recognizing the importance of this investment, several major corporations from a number of developed countries have formed the fledgling International Environmental Bureau to help developing countries plan growth in an environmentally sound fashion. The device of swapping debt for the commitment to protect vital natural areas, pioneered by Citicorp and Bolivia, is a more dramatic example of this new concern.

These are important first steps, but much more needs to be done. Increasing cooperation between government and industry is essential if we are going to generate real strategies for sustainable development. This can be accomplished directly by the establishment of joint advisory councils in individual nations, or indirectly through the use of regional or non-governmental organizations.

Out of such cooperation should come environmental goals, regulations, incentives and codes of private sector behavior that are workable, international and consistent. Nor should industry remain a merely passive compiler. There is much it can do affirmatively, even within the constraints of completion. Hopeful examples of this are the formation in the United States of Clean Sites Incorporated, an industry-funded organization devoted to cleaning hazardous waste sites, and the Health Effects Institute, which receives support from both government and the motor vehicle industry, and which functions as an authoritative source of information on the health impact of auto emissions.

Extending this concept to sustainable development, the World Commission recommends:

• That all industrial enterprises work to establish company- and industry-wide policies governing resource and environmental management, including man-

agement and worker training to incorporate cleaner technologies and environmental planning into work patterns;
• That industries using hazardous materials ensure that information on the risks involved be conveyed, not only to government agencies in the host nations, but also to the people subject to such risks;
• That plants be operated according to the highest standards of safety; and,
• That transnational firms institute environmental and safety audits of their operations in host countries and measure the findings not against the prevailing local standards, but against those in effect in developed nations.

These and similar measures will help to move transnational firms into a position of environmental leadership commensurate with their enormous technical skills and economic strength.

Of course, international agencies also have a major role in the effort toward sustainable development. They have come to realize that in the past, their development aid has often encouraged quick yields of exportable commodities at a terrible cost in environmental degradation and has resulted in the actual impoverishment of large numbers of people—in short, unsustainable development. This is changing, as evidenced by new policy emphasis at the World Bank.

Recently we have seen this reformed policy in action in relation to international funding of roads and railroads in the Brazilian Amazon. The Inter-American Bank has threatened cancellation of this funding because the roads are leading to wholesale destruction of rain forests for cattle ranching and the production of pig iron, using charcoal derived from the forest. This situation is worth mentioning because it is highly symbolic. There is something seriously flawed with an international development assistance program that encourages the destruction of irreplaceable tropical forest to produce a commodity pig iron of which the world already possesses a vast and growing overcapacity.

Beyond this, the World Commission report recommends that a larger proportion of total development assistance go to investments needed to enhance the environment, such as reforestation, fuelwood production, soil conservation, rehabilitation of irrigation projects, agroforestry and small-scale agriculture. Sustainability considerations must be diffused throughout the lending community, starting with the World Bank and the International Monetary Fund, particularly in regard to commodity assistance and other policy-oriented lending. In the past, such lending has served too often to reduce, rather than enhance, the possibilities for sustainable development.

The mandates of international trade organizations, principally the General Agreement on Tariffs and Trade and the United Nations Conference on Trade and Development, should be modified to reflect concern for the impacts of trading patterns on the environment.

Other international institutions should move to recast their research and planning activities in order to strengthen the information base that will make development sustainable. A recent example of this is the Tropical Forestry

Action Plan produced by a cooperative effort of the Food and Agriculture Organization, the World Bank, the World Resources Institute and the UN Development Programme. The plan offers the opportunity for ending the current state of alarm over the destruction of these forests. Its implementation would lead to restored productivity, sustainable use of forest resources, improved food security through better land use, increased supplies of the fuelwood upon which fully half the world's population depends, increased income from locally manufactured products and conservation of endangered species and natural ecosystems. The plan's cost of $5 billion over five years is large in relation to what has been spent on such projects in the past, but it is tiny when compared to what has been spent in recent years on environmentally degrading projects in tropical forest regions.

But perhaps the most important role in creating the conditions for sustainable development will be played by governments, both in the developed and the developing world. Here is where I fear the most difficult problems will lie. History shows how unusual it is for those in charge of governments to take actions that will have effect only over the long term, when they themselves are out of office. It is extremely unusual when the immediate beneficiaries of such actions are people in other lands. It is virtually unheard of when such actions have short-term negative effects on domestic political interests. This will always be true so long as governments are run by human beings.

There is reason to hope that even governments can learn from experience. At the famous Stockholm conference on the environment in 1972, invited delegates of 29 sub-Saharan nations stood and roundly denounced environmentalism as a plot to check development in what we then called the Third World. The dreadful results of 15 years of development projects that have often ignored environmental realities have in many nations had a pronounced educational effect. Recently, Julius Nyerere, the founding president of Tanzania and still one of the most influential of black African leaders, stated, "Environmental concerns and development have to be linked if the latter is to be real and permanent." That would have been heresy at the Stockholm luncheon.

Examples of what happens when there is no such linkage are all too common. Perhaps the most striking is what happened in Costa Rica. I do not mean to pick on Costa Rica; I could have used any number of examples, including many right here at home. I choose it because this nation had and retains so many advantages that so many other developing nations still lack: stable, democratic form of government, enlightened social legislation, a modern infrastructure and a bountiful land and climate. During the 1970s Costa Rica, in common with other Latin American countries, borrowed heavily in international markets. For a variety of reasons these loans did not suffice to establish a viable industrial sector, and so pressure was increased on export agriculture as the only way to earn sufficient foreign exchange to service the loans. Now the nation entered what the World Resources Institute has called "dual debt," the most egregious example of which is in cattle ranching. Large producers of export commodities were subsidized by cheap audit and guaranteed prices. This encouraged them to borrow again, this time against the land itself, clearing forests and bringing marginal land into production. This additional short-term production increase led to yet more borrowing. But the poorer soils supported fewer cattle as the years and the cycle went on, until now, although beef production represents only 6 to 8 percent of Gross Domestic Product, cattle ranching soaks up one-third of all agricultural credit, cattle occupy half the agricultural land, soil erosion has greatly increased, water resources have been wasted, the forestry industry has been decimated and large numbers of people have been driven from the land into the cities and into poverty and unemployment. Costa Rica now has the highest per capita debt in Latin America and is losing forests at the fastest rate in the hemisphere. As I said, my point is not to single out Costa Rica.

If there is a moral to this sad story, it is this: In planning any economic or development policy, developing nations must make sustainability the primary consideration. It can't be secondary, or ancillary, or "nice to have," or something for an understaffed environmental agency to worry about at a later date. If sustainability is not primary, then any natural, political or structural advantage the nation has will be nullified, sooner or later.

How each nation makes the transition to sustainable development will vary with its economic and political institutions and its culture. In the United States, we have created an elaborate and expensive legalistic system based on complex environmental reviews and command and control regulation. This is not necessarily the correct model for the developing world; in fact, I would tend to doubt it, on the basis of my own experience in trying to get it to work properly. Japan has done wonders with its air quality using a quite different system. The point is that developing nations must strive to avoid the development errors that now cost the developed nations tens of billions of dollars each year to fix. If they can afford development, they can afford sustainable development. As we have learned, environmental protection after the fact is too damned expensive.

The national governments of the developed world also have a responsibility here. Resolution of the debt crisis and a resumption of global growth is essential: national programs to help this happen are not in any sense charitable, but rather hard-headed investment in our common future.

Beyond this, national economic policies must be adjusted to encourage sustainable development in the developing world. As I noted earlier, this will cause short-term dislocations in some sectors of some national economies, and governments must prepare to respond to these.

Continued subsidies to agricultural commodities are a major example. Agricultural policies built on shortsighted political responses are becoming a critical economic and environmental problem throughout the developed world. Not only do they divert resources from more productive ends, like investment in sustainable development, but the resultant surpluses depress farming enterprise throughout the developing world. This crisis is now high on the political agendas of the United States, the European community and Japan. It remains to be seen whether these nations will marshall the leadership and wisdom to reform agricultural policy in the face of seductive short-term political temptation.

Protectionism and restrictions on the flow of capital are problems of the same type. The developing world cannot grow in the way it needs to grow, absent from the free flow of capital. Yet trade barriers are rising in the developed world, largely in response to the development success enjoyed by a small group of nations, mostly in east Asia. Should these barriers hold or continue to rise, there is little hope for the kind of development required to preserve and restore the global environment. History shows again and again that such policies impoverish the protecting nations along with those they would protect us against. Our response to global economic interdependence must not be to erect barriers but to accept the challenge that interdependence offers us and lead the world toward an environmentally sound prosperity.

Developed world governments are often moved to action by the efforts of non-governmental organizations. The environmental organizations in the developed nations have, I think, an important role to play. They must become more international and developmental in outlook, so that they can place their ethical force and energy behind the ideas proposed in the world where every day 25,000 people die from easily preventable waterborne diseases. And yet we continue to argue in America about even smaller increments of pollution abatement with diminishing health benefits. This is like putting another coat of white paint on your house while your neighbor's house goes up in flames. None of the environmental values we cherish in the developed world will long survive if sustainable development does not become a reality.

A word should be said here about the notion of pollution havens, since it involves governmental policies in both developed and developing countries. By one estimate in 1980, the industries of developing countries exporting to OECD members would have incurred direct and indirect pollution control costs of over $14 billion had they been required to meet the pollution control standards then prevailing in the United States. In one sense, the developing nations were extracting a subsidy from the environment in order to increase competitiveness.

This is a delicate issue. The developing countries may claim that they cannot yet afford the higher environmental standards, or that our standards are unnecessarily strict. It is probably inappropriate for the developed nations to demand that developing nations simply follow their environmental lead. Yet when the environmental subsidy comes not out of a particular area within national borders nor out of the health of the citizens of one country, but affects the global commons, then it must become the concern of all nations. Working out how the various national policies, developed and developing, affect the common interest is a task we have barely started. Both developed and developing nations must work harder on this issue if the destructive experience of the now developed world is not to be repeated in every corner of the globe, with possibly irreversible effects on the world environment.

Sustainable development is a difficult lesson. How difficult may be seen in the problems we have had in applying one of its minor corollaries, the concept of sustainable yield in the fisheries industry. Across the world, once productive fisheries have been destroyed and fisherman have themselves gone under because of failure to grasp the simple lesson that you can't take fish year in and year out faster than they can reproduce themselves.

Will sustainable development require a miracle, then? Perhaps, but we have seen miracles enough in our time. Millions of people now alive recall Hamburg as a field of stones and Tokyo as an ash pit. India now not only feeds its millions, but exports food and will survive the current monsoon failure without the mass starvation such events have occasioned so often in recorded history. Much of the developed world recognized the warnings of Stockholm and acted on them, and the economic disaster many predicted did not occur.

Enormous changes are afoot, and we must develop economic and political systems capable of coping with them, including especially the ability to succor those injured by the changes incident to a move toward sustainable development. The ecological and human consequences of not doing so are, I believe, intolerable.

And there is another consequence, yet more grim. I have not mentioned peace and security, although that is an important focus of the World Commission report. In the past 20 years the developing world has endured over a hundred armed conflicts, with a total of 11 million dead. The world now spends a trillion dollars annually on arms and not a fraction of that to avoid one of the chief causes of the use of those dreadful weapons, namely resource depletion and the subsequent uprooting and devastation of vast numbers of people.

Former Secretary of State Dean Rusk has written, "One of the oldest causes of war in the history of the human race, the pressure of people upon resources, is being revived in a world in which thousands of megatons are lying around in the hands of frail human beings." Surely, sustainable development is about relieving that pressure for ourselves, our children and our *Only One Earth*.

Drawing by J. Wolf

ECONOMICS AND INTERNATIONAL AID— A DEVELOPING WORLD PERSPECTIVE

Emil Salim

My country, Indonesia, is in the World Bank category, "lower middle-income economies." We have an average income of U.S. $530 per person, as compared to around $17,000 U.S. dollars per person in the United States. We have a total population of 172 million people and, in spite of the fact that successful family planning reduced the population growth from 2.3 percent in 1970 to 2 percent in 1980, we are still experiencing a rapid growth in population. We expect, by the year 2000, to have a population of 216 million, or an additional 43 million people in the next 13 years. This is equal to the size of Thailand's population today.

What does this mean? It means that we have to change our economic structure from an economy depending on land-based activities toward industrialization and surface industries. As a low-income country with high population growth, the pressure is large on the total forest. Out of 193 million hectares of total land area, we have approximately 143 million hectares of forest. It is planned that out of the 143 million ha, we can maintain 113 million ha as a permanent forest. But for this we need development.

Currently, we are assisted by the World Bank, which is working together with us on a development plan incorporating environmental considerations and sustainable development for the years 1989 through 1994. In this effort we are encountering certain serious problems, such as how to give substance to the concept of sustainable development.

One of the major issues is financing conservation and sustainable development. In brief, the issues that we are confronting involve giving substance to the concept of sustainable development—issues such as how to raise the interest of the aid-giving countries to finance environmental programs which have a low internal rate of return (such as financing buffer-zone development around a tropical forest or buffer zones around the national parks) and a very low rate of return on investment; or programs such as land rehabilitation and reforestation, which have a low foreign exchange component and a high local currency component. The trends in aid-giving countries are that foreign aid is to be used to finance the foreign exchange component, and preferably on a donor country's financial base. You receive aid, but it must be spent in the aid-giving donor country. If that is the case, how do you finance land rehabilitation and reforestation, which have a high local currency component?

Second, there is aid fatigue now. Everybody is tired of aid. One gets fed up with aid. So how to raise the total value of aid-flow if you do not only want sustainable development, but want to have it with environmental considerations? Therefore, larger flow is required at a time when the supply of aid is diminishing. Aid for family planning is declining. Aid to the United Nations Environment Program for 1986-1987 is declining. Total aid to the IDA funds (the International Development Assistance Funds of the World Bank) is not forthcoming. So the total flow is declining while, on the other hand, the need is increasing.

Third, how to ensure an integrated approach to development between the numerous United Nations special agencies such as the FAO for agriculture, UNITO for industries, WHO for health, and so on. While in *Our Common Future* the basic notion of sustainable development is an holistic approach, how can you assure an holistic approach if all the special agencies are working separately? How can UNEP coordinate this?

Finally, how will the environmental dimension be treated in the covenants of aid documents? If you have an aid agreement, you must sign a document. There are conditions. How is the environment to be treated? Will it be another conditionality that if you don't do this and that, then aid will not be forthcoming? If that is the case, it will put an additional burden on the developing countries.

These are, in brief, the major issues that we in Indonesia, and I trust also in the other developing countries, are confronted with when wanting to obtain financing for sustainable development programs.

Drawing by Gaston Phoebus, ca. 1390

CULTURE, MAN
and the
ENVIRONMENT

> *"I heard today that economic growth is a necessity and conservation is a matter of importance. We disagree. Conservation is life and economic growth is a matter of interpretation."*
>
> —Chief Oren Lyons,
> Onondaga Nation
> Spokesman for the
> Traditional Elders Circle

CULTURE AND SOCIETY

THE PERSPECTIVE OF TRADITIONAL AND NATIVE PEOPLE

Oren R. Lyons (Jo Aqguisho)

Neyawenhha Scano—Thank you for being well.

Greetings from the traditional elder circle, the chiefs, clan mothers, faithkeepers, men, women and children, even those on the cradle boards, we send greetings to you.

My relations:

The World Wide Conservation of Wilderness is an important consideration. I shall do my best to present the perspective of traditional people, but I am sure that there will be many things left unsaid and not presented. I apologize for this and admit my ignorance of the cultures and wisdom of the indigenous people and nations unknown to me through this hemisphere and the world. One thing that I have been finding out is that the indigenous nations throughout the world do understand the natural law and have fashioned our societies to support and adhere to this great spiritual law.

I am often asked to speak on behalf of native peoples in North America because I am educated in my brother's culture and society. I understand his language better than I understand my own. Because of that I am able to communicate with you our collective thoughts. I have been instructed on what to say and it stays with me.

It is important for you to understand that our societies often choose representatives to convey the thoughts of the people. The thoughts conveyed may be the collective position of the people of the Onondaga Nation, the

Onondaga Council of Chiefs, the Grand Council of Chiefs of the Haudenosaunee or the traditional elders circle of North America, the good minds.

It is not my thoughts nor my wisdom that you read, but the collective thoughts and wisdom of the indigenous peoples who have always been here in these lands from time immemorial. Their knowledge is profound and comes from living in one place for untold generations. It comes from watching the sun rise in the east and set in the west from the same place over great sections of time. We are as familiar with the lands, rivers and great seas that surround us as we are with the faces of our mothers. Indeed we call the earth "Etenoha," our mother from whence all life springs.

My relations: So then let us begin:

We will start with the word wilderness, derived from the word wild. For us there is no word for wild, it is not in our vocabulary. The closest we come to that is free; so then we speak of freedom in the natural order of things with the inherent rules and obligations of freedom. Respect and recognition of the sovereignty of the individuals, whether they be human beings, the animal nations or the living forests.

For us our lands did not become wild until our brothers from across the great Eastern sea arrived upon our shores, and then our lands became wild and untamed—even called the Wild West. Previous to that, this continent we called the Great Turtle Island was a land of peace and plenty, so we do not perceive our habitat as wild but as a place of great security and peace, full of life.

My relations: Listen to what we say:

Our grandfathers spoke of the crystal clear waters of the springs, streams, rivers and lakes and great inland seas. They spoke of the fresh pure waters. The first law of life: water.

They spoke of ancient trees, grandfathers of another age, trees so huge it took six men to circle their trunks.

They spoke of forest so vast, leaves so thick that sunlight barely found its way to the forest floors, and a squirrel could travel from the great eastern sea to the Mississippi River without touching the ground.

They spoke of flowers and medicines that grew in profusion along with the fruits, nuts and berries that fed not only the human families but also the animal nations that abounded and prospered in these vast lands.

They spoke of fish so abundant that in spawning season, the streams and rivers were so full you could run on their backs.

They spoke of the passenger pigeons so plentiful their roosting places were stripped of limbs, their combined weight breaking those limbs, so plentiful they darkened the sky for hours as they migrated north and south.

They spoke of the vast herds of game, deer, elk and massive herds of buffalo that roamed the entire continent, powerful and endless.

But they did end, and so we received our first lesson.

My relations: listen as we continue:

The lesson we learned was that man wanted to dominate, and what he couldn't dominate he destroyed; that mankind was capable of destroying life, both the natural world life and his own. Our people were so closely aligned and intertwined with the order of the natural world that we suffered the same fate as the trees and the wolves, our spiritual relatives.

It taught us that mankind could be motivated to exploit the natural resources and the environments that these resources provided, to the point of total depletion and extinction of the animal and fish life.

It illustrated to us that there were people who were ignorant of the natural law, or who chose to ignore it. It caused our people to gather together in alarm and hold to our bosoms the principles of the great natural law and to protect our ceremonies that celebrated these principles and ensured the existence of the generations to come.

My relations: The natural law as we understand it is the ultimate authority upon these lands and waters. It is the prevailing law of life and the order of life upon this earth we call our Mother.

It is the law the Creator put here, set down here deliberately, firmly and with finality to govern all life in this creation.

This is the way we understand it. The Great Creator planted life upon this earth. He planted all of the nations of life from the grasses to the trees, from the insects to the elephants, from the tiniest life in the waters to the great whales in the seas.

He planted the families of mankind, in the four great sacred colors of black, white, red and yellow.

He gave instructions to these great nations of life, from the grasses to the whales, and they continue to follow these original instructions up to this very moment. To the best of their abilities they carry out these duties—they live in a state of grace. They do no wrong.

For us, the human beings, he gave additional responsibilities. He gave us hands to work with, he gave us intellect and the power of reason, he gave us options to choose our paths to do what is right or to do what is wrong. He gave us the foreknowledge of death and he gave us the insight to life after death. These are responsibilities more than gifts, and he gave each of us a mission in this life that is ours alone. These are responsibilities to be cherished and shared for the benefit of all life.

My relations: This is what we believe: Since you asked, we shall continue:

We are sharing this with you so that you may understand us better. These are our cosmologies. Your stories may be different, but we believe that we all received the same instructions in the beginning.

The natural law is a spiritual law. Its powers are both light and dark. We are blessed and we prosper if we live by the law. It is dark, terrible and merciless if we transgress the law. There is no discussion with the law, there is only understanding and compliance. Its tenets are simple.

A respect for all life, for all life is equal.

Thanksgiving ceremonies for the special forces of nature.

A Thanksgiving ceremony for the thundering Grandfathers who water the earth and the people who freshen the springs, streams, lakes and rivers.

A Thanksgiving ceremony for the four winds who bring the seasons and sow the seeds of life.

A Thanksgiving ceremony for the corn, beans and squash that sustain our lives and give strength to our bodies.

A Thanksgiving ceremony to our Grandmother, the moon, who raises and lowers the tides of the great salt seas, who gives us light at night and who marks the cycles of the female life and the seasons.

A Thanksgiving ceremony for our mighty Uncle the Sun, who unites with our Mother the Earth to bring forth life in all our seasons; who brings us light each day as we wait in the morning to greet him.

A Thanksgiving to those spiritual beings assigned to help the human beings carry out our duties.

A Thanksgiving ceremony to the Great Creator, the master of all life, for the creation and all that we have been given to enjoy, and to protect so that seven generations from this day our children will enjoy the same things that we have now.

Listen to the howl of our Spiritual Brother the Wolf, for how it goes with him, so it goes for the natural world.

My relations: So now we will continue:

The World Wilderness Congress gathers people from the four directions of the earth to report on how it is where we come from. This news is heavy and there seems to be a determined effort to destroy life on this planet. How did this come about and what are some of the problems facing us and the natural world?

What is the relationship between a fast-food hamburger and rain forests in Central and South America?

We as consumers should know, but we don't. And more to the point, even if we did know these connections and understand them, it is very questionable that we would give up the convenience of fast foods for the long-term process of conserving the wilderness and saving our environment.

The discussion then revolves around the values of the societies responsible for the attitudes of their people. What are the societies teaching their children?

Rain forests are cut down for timber and to clear the lands for farming and ranching. Ranching lands are seeded for cattle grazing, a cash crop. The local people do not eat the meat. It is often shipped north to become hamburgers. The people give up subsistence farming for wages and the land use is changed. Cheap labor on that end, more profit on this end. At the same time the manufacture of Styrofoam releases chemicals into the air that affect the ozone layer, the thin lifesaving protection of life on earth.

The rain forests are the lungs of the earth. Trees recycle carbon monoxide back into oxygen, clean air that all life breathes in common, thus continuing the life-giving elements and maintaining the constant atmospheres and temperatures around the earth. If we continue to cut these trees at the present rate, we will have cleared a space as large as India within 30 years. The natural law is simple in this case: we will suffer in exact ratio to our transgressions; the damage done may be permanent in mankind's existence.

My relations: We shall continue:

The scenario is the same in Central and South America—first the timber companies come to clear the great forests and lands are used for cash crops. These crops need help to grow because the cleared lands are fragile, so fertilizers are introduced, and as the cash crops grow, insects invade and insecticides are introduced. These chemicals cost money, so soon the farmer is paying more for chemicals that his cash crops can be sold for, and he finds himself working for the chemical companies. Soon he gives up and abandons the land as it turns to dust and as the timber companies march into virgin rain forests, he follows to continue the cycles. This process is called progress and sometimes economic development.

The natural law is clear in this case: If you destroy the process of the life cycles of the rainforests, which affect climate around the world, then you will affect life as we now know it. The balance is delicate. The Mayans farmed these lands for centuries by working with this balance and they prospered. They are called people of the corn, and they lived in the jungles of these huge rain forests in harmony. They lived with the law in respect and understanding and they prospered.

There are great dams being built in these same areas and they have caused the rivers to cease their annual overflowing to bring silt and fertility to the lands that they covered. The lands lose their fertility and life suffers. We understand that the World Bank, which most often financially supported these projects, is now rethinking its policies, and I for one am grateful. The natural law is clear in this case: damage done quickly takes a long time to repair or renew. Thus, we may cut a tree with a chain saw in 10 minutes, but it will take 100 years for that tree to grow back. So who suffers? Our children. We are profiting at their expense. We are deliberately changing our life in the future and we must question our motivations.

The great seas are the same as the earth.

Man has lived off the abundance of the sea from time immemorial. Its great resources have sustained life and songs of joy and contentment have lifted our hearts up to this time. The energy it produces has galvanized civilizations and cultures throughout the world. But we, even now, endanger our lives by imprudent exploitation without regard to the laws of nature, and again we will suffer the consequences.

My relations: You have asked us what we think and so we will continue:

The herring is gone from the North Sea; it is gone from the diet of the people, the result of overfishing. How did this happen? It happened because we either did not understand the natural law or we deliberately chose to ignore it. We could say that technology caused the demise of the great schools of herring, but technology is a tool. Technology doesn't think, ponder or reason. That is the province of mankind. So we must agree that the destruction of the herring was a conscious decision of mankind. What then is the motivation? The answer is simple: profit. Profit at our expense, for we are all deprived, including the fish life that also sustained itself on this once-great natural resource. Technology unleashed our greed. There were many nations involved in this great kill; they fished in competition and rivalry. They developed fishing nets that allowed larger and larger catches. The great seine nets were the final blow to the herring and coupled with the giant trawlers now prowling the seas they were able to catch in one day what previously took a month of fishing. So it is not technology that is to blame, it is the attitude of the fishermen. The results are the same; we have lost a great resource. It is the law that we suffer.

Brothers: There are many examples of mankind's folly and I use the word "man" advisedly because Western thinking, as we see it, has exploited the women as well. Men have excluded women from decision making, and thus flawed the partnership that is the natural law. Male and female are fundamental to life, partners in work to be done. By excluding the female, mankind has again denied a resource of compassion and understanding that balances the competitive nature of the males. We as men should not fear our mates; we should listen to their counsel. They may be the last reservoir of life. They are just now beginning to fight for life. Mankind should stop and listen to their song. As we plunge ahead to build empires and race for supremacy we should stop and listen to their song of life. For without the female there is no life.

My relations: We come to the close of this short discussion.

Do not take offense as we present the examples of what we consider flawed thinking. The examples abound.

Acid rain has already killed half the forests of Germany. Acid rain is killing life in the rivers, streams and lakes of northeastern America. It is killing the chief of the trees, the maple, as our prophecies foretold.

Great famines are sweeping the earth, particularly in Africa, where the natural law is exacting the price of transgressions against it, and life suffers without relief.

Water is contaminated at the expense of our children. Toxic waste dumps are time bombs of death as they slowly work their way into the freshwater veins of our lands.

The Indian nations of North America have been particular victims to uranium mining, and toxic piles of waste tailings have contaminated the people, aborting life in pregnant mothers and causing defects upon our children who are born in these areas.

How can we discuss the economic problems of wilderness and life without talking about the monster most responsible for the problems of the earth today? And that is the gigantic military complexes of the two most powerful nation-states in the world. Soldiers outnumber teachers and doctors by wide margins. And row upon row of deadly bombs, weapons and aircraft wait for the moment of global war. It is hypocritical for countries to profess the cause of peace when their economies are based upon the sale of military hardware. Something is wrong when arms to developing nations outnumber economic aid three to one.

We are seeing our prophecies come to be, one by one. Our gardens in the Mohawk Nation Territories are stunted and refusing to grow from this dark cloud of pollution that daily rains down upon us. We were told that this would happen, and so it has.

Ninety years ago there were 13 cities with a population of over one million. Today there are 200 cities with one million, with Mexico City in the forefront with 18 million, and we know the problems of that city.

Respect should be given to those indigenous nations who still carry on their ceremonies; following the ancient laws of nature with songs and ceremonies.

We cannot give up. We must follow the spiritual law set down for us so long ago. We are not defeated—if we do not allow ourselves to be manipulated like yo-yos on a string by cosmetic politicians whose interests are not for the natural world or the people.

I have heard that economic growth is a necessity and conservation is a consideration of importance. We disagree. Conservation is life and economic growth is a matter of interpretation.

So, my friends and colleagues, at this time in history we have a task that we cannot leave to our children. We have a choice that takes courage, fortitude and a will inspired by the understanding of the great spiritual law of our Mother this Earth. Take heed to the word of our Grandfathers who instructed us to:

"Take care how you place your moccasins upon the earth, step with care, for the faces of the future generations are looking up from earth waiting their turn for life."

So the decision is simple. Obey the natural law, or perish.

Dah Nay To

THE ZULU TRADITION

Magqubu Ntombela

Editor's note—Eighty-seven-year-old Magqubu Ntombela is an elder of the Zulu people, a living legend of history and the African bush. His father fought in the Zulu War of 1879 against the British at Isandhlawana. His grandfather served the great Zulu king, Shaka and his great-grandfather served Chief Senzangakona. Although Magqubu cannot read or write, his knowledge of history is exact and unfaltering. He remembers everything passed down through the generations, father to son.

Magqubu lives in a thatched cottage, in his kraal, at Machibini, near the entrance to the Umfolozi Game Reserve in Natal, South Africa. He lives with his two wives, many children, grandchildren, a herd of cattle, goats, chickens and sheep.

He learned hunting, tracking and other wilderness skills early in life—like all of his Zulu contemporaries at that time. Tracking skills were required to find lost goats and to hunt and trap for food. White rhino, black rhino, lion, leopard, cheetah, kudu, impala, reedbuck, crocodile and other animals were all part of his daily life.

At age 14, Magqubu was an accomplished hunter and tracker and a guide to hunters who came to shoot in the crown lands adjoining Uluhluwe and Umfolozi Game Reserves. At age 16 he was employed as a laborer by Vaughn-Kirby, the first Game Conservator of Zululand. Magqubu worked for over 60 years as a Game Guard, continuing to study and protect the wilderness resources of his native land.

Magqubu has been involved with the Wilderness Leadership School since its inception. The World Wilderness Congress was originally his inspiration, when he told Ian Player that conservation needed an "indabakulu," or a Great Council. He is a natural teacher and is a favorite leader on wilderness trails. Despite his age, he is always ready to go on the trail, to share his knowledge and understanding, and to provide people with his unique perspective on the need for wilderness and conservation.

The following is a mere glimpse into a rich and varied individual. Sadly, there is no way here to reproduce the animation, gestures and incredibly realistic sound effects used by Magqubu when he speaks of the bush and the wildlife. He is a master mimic, a living repository of the ancient oral tradition of his people. He is a remarkable person.)

Saubona. I would like to greet everybody here today. I would like to greet all the dignitaries from America and all the other nations that are gathered here today.

I was born in the place called Masinda where people used to hide during the times when people were fighting among themselves and stabbing each other with spears. We lived during hard times when our people used to be killed by the British and Boers who used cannons while we only had spears. We were able to survive those hard times and I want to tell you a little of our way of life. I would like to thank all the officials of KwaZulu and the other officials who have helped me give this to you. It is very important for myself and my people that you know a little of who we are.

The month of September used to be respected by our forefathers because this used to be a very important month for the wild animals. There is the call of the wildebeests. The Boers, the white hunters, used to shoot the wildebeest and it used to make a call while trying to escape from the bullets. KwaZulu is the land of the Chiefs, the land of the kings, first Senzangakhona then Tshaka, who turned his clan into the mighty Zulu Nation, then Dingaan, Mpande and Cetshwayo who fought the British. Kwa Zulu was once a land full of wild animals like the elephant, rhino, kudu and crocodiles. We lived with and knew these animals.

I now come to the month of October which is also very important in the lives of wild animals. If we had stuck to the traditional laws, we would be living longer than we are living today. I can agree that the laws of nature, the traditional ones, are very difficult to abide with. If we had abided with the traditional laws of nature, the World Wilderness Congress would not need to happen.

The main reason for the World Wilderness Congress is to save our lives and the lives of our future children and teach our children the laws of nature. That is our main aim.

The white rhino is an animal that I first saw while I was still a young boy. When a male white rhino is proposing to a female rhino, it makes a certain noise. The cow will either accept or reject the male. If accepted, the bull will get on top of her and the female makes a different noise. When it is finished it will dismount. I know the white rhino very well as I was born amongst them. This animal is highly respected by our people. Everybody from Pietermaritzburg and Durban has great respect for the white rhino.

A white rhino only used to be shot when a permit had been granted by the officials in Pietermaritzburg. I can remember one occasion when we had to shoot one for the museum in Pietermartizburg. It had to be skinned very carefully making sure that no bones were broken. It was then put in a place where all the young children could see it.

When I was involved with Operation Rhino I heard a hyena laughing. The hyena had seen a pile of meat from the dead white rhino. The first hyena was laughing and signaled to the others that the meat had been found. The hyenas ate and finished all the meat. The next day the hyenas could hardly move because their stomachs were heavy. We have a description in Zulu which says the time of the hyena. It is that moment between night and day when everyone looks the same. Even the ugly ones.

The white rhino is the animal that I like the most. Dr. Player was the first person I saw touching a rhino. Dr. Player, Mr. Steele and myself worked under hard conditions in Umflozi Game Reserve catching white rhino. They were captured by darting them first and then when they went down, Dr. Player gave them another injection and we steered them into a crate. Some were kept in bomas and then sent to many countries including America. We also sent rhino to the Kruger National Park and other game reserves in Africa. Our work was hard and we worked night and day.

I used to be involved in antipoaching campaigns and we caught many people killing the wild animals. We were protecting the animals against the poachers. Another animal that lives in KwaZulu is the buffalo. We do not point at this animal by finger. We point at it by our fist. It was not called by its name—it was called "the black ones." That is the way in which we respect the buffalo. I grew up among the animals and there were no fences during those times. We did not kill the animals without permission from our traditional king, King Dinizulu. He did not allow people to kill the animals and any person caught was severely punished.

I also grew up with the animals called zebras. The zebras used to make their calls all over the plains. They used to make these calls while they were running back into the game reserve at sunset.

I think it is a very good thing that we should stick to the old traditional ways of living so as to protect the future for our children, so that our children will understand what a wild animal is. When future generations come they will know what wild animals we are talking about and be able to see them. All my life I have been involved in the conservation of wild animals and I have seen many of my fellow Rangers killed by poachers when they were protecting wild animals.

I understand the plants and the animals, birds and insects. I can tell when rain is coming. All this knowledge is in my blood. I know of Hlonipa, the language of respect, which we use when referring to animals and in the presence of our Kings and Chiefs. We once had a way of living in the world and knowing what was happening on the land. We were in tune with all that lived and sang. Chief Oren Lyons and my people speak a common language, "people of the feather." I will present to him the tail of the wildebeest which has been decorated with beads by our women. It is carried as a symbol of authority. Chief Oren Lyons speaks with the wisdom of his ancient people and their values should rule the world.

I wish I could tell you about all the knowledge of my people, about the land, the animals, birds, the plants that are so much of our lives. I have really only just begun to tell you.

Hambani ghalhi.

© Geoff Tischbein

WARDENS OF WILDERNESS

Kailash Sankhala

The Thar, or the Great Indian desert, is an extension of the Saharan Arabian Palearctic desert biome. It is situated between 22 and 32 degrees north latitude in the states of Rajasthan, Gujarat, Haryane and Punjab. It lies across India's western frontier with Pakistan, extending over 270,200 square miles (700,000 sq. kms.). The land forms, such as sand dunes, barren rocks, pavements with stunted and scattered vegetation and tropical grasslands, designate it as a desert. Temperatures exceeding 50° C during May and falling below -3° C at night in January are inhibiting for life. The heat is augmented by vaporless hot winds including whirlwinds and chilled by freezing winds from the Himalayas. The arid conditions further increase when rains miss the region, year after year. Surface water hardly exists except in some ephemeral depressions in lake-like forms. Its salinity is high, and increases in the summer. Pelicans (*Pelecanus phillipensis*) come for fish and are followed by flamingoes (*Phoeni copterus roseus. p. minor*), who feed on microbes in these salt lakes. By mid-summer, water becomes more of brine fit only for salt manufacture. Wells are few and deep. A relay of camels or donkeys is needed to lift water from over 100 meters' depth.

A water point is a center of activities of animals and birds. It is the nerve center of the village, where village beauties gather and discuss all topics. Mother-in-law is a common subject. Since it is a social gathering, ladies change their dress every round they return. The display of the charming forms is splendid. In many cases, people spend half of their life only bringing water from the wells on camels and donkeys and lend a helping head to carry a pot.

RICH DESERT LIFE

Since less than a million years is too short a period to bring about any anatomical change, the story of existence of the wide spectrum of life in the desert is the saga of heroic struggle of survivors.

Uncertain water supply, limited food and scarce opportunity for feeding make life in the desert a risky living, yet, life exists rich in vegetation varying from grasslands dominated by *lasiurus sindicus* to scattered flowering trees of *tecomela undulata, prosopis cineraria, salvadore oleoides* and acacias. Also common are xerophytes on dunes and rocks, and halophytes along salt lakes. These vegetative producers support a variety of first-stage consumers and their predators. In the food chain of the desert pyramid, the energy flows from base to the apex and, provided there are no outside influences, ultimately returns to the base to be again converted for circulation in the endless process of life and death.

The desert is rich in insects. Most of the insect orders are represented here. The dominating ones are the ants. There are 17 species of termites. The desert is the home of the locust, which is the means of sustaining many birds and reptiles. Grasshoppers and their larvae do all the eating of vegetation and in turn they are delicious meals for insectivorous birds. A majority of the land vertebrates live here. They vary from dinosaurian spiny-tail lizard (*uromastic harawickii*), purely a vegetarian, to the dragonian monitor lizards (*varanus bengalensis* and *varanus grisesus*), which are wholly carnivores. Snakes vary from dreaded banded kraits, the Sindh krait (*bungarus caevuleus*), saw scale viper (*echis caenatus*), and Russell's viper (*vipera russelli*), to nonpoisonous large rat snakes.

ANTELOPES

Sure-footed gazelles fly with ease on rocks and are also at home on sand dunes. The open landscape is the home of the black buck, a true antelope (*Antelope cervicapra*). It has its telescopic sight and lives in herds of up to a hundred, dominated by a strong male, black in color with deadly pointed spiral horns. Sometimes a small herd consists purely of rejected bucks who are always on the lookout for their reentry into a full herd, or for an opportunity to fight it out and separate a few does in order to establish a new herd.

There are 25 species of rodents. The desert hare is the largest one (*lepus nigricollis dayanics*). Curious specie hedgehogs (*hemiechinus aurihis*) and many species of gerbils (*meriones hurranae* and *gerbillus gleadowi*) occur.

AVIFAUNA

The desert is rich in birds such as munias sparrows, skylarks and common sand grouse (*Pterocles exustas*). The last one lives in family flocks of about four to six members, but are more gregarious at water holes where over 1,000 birds congregate to drink. This spectacle of birds lasts for but a few minutes every morning just after sunrise. The avifauna is enriched by winter migration of common and demoselle cranes (*grus* and *Anthropoides virgo*). They arrive in large flocks for feeding. Their arrivals and flight formations are sung in romantic songs of the desert. Birds arriving in still larger flocks are the imperial sand grouse (*Pterocles orientalis*). When they take off to visit a water hole it is like a volcanic eruption. The flights are soft and their landing sounds like a waterfall. The rollers (*Coracias bengalensis*) and bee eaters (*Merops phillippinus*) lend color to the desert. The grace of the desert is the "ostrich" of India—the Great Indian Buzzard (*Chirotis migracaps*). This miniature ostrich flies, but lot of effort is needed to be airborne. After a short distance, it glides to land. The lesser buzzard is a migratory bird which arrives in pairs from Arabia and Iran. The buzzard is the falcon legend of the Arab Emirates. Falconry, an expensive sport where one bird costs over $6,000, is a sport now banned in India.

Masters of the sky are the eagles and falcons, the largest of which is the tawny eagle (*Aquila rapax*). The lagger falcon (*Falcob armicus*) is the fastest in picking up partridges. Both raptors breed in the desert. There are two species of flying foxes—the common fox (*Vulpes bengalensis*) and the desert fox (*vulpes*).

They feed on desert fruits, insects, lizards, birds and mammals. They are at the apex of the biological pyramid and maintain the balance of nature in the desert. For vultures, there is enough to eat since cattle population is large and their underfeeding results in many deaths. The scavenging vulture (*Neophron percnop-terus*) is bold and aggressive. The king vulture is big but shy. Its red wattles give it regality. All the same, they are scavengers. They start eating even without waiting for the formality of death.

DESERT FLOWERS

The desert blooms twice a year, first in spring when woody plants like tecomela and capparis decide to flower, and then during the rains when the annuals flower. They range from large cucurbita to macroscopic indigofers. Fruits of salvidore oleoides are juicy but slightly pungent. Plums of capparis are the delicious fruits. Cricket ball-like melons are called bitter melons (*cucurbita spp*) due to their taste. But rodents love them. They are also a source of water in the desert.

DESERT MAN

In terms of human settlement, the region is cosmopolitan—Hindus, Muslims and Jains. Except the Jains who are traders, all others are semipastoral, marginal agriculturists. There are traces of civilization which existed here even 2,500 years before Christ. Even the recent ruins of Kirada near Barmer are over 1,000 years old. Artists' concepts of what the desert was when man was part of the ecosystem are often presented in the miniature paintings of the desert school of art. It was a harmonious existence of man and animals, marking the time of the golden era of the desert.

This attracted outsiders. Loot, plunder, conversion and killing became the order of the day and influenced the way of life of the people. The open society changed to a closed culture, fortified in forts. Needs gave way to greed. Reckless cutting of trees and killing of animals began in any name shikar and trade. The land became treeless and lifeless. Droughts, famines, migrations, death and poverty prevailed, and desertification increased.

JAMBASHWARH'S BISNOI

Moved by the lot of the people, the heir apparent of Panwar Jagiradars of Pipasar left his fortress and preferred to roam in the desert to understand the problems of the people. He meditated for years on sand dunes. As a result of his meditation, he discovered that ecological disorder was the cause of their misery. He had no education and his arithmetic was limited to counting up to 20, that also because it was easy to count fingers and toes. But he had nine more things to teach. He added nine to 20 (Bis) to make 29, creating Bis-no (20 plus nine). The followers became Bisnoi. It was the need of the hour and the awakening spread like wildlife among semipastoral and marginal agriculturists of the desert. The Guru came to be known as Jameshwarji or, in short and with reverence,

"Jamboji." He preached the significance of trees and animals. He symbolized Khejari (*prosopis cinraria*) among trees worth a worship and black buck among animals as indicators of environmental quality. This was 500 years ago when ecology was unknown.

In every Bisnoi settlement, village or hamlet, antelope, gazelles and birds have a part to play. The howl of jackal is a healthy sign, and disappearance of that howl is supposed to bring disaster on the village. Therefore, jackals, foxes and even wolves are given protection.

Bisnoi men are tall and handsome, clad in snow-white clothes and large turbans, with a camel. The hard work of the Bisnoi women shape their forms. They are bold and colorful, and continue to be custodians of their culture. They surpass the menfolks in charm, beauty and jubilation.

AGRICULTURAL PHILOSOPHY

Their agriculture is full of chance, and they play this gamble every year for the opportunity to raise a crop of bajra. Their fields are open and the damage done to crops by wild animals and birds is considered a fair share, according to the Bisnoi farming system. Their philosophy is that sometimes their harvest is good because of the luck of birds and animals. Good luck of the animals complements the Bisnoi in their mutual search for existence in the desert.

KHEJARLI—AN ULTIMATE SACRIFICE

The Bisnoi passion for environmental preservation has no parallel in the human history. Some 250 years ago, when the 400-year-old fort of Jodhpur needed repairs, the Maharaja's man could find no sizeable trees to cut except in the Bisnoi village of Khejarli, which was known for its Khejari trees. This is hardly 20 kilometers as the crows fly from the fort. But it was not easy to cut trees—the symbol of Bisnoi culture. Bisnois hugged the trees to protect them even at their life's cost. The first to fall victim in protecting her trees was Amrita—a lady. Then her family was slain, and thereafter the sacrificial ceremony was simple. One by one, a Bisnoi came, took a bath and got his head chopped off. Three hundred and sixty two trees were cut only after 362 men were beheaded. When the Maharaja came to know of the bloodshed, he immediately issued a declaration that "No one shall cut trees and kill animals and birds in the territories of Bisnoi villages throughout the State of Marwar." No tree is cut and no animal is killed in these villages. The result is the richness of the environment. The Bisnois continue to be the custodians of the flora and fauna in the name of their Guru.

The incident can easily be passed on as a fiction. But the rich environment in density of trees and number of birds and antelopes, in stark contrast with the adjoining overfelled and overdestroyed land, is proof in support. The spirit of sacrifice is still demonstrated if anyone happens to stray from the main road. The whole village—men, women and children—come to stand between the wild animals and the hunters' guns. The animals have also realized to rush to the villages and hamlets for shelter. The confidence placed in men by the animals is a unique example. A herd of antelopes, clean prosperous houses, healthy, charming and happy inhabitants loaded with silver and gold ornaments in casual innocence are the characteristics of a Bisnoi environment. Bisnoi settlements are not showpieces or demonstration plots, but extend over 30,000 square miles from Punjab, Haryana to the southwest end of Rajasthan—all a desert environment.

ENVIRONMENTAL TRUTH

There has been no second Guru in the last 500 years to rejuvenate the Twenty-Nine Principles, but their spirit has not faded. Five centuries is a sufficient period of time to test the truth. There is no second example in the world of a conservation culture of such commitment. People come to the Khejarli to pay homage to the heros who gave their lives to protect the trees. Men and women pledge for the supreme sacrifice in defense of their environment in front of the sacred fire. They assemble there every year in September to recharge their commitment. They also visit Mukam where the Great Guru rests in peace, to pay their homage to the Guru for the Twenty-Nine Principles he gave them for their prosperity. The ceremony starts with lighting a fire in front of the Samadhi, with praises of the Guru.

One must not carry an impression that they are backward tribals and that preservation of the environment is just a tribal custom. These are reformist Hindus, enlightened people who are part of the mainstream of India. Many are prominent in our national politics. Our Minister for Environment and Forests in the Central Cabinet, Shri Bhajanlal, is a Bisnoi. The Bisnois are in all walks of life, including business. They are masters of the land they plough. They have mechanized their farms and are proud owners of tractors, having replaced their camel carts.

IN PRAISE OF THE GURU

In the present context, their contribution to conservation is meritorious. But for the Bisnois, the desert would have been a barren land, depleted and deserted. It is their concept of the Biosphere Reserve, initiated five centuries ago. And all goes to the credit of the great ecologist, Guru Jambeshwarji, who is sung to every day with reverence and in thanksgiving.

Jai Jambeshwarji Maharaj ki Jai

PRAN TARANG— THE FLOW OF LIFE

Jasmine Shah

Pran Tarang takes you back through the corridors of time to a vision of the natural world rooted in antiquity. The earliest expressions of this vision are to be found in the *Vedas*, the ancient Sanskrit scriptures of the Hindus. "Knowledge," "vision," "wisdom" and "science" are some of the meanings implied in the Sanskrit word *Veda*. The earliest glimmer of this vision began more than 30, perhaps 40 centuries ago. The *Vedas* have come down to us unchanged, recited daily by an unbroken chain of generations "traveling like a great wave through the living substance of the mind."

These texts of philosophy were composed in Sanskrit, the classical language of India, which is ideally suited to describe the nature of phenomena, from the spiritual level to the physical. This range of applicability in the realm of nature makes it the language of nature.

The *Vedas* are the fountainhead of Indian philosophy from which have evolved not only the tenets of Hinduism, Janism and Buddhism, but also a rich tradition of mythology, classical music, dance and literature in India. Common to all of these are a deep sense of identification with, compassion and respect for all aspects of creation.

Beginning with this philosophical background, Pran Tarang presents these perceptions of nature through a rich combination of visuals, music and narration. The audiovisual opens with the sounds of the timeless conch and verses from the beautiful Hymn of Creation of the oldest *Veda*, the *Rig-Veda*. Chanted in Sanskrit by voices from ancient South Indian Temples, these verses dwell upon the evolution of life from a single primordial cause, the primary or eternal principle, the *Hiranya Garbha*. This hymn is remarkable for the beauty of its pure abstract, which was born out of a strong identification with nature.

Life is seen to have evolved from that single point of potency; all forms of creation are considered manifestations of the same basic living energy. There is a sense of unity linking all forms of life—human, plant and animal, mountain, river and earth in a primary kinship. Nature is not to be conquered or dominated. Instead, it is seen to be full of fertility and generosity. The difference between man and animal is not one of kind, but of degree. All forms of life, grand and small, are celebrated and respected.

In Indian mythology, animals represent life/energy, fertility and wisdom, and are associated with the gods as their vehicles and companions. Ganesha, the elephant god whose vehicle is the mouse, is the symbol of wisdom and humor. They show us that the biggest and smallest of all creatures are equally important.

Traditional Indian art in all its forms of expression—sculpture, painting, terra-cotta—is part of this same vision. The traditional Indian artist has seen in nature the thousand-fold reflections of ideas. The whole aim in his art is the expression Rasa or the passion which animates nature. Classical Indian literature, as in the verses of the immortal Sanskrit poet Kalidasa, continually reminds us of the grand qualities associated with mountains, rivers and clouds and the delicate emotions felt by trees and animals. Classical Indian music keeps man in close touch with nature and its melodies reflect nature in all her seasons and moods.

This integrated vision of life and creation is a philosophy which finds expression in every aspect of traditional Hindu life. Carried on the magic carpet of sculptures, scriptures, music and dance, and the deep resonance of Sanskrit hymns echoing around us, we receive a message which lingers and lives in our minds beyond the show.

ON LIVING IN HARMONY WITH NATURE

Hind Sadek

We should acknowledge that this sapient species of the genus Homo has not always been the despoiler of nature and the destroyer of life on earth. *Homo sapiens sapiens, Homo sapiens neanderthalensis, Homo erectus,* and many others before us have lived on this earth and shared the natural world with other living creatures. They extracted a livelihood and survived in both friendly and hostile environments through sheer ingenuity and technology, without polluting, destroying or marring the environment. And they did so for many hundreds of thousands of years.

Anyone who has visited the caves of Lascaux or Altamira cannot fail to recognize in the paintings not only great art, but the testament of an intimacy with nature and with life that can only be borne of love and of respect for life. There is an indefinable sense of spirituality on the walls of these 15,000 to 20,000-year-old caves. Looking back as you exit Lascaux is indeed a humbling moment.

The alleged pagan worship of animals of so-called primitive societies is neither pagan nor worship. Today, yesterday and for millennia, the attitude of these societies has been one of brotherhood with the animate and inanimate world, including rocks, plants and animals. Hunting and gathering activities were aimed at human survival, not at the extinction of species nor the destruction of the natural world. And so, for millennia, the animals continued to roam and the forests continued to provide shelter and sanctuary for all.

The extraordinary phenomena of the modern world—the successes and excesses of modern technology which we identify with progress—are based on the inventiveness, creativity and industriousness of men and women. Its advances have helped alleviate much human suffering, cured men and women and children of disease, and much more. Yet, there has also been extensive degradation of land, resources and people. But I have a new hope that reversing that vicious cycle of development-equals-destruction is possible. It is a hope inherent in the concept of sustainable development; development that encourages economic growth and yet does not lose sight of the environmental imperatives.

Is poverty the single most important cause of environmental degradation, as has been suggested by some? I think not. Though it is true that in developing nations, parents who cannot feed their own children can hardly be concerned about clean air for their grandchildren, it is equally true that acid rain is certainly not caused by poverty or by primitive technologies. While slash and burn have no doubt contributed to the destruction of forests, and erosion of overgrazing has aided in the desertification and agricultural lands, so has the indiscriminate use of chemical fertilizers and pesticides, both products of highly evolved technologies. Another product of superior technology and of wealth, rather than poverty, is the dumping of toxic wastes by the millions of tons, which poses severe threats to human health and causes loss of habitat and species, with grave consequences to both developed and developing nations.

Damages to the environment and natural resources, which are accelerated by increasingly more efficient methods of exploitation, aggravate rather than relieve the overexploitation of native raw materials which, in turn, add to what the NCED has rightly identified as the "hidden costs" of environmental degradation. Since developing countries are compelled to pay these "hidden costs," the inevitable consequences to these countries and to their economies is financial debt, which translates into such statistics as: high illiteracy rates, poor national health services, low average per-capita income, and, yes, poverty! Furthermore, the high birth rates and alarming population growths which today characterize most developing nations accentuate their plight.

The fact is, however, that it is not poverty, but the *cause* of this modern, devastating poverty that constitutes our main concern. We must find alternative solutions for the cause, and not just focus our efforts on curing effects. Some may argue that this is too long term—not so. Both are needed—long-term projects as well as "specific, short-term projects" and "resolute action right where the problems are," to quote Mostafa Tolba of UNEP.

Debt-for-nature conservation swaps appear to offer immediate solutions involving governments and banks. But it is the involvement of the citizenry of both the developing and the developed nations that is of greater and more profound significance. The fact is that we are now talking to each other and that we must find ways and means of talking to concerned citizens outside of our circles and we need to make sure we are being heard and understood. It is indeed a literacy campaign and one that must begin at the grass roots level of life. Young and old, developed and developing, must learn the language of conservation and sustained development.

THE ROLE OF NATIVE PEOPLE IN SUSTAINABLE DEVELOPMENT

Norma Kassi

I am of the Vuntat Gwich'in Nation—The People of the Lakes—of the far northwestern part of Canada. My village, Old Crow, is the most northern community in the Yukon Territory. I am a member for Old Crow in the Territorial Legislature. Since being elected just over two years ago, I have had the privilege to attend meetings across my country, to speak and to learn.

I am both a legislator and leader of my community and must constantly struggle with how to assist governmental officials, politicians and decision-makers to understand that the environment, to indigenous people, is not a matter of perspectives or forums. It is our life and our survival. Let me explain.

The Yukon is changing, and I want to share with you what those changes are all about, mostly by using examples from Old Crow, my community of 300 people.

Changes are taking place as well in the territory as a whole. For the first time in history, the new democratic government of which I am member has a majority of aboriginal elected members, including two cabinet ministers and the speaker of the legislative assembly. Even with this majority, it is sometimes difficult to create a cultural balance.

It is important to understand that in the Yukon, the land claims of the aboriginal peoples have never been settled. No treaties were signed and no conquest ever occurred. Our land claims negotiations are a difficult process. The claim involves more than land ownership. It also must address aboriginal self-government—the right to decide what happens to our people and to all important resources of our lands; the right to continue to protect our resources, in other words, our environment.

My people have governed their environment for thousands of years in order to sustain their communities and lands for generations to come. Southerners and Northerners, white people and aboriginal people must come to an understanding and accommodation which allows the environment to sustain us both for all time.

Old Crow is located below the junction of the Crow River and Porcupine River. These rivers meet and then join the Yukon River, which flows through Alaska to the Bering Strait. Much like this great river system, the Gwich'in Nation extends throughout the Northwest Territories, the Yukon and Alaska. We have a language of our own and a strong culture based on the land. It has been documented that we have been a self-determined people for 30,000 years.

Through all these years we have lived and managed the resource in a sustainable manner. We have conserved and protected the caribou and other animals, and we have lived in harmony with the natural world. While you may think of us as living in the wilderness of northern Canada, we think of ourselves as being of the wilderness. We and our activities are part of our natural wilderness system and have been so for tens of thousands of years.

Our ability to live with our environment has always depended on our Old Ones, our Elders, who command the respect of the community and whose direction we must follow. The Elders train their children and educate them in our traditional ways. We are taught to conserve Mother Earth and all the resources she holds that are given to us so freely. By this I mean the basics of life that we cannot survive without: the air we breathe, the water we drink, and the plants and the wildlife that we eat and use. The land is not something which lies pristine and dormant, stretching away empty around my village. Every spring, for example, the village of Old Crow becomes nearly deserted as many families leave town to go muskrat trapping, or "ratting" as we call it, in the Old Crow Flats, many lakes north of the village.

From the month of March until June, our culture thrives on a springtime of hard work, traditional training and personal as well as family-unit development. The muskrats we get are an essential part of our yearly income. Their harvest is a focal point for our traditions. This is also true for many northern communities where fur trapping is a very significant activity where most people are not part of the wage economy.

Animal rights activists in the south and overseas who attack fur harvesting ignore the fact that Yukon's wilderness provides a basic subsistence living for most people. The antifur campaign is an attack on the survival of my community and the Gwich'in Nation.

My people are of the wilderness. We use the land and the animals. It is our life's foundation. Aboriginal people are an important part of the environment where I live—there may not be villages or roads everywhere, the evidence which you may associate with human use, but we do use the land. So when southerners think about northern wilderness, they need to think about allowing traditional use of the land and wildlife by a culture much different from their own. It is good that some areas are set aside to protect wildlife and it is good that there are controls on industries and road building, but southern ideas of excluding all human activities from all wilderness areas is not an idea that my people can ever agree to. We conserve the resources and we have to use them to survive. We need the wilderness—for food and for life in general.

This spring I spent a month on the flats, a place which nourished me spiritually. But beautiful as it may be, I have seen a lot of changes there, changes that have taken place since I was last on the Old Crow Flats. Subtle changes, slow changes that the Elders talk of. In the environment, lakes are drying up here and there. Our snow water doesn't taste like it used to. Small animals—ptarmigans, rabbits, birds, ducks, migratory birds—are not as abundant as they used to be. As well, the behavior of the caribou has changed; it's different from what the Elders remember. There are more airplanes flying over our camps, including U.S. military jets flying tests. This is upsetting.

My Elders speak about these changes. They speak about them often and with concern. We suspect that many of the changes are the result of industrial developments in the south and in Alaska, and we fear the effects of nuclear testing, oil spills, chemical waste deposits, pollution and the influx of more people who see wilderness only as a resource to be exploited. We are very concerned. How much more can the land and the wilderness tolerate?

In Old Crow, the people believe that our future relies on our renewable resources. We are not interested in the exploitation of nonrenewable resources such as oil and gas. Huge developments such as the MacKenzie Valley Pipeline have been proposed for our area. Our village fears developments. The benefits from such exploitation of our lands flow all in one direction, and it isn't to our people. I do not believe we need a pipeline, a road or a port facility on the north coast to give us wage work. We have learned that oil industry work is unreliable; it comes and goes with the price of oil and gas. The large-scale developments such as the proposed oil and gas developments on the Alaskan North coast will be devastating for our people. We rely on the caribou that use the coastal plains. The caribou are our main source of food. We eat caribou meat three or four times a day—boiled, dried, roasted—from the nose to the insides, and we use the hides for clothing. It is the very essence of our survival and we intend to protect our future through the development of a local conservation strategy. We may have to make accommodations to other interests in the vast North, but we will fight to make our priorities known and included when decisions are made.

Our local conservation strategy will focus on six specific renewable resource issues of immediate concern: water, fuel, wood and timber, fish, fur, caribou, waterfowl and our involvement and control in the operation of the North Yukon Parks. With the support of the Yukon government, we will build a strategy that makes sure that the resources are not overused and that they will continue to be available to us for all time. This strategy will involve our traditional laws and practices concerning our land and environment.

Scientists like to use big words when they talk about conservation—words like sustainable development, biological diversity and ecological stability roll off their tongues. But to my people of Old Crow, it all means one thing—our survival. There really is no acceptable alternative to conservation for my people—at least if we want anything like our present lifestyle and if we want a future which follows our tradition.

With a conservation strategy in place we will have a more secure future, but getting the strategy in place will mean hard work. If we have the strategy we can continue to hunt, fish, trap and survive with some certainty in our lives. The aboriginal people of our countries have the skills of conservation. We follow our traditional laws. When we take, we have ways of giving back. If we go out on the land and take a caribou, we give back some, we have our traditional ways of doing so because of our spiritual ties to the land. If we take fur, it is in balance with the muskrat that are available to us. We share with everything. We are part of the natural cycle and must live that way to maintain a balance between our needs and the available wildlife resources.

If we destroy the land and resources on which we depend, and with which we live, then we are destroying ourselves. The Vuntat Gwich'in Conservation Strategy will help us ensure that there is a future for the children of Old Crow, but it cannot stand on its own. Cooperative arrangements must be made with other organizations that share the responsibility for managing the resources on which we depend. Our Vuntat Gwich'in Conservation Strategy will stand a better chance of helping us because it will mesh with a strategy for sustainable development which my government is working on for the whole Yukon. But what about the world beyond the Yukon's borders?

The caribou on which we depend recognize no political boundaries. In Canada, they move between the Yukon and the Northwest Territories. Internationally, the herd moves from Canada to Alaska and back. We have recognized this fact.

The Gwich'in people in the Northwest Territories, the Yukon and Alaska are now all represented on the boards that make decisions on the management of the porcupine caribou herd that has all user interests represented, a majority aboriginal membership and an aboriginal chairperson. The government of the Yukon also has representatives on the board. The board has responsibilities for harvest allocation and deals with management issues, for example the decision that no commercial harvest of the herd will be allowed except for traditional practices of sharing food within the aboriginal communities.

This year an additional management mechanism was put in place. I represented the Yukon government in Ottawa this summer when the governments of Canada and the United States signed an international agreement for management of the herd. This agreement will establish a management advisory board designed to improve the cross-border communication of information about the caribou. It took a long time to negotiate this agreement.

Unfortunately, in spite of all this, the caribou herd is still threatened. The U. S. Department of Interior is proposing to open the last 10 percent of the Alaska Coastal Plain to development—in the heart of the calving grounds of our caribou. They are doing this in spite of scientists' warnings about the potential effects on the animals, not just the caribou, but the birds, the bears and the muskoxen that use this area. I'm aware that there is considerable opposition to the oil and gas proposal in the United States, and I am grateful. The proposal is frightening to my people and it must be stopped.

Because we are opposing these particular oil developments in Alaska, we have been accused by some government officials and developers in the United States of being antidevelopment. Well, yes, we are, if "development" is always defined in their terms. Development to us is "preservation," and we have been successful to date in preventing their kind of developments in the caribou habitat in Canada. We depend on the caribou and our survival depends on their protection. We cannot tolerate any harm to these renewable resources that have sustained my people and our ancestors for many thousands of years. My people have contributed to the development of conservation policies that are now in place for the Northern Yukon. We now have the North Yukon National Park, which was established through the land claims settlement on the north slope, and we are negotiating a new land settlement for the Old Crow area. In time we hope to ensure even more protection for the caribou through a regional land-use planning process. But the developments proposed for Alaska National Wildlife Refuge lands will potentially destroy not only the habitat of the caribou, but of migratory birds, polar bears, foxes, grizzly bears and many other species of wildlife which live in the Alaska coastal plain and the north coast of Canada. It is time for our kind of development.

The migratory birds that use the area, for example, are the same ones that sustain people on Banks Island in the Canadian arctic, and they are the same ones that are hunted for sport in British Columbia, Washington, Oregon and California. The habitat pressures on these birds are growing all along their flyway, especially in places like California where wetlands are being converted to agriculture at a rapid pace. We need to be aware that these international resources are at very great risk. The world is linked together—we need to be responsible for one another's well-being and get away from this myth that we are only having little local effects with projects like those proposed for the Alaskan coastal plain.

Consider issues like acid rain or ozone depletion or the Chernobyl accident. The human species is affecting the entire planet now. With our waters poisoned, our plants and animals dying, then *we* are next. Everything *is* linked to everything else. We need to wake up to this reality *now*.

This message is one that definitely was heard by the World Commission on Environment and Development. Prime Minister Brundtland and the other commissioners heard the message being delivered by communities like Old

Crow and I hope in my heart that the world's leaders will also hear the message.

Similarly, we need the leaders of the U.S. government to hear the voices of the Gwich'in nation. The people of Old Crow must be heard, and I ask you for your support. I urge any of you with concern or influence over decisions about the Alaskan Arctic National Wildlife Refuge to try harder still to protect it from development. The very survival of our northern native communities is at stake.

As you can see, conservation and sustainable development are ideas that are very much alive in our minds. In our tradition we have always been aware of our unity with the life and the land around us, of our activities having an effect on the world beyond that which is immediately obvious.

As the Gwich'in people, we have hopes and aspirations for the future. We hope that the world will come together to conserve what we have left, and we hope that the cultural and traditional values of the world's people will follow the natural laws. We believe that our Mother Earth has had enough destruction and can't handle much more. The world is trying to deal with nuclear experimentation and pollution that has gone beyond our control. We see more and more people suffer and even we are affected where we live.

In Old Crow, we want to take care of what we have left and share it with whomever will respect it and do the same. The World Wilderness Congress is an effort in cooperation, just as is the work we do—together we can make the world a better place. I want to believe that my people can sustain our traditional lives— the environment demands it of us and we have grown to enjoy and believe that we, the Gwich'in Nation, can live forever in harmony with our surroundings. *Mahsi-cho!*

HONORING LIFE'S INHERENT DESIGN

Michael Burghley

I'm sure that many of us have been thankful for the availability of our wild places as settings for true inspiration and education. I'm especially aware of this because for many years now I've had an association with an outdoor adventure school in central British Columbia, the Educo School. I've seen thousands of young people pass through the school over the years and have been aware of the specific contribution that the wilderness has made to their discovery of inner character and inner worth. Obviously that is not the only element involved in such a situation, but it is a crucial one.

The massive urbanization which has been occurring in recent decades emphasizes the importance of the natural world as a place for reminding us all of the way life really works. In Canada only 2 percent of the population still live on the land. This has had a profound effect on the way in which life is looked at. When we look at the designs of nature we can see the delicate and yet powerful way in which the natural systems of life fit together such as a spider's web, with all its precision and geometric exactness. Such a simple, silent thing hanging there, and yet representing a factor of absoluteness that is present throughout the natural world and, for that matter, is present in our own bodies and in our whole experience of life wherever we may be. The problem for us has been that so often we tend to be distracted from that awareness of absolute design.

We are keenly aware of the degradation that is occurring on the planet as a whole. I would like to remind you of some of the words of the Denver declaration:

"The productivity of the earth's natural resource base is rapidly deteriorating, as evidenced by desertification, deforestation, accumulation of toxic wastes, polluted drinking water and oceans, diminution of wilderness habitat and loss of genetic diversity. It is clear that, under the demands of increasing human population, the overall situation will continue to deteriorate."

We have in that description a summary of where human experience is today. The world condition reflects the inner state of its human inhabitants. Furthermore, the true severity of the deterioration of the world's economic and environmental conditions, for the most part, has not really been grasped. We do not have much time left. In fact, the repercussions of many of the things that have already been instituted on this planet in the way of degradation will have to be played out, and there will be heavy effects which will impact us all. There is the inclination, especially in North America, to look out at the broader picture and say that those in Third World countries need to deal with their population problems, as though somehow we weren't on the same boat! Only their end of the boat may be sinking, but we all go down if it goes.

There is much evidence of a huge destructive momentum moving in many fields. So often those who are knowledgeable in a particular field are very concerned about it; they see a disastrous situation looming. But they often feel that, while this is true in their individual realms of responsibility, the rest of the world is hanging together pretty well. However, at this 4th World Wilderness Congress we have begun to realize that everything is interconnected, and that there are serious problems in the whole fabric of the earth.

Chief Oren Lyons remarked, "The natural law is a spiritual law. Its powers are both light and dark. We are blessed and we prosper if we live by the law. It is dark, terrible and merciless if we transgress the law. There is no discussion with the law. There is only understanding and compliance. Its tenets are simple....The decision is simple. Obey the natural law or perish."

These are wise words, spoken by one representing a people who, in their history, have been more closely connected with the Earth Mother than most of us, and who have lived in an awareness of the Great Spirit. These words must be heeded. Indeed, the leaf emblem of the Wilderness Congress represents this wisdom. As you probably are aware, the idea for that emblem came from Magqubu Ntombela, the Zulu elder. The two smaller leaves lower down on the stem represent man's relationship with man and man's relationship with the earth. But the central frond, pointing upward and much larger than the other two, represents man's relationship with God.

This isn't the God of common and religious belief, but one who simply represents the way life works: a symbol of the universal law, the universal spirit, which informs us all. We have violated the laws that govern nature and which are evident throughout this planet and beyond. Oren Lyons stated that the tendency to ignore the law brings certain repercussions. It is of no ultimate avail attempting to deal with nature's laws without an acknowledgment of this point.

We need to admit that there is something that goes beyond our own immediate abilities, so that we step back to a place of greater humility and stillness in ourselves. Then we may have the space internally to perceive and respect natural systems and to sense what our relationship with them actually should be. If we are too taken up dealing with the problems that are immediately at hand in the external sense—though they certainly do need loving attention—to the exclusion of respect for life's inherent design and purpose, then the actions we take will inevitably create further problems.

The real point here is that we belong to life. Life does not belong to us. Many things have been said about the benefits that wilderness can give us. How about asking the question, what is it that we should be providing for the world in which we live, rather than all the time thinking about what we can take away, what may benefit us? Oh, we'll provide a little protection here, a little care there, so that we can have what we want. But the question is: What does life want of us? That never seems to be considered.

Population is a major issue on which the World Wilderness Congress needs to focus. In the external sense the population explosion is the ultimate problem that we're all facing, so much more discussion is needed. Perhaps we think it inevitable that population growth will continue until we have standing room only on the planet and all we can do is see if we can devise ways of accommodating this. There is certainly more to the issue than resignation! Does not the population problem epitomize the feeling extant in the human race that we want the right to have the sexual aspect of our lives to ourselves? We talk about the need for education in this field, about the need for people to be aware of the impact their actions have on the planet as a whole. But people love children, and people feel insecure. They feel that if they surround themselves with sizeable families, that is security. I'm a fine one to talk about this: I have two children and live in wealthy North America!

It has been said that those who live in the developed world and who don't think they have a population problem need to look at their consumerism, because that is the same expression of wishing to fill out one's life in a way which is satisfying, fulfilling, secure.

Chief Lyons impliedthat the place fulfillment comes from relates to harmonization with the natural, spiritual Law, not from surrounding ourselves with glitzier surfboards or larger families. I'm talking about sacred things here. In the end we are all brought face to face with ourselves personally. It is not a matter of arranging the rest of the world, but of considering what my stance is toward the world where I live, toward life and the laws of life. Am I willing to put aside the well-established self-preoccupations that have been present for me, so that I have the openness to accommodate the requirements of the universal law and so that I can sense what it is that life actually calls for me to do?

There is a statement in the book *Touch the Earth* which speaks of the native American, but which really speaks to each of us and the genuine potential in each of us: "He believes profoundly in silence—the sign of perfect equilibrium. Silence is the absolute poise or balance of body, mind and spirit. The man who preserves his selfhood is ever calm and unshaken by the storms of existence—not a leaf, as it were, astir on the tree; not a ripple upon the surface of the shining pool.

"If you ask him, 'What are the fruits of silence?' he will say, 'They are self-control, true courage or endurance, patience, dignity and reverence. Silence is the cornerstone of character.'"

With the increasing pressures of our day and the crises that face us all in one way or another, it is only that individual who has come to a place of inner stillness and silence who will be in position to stand steady and act wisely with respect to what arises. When the pressure rises, pleasant ideals tend to fade away. Should the economic situation collapse, should the environmental situation go from bad to worse, should the population situation be uncontrollable, what then? Who will be calm and unshaken? Who will be able to provide any wisdom and perspective? That is the challenge I leave with you.

It is something that, for myself, I must ponder deeply, knowing that my actions in the external sense will carry healing and blessing only if they spring from this clear, still place of harmonization with the laws of life. They are there to be sensed and related to if our inner eyes and ears are open to them, if we are not taken up with our own adventures, our own goals and ideals, our own opinions and beliefs, but are still, in a place of silence. There life speaks like thunder for those who are listening.

WILDERNESS AND THE SOUL

John A. Sanford

As a Jungian analyst, my focus is on one individual person and the inner life of that person, which I like to call the soul. It is a very different kind of focus than most people consider when they deal with conservation. The question might be, of course, what does the soul of a single individual have to do with the larger theme of the conservation of nature with which we are all very concerned?

There are three aspects of my work with the soul of a given individual that can be related to the issues of conservation. The first concerns what we call in the language of my psychology, individuation. The process of individuation revolves around getting the bad news about yourself, facing the things you would rather overlook if you could. C.G. Jung observed that the people who kept coming to him over the years were engaged in a process, a lifelong process, of becoming a whole, completed personality. This process, he felt, was not something that they chose or decided upon, it was a process that was thrust upon them from an unconscious source buried deep within them with such strength that it became an inner necessity.

Jung named this process "individuation." He chose that name for several reasons. First, because he believed that process was seeking to bring that particular person into his or her unique fruition as a human being. Because, of course, while we are all members of the same human race, no two of us are ever alike. Each one of us has his or her own destiny and personality calling for fulfillment. This very individual quotient to our personality can never be discovered by a collective means. It must always be discovered individually and personally. Jung called it individuation because he believed that this process was attempting to bring about a person whose personality was no longer divided, a person in whom the conscious personality and the unconscious personality were now in harmony and accord. It is of course an ideal goal. No one ever reaches it completely. But the striving for it lends to life a sense of meaning even when things are going badly.

Now, to many people this may seem perhaps an esoteric idea, but actually it is very commonplace. In fact, we see something very much like this everywhere in the natural order. Everything that lives is impelled to its proper goal and fruition by its own inner dynamic force. If we went out into the hills and mountains and we came across a great oak tree with its great spreading branches, great massive trunk and its firm strong root system, we could say there is an acorn that has individuated. There is an acorn that has reached its proper destiny, fulfillment and goal, for it is true that contained within the acorn there was, in potential, the mature tree.

So in nature too, everything individuates. Jung once said, "Everything living dreams of individuation, for everything strives towards its wholeness." It is, in the final analysis, this power that heals. The psychotherapist knows that he or she never heals anyone. They heal themselves, and they are able to heal themselves because each person has within himself or herself exactly that same power that lies within the acorn—a built-in knowledge and striving of the goal toward which we are summoned. And the healing process is to realize the goal and make it a reality.

There is, however, in human being, a difference between us and the oak tree. In the life of the oak tree, so far as we know, it all proceeds along biological and natural lines. In the life of the human being, this process of individuation that moves toward wholeness must be consciously understood and realized. It all must go through an ego that has been awakened into consciousness. So on the level of our human life this otherwise very natural process has a markedly psychological and spiritual aspect.

The second thought I would like to suggest to you revolves around the idea of what we can call the "center." In this process of growth, of individuation, we discover that a process takes place in the personality. The personality is centered originally around the ego, the "I" part of us which lends to our personality an irritatingly egocentric quality. We find that as that person moves toward wholeness, the center of the personality shifts from the ego to a much greater center within us, a center which Jung called the "Self." And so in our psychology, there are two centers to our personality rather than one, the lesser center of the ego and the greater center of the Self. The process of individuation requires that the ego, while vitally important for the accomplishment of this process, must eventually subordinate itself to the greater and larger reality of the center within. Only in this way can we be healed, only in this way can we be fulfilled.

In a religious language this greater center within can be likened to the will of God, and has been so described in religions of all sorts. To mention just one, from Saint Paul, where he declared, " It is no longer I who live, but Christ who lives in me," meaning in psychological language, his life is no longer organized around the striving, wishing, willing "I" (the ego), but around a much greater reality within himself that he termed, "the Christ within." It is out of this larger reality there emerges our unique identity. Out of this larger inner reality that there emerges the purpose of our lives. And I think it is this larger reality, the self, which embodies a natural law of which indigenous people speak.

Nature also has a center. In nature, all forms of life are interrelated. No unit or species of life in nature exists by itself. There is an interconnection amongst all things. Left to itself, nature will achieve a balance. It is as though there is within the natural order an invisible center. Indeed, sometimes within a certain species there appears to be an invisible center. If you study a colony of ants you notice that each ant seems to know exactly what to do. But, according to a study done on ants, if the colony of ants were reduced to a number below 200, the individual ants became disoriented and no longer knew what to do. We could say that the center of the ants was within the colony. Among the ants there was an invisible center guiding and regulating the life of each individual ant.

So nature, too, has her center and we call this in the language of ecology, the "ecosystem." We know in that if the balance of nature is disturbed, which it is by the intrusion into nature of egocentric human beings, then the ecosystem is disturbed and everyone in time will suffer. In the same way, if that same arrogant, egocentric ego tries to dominate the personality of the individual, then that individual's balance is disturbed and illness results.

The third thing I would like to mention has to do with dreams. How might we find this inner center? How might we know about the greater life of the self? There are many ways, but one way is the analysis of our dreams. In the course of a great deal of this kind of analytical work, dreams are very important. They are not the only thing that is important, but they are very important in the work for several reasons. First, dreams relentlessly portray to us the truth about ourselves. They lay out for us the way things are in the state of our souls. To look at dreams, therefore, is to look at the way things really are within us, and sometimes things within us are much worse than we thought, and sometimes things within us are much greater than we thought. The dreams are also endlessly creative. One thing at which I marvel is that in the tens of thousands of dreams about which I have listened to and examined, of myself and of my clients, with only infrequent exceptions, has there ever been a duplication. The dreams are endlessly original. They may bring up the same motif, but each one says it in its own uniquely clever way. It is as though the dream story fabricator within us is a brilliant author, constantly thinking of original plots.

So there is in our dreams evidence of the endless creativity of the Creator. And then, too, the dreams emanate from our deep self. When heeded and listened to they lead us into a relationship with this deep Self and therein we find our purpose. Although we use our dreams in depth in psychology and we think perhaps of people like Freud and Jung bringing this to our attention, analysis itself is very ancient. The first Jungian analysis, to make a small joke, was the prophet Daniel in the Old Testament. He summed up the essence of Jungian thought on dreams in one sentence, "King Nebuchadnezzar of Babylon had a dream. He could not understand his dream and his various magicians and dream interpreters were unable to interpret it. But he heard that the Hebrew prophet Daniel was skilled with such things and so he summoned Daniel and he told Daniel his dream. And Daniel interpreted King Nebuchadnezzar's dream. And after he had finished the King said to Daniel, 'Why did the dream come to me?' And Daniel said, 'The dream has come to you, O King, in order that you may know the thoughts of your inmost mind.'" And there it is in a nutshell. The dream brings to us the thoughts of our innermost, unconscious mind, for the purpose that we may know, understand, and become conscious.

Others, too, relied on dreams by our time. I could make quite a list. The American Indians relied on dreams. They said that the Great Spirit knew, that we would wander in darkness and error in this world, and so he sent us dreams to be a light and a guide to the soul. And so did inspired spirits in all ages. In the nineteenth century, for instance, that most materialistic and deterministic and mechanistic of all centuries, we find such persons followed their dreams as Abraham Lincoln, who has left a record of them, Dostoyevski, Robert Lewis Stevenson(who dreamt the plot of Dr. Jeckyl and Mr. Hyde) and Emily Brontë.

Dreams also are filled with symbols drawn from nature. Earthquakes, forests, streams, rivers, meadows and flowers abound. As an analyst I could always tell how well someone is related to their unconscious psyche by examining their dreams to see if they are in a good relationship with the animals that appeared in their dreams. Just five days ago a man brought to me a dream with a sketch of a magnificent spider web. In Jungian understanding, this is a dream of that center I mentioned earlier which, like a spider, catches disparate things and brings them together into its web and its center.

Does nature dream? We know that animals dream. Maybe Jung is right. Maybe everything dreams. I would rather quote the American Indian shaman, Lame Dear: "A human being is many things. We must learn to be different, to feel and taste the manifold things that are us. The animals and plants are taught by Wakantonka what to do. They are not alike. They all have their own ways—the leaves of one plant on the same stem. None is exactly alike. The Great Spirit likes it that way. All creatures exist for a purpose. Even an ant knows what that purpose is, not with its brain, but somehow it knows. Only human beings have come to a point where they no longer know why they exist. They don't use their brains and they have forgotten the secret knowledge of their bodies and their senses and their dreams." Whether we have recognized it or not, many people are conscious today of such hunger in themselves. Our souls are empty and they yearn to be filled.

20,000 YEARS OF ANIMAL ART

David M. Lank

Our legacy of wildlife art provides the most enduring record of how man has seen—and interacted with—the world around him. In the earlier years, the artistic outpouring seldom consciously segregated man from his world, for man never questioned that he was one with his surroundings. Reviewing 20,000 years of creativity is, therefore, not only an aesthetically delightful exercise, but also a trustworthy way of gaining insight into our own social roots. It is my firm conviction that any civilization worth its salt must be judged on how it views and treats the world around it. The written record covers too short a time span, and changes of words, language and meaning distort our ability to understand fully the tempers of people past. The visual record is a far more trustworthy guide.

It is a rather extraordinary task to present 20,000 years of art in a paper such as this covering all cultures and all mediums. You will therefore be glad to know that during the introductory paragraph we covered the first 13,000 years. It is a shame to gloss over time and art, the two elements that most firmly establish our place in the total scheme of things.

We are part of the animal kingdom, the biosphere and the ecosystem. But the dividing line between man and animal is now being examined more closely than ever before. Our traditions taught us that we were "Man the Thinker." We now have extensive empirical data showing that a lot of animals can consciously think, at least to a limited extent. We have long talked about "Man the Toolmaker" as a dividing criterion, but then we see Secretary birds grabbing large pebbles and hurling them at ostrich eggs. Chimpanzees and the great apes pile up chairs to get at the last banana, and the Darwinian woodpecker finch uses a tiny thorn to pry a grub out of a rotting Palosanto tree in the Galapagos Islands. So, "Man the Toolmaker" isn't quite as good as it used to be to separate us from the rest of the animal world.

What about "Man the Artist?" Man the artist is unique. I do not consider finger painting by a chimpanzee to qualify, even though it is more than qualified to hang in some of the more trendy art galleries.

Long before man had been dissected and studied by anthropologists and sociologists, before we were conscious of skin color or contending religions, the artistic impulse appears to have been at the forefront of our entire civilizing evolution. And art has continued as a vital part of all cultures over the 20 millennia since man emerged from prehistory into protohistory. In the lime-stone caves of Lascaux and Altamira and the Pyrenees region between France and northern Spain, some of the greatest animal art of all time was created *NOT* to be seen. The artists selected the darkest almost impenetrable recesses where few could have gone. Art was the vehicle chosen to underline man's inexorable participation in nature—man and animals meant man and life.

There is an artistic message that comes across the centuries. The various species, the movement, the character are all forcefully depicted yet sparse in detail. You cannot see every hair. The artists felt no need for the microscopic detail which tragically, from my prejudiced point of view, seems to be the leading religion of many of today's wildlife artists. Let me sound a cautionary note: most of the Limited Edition Art Prints—or prints in unlimited numbers with limited art—are to serious art what pop stars are to serious music.

In cave paintings the essence of the animal was there, whether on monumental or diminutive scale. This applied to primitive sculpture, whether in clay modeling of an extinct European bison from 13,000 B.C. or a flotilla of tiny seabirds of ivory from the Inuits of St. Lawrence Island in the Bering Sea.

The currents of art run deep. After thousands of years of isolation, the Quechua Indians of the Inca Empire would put little totemic figures of llamas into graves for use in the afterlife by the deceased. Parallels can be found in all primitive cultures throughout the world. Primitive animal art was less a celebration of the animal itself than it was an attempt to integrate animal life into human activity. Animal art, as we shall see, assumes a very different meaning as we enter the modern era.

Styles obviously change. The Egyptians knew how to draw, but their style appears distorted and flat to our eyes. They understood that perspective is a trick of the eye and that the farther away something is, which is the same size as you are, the smaller it appears, not the smaller it becomes. To compensate for this optical distortion, they made all of the cattle the same size, even though some are farther removed from the viewer than others. And yet in their art you can feel the powerful movement of that herd—almost hear the lowing—as it walks to its destination. It would appear similarly when they depict a gaggle of geese—the rules of perspective that we insist on today would be ignored. But the bustle and the imminent chaos would still be there.

I use the Egyptian experience to emphasize that there is no one right way of making art. There are lots of different approaches, each of which, when excellently done and conceived in the right spirit, is equally meritorious.

The Greeks knew that art and utility were not in conflict. Some of the finest classical art is to be found on pottery intended for domestic use. For example, there is this wonderful black-figure kylix of Dionysius returning on his little vessel with the grape arbor mast. Joyously guiding him home are dolphins leaping and sporting. They are not "accurate" in the modern Richard Ellis sense of underwater painting, but there is no doubt as to what they are doing.

The Scythians were considered barbarian nomads, but they appreciated the work of their captured Greek goldsmiths. On a 2,000-year-old pectoral, there is a 3/4-inch long sheep being milked, which is a study of the mutuality of interest between flock and shepherd. In no manner should size determine artistic greatness.

In the Pompeiian frescoes, even with the passage of two millennia, one has no difficulty at all in recognizing a magpie or a guinea fowl. There are no guinea fowl in southern Italy, nor have there ever been. It is an imported species from Africa. Animal art begins telling us where people traveled and traded. When Vesuvius erupted in 79 A.D., the magnificent Roman frescoes of Pompeii and Herculaneum were snuffed out, and for almost 1,800 years were lost.

The development of our Western animal art really sprang from indigenous roots whose continuity was snipped off from the classical world. The thrust of Western animal art has been profoundly influenced by *Genesis* 1:28, in which God gave man "dominion over" everything that flies, swims, walks and crawls. Not surprisingly, this conceit led to a corpus of art with animals in the service of man, not of animals in their own right.

Above all, animals represented food. Food meant hunting or domestication.

Food also meant cooking and eating. There are thousands of examples of animals in art depicted in one of these settings. Even as great an artist as Rembrandt could portray a flayed ox.

With status came institutionalization of killing. There is a subtle difference implied between killing for food—hunting—and killing for fun—sport. Based on hunting paintings, if you are a scorekeeper, the animals were not winning. They are usually shown at the wrong end of someone's spear, gun, trap, net or fishing rod. Such paintings number in the thousands.

In all such cases the animals were in the service of man. Overwhelmingly, animals in their own right were ignored. Great painters such as Titian, Tintoretto and most of those we associate with the Italian Renaissance boasted about the fact that they knew nothing about animal anatomy because the church taught that animals had no soul and, therefore, animals were beneath the dignity of a serious artist. The examples of awful animal renderings in so-called masterpieces are truly embarrassing. Leonardo, Albrecht Dürer and Bruegel are real exceptions.

In order to trace the evolution of animal art as we know it today, we find the real thread of continuity, tenuous though it might be, in books. Some of the earliest admittedly paralleled the developments in other art forms. The illuminated manuscripts in the sumptuous Books of Hours for the Duc de Berry have gem-like butterflies, flowers and birds in the margins for use as decorations, religious symbols or real participants in historical events—but always in the service of man. Not surprisingly, some of the earliest books containing animal art dealt with hunting and falconry.

But sometimes the tables were turned—engravings of man in the services of animals. One of the most delightful examples dates from 1633 in Olina's book on birds, presenting how to recognize them, take care of them, feed them and—back to the service of man—how to eat them. One plate on how "to stimulate the nightingale to sing" shows several clusters of musicians on lutes, dulcimers and celestes playing for their stimulation. Another plate shows how to prepare special food in a noble's kitchen, but another gives graphic instructions on how to impale little birds on a tree, before roasting 16 at a time on a skewer, before popping them into your mouth.

Then as now, art needed patrons. The church—directly and indirectly—was the largest patron and animals, therefore, could not expect much support. Ironically, a pre-Christian author was largely responsible for the lack of change in attitudes. Pliny, who died in the eruption of Vesuvius, wrote in his *History of the World* about whales that were 600 arpents long and three feet wide which, conveniently, lived in the deserts of Arabia where verification was difficult. This total divergence of fact and reason suited the church just fine. Down to 1634 with the first English translation, Pliny's 2,000 year out-of-date natural history was widely accepted as a sort of parallel gospel.

But the first glimmerings of what we would call science were discernible by the mid-sixteenth century. Pierre Belon of France and Conrad Gesner of Zurich produced major works which included hundreds of woodcuts of birds, animals and fish to accompany texts that, while incorporating some new material, relied heavily on Pliny, Aristotle and even earlier naturalists. It was Ulysses Aldrovandus of Bologna who was the first man ever to hold the title professor of natural history as opposed to natural philosophy. His multivolume sixteenth century work included firsthand field knowledge, and represents a significant pushing back of the frontiers of ignorance.

Woodcuts from the sixteenth century are stiff, but only because of the technical limitations imposed by the grain against and across which the engraver had to incise his lines. The original watercolours from which the cuts were made show that art was filled with subtle and fluid lines when the medium permitted.

Before being too quick to criticize the crude-looking cuts, let's admit that most of the species are instantly recognizable, which was no mean feat without the aid of colour. And remember, too, that 400 years ago, when these were done, Copernicus was still alive, Kepler had not yet discovered the laws of planetary motion, Newton had not yet been hit on the head by the apple, Descartes had not yet begun to think and therefore wasn't, the earth—not the sun—was the center of the official universe and, of course, Galileo had not been forced to recant. The woodcuts in the books of Belon, Gesner, Aldrovandus and their contemporaries are a visual link with the dawning of intellectual scientific thought in our Western civilization. In effect, they come from a world as different from ours as are the planets revealed by modern space probes.

Freedom of artistic expression in books was accelerated by the introduction of new technology. This is part of the human experience: technology allows leaps forward, not just leaps backward.

Copper engravings were used successfully for the first time at the end of the sixteenth and beginning of the seventeenth centuries. The birds and fish found in the books of Willoughby and Ray are a quantum jump beyond the woodcuts on which many were based. The most obvious next step was to combine the freedom allowed by copper with the artistic potential inherent in colour.

The first natural history book published with colour plates (as opposed to black and white intended for future colouring) was Eleazar Albin's *Natural History of Birds* from 1728 to 1731. On the title page of the first edition we read that the book was "published by the author, Eleazar Albin and carefully coloured by his daughter and self." She was so much better an artist that her name was taken off the title page of the second edition by her jealous father. In Elizabeth's work one notices not just a bird, but decorative elements that add an appropriate touch to the scene.

Mark Catesby was working on *A Natural History of Carolina, Florida and the Bahama Islands*, the first comprehensive natural history of North America. As a botanist Catesby taught himself how to engrave plates. He was beyond his predecessors in that he introduced birds and animals doing something, rather than just sitting there. His meadowlark and blue jay are classic examples of poses that show an activity associated with a particular species.

Catesby did magnificent plates of snakes, and this brings to mind the fact that we in North America tend to be species-oriented rather than art-oriented. A really bad painting of a bald eagle will surely sell more easily that the greatest portrait of a Wampum snake. Catesby achieved new levels of layout and artistry in his snake plates, but they can hardly be called popular.

Catesby also pioneered placing his animals and birds into settings that incorporated appropriate ecological elements. For this he is often called the "Colonial Audubon." If some of his figures are less than perfect, we can kindly remember that they had been collected 20 years previously and had been stored in kegs of dark navy rum. Catesby had to reconstruct a lifelike rendering from a soggy mess and copious field notes.

The evolution of animal art picked up speed as we approached the close of the eighteenth century. Peter Paillous was producing imposing life-sized raptors and water fowl for Thomas Pennant's *British Zoology*, one of the most important books on natural history of all time. Perspective, foreshortening, creative torsion and tension in the bodies were now standard elements.

At that time, there were even artists/naturalists who were trying to make a living in the publication of natural history books. Edward Donovan was one such entrepreneur. He could rightly point out that the more than 2,000 hand-coloured copper engravings in his 30-odd volumes were individual works of art. The underlying engraving was so faint that it basically ceased influencing the tonality of the finished plate. He laid on the colours in lavish amounts and completed the detail where necessary with a single-hair brush. On his insects, he added gold leaf and individually varnished the wings of dragonflies. The process was too expensive and too time-consuming to be economically viable, and so Donovan's books are considered among serious collectors to be little more than highly treasured oddities.

The artist who had the biggest impact was Donovan's contemporary, Thomas Bewick from Newcastle-upon-Tyne. Bewick's *Birds and Quadrupeds* revolutionized the art of the time and the art in books. By the simple act of turning the wood blocks on end to remove the impediment imposed by parallel grain, he was able to move his graver with the same freedom as would a silversmith. His birds—drawn from life—were brilliantly alive, and the textures of feather, rock, leaf and water were wondrously differentiated. Everything was accomplished with only black and white lines. His creatures were seldom more than an inch or two long, frequently far less, but they proved that monumental art could be achieved on a miniature scale.

Bewick is worth mentioning for another special reason. In 1790 he recognized the uniqueness of his thumbprint, and used an engraving of it as a receipt for copies of his *Fables of Aesop*. This was a century before Francis Galton published his great study on thumbprints which laid the foundation for a branch of forensic science. A hundred years earlier, an artist had anticipated a scientist. This is one of the reasons why I am pleased that art is treated seriously at the 4th World Wilderness Congress, because artists have every bit as much right to have input into the environmental consciousness as do those of a scientific bent.

The turning point between the old and the new was focused on Alexander Wilson. After this Scottish poet wrote some unnecessarily accurate verses about the good burghers of Paisley, he found himself on the next boat to America, where he devoted the rest of his life to the first comprehensive bird book of the new world. As he had been trained as a poet, it is not surprising that his text was magnificent. As an artist, at his best he was better than any who had come before, but at his worst he had little to commend him. Yet, the whole of Philadelphia fell over themselves to become his champion and his patron. Ironically, the adulation of Wilson closed the eyes of Americans to the greatness of John James Audubon who, when he had seen Wilson's birds, rightly published his own.

Audubon's start was quite modest. After Wilson's early death, Charles Lucien Bonaparte published what is known as *The Continuation of Wilson*, being those birds that the Scot had not seen. One of the plates in Bonaparte's book was of the great crow blackbird, known to us as the boat-tailed grackle. In the picture, the male in the foreground was by Rider. It was obviously nailed to the branch. There was no accuracy or truth in the rendering of the body or feathers, and the muscle and skeletal structures were completely lacking in conviction. It was, in short, a typical bird painting of the period. However, the female in the background could not have been done by the same artist, and it wasn't. The bird is alive, full of tension, and exhibits the essence of species. And it was the first painting by Audubon to be published.

But Philadelphia scornfully rejected the man who would change our way of viewing wildlife—and by extension, the way we see ourselves in relation to wildlife. Audubon took his portfolios over to Edinburgh and London, where he was to publish the greatest bird book of all time, *The Birds of America*, four double-elephant volumes with 435 hand-coloured copper plates.

To say that Audubon was a mere illustrator or just a wildlife painter says more about the critic than it does about this man of towering genius. History had, however, perhaps been too lavish in its praise of Audubon's originality, for many of the things that Audubon is credited with were actually pioneered by others. Others had painted birds life-size, but not up to the size of the whooping crane. Others had used proper ecological backgrounds, but never had they been so spectacular. But working away in Henderson, Kentucky and other backwoods areas, Audubon had not really had access to what others had done before. He independently arrived at the solutions and, in the process, far surpassed anything done by anyone before.

Time and again its so-called distortions have been proven incredibly accurate through the advent of high-speed photography. And time and again have critics pointed out specific faults in a small number of plates in order to condemn the whole. Despite admitted failures and even occasional plagiarism, it can be said that John James Audubon marks the transition from the old to the modern, and that he represents the first truly great wildlife artist in history.

Audubon did not just represent wildlife art; he represented art. His Great

Eskimo Curlew is a case in point. The upward motion of the neck and the slight swelling of the guttural sack tell of notes you can hear if your eyes become your ears. The angle of the beak is echoed by the countermovement of the waving grasses. In his plate of the yellow-breasted chat there is a visual bond between the male and the female on the nest. The two birds flying with their feet hanging down are not a mistake— that is the way chats fly during their nuptial dance. We are seeing birds as they are in nature, not artificially composed decorations conforming to the dictates of some passing taste.

The Birds of America overshadowed Audubon's other great project, The Viviparous Quadrupeds of North America, perhaps the greatest animal book of all time. An author stated recently in a leading wildlife magazine that Audubon did not know his animals as well as he knew his birds. To show that the poses were contorted, the author chose as his example the grey fox. I once spent a day with a grey fox. Every time it changed direction or something caught its attention, the fox would hunch his back and raise his paw for just a split second. By studying the picture carefully, at the extreme top right of the plate you can notice a small feather wafting down. The bird has just escaped, and the fox strikes the exact pose I had seen so fleetingly. Genius manifests itself in unexpected ways. Audubon's powers of observation were phenomenal, and so was his art. Give genius a chance, and mere talent is silenced.

Once Audubon—and his sons Victor and John Woodhouse—had showed the way, there were many other artists waiting in the wings. John Gould in England was one person who immediately understood the potential in publishing animal and bird art in this new form. He himself rarely completed a painting although surviving sketches and watercolours indicate that he possessed a fair amount of talent. Rather, he engaged the services of others, including his wife Elizabeth and artists such as Edward Lear of The Owl and the Pussycat fame. Hart and Richter were two more of the artists who worked for Gould. Altogether Gould published 40 folio volumes containing 2,999 hand-coloured lithographs which, for quality and consistency, constitute the most ambitious publishing venture undertaken during Victorian times.

The greatest of the artists who worked for Gould was Joseph Wolf, known in his day as "peerless," "impeccable" and by other similarly adulatory words. Wolf was only 20 when he did his famous portraits of falcons for A Treatise on Falconry, before emigrating from Germany to England. By the time he died in 1899 he had completed thousands of paintings and sketches, none of which were more beautiful than those done for Daniel Giraud Elliot's monographs of the Pheasants, Birds of Paradise, and The Cat Family, considered by many today to be the most sumptuous books of all time.

The finished plates were hand-coloured lithographs that had been translated onto stone from Wolf's original charcoal sketches by two other artists, Joseph Smit and John Keulemans. From the artistic point of view, these sketches far exceed the final product, because they bring you face to face with that once-in-a-lifetime microsecond when the artist sees and experiences nature. You share his reactions before he has a chance to go back into the studio to polish, change, edit and thereby lose the magic of the moment.

In Wolf, art and science were finally reconciled. The artistic approach was carried on by younger men such as Keulemans who, during a working career that spanned 50 years, produced more than 30,000 paintings and drawings of remarkable quality. But Keulemans was the sunset of the Victorian style. He overlapped with a newcomer, Archibald Thorburn, who can be called the first of the truly modern painters. In his early paintings for Lord Lilford's *Coloured Figures of the Birds of the British Islands* (1885 to 1897), we find for the first time an understanding of the role of light. Thorburn saw reflection and refraction and light diffused by differing atmospheres. He also understood how birds flew and floated, and how they interacted with gravity. He built up his paintings in planes of perspective that started at the viewer's feet, so that the viewer became a participant in the painting, not merely an observer. In Thorburn's paintings the animals owe nothing to man. There are no cooks, farmers, hunters or sportsmen. There are only animals for their own sake. Perhaps this signaled a new degree of maturity in our civilization.

As animal art concentrated less on man and more on animals, the vast majority of works came from artists whose mother tongues were not Romance languages. The French, Italians, Spaniards and Portuguese did not paint wildlife. This strange fact may in part be accounted for by a parallel lack in any of their languages of a word for "wilderness." Each has a phrase or two that defines part of the concept, but nothing that is all-embracing. No single word comes down from the time when wilderness still existed in the Mediterranean world. Statistically, out of all proportion to their populations, the greatest animal painters have come from Northern countries: England, Scotland, Germany, Holland, Canada, the United States and Scandinavia. In fact, the greatest animal painter of all was Bruno Liljefors of Sweden, and in my opinion the finest bird painter was a Swiss, Leo-Paul Robert.

As unbelievable as Robert's bird paintings were, he always claimed that his greatest masterpieces were the 500 life-sized portraits of the caterpillars of his native Jura Mountains. Just as Catesby's snakes proved two centuries earlier, Robert's caterpillars emphasize how we tend to be species-oriented rather than art-oriented.

For centuries, animals in art played a subservient role and, within the total framework of art, animal art—or more accurately, animals in art—did not constitute a very large proportion. In fact, a case can be made for surprise as to how much there was, given the lingering prejudice of *Genesis* and the divinely bestowed "dominion." By the nineteenth century, quality and quantity of animal art took a quantum leap forward. Who were these people to whom we owe so much? I've described some, but many remain anonymous. In 1834, in Edinburgh, there appeared the first volume of *The Naturalist's Library*, an encyclopedic work that would span a decade and consist of 40 volumes. There were over 1,700 hand-coloured, copper engravings in each edition, and there were an average of at least 5,000 copies of each volume. Simple mathematics shows that almost 50 million beautifully hand-coloured engravings were required for this one publishing venture alone. In one of the volumes there was an interesting publisher's advertisement which stated: "Altogether independent of the gratification which these plates have given to the public, the publication has opened up a source of agreeable, permanent, and profitable employment, to a very numerous class of most deserving and industrious persons in Edinburgh, whose rank in society and whose education precluded them from applying themselves readily to any other occupation than that of colouring." Men and women of towering genius have combined with the lowest of the low to bring us 400 years of animal art in books.

The importance of the development of animal art in books cannot be overestimated, as the chief repository of animal representation was found in the engravings and later the lithographs that accompanied a vast outpouring of books dealing with science, travel and sport. It has been rightly remarked that, until the popularization of the camera, more about science was learned through the sights of a gun than through any scientific instrument.

The patronage for wildlife books—even spectacular folios with hand-colored lithographed plates—was relatively widespread compared to the support given to wildlife paintings. It was only in 1874, after all, that the U.S. Congress finally authorized the unheard-of expenditure if $10,000 for a large painting of the Grand Canyon, by Thomas Moran, to hang in the Senate lobby. Even though it is dangerous to ascribe precise motives to the actions of others taken in other times, perhaps we can state that the Grand Canyon painting does mark a turning point in the official view of the importance of wilderness, and by extension, of wildlife. Since then the interest in and appreciation of wildlife and wilderness art has grown to the extraordinary levels they enjoy today.

© Drawing by Catesby, ca. 1731

CULTURAL CARRYING CAPACITY AND THE DEFENSE OF WILDERNESS

Garrett Hardin

Although environmental issues are steadily gaining support among economists, it is still true that our most vigorous opponents are found in the business and economics community. Even extreme statements of one's enemies should be taken seriously, because it is always possible that they may prevail. One of the strongest condemnations of wilderness lovers was made several years ago by one of President Reagan's most valued advisers. The wealthy industrialist Justin Dart, after admitting that he "loathed environmentalists," went on to say:

"I am for preservation. I say we should preserve the redwoods, sure, maybe 100 acres of them, just like the way God intended them, to show the kids. Those environmentalists who talk about preserving the wilderness in Alaska—how many goddamned bloody people will end up going there in the next 100 years to suck their thumbs and write poetry?"

In the academic world, unfriendly "growthmaniacs"—Herman Daly's term— may speak less colorfully but more effectively. Julian Simon and Herman Kahn have attacked one of the fundamental concepts of ecology in these words:

"Because of increases in knowledge, the earth's carrying capacity has been increasing throughout the decades and centuries and millenia to such an extent that the term carrying capacity has by now no useful meaning."

This statement raises several important points. The authors either deny— or do not understand—the centrality of the Malthusian model of population regulation. What Malthus asserted can be cast in the modern language of cybernetics. The temperature of a room is kept nearly constant through the suppression of departures from the "set-point" by negative feedback. In a similar fashion a population of animals is normally kept near its set-point—which is determined by the carrying capacity of the territory—through the negative feedbacks of Malthus's "misery and vice" (on the upside) and excess reproduction (on the downside). The logical entity that accomplishes this equilibration is called a *demostat*.

Most criticisms of Malthus rest on his failure to realize that the demostatic set-point was being moved upward in his day by technological advances in the production of food and other necessities of life. In our analogy, we would say that the temperature of a room was thermostatically controlled even if an unseen hand were to slowly turn the set-point to a higher level. So also is population demostatically controlled even when the set-point undergoes a slow secular drift (due to technology or whatever).

Malthus was not alone in failing to see the significance of technology. At its beginning, every historical trend is hard to see. Recall that the Renaissance in Europe was not named until four centuries after it started. All we have to do to make Malthus up-to-date is this: add the possibility of secular drift to the implied demostatic set-point.

Modern economic theory is such that economists experience difficulty in taking time seriously if it extends farther than five years into the future. Communist leaders and capitalist planners both find five-year plans adequate for most of the challenges that face them. Economists who say that Malthusian theory is useless because the set-point has risen for two centuries thereby reveal deficient imaginations. Human beings have been on this earth for at least a million years. During most of this time the change in set-point has been imperceptible during a single human lifetime. Not so, during the last 200 years.

But what are two centuries out of 10,000? No more than a "blip" in a curve. We hope that the human future will extend for at least another 10,000 centuries. If it does, what is the chance that the earth's carrying capacity will increase for 10,000 centuries as it has during the mere two centuries of the immediate past? *Zero.* There is not material enough, energy enough, or enough elbow room on earth to nourish forever the compound interest growth of technology of the past two centuries. (Migration into space is another matter, suitable for contemplation by those who believe in "Star Wars." In any case, this possibility won't help whatever human beings are left behind on earth.)

Some economists seem not to know that every rigorous science must be built on a foundation of conservation principles. Too many economists are like Dickens' Mr. Micawber in believing that "Something will turn up." Their childlike faith in the power of future technology justifies (they think) their walking away from the work of paying attention to the foundations of political economy. The economists' "trickle-down" hypothesis holds that no one need be concerned with distribution problems because riches will automatically cascade down from rich to poor. This seductive hypothesis is not part of technology, it is not part of science and it is not a proper part of political economy. It is a religious belief (and a very convenient one for those in power).

The belief that carrying capacity is a meaningless concept is equally convenient, but we cannot let economists get away with such an assertion. The concept of carrying capacity is as basic to ecology as is the conservation of energy to physics. Let's see what carrying capacity means when it is applied to animal populations.

The carrying capacity of a territory is that number of animals that can be supported year after year without degradation of the environment—that is, without lowering the carrying capacity. Because capacity is subject to both seasonal and secular variations, the carrying capacity figure adopted must, in practice, be the lowest in the time series; or, that failing, massive die-offs will take place whenever capacity takes a downward turn.

When we turn to populations of *Homo sapiens*, capacity theory needs to be elaborated. In 1967, the economist Colin Clark concluded that "the full support of one person requires the continuous cultivation of an area no larger than 27 square meters [of agricultural land]." Estimating the ultimate extent of the earth's agricultural land at 9.33 billion hectares, Clark concluded that earth could support 346 billion people. Wherever there is today a single human being, in Clark's Brave New World 69 human beings would ultimately have to be accommodated.

Are we, then, to say that the carrying capacity of the earth is 346,000,000,000 people? Only if we are reconciled to the thought of restricting *everybody* to the minimum number of calories required for the barest living. No automobiles, no airplanes, no movie theaters, no sports arenas, no museums, no orchestras, no universities and perhaps no schools of any sort. Amenities that are conspicuous squanderers of energy would be forbidden: meat, baked food (boiling is more efficient), all sports and all vacation trips. Even complaining would have to be forbidden—it, too, "wastes" energy. Each adult would be held to a maximum daily consumption of 2,300 calories.

If you want a view of what such a world would be like, go to Bangladesh, where energy consumption is less than the present American standard by a factor of 140, in round numbers.

Now we see a good reason for being wary of "carrying capacity," but it is not the economists' reason. The concept is not meaningless; on the contrary, it has too many possible meanings. Calculations of the carrying capacity of the earth are necessarily based on the level of amenities assumed, whether stated explicitly or not. Focusing merely on energy, we note that Americans use 100 times as much energy as they need for the barest living—some 2,300 calories of energy per person per day.

Energy is a convenient yardstick of living, but it does not give the whole measure. A growing proportion of the population realizes there are real human values to be imputted to uncrowded beaches, to wild rivers, to the odor of pine forests unmixed with the effluvia of industry and automobiles, to extensive and lonely wilderness, and to all of the arts. Though the cost of such goods might be stated as energy production foregone, this approach hardly seems adequate.

We are deeply concerned with the values of the culture, where "culture" is used in the anthropologist's sense to include all the things, both material and immaterial, that are significant elements in the life of a people. If we want to make a meaningful assay of the potentials of our earth, we must replace the simple concept of carrying capacity by the richer concept of *cultural carrying capacity*. The semantic change does not automatically give us the answer to our problem; it reminds us that there can be no answer without an agreement on values, on standard of living, on "the quality of life."

Bluntly put: whenever someone asks you for the carrying capacity of the earth, the United States, or whatever, you must, at the outset, refuse to give an answer. You must convert the question into an inquiry into values. Most social scientists (including most economists) evade value questions, hoping thereby to make their disciplines more "scientific." But without values, explicit or implicit, what use are social studies? (Whether the studies are to be called sciences or not is a definitional issue.)

Cultural carrying capacity is inversely related to the richness of the culture.

What then are the consequences when different nations adopt different standards of living? Many idealists regard national boundaries as indefensibly arbitrary; they hope to weld the many nations into "One World" that lives by Marx's ideal of "From each according to his ability, to each according to his needs!" Even in 1875, when Karl Marx first coined this slogan, the ideal could not be successfully defended, because of a fundamental analysis carried out almost half a century earlier by William Forster Lloyd. But the significance of Lloyd's work was not realized until 1968.

Now we know that a global Marxist sharing according to need will produce universal impoverishment. Just as free competition among different forms of money results in bad money driving out good money, so will free competition between different living standards (if need is the paramount consideration in distribution) produce a Gresham's Law of the Environment: Low living standards will drive out high standards. In a truly Marxist distribution, ultimately all grades of cultural carrying capacity become irrelevant, as the barest form of "carrying capacity" determines the outcome. Turn all the means of subsistence into common property and a "tragedy of the commons" is set into motion.

I am not sure that we who love wilderness appreciate fully the difficulties facing us. It is easy to perceive the threat of commercial greed, in such statements as the one quoted earlier from a Reagan adviser. It is much harder to recognize the latent dangers of idealism. Yet history presents us with minatory examples that should give us pause.

The growth of concern for animal welfare and the rise of the concept of the "sanctity of (human) life" in the eighteenth and nineteenth century may have seemed innocent enough in the beginning. But today we reap the unforeseen harvest of these idealistic movements. Medical research facilities are now being "trashed" by self-styled animal lovers who are made furious by the use of dogs and cats in experiments. Birth control clinics dedicated to improving the lives of women are bombed by "Right-to-Lifers." Both kinds of violence are carried out by people who express the most elevated concern for life.

What about wilderness? Is it possible that we may some day encounter a kind of idealism that threatens the preservation of wilderness? I think it is possible. The idealists who pose the greatest threat to the preservation of wilderness are those who most eloquently put forward *equality of distribution* as a paramount good.

Like so many other ideals, this one also dates back to the eighteenth century. In 1796 the radical French revolutionist who called himself Gracchus Babeuf published a *Manifesto of the Equals,* in which the following significant passage occurs:

"We henceforth intend to live and to die equal, just as we were born; we want real equality or death, that is what we need. And we shall have it, this real equality, no matter what the price. . . .Woe to anyone who would offer resistance to so keen a desire!. . .may all the arts be destroyed, if need be, as long as we have real equality."

Within nations, and between nations, those who place a Marxist distribution according to need at the pinnacle of the ethical system are following in the footsteps of Babeuf. It will be a sad day for wilderness if society adopts the Babeuvian idea, May all art and beauty be destroyed, if need be, to achieve equality of distribution.

Wilderness can be preserved only by explicitly asserting that equality of distribution, desirable though it may seem, must not be made the paramount goal of society. If we are deeply concerned with the well-being of our descendants, our paramount goal must be the acceptance of a level of cultural carrying capacity that includes "all the arts" and such precious amenities of life as wilderness.

© Sankhala

WILDERNESS AND HUMAN POTENTIAL

HOW WILDERNESS FACILITATES PERSONAL GROWTH

John C. Hendee and Michael Brown

The general notion is that in the wilderness you can learn about yourself, your companions and nature. In wilderness, away from the social intensity and distractions of daily life, participants test themselves, heighten self-confidence and esteem, clarify their identity and personal values and address the central issues in their lives. While in such environments and while benefiting from awareness, plans to change troublesome behavior can be laid and patterns redirected toward more inspired purposes.

How do programmed wilderness experiences facilitate personal growth? When and under what conditions is it most likely to occur? How much is possible? What is the right mix of hard skills, such as rock climbing, and soft skills, such as group dynamics, exercises and solo time? Can experiences be prescribed to produce desired results? Can we, as practitioners and proponents of the use of wilderness for personal growth, therapy and education, synthesize collective evidence from studies into a practical conceptual framework?

Scores of studies have been conducted on wilderness experience programs to determine their effect on participants. Hundreds of investigative and popular articles have been written about wilderness adventure programming and outdoor leadership, and courses are offered at many universities. Scientifically, one can conclude from the research evidence that many wilderness programs yield small but significant increases in self-esteem, improved self-concept, a shift in locus of control from external to internal and heightened self-awareness among some participants.

Despite several analyses of the experiential process, there are not yet agreed-upon principles to guide the training of instructors and practitioners in the use of wilderness for personal growth, therapy and education. Neither is there any agreed upon theory, model or framework to guide further research or program design.

This paper offers a conceptual model that synthesizes previous research, personal experience and years of dialogue with instructors of wilderness programs, their participants and other wilderness users.

Our goals in developing this theoretical model are: to create a useful tool incorporating previous research and experience to help practitioners improve their programs and train instructors; to focus additional research; to help users understand how to use the wilderness for their own greater inspiration and benefit; and, to increase understanding by resource managers about how the natural environments they manage can contribute to the development of human resources.

PERSONAL GROWTH

First, some definitions and assumptions: By personal growth, we mean a range of effects toward expanded fulfillment of one's capabilities and potential. We see a continuum of personal growth outcomes ranging from insight at the low end of the spectrum, clarified purpose in the middle, to transformation or redirection of one's life on the high end.

We define growth motivation as including all motive patterns which aim toward personal development and self-actualization. For example, personal growth begins with an increased awareness of one's desires, abilities and values, which makes possible the satisfaction of needs and the achievement of goals that are important and different for each individual. For some it may be more power and possessions; for others it may be enhanced love and relatedness to humanity. But many people may also be struggling with deficiency needs such as dependency, low self-esteem, a poor sense of identity, or a lack of direction or self-confidence.

Postulate 1

Personal growth depends on receptivity: Personal growth from a wilderness experience depends on the participants' receptivity. Do they want to go? What are their incentives to participate? Are they ready to change? Readiness for change may depend on conditions preceding the experience which affect one's motivation to grow or change, and also one's stage in life. For example, people struggling with deficiency needs or those who are already striving toward self-improvement are likely to be more receptive to personal growth. So are people in transition from one life stage to another, such as from adolescence to adult-hood, mature adult to middle age, from illness to health, from marriage to divorce. Likewise, people coping with change or emotional trauma—such as a new job or the loss of a loved one—are good candidates for personal growth and can benefit from clarified values and heightened self-esteem which may stimu-late renewed direction and meaning for their lives.

We believe that one cause of clouded results in the hundreds of studies of par-ticipants in wilderness programs is that they include persons who are not in a re-ceptive mode. Such studies include participants along the whole continuum of growth motivation, including persons who are comfortable in a steady state per-iod of adjustment and not motivated to explore themselves. Others may be in a stage of denial which often precedes growth and would cause them to resist a process of change. Unreceptive participants are not likely to experience growth.

Postulate 2

Personal growth depends on optimum stress from the experience: Personal growth depends on the right degree of stress from the wilderness experience—physically and emotionally—and this threshold will vary with the physical condition and previous experience of each individual.

Natural environment experiences are diverse in their intensity, from gentle hikes near town to wilderness experiences requiring rigorous and skillful physi-cal activity like backpacking or technical rock climbing. Stress comes from dealing with the rigors, discomfort, danger and uncertainty of outdoor experi-ences. A sudden snowstorm can turn a day-hike into a survival situation. The stress is physical and psychological, as anyone knows who has gritted his teeth with determination to fight pain and fatigue those last few miles back to camp at the end of a hard day. With extreme physical stress may come psychological breakdown as anyone knows who has unravelled wilderness disasters where the difference between death and survival was panic and illogical decisions.

There is wide belief that the greater the natural environment intensity, and the harder it is to access and enjoy the environment, the greater the potential for personal growth.(No pain, no gain!) It is thought that the more natural, primitive and remote the setting and camping style, the greater the likelihood for personal growth to occur.

But this is not necessarily true. There are limits, and each person has his or her own unique threshold of tolerance for intensity of contact with the natural environment which must not be crossed if the experience is to be positive and productive. Beyond a certain point, the individual may become overwhelmed by the challenge, demands, uncertainty or dangers, and then the experience can "short circuit" with negative results. Excessive stress may trigger a whiplash effect. For example, too much stress may provoke uncontrolled emotional release beyond a constructive threshold and result in denial, repression of exposed weaknesses and mobilization of defenses—a regressive rather than a progressive growth effect. Furthermore, excessive stress once survived can lead some to inflated ego and self-aggrandizement—a survivalist effect that can produce a macho or authoritarian attitude and self-concept that will thwart cooperation.

Prescribing the right degree of environmental intensity is thus extremely important and will vary depending on individual differences. Some things to consider are willingness to risk, personal growth motivation and needs, physical health, previous outdoor experience and skill, responsibility and maturity, the psychological readiness or receptivity or the goal orientation of the participants, and the individual or group outcomes desired.

The purpose is to create just enough stress with which the individual can successfully cope, but enough to also bring core behavior and psychological patterns into awareness where they can be identified, clarified, evaluated and redirected if desired.

Postulate 3

Wilderness experiences provide change and attunement: Wilderness experiences provide a reprieve from cultural influences, external constraints and stimuli, providing a change of pace and the opportunity for attunement to oneself and the immediate environment. For many people whose lives are intense, an immediate effect may be a slowing down. For others, the effect may be liberation from the external forces that govern their daily lives.

With this liberation from the patterns of our daily lives, latent feelings, emotions and physiological functions may emerge. New perspectives may evolve. Enhanced potential for insight and a sense of renewal may follow as core patterns of behavior and values are viewed from a new perspective.

In wilderness, attuning to ourselves and the natural world, we can experience the functions of the right side of the brain. We can relax, slow down and access higher levels of awareness, imagination, intuition, creativity, empathy, and insight and enjoy the energies these functions deliver: awe, wonder, hope, inspiration and vision that connect us to a sense of the values, meaning, purpose and density in our lives. In the wilderness, we can experience, once again, the true significance of our lives in the natural order. This experience, of seeing ourselves in true perspective, both humbles and empowers us.

Postulate 4

Wilderness provides metaphors. Wilderness activities can provide metaphors to strengthen desirable qualities for application back home. The most simple metaphor may come from success in dealing with stress from the environmental intensity of experience and discovering previously untapped resources and a sense of accomplishment. This is why optimum stress from the environment is so important to provide challenge, but allow for successful coping.

The opportunities for metaphors are diverse using programmed activities which may reveal and allow development of native abilities of leadership, creativity, enhanced reasoning and problem-solving, communication, cooperation and teamwork, trust, delegation and negotiation. Metaphors provide new ways of seeing reality and the opportunity to reframe old ways of doing things. For example, the cooperation and teamwork required to get a squad over a 12-foot wall. Trust is required to be lowered on a rope in a rock climbing and rapelling exercise. Group dynamics exercise may require communication, cooperation and negotiation. Visualization exercises, enriched and stimulated by the natural environment, can provide a blueprint for growth in new self-concepts: for example, I am like an oak tree with deep roots and strong branches, I am like the river, with greater depth when moving steady and gently than when rushing wide but shallow. Encouraging these images can shape and guide behavior, inspire effort and build self-esteem.

HOW THE WILDERNESS WORKS: FOUR HYPOTHESES

How do wilderness experiences facilitate personal growth? The foregoing postulates are assumed to be true but, of course, each one provides a focus for additional research. They are important, because if we can isolate and understand the processes and conditions which enhance opportunities for personal growth from wilderness experiences, then we can more effectively prescribe experiences, conditions and programmed activities to maximize growth potential. These postulates lead us to four additional ideas or hypotheses about how wilderness experience can lead to personal growth that are both sequential and interrelated. They assert that wilderness experiences can lead to (1) increased per-sonal awareness, leading to (2) a threshold of growth motivation or what could be called one's growing edge, (3) which in turn can result in increased social awareness. All of these states are enhanced by the primal influences of wilderness and the experiencing of ourselves in true humility to the natural world.

1. *Personal awareness*—Wilderness experiences can reveal core patterns of personal behavior, values, emotions, fears, drives and tendencies, thus fostering heightened self-awareness, a first step toward personal growth. When we begin a wilderness experience we bring with us our worries, anxieties and concerns, and usually have had to forcefully carve out time for the trip from the overwhelming fullness of our lives. Our minds and bodies want to slow down and relax even as our spirits want to soar. It takes a while to shuck worries, tensions, concerns and fatigue, and even longer to throw off the patterns that drive us in our daily lives. One of the principle values of outdoor experiences is the opportunity it provides to notice just how patterned we really are.

The wilderness environment provides a mirror with which to see reflections of our inner worlds. We are uncomfortable when our normal patterns do not work, or when they stand out in stark contrast in a new and unstructured setting, and this discomfort heightens our awareness. The novelty of the wilderness experience strips us of the normal social basis for personal identity and provides many opportunities for acute personal awareness. In the absence of our masks, roles and other social mechanisms for dealing with one another, we must confront ourselves. We can develop insight and glean new perspectives about who we really are inside.

Why does this occur in wilderness? Because it is so far removed from the influences of our daily life. Our patterns, values and beliefs emerge in bold relief. They become clear to us and our companions. We cannot blame troubling patterns in the outdoors on our partners, boss, kids, parents, society. We are the authors of our wilderness experience and by example we may come to learn that we are also the primary authors of our lives back home. Such heightened personal awareness is often an uncomfortable revelation, but it is often quite liberating, too. Heightened awareness is the first step on a path toward change.

2. *Growing edge*—Wilderness and outdoor experiences, by heightening personal awareness of core patterns, beliefs and values, place the participant at a growing edge where these personal qualities can be evaluated and change can be initiated if desired. The wilderness experience provides space for something new to happen. If unconscious patterns and values become clear, it can lead to important questions: Is there a better way? What is the meaning of my life? What goals should I pursue? What's worth living for, what's worth dying for? Simply stated, the growing-edge hypothesis asserts that as personal awareness is heightened under the stress of coping with the outdoors, core patterns will become clear and be available for evolution and potential change.

It is possible to go into the wilderness and simply replicate our standard patterns and routines. The hard-driving business executive may go with his son and hike 15 miles a day, carrying 65 pounds of gear. The immature young adult may go with his friends for a weekend beer party and leave beer cans strewn along the trail. People seek escape from the unhappiness of their lives and use the outdoors as a space simply to get away, with no intention of confronting their inner selves. In fact, many outdoor enthusiasts adamantly resist combining outdoor recreation with programmed activities in search of personal growth. It would spoil the fun! Such participants may be unreceptive to the personal growth opportunities of programmed wilderness experiences.

We assert that outdoor environments, even on these terms, provide unique space for nurturing the growth of the human spirit. The 15-mile-a-day executive may have no other forum with which to reach his son. The young adult is asserting his independence, testing his new wings and beginning to claim life for himself. If he finds part of himself in the wilderness, he may return to search for more. Conservation and environmental ethics will hopefully be learned along the way. Unhappy people can find a certain peace and calm, and enjoy the quieting effect of wilderness and the much needed change of pace and opportunity for attunement. Values have a way of getting clear, almost by themselves, in the company of solitude and silence.

Participants in a receptive mood, experiencing a proper degree of environment intensity, liberated from their normal routines and enjoying a much needed change of pace and the opportunity for attunement, may find their growing edge even without the help of programmed activities directed toward self-discovery.

3. *Social Awareness*—Wilderness experiences in groups reveal individual patterns of social interaction that can then be evaluated. New patterns can be shaped and learned if desired.

Every wilderness group is composed of unique individuals who are required to interact for the duration of their trip. If strangers, they will be without the customary social identity of their daily life. Each unconsciously brings his or her patterns, defenses, masks and roles. But then each may begin to slow down, to relax, to tune in to the environment and to themselves. In the outdoors people begin to socialize in remarkably different ways. Status differences dissolve, stories are told, secrets are revealed, pains are shared, new alliances and friendships are formed, existing friendships or family bonds can be strengthened.

Unshielded by status and other conventional social bases for identity, we have many opportunities to see ourselves as others do, see into others like never before, and recognize and appreciate our common human condition. In wilderness, enhanced trust among interdependent companions can reduce the risk of self-disclosure, and patterns of social interaction that are functional, effective and inspired can be developed and shared. With participants moving toward heightened self-awareness and their growing edge, new and more effective patterns of social interaction can be cultivated, tested and learned.

4. *The primal experience*—Wilderness experiences directly expose participants to the primal influences of nature and the elements, which foster a sense of humility in relation to the natural world. The exposure to primal influences distinguishes the wilderness as an extraordinary place for personal growth compared to other locations such as a playground, counseling center, classroom or retreat facility.

In wilderness we must pay close attention to what is going on around us and continually adapt and respond to changing circumstances. Our awareness must return to the basics, to the essentials, to the primal truths of existence. We confront the natural world and sense its indifference to us, regardless of our social status back home. We feel relatively insignificant in the face of nature's awesome power, the perfect antidote for a self-absorbed ego. We learn we must be responsible for ourselves and for each other, in ways that are immediate and direct, for ultimately there can be lives at stake. We must pay the price for any mistake. We see ourselves more clearly under such conditions, and we may be both humbled and inspired by the beauty and power of the natural world.

Dealing with the natural world in a direct and unmediated way allows basic levels of awareness to be activated. Structures of perception and ways of knowing that lie below the ego and the personality are activated. We experience an awareness that is fully present to the moment. We remember with our bodies and souls the ancient language of survival. This is how the creatures in the wilderness survive, responding naturally to life and the threat of death.

This, too, is our potential: to experience the world in a primal, immediate undistorted way. For a moment we take our rightful place beside the creatures of the wild. Our original selves reemerge, long buried beneath the artificial constructs and patterns of society and culture. We sense the mystery of the natural world. We are a part of the timeless dance of life and an expression of its mystery. This is the real meaning of recreation and renewal: to be reborn with renewed perspective about who and what we are. Such moments of realization are extraordinary when they happen, are never forgotten, and are moments upon which lives of integrity and meaning can be built.

The model presented here is a guide to how wilderness experiences can work for personal growth. We hope and expect that the model will be a focus of debate that will generate additional ideas and inspire future research. In the meantime, it provides a valuable framework to guide: (1) the design of wilderness programs to increase their potential for leading to personal growth, (2) the instruction of wilderness program leaders in concepts and processes effective in increasing the growth potential of wilderness program participants, (3) wilderness visitors toward more enriching experiences. The model can also increase the understanding of wilderness managers so that they can better protect wilderness for personal growth and the development of human potential.

APPLYING THE MODEL

These ideas are presented in a scientific framework of postulates and hypotheses. Let us tell you more directly how they might be applied to increase the personal growth potential of wilderness experiences.

First, diagnose and cultivate receptivity to personal growth and change. It is unrealistic to think that maximum growth is possible among random participants merely by running them through a wilderness program.

Second, create the right degree of stress through program activities and contact with natural environment. The objective is not to break individuals down but to bring each of them to their growing edge by creating optimum stress for each individual. Recognize that the tolerance for stress of each individual is different and that proper challenge for one may be too much for another. A balance is needed between hard activities like rock climbing and soft activities like introspective exercises and group dynamics. In the final analysis what the wilderness location and outdoor activities really do is set the stage for something introspective to occur.

Third, to take full advantage of the new environment and activities in wilderness, time and encouragement are needed for attunement to oneself, the group and the natural environment. There must be time and activities that encourage personal reflection, social interaction among group members and communion with nature. This focus on reflection, social activity and environmental interaction may be most effective if gradual at first and then in increasing depth.

In conclusion, the model suggests that optimizing the personal growth potential of wilderness programs depends on: receptive candidates who are ready for change; optimum stress from contact with the natural environment and a balance of hard and soft activities; a sufficient change for attunement to oneself, the group and the environment while in the wilderness and away from daily routines and roles; and, the conscious use of metaphors from the wilderness experience and program activities. The goal is to allow core patterns, feelings, beliefs, values and social interaction to emerge, and to use this heightened state of personal and social awareness to bring one to a growing edge where one's behavior can be understood, addressed, evaluated and affirmed or redirected.

Finally, the model suggests, and we firmly believe, that these goals are facilitated by the primal influences of wilderness that allow participants to see themselves in their true perspective to the natural world—a view and realization that is humbling, inspiring and empowering.

THE WILDERNESS LEADERSHIP SCHOOL

Ian Player and Wayne Elliot

The idea of the Wilderness Leaderhip School was conceived in 1957 when I was a game ranger stationed at Lake St. Lucia, a reserve under the control of the Natal Parks Board. A group of six schoolboys from my old school, St. John's College, was visiting the lake reserve and accompanied the game guards and me on patrol. The schoolboys' wilderness experience amongst the hippo, crocodile, flamingoes and pelicans and the coastal dune forests inspired a response that has become common to participants and a refrain Wilderness Leadership School trails since: "This experience changed my life."

The beginnings of the Wilderness Leadership School are founded in the steadfast belief that the future of mankind lay in an informed public—particularly people in leaderhsip positions—who will lead others to appreciate the necessity to conserve the natural resources of our planet, particularly the wilderness areas. The original objective of the Wilderness Leadership School was: "To enable people to go into the wilderness and wild places of southern Africa, under experienced guidance, in order to gain understanding of and to receive instruction in the conservation of natural resources, of nature and of wilderness."

The Wilderness Leadership School continues to believe that the leaders of today are mankind's most precious resource, and that they can be strengthened in spirit, mind, body and character by a wilderness experience. The school allows people the opportunity to experience firsthand not only the important role wilderness areas play in maintaining a healthy, vigorous world, but also to understand the relationship between the environment and human nature.

The symbol of the Wilderness Leadership School since inception has been the *Erythrina caffra* leaf chosen by Magqubu Ntombela. The three points of the leaf represent "Man to God, Man to Man, Man to Soil," the fundamental philosophy of the school.

More than 10,000 people from many countries have now experienced the trail with the Wilderness Leadership School. As a result, the school has become a vital part of an international movement and is able to influence conservation policy decisions.

The Wilderness Leadership School employs four full-time field officers who conduct the trails, two in the Province of the Transvaal and two in Natal. There is a volunteer staff of 25 field officers in engineering, architecture, building industry and others too numerous to mention. These volunteers perform a most valuable function by conducting weekend trails for interested members of the public who are only able to be away for two days instead of the normal five. The volunteers have been highly trained by the professional staff. They are unpaid and are able to expand the work of the school without being a financial drain. Plans are under way to train volunteer field officers in the Province of Natal. A branch has been formed in the Cape Province where experimental trails are being conducted by a psychiatrist with patients from a local hospital. There is strong belief that the wilderness has powerful therapeutic properties which can assist in the healing of the mentally ill.

Financially the school receives one-third of its income through trail fees and the remainder in donations from commerce, industry and individuals in South Africa, and from conservation organizations in the United States, including the International World Leadership Foundation. The IWLF has made it possible for many young American leaders to participate on Wilderness Leadership School trails through the provision of scholarships. The IWLF has also sponsored the four World Wilderness Congresses.

A review of the Wilderness Leadership School's activities over the last 30 years shows that the school provides two kinds of experience. First, it gives all the people of South Africa—irrespective of race, colour or creed—as well as visitors from overseas, the opportunity to experience the wilderness, to feel the rhythm of Africa, so aptly described by Jan Smuts, who wrote the following in 1929:

"The mysterious eerie spirit which broods over its vast solitude, where no human pressure is felt, where the human element, indeed, shrinks into utter insignificance and where a subtle spirit, much older than the human spirit, grips you and subdues you and makes you one with itself."

This is achieved by walking through the wilderness areas of South Africa like the Umfolozi game reserve and Lake St. Lucia reserve and areas in Northern Jululand adminsitered by the KwaZulu Bureau of Natural Resources. The Pilanesberg National Park and the Borakalalo National Park in the independent homeland of Bophutatswana are also used. The walking is done at a leisurely pace, each trailist carrying his own backpack and food for the trail. Encounters with the large mammals of Africa—black rhino, lion, Cape buffalo and white rhino—heighten the experience. Canoeing amongst the hippo and crocodile adds the spice of physical danger which heightens the awareness of the trailist. The scream of the African fish eagle in the early mornings and the sound of nocturnal predators and birds make campfire talk a special experience. All trailists are expected to keep watch alone for at least an hour each night, and this is the time for introspection.

Second, and depending upon the knowledge of the field officer, trailists can become aware that there is an inner wilderness—a personal, often unconscious, reality from which springs our personality and our actions. By allowing nature to become the teacher, there is a realization of the inward journey toward the self as understood in Jungian psychology.

The dreams of those participants sleeping on the African earth for the first time are often revelations that lead the dreamers to a better understanding of their own personal inner and outer states. Through knowing themselves better by a wilderness experience, they become more aware of their fellow men. And they learn the importance of wilderness to the continued existence of mankind. The wilderness enables them to be free, albeit for only a short while, from the technologically controlled lifestyle of the modern world and man's dominating attitude toward nature. The trailists are brought back to their aboriginal fears and become watchful, humbled and, importantly, awed by nature. The spark to tread the inner and outer paths toward wholeness can come from the wilderness experience. Many participants are deeply moved to a state beyond words by the darkness of a moonless African night, the penetrating silence, the solitude, the presence of the unknown and unseen, the crossing of a river in the presence of crocodiles, the fresh track of a lion in the mud, the weird call of the hyena and the comfort of a campfire.

Professor C.A. Meier, a Jungian analyst, in a paper entitled "Wilderness and the Search for the Soul of Modern Man," presented at the 3rd World Wilderness Congress (Scotland), noted the importance of a balance between the inner wilderness and the outer wilderness. Professor Meier states the wilderness within would go wild if one should badly damage the outer wilderness. The great dangers facing modern man will continue until man appreciates that his continued well-being lies in the understanding of the natural world and the rhythms of our planet.

To this end the Wilderness Leadership School continues to work.

WILDERNESS VISION QUEST

Michael Brown

"Climb the mountains and get their good tidings. Nature's peace will flow into you as sunshine flows into trees. The winds will blow their own freshness into you and the storms their energy, while cares will drop off like autumn leaves."
—John Muir

"I went to the woods because I wished to live deliberately, to confront only the essential facts of life, and see if I could not learn what it had to teach, and not, when I came to die, discover that I had not lived."
—Henry David Thoreau

Let's take a trip into the high country of concepts and ideas and talk about *how* we can connect with the peace, freshness and energy that Muir speaks of. Like Thoreau, let's deliberately confront some essential facts about how we can explicitly use our wilderness experiences for personal and spiritual growth.

I would like to share some of the latest research on how the brain works and talk about how we need to balance adventure-related activities with inner-directed processes to get the most out of our experiences in nature. I would like to introduce the field of transpersonal psychology, talk about the rituals, ceremonies and rites of passage people have used throughout time to provoke transformative experiences in nature, and I will discuss some specific methods we can use to enjoy a much more profound contact with the natural world.

As a human resources consultant living in Washington, D.C., I conduct a wide variety of innovative training programs for public, private and governmental organizations throughout North America. My primary commitment is to help people develop their latent human resources so that they can participate most fully in the joy of living. My expertise involves the development of creativity and the process of self-actualization.

Twenty percent of my work takes place in wilderness and back-country settings, on a retreat program I call the Wilderness Vision Quest. Since 1976, I have led more than 600 people on outdoor retreats which, at various times, have involved backpacking, trail rides, ropes courses, canoe trips and other adventures in nature. This is a small program, in comparison to those of Outward Bound, the National Outdoor Leadership School and the African Wilderness Leadership School. The work I do with participants is intensely personal and I have always been the sole leader on these trips.

SPIRITUAL GROWTH

I believe it is time for us to speak openly, and with a clear voice, about the spiritual value of our experiences in the natural world. I believe it is time to acknowledge the fact that perhaps the highest use of wilderness is as a site for self-discovery, and for the exploration, enrichment, healing and growth of the human spirit.

Sigurd Olson, a prolific writer and one of the founders of The Wilderness Society, said that wilderness to the people of America is a spiritual necessity, an antidote to the high pressure of modern life, a means of regaining serenity and equilibrium.

Arthur Carhart, a Forest Service employee in the 1920s who helped lay the foundation for the National Wilderness Preservation System, said perhaps the rebuilding of the body and spirit is the greatest service derived from our forests, for of what worth are material things if we lose the character and the quality of the people who are the soul of America?

We have many needs when we enter the natural world. We need a change of pace from the routines of our daily lives. We need to release our constant, grinding, inner stress. We need to discover who we really are inside. We need to experience beauty, adventure, wonder and renewal. Nature has a tremendous impact on the human spirit, even if we are a bit reluctant to identify spiritual growth as the reason for or the end result of our trips into wild country.

TRANSFORMATION

Although our experiences in nature can be exciting, educational, meaningful, significant and touch us in many ways, they are not always transformative. It is about the process of transformation I wish to speak. There is a tremendous difference between recreation, stress management or adventure, on the one hand, and the life-changing experience of transformation on the other.

The concept of transformation is powerful and complex. It represents a complete change of being and a shift to a higher mode of operating. It implies the awakening of new levels of awareness; a fundamental resolution of the internal causes of stress; the discovery and clarification of essential values; the creation of new goals through which to manifest these values in the world; and the redirection of life energies toward a higher and more fulfilling purpose.

It is obvious that something very powerful must take place for real transformation to occur. Unfortunately, this does not always happen on our back-country trips. Our experiences may change us for a while, but our roles, masks and personality patterns too readily assert themselves again. Unhappily, much of the positive energy we generate on our outdoor adventures simply decays over time, and all too often only vague memories remain of the fun, difficult or exciting times we have had outdoors. How do we reach for, experience, or facilitate self-actualization or transformation on our wilderness and back-country trips? Where can we turn for guidance when trying to understand this process?

Important insights into the process of transformation are being discovered these days in transpersonal psychology. Transpersonal psychology represents the cutting edge in psychological research today, exploring hidden dimensions of the human psyche and blazing new trails on the frontiers of human resource development.

In Latin, trans means "on the other side of," as implied in the words transatlantic or transcontinental; or "above and beyond" as implied in the word transcend. In Latin, persona means "mask." At the broadest level, then, transpersonal psychology seeks to help us:

1. Understand how to "get above or beyond" our personalities so we can see them clearly, understand their origins and dynamics, integrate their functions and transform them when possible;

2. Look "on the other side of" these roles, patterns and masks to discover what is hidden, blocked, defended, or unknown within us;

3. Develop new levels of awareness and latent human resources;

4. Consciously play roles in life that manifest our deepest values so that we can and bring into the world our best talents and abilities and thereby live meaningful, productive, wise and loving lives.

To accomplish these goals, transpersonal psychology investigates and explores the deepest realms of the human consciousness. It seeks to understand how extraordinary and unusual events impact and affect the human psyche—such events as the wilderness experience, profound grief, the near-death experience, altered states of consciousness, the use of psychedelic substances, meditation and yoga, psychic phenomena, trance and mystical states and other deviations from what are considered normal levels of awareness. Focused in the fields of education, therapy or organizational development, transpersonal psychology carefully employs specific methods and techniques to help us develop and enjoy the use of our most important human resources such as imagination, intuition, creativity, inspiration and insight. These methods and techniques will be discussed later. In its research, transpersonal psychology has discovered three important steps that must be honored in the transformative process: preparation, exploration and integration.

Transformation requires us to be willing to take off our masks and be ready to explore our inner depths. It requires us to be willing to experience ourselves in new ways (to face our fears, for instance; to release our emotions; to be touched by wonder; to have the primal forces of nature move powerfully through us). And transformation requires us to take responsibility for the new things we learn about ourselves and integrate our new insights and energy in daily life.

But what does all of this have to do with wilderness? Let's consider how the brain operates and look at what happens on wilderness and backcountry trips.

HOW THE BRAIN OPERATES

What does consciousness mean? Websters defines consciousness as the awareness of one's thoughts, feelings and impressions. But who, or what, is conscious? It is the self within us that is conscious and it is the brain that is the organ of awareness. The brain is divided into two hemispheres, left and right, and recent neurophysiological research shows that each side of the brain has different functions.

> Left Side of the Brain
> > Outer-Directed, Purposeful
> > Rational, Logical, Analytical
> > Will, Strength, Endurance

The left side of the brain helps us handle outer-directed activities and controls the rational, logical and analytical functions of the self. The left brain helps us perceive, understand and respond to realities in the world around us and helps us fulfill our chosen purpose. When stimulated, the left brain provides us with the energy required to achieve specific goals—energies such as will, strength, and endurance.

Most wilderness and backcountry programs single-mindedly stimulate the functions of the left side of the brain. "Hard" skills and technical abilities are needed to survive in the wilderness. Rock climbing, canoeing and cross country skiing, for instance, require a high degree of left brain activity.

> Right Side of the Brain
> > Inner-Directed, Meaningful
> > Receptive, Intuitive, Symbolic
> > Compassion, Empathy, Love

The right side of the brain helps us handle inner-directed activities and connects us to the meaning dimension of life. It controls the receptive, intuitive and symbolic functions of the self. The right brain helps us perceive, understand and respond to the powerful dynamics within us. When stimulated, the right brain provides us with energies which enhance the quality of life such as compassion, empathy and love.

"Soft skills" such as relaxation, reflective writing, poetry, dream work, visualization, art, music, dance and mime turn on the functions of the right side of the brain. These methods can help us understand, find the meaning of and integrate the effects of our adventures in the world.

Balanced communication between the left and right sides of the brain results in a state called whole-brain thinking. To be powerfully transformative, wilderness treks must provide us with the opportunity to experience this whole-brain thinking. Far removed from the demands of civilization, wilderness is the perfect context in which to link the left brain (conscious personality or "I") with the right brain (unconscious functions through which the self communicates). Through this link we discover the meaning and purpose of our lives at any given moment. In wilderness we infuse our goal-oriented behavior with essential values and experience our full humanity, self-actualization!

Whole-Brain Thinking
   Discovery of Meaning and Purpose
   Goal-Oriented Behavior—Informed by Essential Values
   Full Humanity

RITUALS, CEREMONIES AND RITES OF PASSAGE

Just to stretch our imaginations, let's consider some of the powerful ways people throughout time have employed to shut down the left brain, set aside their worldly concerns, turn on the right brain, develop the latent resources of the self and experience the unity that underlies creation. Special rituals, ceremonies and rites of passage have been developed since time immemorial to experience the regenerative effects of the transformative process.

For centuries in the Hindu and Buddhist traditions, people have gone to caves, mountaintops and other remote places to practice yoga, meditation and other spiritual disciplines directed toward the realization of the self. The history of Christianity is full of stories about people like Saint Francis and Saint Claire of Assisi—hermits, mystics and monks, who, through prayer, fasting and severe discipline have developed their spiritual potential. Aborigines in Australia undergo the rigors of a yearlong Walkabout as a rite of passage from adolescence to a mystical relationship with the world around them. Shamen in Siberia, through drumming and chanting, experience intense trance states and what is described as spirit flight, to understand and learn the secrets of the healing arts. The Huichol Indians in Mexico use the hallucinogenic peyote cactus in night-long spiritual ceremonies, then share the lessons they learn about themselves and creation by making beautiful yarn paintings. The Sioux, Cheyenne, Pawnee and other native people in North America prepare for spiritual ceremonies through the purifying heat of the sweat lodge. Some undergo rituals of severe physical stress and pain, such as the sun dance ceremony, to provoke altered states of consciousness, to discover that they are truly more than just their physical bodies and connect in a primal way to the Great Spirit of life. Many native Americans go on the vision quest: retreat alone in nature and fast from food, water or sleep for as long as four days to learn powerful lessons about the meaning and purpose of their lives.

These rituals, ceremonies and rites-of-passage are rigorous and demanding. They are always approached with reverence and are conducted or supervised by wise elders of the community with experience in using the methodology.

The exploration of consciousness is not as widely validated in our culture as it is, and has been, elsewhere. Few of us are willing to participate in such unusual or powerful experiences today. They seem irrelevant at best; dangerous and threatening at worst. We scoff at native and primitive practices while, at the same time, many of us are bored with our lives, lack enthusiasm and passion, only superficially interact with others and lack any sense of the meaning or purpose of our lives.

Few of us really know how to renew ourselves at the deepest levels or heal ourselves from the tragedies that befall us. Few of us know how to make a good transition from one stage in life to another, how to tap and experience the mysteries of nature or how to set the stage for an experience of the eternal, the ineffable, the infinite.

Organizations that lead people on wild country excursions offer their participants many important experiences. They care about safety, focus on the development of technical skills or leadership potential, teach people the ethics of wilderness travel, deliver high adventure. And they do a superb job achieving their goals. They know that powerful transformative experiences can occur in nature, and they know, implicitly, that this is what many of their participants seek.

But few organizations are willing or able to provide the delicate kind of guidance required to help participants fully take advantage of their right brain potential on wilderness or backcountry trips. Few organizations take advantage of the many excellent methods currently available to help participants experience themselves in wholeness, and so, many people are unable to gain the very most from their contact with the natural world or from their outdoor adventures.

We can all do more to balance adventure related activities with inner-directed processes on wilderness or backcountry trips, whether we are alone with our families, friends or colleagues or work for organizations commissioned to guide people on outdoor treks.

I would like to end with some practical suggestions about how one can more deeply tap the transformative potential of wilderness and backcountry experience if you wish to. The procedures I am about to share are distilled from the methods described throughout this talk. They have formed the core of the Wilderness Vision Quest program I have been running internationally for the past 11 years.

SUGGESTED ACTIVITIES

1. First thing in the morning, take the time to do some gentle exercise. Feel the earth. Breathe deeply, release your physical stress and psychological tension through slow and conscious movement. Enliven and enjoy your body, stretch, touch the sky, reach out and embrace the world around you.

2. Seek solitude whenever possible! Come to a complete stop for a significant period of time. Shut down the left brain and turn on the right. Sit quietly and attune yourself to the natural world. Move beneath persistent thoughts and the ever-talking mind and absorb the peace of nature. Feel the warmth of the sun. Listen to the music of the birds, to the wind, to the whispering trees. Empty your mind and let nature fill your senses.

3. Take a minimum of food on your wilderness or backcountry trip. Get a little hungry. Break your pattern of eating by the clock and eat only when you really need to. Fast for a day or two if you really want to heighten your awareness and experience yourself in some exciting new ways. Let profound contact with the natural world nourish you and satisfy your appetites.

4. Take a journal along and enjoy the finest functions of your left brain: evaluation, analysis, and reason. Write about your important experiences. Reflect on the seasons, the elements, your triumphs and disasters outdoors. Note your patterns, motives, behaviors and responses as they become clear and discover what really moves you. Reach for inspiration, maybe document your insights in poetry or song.

5. Draw pictures of your fascinations on the land. Conscious penetration into the symbolic and metaphoric dimension of the right brain is a critically important part of the transformative process. Take the time to really see nature as you sketch, paint and draw, or portray the meaning of your experiences in symbolic art.

6. Be creative, take some chances and get your body involved in kinesthetic imagery. Expand your potential for self-expression by physically identifying with nature. Become the forest, move like the trees, identify with the life around you. Open the channels of your physical body to the powerful and unsuspected currents of energy that lie dormant within you.

7. Take the time to discuss your discoveries with other people. Listen with respect to the experiences of others and take the risk to share what moves you in open and honest ways. Interpersonal skills can greatly improve through sharing the meaningful and significant events that occur to us on our outdoor adventures. As we do, we come to fully appreciate the meaning and the joy of community.

8. Finally, before you walk out of the wilderness, make an action plan. Consider the insights you have gleaned, the inspiration that has moved you, and decide how you can use them in specific, practical ways to renew your life back the regular world. Take responsibility for grounding and integrating your insights and inspiration by drawing up an action plan for the week or two immediately following your trip.

With clarified visions, renewed energy, and strong intention we can return transformed from our experience of the natural world.

OUTWARD BOUND USA

Stephen Bacon and Donna Thompson

Outward Bound is the largest and oldest adventure-based education organization in the United States. The Outward Bound system in the United States consists of the National Office and five independently controlled schools. The system is a nonprofit, tax-exempt organization supported by contributions from individuals, corporations and foundations.

Outward Bound grew out of the need to instill spiritual tenacity and the will to survive in young British seamen being torpedoed by German U-Boats during World War II. What began as a training exercise for apprentice British seamen and youth in Wales has since evolved into a modern-day program for self-discovery and personal development.

Today, Outward Bound's purpose is to develop and enhance in its participants self-confidence and self-esteem, leadership qualities, teamwork and empathy for others, service to the community and sensitivity to the environment.

The essential concept is to impel people into value-forming experiences. The process assumes that learning and understanding take place when people engage in and reflect upon experiences in challenging environments in which they must make choices, take responsible action, acquire new skills and work with others. Teamwork among participants is vital. Instilling a love and appreciation for the wilderness environment in which our courses take place is an integral part of what has come to be known as the "Outward Bound experience."

All courses include teaching core components of skills, training and physical conditioning, one or more extended expeditions, a solo experience, a service project and a marathon event. The curriculum emphasizes personal growth, teamwork and the development of compassion and social responsibility.

We remain committed to making our program available to all who wish to participate and seek to provide an adequate level of scholarship funds so no qualified student is turned away. At present, one of every five students receives some form of financial aid, and the goal is to offer at least 40 percent of young applicants financial aid even as enrollments continue to grow.

Outward Bound is an interpretation of the educational philosophy developed by Kurt Hahn. Hahn was an innovative educator in Germany and the foremost developer of the experiential education concept. He said, "No student should be compelled into opinions, but it is criminal negligence not to impel into experience."

Hahn emphasized developing and maintaining "strong awareness of responsibility for others along with the belief that strength is derived from kindness and a sense of justice." This dual emphasis on the development of self and connecting with one's community pervaded all Hahn's thinking.

To a remarkable degree, today's Outward Bound programs remain faithful to Hahn's philosophy. His experiential approach to education (learning by doing) has become a powerful complement to mainstream education. The power of his thought is demonstrated by the fact that his ideas are as relevant today as they were at their inception 50 years ago.

Our primary mission is to serve the needs of youth, but we also work with adults and special populations. Model programs have been developed to serve troubled youth, alcohol and substance abusers, the handicapped, Vietnam veterans, battered wives and others.

From the start, it was evident that Outward Bound's impact would be limited if it concentrated its efforts solely on operating its own course. Instead, it adopted a model-program strategy that encouraged imitation and provided help and consultation to r-plicators. These programs come in endless variations, from copies of Outward Bound to derivatives concentrating on some particular component.

Many of these programs were begun under the leadership of former Outward Bound instructors and students. Among them are the National Outdoor Leadership School, the Leadership Forum, New York City's Civilian Volunteer Corps, the Connecticut Wilderness School, the Santa Fe Mountain Center and Project Adventure. In addition, Outward Bound was the founding force behind the 400-member Association for Experiential Education.

The therapeutic use of the process has also been replicated. Many social service agencies have successfully developed programs similar to ours within their own communities, and at least 20 states used similar principles for statewide youth rehabilitation programs.

The philosophy and methods pioneered by Outward Bound have also been adopted by more than 3,000 public and private schools, colleges and universities in this country. The relevance of Outward Bound to education has been confirmed by many studies. Research indicates that participants achieve higher levels of self-concept, interpersonal competence and motivation.

First established in Great Britain in 1941, Outward Bound is a worldwide network and includes 46 schools and centers on five different continents. Founders and leaders of the Outward Bound movement in the United States were Joshua L. Miner, who taught at Phillips Academy in Andover, Massachusetts, and F. Charles Froelicher, at that time, the headmaster of Colorado Academy in Denver.

Since conducting its first course at the Colorado school in 1962, almost 160,000 individuals have been served by Outward Bound USA. Every year more than 17,000 people participate in courses conducted at five American Outward Bound schools in Colorado, Hurricane Island, Maine, North Carolina, Pacific Crest, Oregon and Voyageur, Minnesota.

The Outward Bound National Office and the five schools are organized independently, governed by separate boards of trustees and bound together as a federation. The schools adhere to the essential Outward Bound curriculum, to national safety policies and to uniform enrollment procedures. The National Office is responsible for chartering schools and supporting and developing the Outward Bound movement in the United States.

Outward Bound serves a wide range of people:

• Young people—Outward Bound today, as 45 years ago, is an educational experience aimed at helping youth develop leadership and teamwork skills, responsibility, self-confidence and self-esteem. Courses have been designed specifically for 14- and 15-year-old boys and girls. Outward Bound has proven to be an especially powerful rite of passage for young people 14 to 20 years of age.

• Youth at risk—Young people in trouble with the law or on the verge of making long-term decisions are helped by special Outward Bound courses staffed by clinically trained instructors. Positive impact is made when these participants realize, perhaps for the first time, that they are responsible and directly accountable for their own actions, not only in the wilderness but also at home with family and peers.Outward Bound also operates wilderness rehabilitation programs for adjudicated youth in Florida, Maine and Washington. A strong body of research indicates that the Outward Bound approach is a "treatment of choice" for these young people.

• Adults—Although Outward Bound was originally intended for young people, there has been an ever-increasing demand for the experience by adults. The median age of Outward Bound students is now 22.

• Executives—Each year, more than 2,000 executives and managers enroll in Outward Bound's professional development courses to build camaraderie, improve communication skills and refine leadership abilities.

• People with physical problems—Again, Outward Bound has been a proving ground to illustrate graphically to those with handicaps or chronic illnesses that many limits are self-imposed and can be overcome when challenged. Special programs for the physically handicapped, hearing impaired and those with chronic illnesses such as juvenile diabetes and juvenile arthritis have been established by Outward Bound schools. Pilot programs have demonstrated to professionals in the rehabilitation field that people with severe disabilities are more capable than was previously supposed. The impact of witnessing these courses on able-bodied students and instructors has been extraordinary.

• People in crises—The Outward Bound model was applied to another group when a founding trustee of the Colorado school proposed working with the Alcoholism Recovery Unit of St. Luke's Hospital in Denver. In October 1978 for the first time, a group of alcohol-dependent patients went into the mountains as part of the rehabilitation process. Today more than 2,000 alcohol and drug abusers are served by Outward Bound.

Based on its continuing effectiveness, Outward Bound has a strong agenda for the future:

• The social mission and the city—Although Outward Bound has functioned as a wilderness school in the United States, it has always had a strong commitment to serving urban populations, especially underprivileged youth. In the main, this commitment has been fulfilled by offering scholarships to wilderness programs and by special contract courses designed for urban dwellers. In the past five years, Outward Bound has begun to expand this commitment by establishing urban centers for recruitment, course preparation, urban programming and follow up. Such programs have begun in Minneapolis and Baltimore and will soon begin in New York City and Boston. This increase in urban activity marks a reemphasis of Outward Bound's social mission and a rededication to the belief in the primacy of the values of compassion and interdependence.

• The mainstream education initiative—As mentioned above, the Outward Bound process has already had a strong impact on education. Some kind of Outward Bound component is included in the curriculum of hundreds of public and private educational institutions in the United States. Outward Bound seeks to expand this influence by developing additional programs which will integrate the process into academic training, drop-out prevention programs, literacy programs and other areas where it might complement existing pedagogical efforts. Such initiatives are under way across the country.

• Wilderness therapy—Outward Bound's treatment programs for troubled youth, alcoholics, Vietnam veterans, victims of domestic violence and others have received strong paeans from therapists, research scientists, and clients and their families. In addition to replicating these models, Outward Bound seeks to articulate its methodology and document its outcomes to the point where the process has a significant impact on how psychotherapy is performed in the United States. To this end, a number of outcome studies are under way. Wilderness therapy theory is being articulated and documented, and programs and treatment centers are being expanded.

THE NATIONAL OUTDOOR LEADERSHIP SCHOOL

Philip James Ratz

The National Outdoor Leadership School's (NOLS) mission is to be the best source and teacher of wilderness skills and leadership which protect the user and the environment.

The purposes of all NOLS courses are:

• To teach, study and develop the necessary techniques, skills and methods to safely live and travel and still conserve the wilderness environment;
• To teach, study and continually improve techniques of low-impact camping, outdoorsmanship and outdoor leadership;
• To develop the best outdoor leaders possible—people who are technically capable and academically well versed in all areas;
• To promote leadership that is able to meet the varying demands of outdoor wilderness users and the changing needs of the environments they use; and,
• To have an enjoyable, enlightening and intellectually stimulating wilderness experience that might serve as a means to further pursuits in the natural sciences and recreational activities.

NOLS believes that the education of users in the skills and ethics of wilderness travel is the key to continued use of wild lands without creating adverse environmental impact. Safety of the individual and care for the environment are the priorities. Outdoor living skills, leadership insight and enjoyment result as additional benefits.

Toward these goals, NOLS offers 14- to 95-day courses of various types in wilderness areas worldwide. NOLS courses are expeditions. We don't offer short courses or weekend excursions. We immerse our students in the wilderness environment where they have time to learn and appreciate leadership, skills and their surroundings, in order to become well-rounded outdoors people.

In addition, NOLS sponsors conferences on specific wilderness-related educational topics and conducts research on minimum impact, environmental conservation, user benefits and leadership.

NOLS is a nonprofit, educational organization, incorporated as a private licensed school in the state of Wyoming.

The NOLS International Headquarters is located in Lander, Wyoming, which oversees five branch schools in Wyoming, Alaska, Washington, Kenya and Mexico. The administrative staff, headed by myself, reports to a 12-member Board of Trustees. The instructional staff is selected by NOLS after a rigorous and extensive in-house training, apprenticeship and certification program. To maintain high standards of quality and safety, the school only employs NOLS-certified instructors for fieldwork. There are currently 200 active instructors working at NOLS.

NOLS seeks to enroll a mixture of people of different backgrounds and capabilities and teaches them how to be competent expedition members. Students have come to NOLS from all over the U.S. and the world. They have ranged in age from 14 to 71, with the average age in 1987 being 22 years old. This last year NOLS had 2,000 enrolled students.

The NOLS program is based on learning by doing, improving judgment by making one's own decisions, assuming responsibility and being aware of the effects those decisions have on others and on the natural world. Lessons and facts are important because they are real, not contrived. The means by which we serve the mission statement are contained in six elements of the core curriculum.

SAFETY AND JUDGMENT

From the first day of an NOLS course, students are impressed with the emphasis on safety and their own responsibility for the safety of their fellow students. Accepting responsibility for themselves and the expedition is the first step in the NOLS safety program.

To provide students with specific safety skills, the mandatory curriculum of every course includes basic first aid, safety and accident prevention, hazard evaluation, heat- and cold-related accident prevention, and treatment and rescue techniques.

Accident prevention, first-aid training and emergency medical care are part of the NOLS instructor certification. Quality equipment is provided to all students, a low student-to-instructor ratio is maintained, and drugs and alcohol are prohibited dueing courses. Evacuation procedures are in place 24 hours a day.

The NOLS safety officer monitors injuries, reports annually to the Board of Trustees and consults with loss-control experts, physicians and other outdoor education program managers for insight into ways to improve both field and in-town safety. Safety is closely monitored at NOLS and is evidenced by its excellent safety record.

LEADERSHIP AND EXPEDITION DYNAMICS

Real problems, conflicts, varying terrain and weather conditions allow students to observe and experiment with the effectiveness and appropriateness of various leadership styles.

"Leader of the day" opportunities give students the experience of testing their own style and abilities for leading their peers. What do you do if there is a slow member in your group who cannot keep up with the others and you are faced with severe stream crossings? What happens when the summit is close but the weather looks questionable and time is running short?

The NOLS program encourages students to figure out what questions need to be asked and to use their judgment to find solutions that work best in each particular situation. NOLS gives students an education far beyond the scope and depth of that provided by the traditional classroom.

Since 1965, NOLS has pioneered the teaching and development of practical conservation techniques designed to minimize impact. Over the years, the techniques have been continually tested, refined and improved. The NOLS conservation practices are a summary of the state of the art techniques taught in the core curriculum.

ENVIRONMENTAL AWARENESS

Geology, weather, flora and fauna identification and ecosystem relationships constitute the curriculum of environmental awareness.

Using common examples such as flowers on the edge of the trail, shells picked up from the beach, animal and bird calls, the teaching aids for lessons are everywhere and students learn to use their senses and become more observant.

Ecosystems are made up of intricately interrelated components, from minerals to insects to more complex organisms. Each component has a value and purpose, including the human visitor.

OUTDOOR LIVING SKILLS

Cooking and baking, nutrition and rationing, fishing techniques and ethics, climate control, physiology, equipment care and selection—many of these skills are part of the lesson the very first day. Practice leads to refinement and creativity, until students find themselves not merely surviving, but comfortable and living "in style" in the outdoors. Yeast and quick breads, fly-fishing for trout, quinzhee snow shelters, telemark skiing—all of these are part of living "in style," affordably, comfortably, enjoyably, safely.

TRAVEL TECHNIQUES

NOLS courses are expeditions, learning how to get from one place to the next. This includes the principles of energy conservation, trail technique, paddling technique, map reading and compass use, navigation, route finding and time-control plans.

Quality, safety, minimum impact, wilderness ethics and leadership in teaching and research in the outdoors will always be fundamental concepts of the NOLS mission. We will continue to build on our foundation of excellence in the education of future outdoor leaders and wilderness users. We are constantly evaluating curricula for improvement and creating new courses to satisfy wilderness users with more diverse and sophisticated needs. Courses targeted for special attention are the instructors' courses and outdoor educator courses. In addition, we are giving increased attention to our Wilderness Skills Courses which are designed to serve our older students in their thirties, forties, fifties and perhaps beyond.

Our third annual NOLS Wilderness Research Colloquium was cosponsored by Dr. Robert Lucas of the USDA Forest Service Management Research Laboratory in Missoula, Montana, on the subject of identifying wilderness qualities. The participants included a mixture of academic researchers and forest management personnel. Our role is to serve as an intermediary to help translate the research findings into usable concepts for on-the-ground managers, and in turn, to translate the managers' needs to focus the researchers' efforts on the real problems.

Significant challenges face the school in the years to come, in terms of translating the wilderness education techniques that we have developed in our programs overseas—Kenya, Mexico, our expeditions in Canada and South America—into programs of value to other countries seeking to expand their human potential through wilderness activities.

We don't wish to expand overseas for the sake of adventure travel. We want to contribute and know that the value of the NOLS curriculum does not stop at national borders.

It has been 22 years since the founding of NOLS in 1965. During that time, the school has matured into an organization of size, scope and reputation of which all those who have ever been a part of the NOLS community can be proud. I believe that over the next 20 years, the school will grow responsibly, with direction and style.

Our goal is not to be the largest, but we do see ourselves as a primary source of leadership and ideas that will allow this field of wilderness education, therapy, and personal growth to expand nationally and internationally for years to come.

SUPPLEMENTAL INFORMATION

"We will establish forever the fact that wilderness not only is from gound level to the tops of the trees, but it extends underground, under the water and above the trees for an unlimited distance."

—William Penn Mott, Jr.
Director, USDI
National Park Service

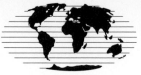

KEY THEMES
AND
ACTION ITEMS

In addition to being an enjoyable and interesting international event, the World Wilderness Congress is an action-oriented process. Possible solutions to matters of current worldwide conservation concern are developed during the several years of congress planning and then are integrated into the congress program. The Executive Committee of the 4th WWC focused specifically on the global aspects of wilderness policy and natural resource inventory; finance and economics; the sharing of information and services; non-governmental cooperation; media and public education; science; and, art and culture. Much of what has been presented in this volume addresses details of these concerns, the collective results of which are summarized here briefly.

WILDERNESS SANCTUARIES

Harold K. Eidsvik

The single green leaf is the symbol of the World Wilderness Congress and, by extension, of wilderness. The single leaf is both compound in structure and complex in nature, and through its veins flow the juices which sustain forests. In a similar manner, wilderness courses through our veins and sustains humanity in many manifestations.

At the 4th World Wilderness Congress, many different cultures and nationalities presented perceptions of wilderness: to the Inuit, wilderness is the wild and unkind urban jungle; to those from the urban jungle, wilderness is the vast forest, the untamed jungle or perhaps the northern tundra; to our Spanish or French speaking colleagues, wilderness is a difficult term to define, perhaps best expressed as *les aires sauvages* or, in Spanish, *los areas salvaje* or *tierras virgenes*. Whatever the perception, wilderness is that which is untamed, primitive, remote and elusive.

Thus, the 4th WWC, like the 1st, 2nd and 3rd congresses, had great difficulty arriving at a definition of wilderness which is simple, crisp and agreeable to all countries. Good progress was made, however, but let us first clarify the need for legislation and definition of wilderness, because to some people this may still seem unnecessary.

Quite simply, history shows us an inexorable destruction of wilderness. Progress has always devastated wild lands, whether one considers the Roman influences on the Middle East and North Africa, the urbanization and acidification of Europe or the leveling of tropical forests. However, it was through the mounting pressure of agricultural and industrial expansion in North America over the last 100 years that the need for an enduring defense mechanism (and the need to define what had to be protected) became clear.

In response, before the turn of the twentieth century, the pioneers of wilderness conservation began to emerge. Some, like Henry Washburn, George Catlin and John Muir, had visions of "public pleasuring grounds." Thoreau placed nature in command. Others, advocates of public lands such as Gifford Pinchot, Stephen Mather and Bob Marshall, put bureaucratic models in the forefront. Government began to play an important role, prodded by the will of such visionaries.

As a result of this steady upswing in America over concern for wilderness conservation, contemporary leaders such as David Brower, Howard Zahniser, Sigurd Olsen and Olaus Murie worked through the Sierra Club, the Wilderness Society and other movements to help codify the concept of wilderness. The pressure of American conservation groups (non-governmental organizations) eventually culminated in the passage of the 1964 Wilderness Act, and wilderness work moved into the lawyer's world—an unfortunate but necessary change in a concept perceived to be intrinsically good and, in its true state, unhindered by restraints or definitions.

For years, the concern with wilderness conservation was seen as a particularly American phenomenon. But, as industrialization marched on and the tropical forests fell, the concept continued to grow. Species extinction raised concerns about biological diversity, which led to concerns about genetic diversity, which intertwined with island biogeography, all of which have begun to be overlaid with economic, medical, agricultural and industrial concerns. The resolution of these problems can readily be linked to undisturbed wilderness areas.

Other countries became involved in the international wilderness debate, New Zealand and South Africa among them. Most notably, Australia entered the fray and new protected area concepts such as World Heritage assumed a critical role. Tasmania and the Queensland rain forest joined the Amazon and Alaska as new testing grounds for an already tested ideology: in wilderness is the preservation of the world.

The World Wilderness Congress has given wilderness an international platform. It has dealt with the concept, the reality, the difficulties and, most importantly, the need for wilderness. Progress has been made, and wilderness is now on the international agenda in a serious and considered manner. For example, the IUCN's Commission on National Parks and Protected Areas is currently pursuing the extension of its work to incorporate wilderness.

Ever pioneering, the 4th WWC presented new concepts of wilderness for consideration. The resource of the 72 percent of nonterrestrial earth became the testing ground for a new perception, "marine wilderness," which was the central subject of a seminar at the congress coordinated by the National Oceanic and Atmospheric Administration.

The need for a universally accepted definition of wilderness is important, in spite of the myriad cultural differences that influence such a definition. Each World Wilderness Congress has grappled with this question, and progress has been made slowly but steadily. The following modification of the 4th WWC Resolution on wilderness definition can be applied to marine or terrestrial areas:

"Wilderness is an enduring natural area, legislatively protected and of sufficient size to provide the pristine natural elements, which may serve physical and spiritual well being. It is an area where little or no persistent evidence of human intrusion is permitted, so that natural processes will take place unaffected by human intervention."

In addition, the Director of the U.S. National Park Service, William Penn Mott, Jr., during the proceedings declared the intention of his agency to investigate the feasibility of underground wilderness and silent, flightless zones over parks as new extensions of the wilderness concept. These steps toward better classification and definition are good, progressive steps. They are further recognition that untouched space, untamed frontier and unexploited resources are essential to man and nature. . . .

Beyond the definitions, concepts and the policies, it seems that wilderness must remain within each of us as a secret corner and a special place. Solitude for contemplation, security of mind and security of place, a touchstone of the past and a home for the future. Whatever the legal manifestation, we can find no better place than the wilderness for this to occur. Wilderness is not a resource but a sanctuary; it is a simple leaf—a complex vein.

FOLLOW-UP

MARINE: Dr. Nancy Foster, Director, Office of Protected Resources
National Oceanic and Atmospheric Administration,1825 Connecticut Ave.
#805,Washington, D.C., USA 20035 or

Graeme Kelleher, Great Barrier Reef, Marine Park Authority
GPO Box 791, Canberra, Act 2601,Australia

TERRESTRIAL: Harold Eidsvik, Environment Canada,
IUCN Commission on National Parks and Protected Areas
135 Dorothea Drive, Ottawa, Ontario K1V 7C6, Canada or

Vance G. Martin
International Wilderness Leadership Foundation, c/o Fulcrum, Inc.,
350 Indiana St., Suite 510, Golden, Colorado, USA 80401

A WORLD WILDERNESS
INVENTORY

Peter Thacher

With our global population passing the five billion level and industrialization
spreading to more remote areas, how much of the earth's land areas are still
relatively undeveloped and wild—dominated by natural forces alone?

A World Wilderness inventory was conducted to be presented at the 4th
World Wilderness Congress. As we learned in this first survey-level inventory,
some one-third of the earth is still in a wilderness state.

This inventory should serve as a benchmark, to be refined where appropriate; against which measurements of future trends in the status of wilderness
stocks and updated inventory results will be evaluated.

A novel characteristic of the World Wilderness Inventory was that inputs
came from a mixture of organizations; a large membership, non-governmental

organization—the Sierra Club (U.S.); a global non-governmental organization, which includes governments in its membership—the International Union for the Conservation of Nature (IUCN); and the principal, global intergovernmental organization devoted to conservation—the United Nations Environment Programme (UNEP).

Each of these organizations has ongoing programs to which non-governmental organizations can contribute to keep the "inventory" process going (see box location for how to contribute to phase two of the World Wilderness Inventory). Also, the World Resources Institute is prepared to receive and forward contributed databases to any of the three major participants, or to others, such as the World Bank, who play supporting roles.

A SYSTEMS APPROACH TO PRESERVING SPECIES RICHNESS

Extinction of species is a major concern among conservationists and environmentalists, and it is increasingly recognized as such by the international development community—ranging from the World Bank, regional development banks, UN Development Program and other international funding agencies, to the rich mixture of bilateral foreign aid programs, such as U.S. AID (Agency for International Development) which has been directed by the U.S. Congress to pay particular attention to the protection of biological diversity.

Species extinction is a worldwide problem. An estimated 1,000 species are becoming extinct each year and the extinction rate could reach as many as 5,000 per year in the near future. The U.S. Fish and Wildlife Service lists 946 species as endangered or threatened. An additional 3,000 species have been documented with sufficient information to propose listing as endangered or threatened.

History also provides many examples of widespread, common and abundant species that are currently extinct or endangered. Since 1620, over 500 species and subspecies of native plants and animals in North America, and more massive losses in the world's tropical rain forests, have been recorded. The passenger pigeon (*Ectopistes migratorius*) and the plains bison (*Bison bisan*) are but two familiar examples. If history is any guide, without appropriate ecosystems-level conservation actions (based on sound biophysical, ecological, socio-economic and geopolitical foundations), a number of species currently abundant will soon join the ranks of the endangered or extinct classes.

With our current knowledge we are not even able to begin to assess our species losses. Public and private data bases commonly restrict themselves to the monitoring of less than 10 percent of the rarest of all species or those species that are hunted. Monitoring efforts for rare species—while addressing the immediate need for protecting these species—give us no overall framework for analysis of long-term trends in biological diversity.

In the last century the conservation movement has begun to recognize the need for the protection of natural diversity. Yet as scores of rare species have approached extinction, both public institutions and private organizations have been forced to use heroic measures to save, on remnant patches of habitat, the last individuals of endangered species. And while the list of endangered species grows, no assessment of the distribution of biological richness, relative to the location of management areas, exists from which to determine the scope of our global conservation need.

It is a sad commentary that the current practice of what may be called "emergency-room conservation" serves to channel most of our economic and emotional support toward those few species which may be least likely to benefit from it. Such efforts, while commendable, suffer from a lack of perspective of preserving the overall biological diversity on this planet.

This latter objective is better served by applying the tools of conservation biology and modern geoprocessing technology to the analysis of the majority of the earth's species to determine how and where they might persist in relatively undisturbed situations, and then managing ecosystems rather than individual species. A major problem lies, however, in our lack of current knowledge on where to focus our management efforts. What is required is a program to assess the numbers of species that are encompassed by existing preserves and where future preserves could be located to protect the most species.

This objective can be met through the use of a Geographic Information Systems (GIS) in which data on species distributions are combined with data on boundaries of existing preserves and other environmental and socioeconomic data. Such a system, constructed with the appropriate layers of data and additional historical information on population and land-use trends, can:

• Improve significantly the effectiveness of current multispecies management practices; and,
• Anticipate the endangerment of a population, species or community.

This is the approach called for in the Brundtland Report—the 1987 Report of the World Commission on Environment and Development chaired by the Prime Minister of Norway, Gro H. Brundtland—which specifically called for drawing up inventories and descriptions of "lands, forests, and waters that are detailed enough to provide a basis for delineating land categories. . . using satellite monitoring and other rapidly changing techniques" to strengthen national planning for sustainable development.

Toward this end, the commission proposed that "development agencies, and the World Bank in particular, should develop easily usable methodologies to augment their own appraisal techniques and to assist developing countries to improve their capacity for environmental assessment." The presentation of the inventory during the 4th World Wilderness Congress was a demonstration of the feasibility of this approach. It is one which should be expanded and continued with the support of private, academic and corporate groups holding data about natural resources.

The WWC adopted a detailed resolution specifically intended to encourage this process whereby the "inventory presentation could be further improved in quality and scale," and which highlighted the role that could be played by the Global Resources Information Database (GRID) set up by UNEP in Geneva and at its world headquarters in Nairobi.

When fully developed, GRID will serve a network of regional centers located in the regional headquarters of the United Nations or other appropriate inter-governmental bodies. Each center will be equipped with mini- or advanced microcomputers, image analyzers and a GIS and will serve as a training center, the nucleus from which national nodes may be assisted.

Global and regional data sets, acquired from organizations such as FAO, WHO, WMO, UNESCO, NASA, Spot-Image and others will be transmitted to national nodes, which in turn will contribute their data toward the build-up of global data sets to improve understanding of global trends and processes, thus aiding such global programs as the International Geosphere Biosphere Program (IGBP).

Presentations by IUCN and UNEP on the opening day of the 4th World Wilderness Congress made clear that composites of information can:

1. Identify those wilderness areas where investments would yield the greatest returns in terms of safeguarding areas of high value for the future (such as the areas known to FAO where rich genetic diversity can still be found for food crops of present and future importance); and,

2. Determine high rates—or risks—of deforestation, soil erosion or other forms of degradation that reduce the ability of the land to support future economic growth.

In the final analysis the success of efforts to preserve biological diversity will not be judged on whether we save the California condor or the black-footed ferret, but on the number of species surviving in the year 2100 and beyond. The time to save a species is when it is still abundant. The technology and the raw data exist to begin to develop this type of systems approach to preserving biological diversity. By focusing our efforts on species-rich areas we can hopefully retain maximum diversity in the minimal area in the most efficient and cost-effective way while not abandoning the concept of protecting individual threatened or endangered species. There exists a pressing need for the conservation movement to augment existing programs with a systems-level approach to the preservation of biological diversity. It is such an approach which currently offers the best chance of saving the largest number of cogs that keep turning this closed life-support system we call earth.

WORLD WILDERNESS INVENTORY—PHASE TWO

The Sierra Club is now ready to launch the next phase of its pioneering inventory of global wilderness areas. This involves verification and further refining of its data, to yield a more exact and current overview of the size and boundaries of thes areas. To accomplish this, NGOs, national parks agencies, scientists, managers and educators from all countries cited in the study are encouraged to send data base information and/or current knowledge of wild lands cited in the original study. Participants will not only help substantiate the report, but will also form a network which will eventually identify smaller areas and help monitor changes to the World Wilderness Inventory. (Follow-up: see page 357.) Copies of the original studies are available and further information can be obtained from Michael McCloskey, Chairman, The Sierra Club, 330 Pennsylvania Avenue SE, Washington, D.C., USA 20003.

INTERNATIONAL CONSERVATION FINANCE PROGRAMME

I. Michael Sweatman

When planning began for the 4th World Wilderness Congress, the International Wilderness Leadership Foundation (IWLF) established as a priority agenda item the linkage between a healthy economy and a healthy environment, particularly in developing nations. It was evident that a combination of economic forces were having a detrimental impact upon the natural resource base of developing nations, and that a major new initiative combining international finance and conservation needs would be necessary in order to address the increasingly urgent problems.

In 1984 the concept of a World Conservation Bank was developed by the IWLF. Consultations and meetings were held with non-governmental organizations and the private and public sectors, including many of the advisors to the 4th World Wilderness Congress. An initial concept paper, "The World Conservation Bank," was presented to the World Commission on Environment and Development (WCED) at its Ottawa hearings in May 1986. As a result of this submission and the rising tide of evidence concerning the impact on the environment from the activities of multilateral development banks and other agencies, in its final report, *Our Common Future*, the Commission urged that "serious consideration be given to the development of a special international banking programme or facility," with the objective of sharply increasing "investments in conservation projects and national conservation strategies that enhance the resource base for development," which could "provide loans and facilitate joint financing arrangements for the development and protection of critical habitats and ecosystems, including those of international significance, supplementing efforts of bi-lateral aid agencies, multilateral financial institutions and commercial banks."

This initiative was a matter of thorough discussion during plenary sessions and in a three-day caucus session at the 4th WWC. The United Nations Development Programme (UNDP), the World Resources Institute (WRI), the International Union for the Conservation of Nature and Natural Resources (IUCN) and other organizations announced their intention to draw up a proposal for a feasibility study for such a program. A resolution supporting this was passed by the plenary session of the 4th World Wilderness Congress.

The UNDP and WRI have acted decisively on this resolution and are now planning to conduct the feasibility study along the following lines:

PURPOSE

In order to carry out the serious consideration called for, the WCED, WRI, UNDP and others propose an intensive 15-month effort designed to facilitate broad international consideration of how best to respond to the need identified by the Brundtland Commission. The process itself should lay the basis for appropriate actions by governments, intergovernmental bodies, the private sector, and non-governmental organizations.

OBJECTIVES

First, a more careful and precise definition will be made of unmet needs and unrealized opportunities for conservation funding and investments in developing countries. This effort will require identification of related programs and activities, types of projects that are currently underfunded, and institutional and other barriers to increase support in needed areas.

Second, the process will identify and provide a common basis for international review of, alternatives for responding to these needs and opportunities. This will have two distinct but closely related dimensions: (a) what functions need to be strengthened, what new services provide, and what new or enlarged sources of support can be made available; (b) possible institutional arrangements for performing these functions, mobilizing support and meeting the needs identified.

Among the institutional options to be examined are:

• A freestanding new entity—perhaps intergovernmental, perhaps a non-governmental organization, perhaps a new public-private hybrid;
• An entity created by a consortium of principally governmental bodies but perhaps also including private sector institutions;
• An entity adjunct to or associated with an existing intergovernmental institution such as the World Bank, UNEP and IUCN; and,
• Strengthening existing institutions and programs.

Third, the process will stimulate broad and open international deliberation on the various options. Key participants in these deliberations will be experts from developing country governments, the international development assistance community (bilateral and multilateral development assistance agencies, multilateral development banks and others), the private banking community, environmental and other NGOs in both industrial and developing countries, multinational corporations and others.

This process of informed international deliberation, carried out on the basis of a common identification of the problem and of the principal options for action, will hopefully bring consensus around a common agenda. The goal of this 15-month project, then, is to provide a springboard to action through facilitating open and informed deliberation on a matter of urgent international concern.

THE PROPOSED PROCESS

1.The Needs and Options Paper: Intensive discussions will be undertaken with all relevant parties to provide a careful definition of the options for action and spell out the pros and cons of each. Each option would be defined in terms of (a) institutional innovation (if any) involved, (b) functions performed and services provided and (c) funding and operating mechanisms.

2.Constituency Development and Consultations: Bringing new ideas to life requires leadership, entrepreneurship and the careful development of a broad and informed constituency. Providing leadership in these areas requires a major continuing commitment for the life of the project. It is further proposed that the originator of the World Conservation Bank proposal, banker Michael Sweatman, will be joining WRI as a Visiting Fellow to provide leadership in these important areas and also to provide financial expertise.

3.International Symposium: This symposium will be coordinated with, but will be in addition to, the extensive consultations, meetings and briefings that will be occurring throughout the project. It will be held after the final needs and options paper is available, probably in a developing country. It will not be large (35 participants) but will include representation from all the project sponsors and relevant communities, including those that would have to be involved in or affected by the various options under review.

ORGANIZATION

A small but broadly representative advisory committee will be convened, including representation from developing countries and other key communities. The role of World Resources Institute will be to produce the needs and options paper, to provide a base for the consultations and outreach work of Michael Sweatman and others, and to work with UNDP and the project funders to plan the symposium and otherwise to promote wide international deliberation of the issues and ideas surfaced in the process.

FOLLOW-UP

I. Michael Sweatman, Visiting Fellow, World Resources Institute, 1735 New York Avenue, NW, Washington, D.C., USA 20006.

THE NEED FOR A WORLD CONSERVATION SERVICE

Joan Martin-Brown

Environmental challenges now loom very large and are simply greater in scale and complexity than can be dealt with by any single organization or nation. At the same time there is an increasing proliferation of governmental agencies, non-governmental organizations, research institutions and data bases that are trying to cope with parts of the problem. One of the greatest challenges is to bring the best available expertise (in the form of professional conservationists and scientists who have the most current information) together with the managers, volunteers or field workers who can actually work directly on the problem.

In recent years, many non-governmental organizations have considered the need for a means by which they can officially network their conservation knowledge, needs, resources and techniques, in order to encourage other efforts and improve those that are already involved in this field. In addition, many governmental agencies are considering the establishment of some type of service corps dedicated to environmental management and natural resource protection. This concept has been referred to under the generic title, World Conservation Service.

Because of the need for conservation cooperation and for increased interchange of techniques and information, the 4th World Wilderness Congress Executive Committee identified this area as one of its Worldwide Conservation objectives and agreed to explore the matter at greater length. A caucus session was established to serve as a focal point for discussions and presentations during the proceedings. Eight case studies were presented during this session, illustrating a variety of vehicles through which global-conservation needs can be addressed and met. The case studies were:

• CARE—"The Role Played by CARE in Conservation Projects in the Developing World"—John Michael Kramer, Vice President, Science, 660 First Avenue, New York, NY, USA 10016;
• EarthWatch—"Bringing Scientific Expertise and Public Volunteer Assistance to Environmental Challenges Throughout the World"—Brian Rosborough, President, 680 Mount Auburn Street, Watertown, Massachusetts, USA 02172;
• Peace Corps—"Conservation and the U.S. Peace Corps"—Arlan Erdahl, Deputy Director, M-900, 806 Connecticut Avenue, NW, Washington, D.C., USA 20526;
• Youths for Environment and Service (YES)—"A Model for a World Conservation Corps"—Ira Kaufmann, Director, and Sureya Ozkizilcik, 111 South Patrick Street, Arlington, Virginia, USA 22314;
• ECONET—"A Computer Network for the World's Environmental Commu-

nity"—Dusty Zaunbrecher, Director, 3228 Sacramento Street, San Francisco, California, USA 94115.

• Australian Trust for Conservation Volunteers—"Organizing Voluntary Manpower to Benefit the Environment"—Tim B. Cox, National Director, P.O. Box 423, Ballarat, Victoria 3350, Australia.

• California Conservation Corps—"International Youth Work Exchanges: Bringing Together Two Precious Resources—Youth and the Environment"—Tim Rochte, Administrator, International Work Exchange Programs, California Conservation Corps, P.O. Box 1380, San Luis Obispo, California, USA 93406.

• Involvement Corps—"Conservation and Corporate Sponsorships—an Emerging Issue"—Ellen B. Linsley, President, 15515 Sunset Boulevard, Suite 108, Pacific Palisades, California, USA 90272.

As each case study was presented, there was thorough discussion and feedback from caucus participants, who included conservationists from the public and private sectors in Australia, Botswana, Canada, El Salvador, Ghana, India, Norway, the Philippines, Qatar, St. Lucia, Sri Lanka and the United States.

The proposed World Conservation Service would function as a hub for both governmental and non-governmental organizations, working internationally to connect scientific and managerial information to practically applied volunteer exchanges in support of environmental management. A fundamental requirement is to carry out work that is needed to benefit environmental stability, and to do so through cooperative ventures between different nationalities and cultural approaches. One of the first and continually important aspects is a communications program that will assist non-governmental organizations in finding information and in locating assistance which will enable them to meet the demands of local and regional conservation challenges.

In summary form, the resolution adopted in plenary session of the 4th World Wilderness Congress requests:

1. That the Australian Trust for Conservation Volunteers, in cooperation with other concerned organizations and individuals, form an international association of practical conservationists before October 1, 1988 and report to all participants of the WWC before that date.

2. That this association be developed with the assistance of the United Nations Environment Programme (in cooperation with other United Nations agencies), which will provide the coordinating mechanism for activities of the initial 12-month period and facilitate the formation of a full steering committee which will address the needs of communication and information, funding, membership and the active role of the proposed World Conservation Service before October 1, 1988.

Meetings are being hosted by the United Nations Environment Programme to determine follow-through on this resolution. A newsletter is planned to facilitate initial communications and information sharing.

A pilot project has been agreed upon between the Australian Trust for

Conservation Volunteers, the California Conservation Corps, Los Angeles Conservation Corps, San Francisco Conservation Corps and East Bay Conservation Corps. There will be an exchange of composite teams of staff, participants and volunteers, each taking part in the field operations of the host organization as well as attending relevant training courses. Conservationists from developing nations are encouraged to participate, as are all parties representing organizations or participating privately. Coordinator for this initial phase is Tim B. Cox of the Australian Trust for Conservation Volunteers.

FOLLOW-UP; World Conservation Service, Joan Martin-Brown, United Nations Environment Programme, 1889 F. St., Washington D.C USA, 20006; Tim Cox, Australian Trust for Conservation Volunteers, P.O. Box 423, Ballarat, Victoria, 3350 Australia.

INTERNATIONAL NON-GOVERNMENTAL COOPERATION

Susan Abbasi

International cooperation among non-governmental organizations (NGOs) was an item of major attention at the 4th World Wilderness Congress. As well as plenary presentations covering successful non-governmental approaches to sustainable development, a three-day caucus convened, under the chairmanship of Edgar Wayburn, facilitated by Diane Lowrie, which explored a variety of models in regional and international NGO networks.

UNITED STATES—The Natural Resources Defense Council highlighted the very successful cooperation between numerous American NGOs to promote environmentally sound economic development policies by the U.S. Agency for International Development (AID), the World Bank and other multilateral development banks (MDBs). This collaborative approach in lobbying key members of the U.S. Congress resulted in legislation being passed each year for five years requiring the U.S. to influence the MDBs on environmental policy and also increasing priority for forest and wetlands' protection and the preservation of biological diversity.

ASIA/PACIFIC—Sahabat Alam Malaysia (Friends of the Earth Malaysia) presented the work of APPEN (Asian Pacific People's Environment Network), which links NGOs of a great many countries from throughout that region. This network has begun to be effective despite the challenges inherent when operating in countries less open to dissent and public criticism than are Western, developed nations.

LATIN AMERICA—Conservation International (USA) convened colleagues from: Bolivia—Maria Teresa Ortiz (Conservation International 1015 18th Street NW, Suite 1002, Washington, D.C., USA 20036) presented the U.S.-Bolivian cooperation on the first successful conservation/debt swap; Venezuela—Aldemaro Romero (Executive Director, BIOMA, Apartado de Correos 1968, Sabana Grande, Zona Postal 1050, Caracas, Venezuela) discussed the increase of NGO networking within his country; Mexico—Ramon Perez Gil, (Instituto de Historia Natural, Apartado No. 6, Tuxtla Guitierrez C.P., Chiapas 2900, Mexico).

CANADA—The Western Canada Wilderness Forum (a coalition of many environmental NGOs) illustrated how their collaborative efforts have focused on the west coast of Canada, culminating successfully in protective statute being granted to the unique Port Moresby area and ensuing action being taken on adjacent areas under threat principally from energy and timber development;

EUROPE—Two examples of regional cooperation were presented, including the British/Swedish work on Acid Rain mitigation (Crister Aagren, Swedish NGO Secretariat on acid rain, Miljovard, Vallgatan 22 S-411 16 Gotegborg, Sweden) and a coalition now working successfully on protecting from increasing pollution the coastal/wetland areas of the Waddensea (Karel van der Zweip, Waddenvereniging, Waddenhuis, Harlingen, Netherlands).

Despite the nature of the political system in which they operated or the level of staffing and funding they achieved, all of the NGO case studies illustrated similar key functions:

1. Problem Identification—NGOs often provide a "watchdog" service to the public, identifying public health hazards, wild land values that may be lost if unwise developments occur, and environmental impacts of nonsustainable development which may be overlooked by proponents of that particular project;

2. Public Awareness and Education—Once problems are identified, NGOs play a critical role in educating the public about the nature of the problem and the policies needed for remedies;

3. Directly Influencing Policy—Known as 'lobbying' in the United States, the role of persuading policymakers and presenting options for policy changes has been a critical one for NGOs. Such efforts are particularly effective when groups work together in sizeable coalitions; and,

4. Information Sharing—This is perhaps one of the most important benefits of regional and international networking. In most cases the expertise of one organization was effectively combined with the information of regional or national situations contained by another organization. This was especially relevant in examples of cooperation between developed and developing nation NGO's. The ensuing solutions proved to be more coherently implemented, cost effective and labor efficient.

Progress on environmental issues has long been associated with the activities of non-governmental organizations (NGOs). These public conservation organizations are usually involved with organizing popular, grass roots involvement in conservation issues, in doing research and/or lobbying elected officials. Until recently, NGO activity has occurred almost entirely within developed nations.

In recent years, as environmental problems have increased in complexity and scale, a new aspect to NGO action is beginning to emerge. A unified, or at least cooperative, approach among non-governmental organizations is increasingly called for. This is true not only within nations themselves, but also regionally and internationally. The role played by NGOs will continue to increase, a fact which is emphasized in *Our Common Future*, the report of the Brundtland Commission.

Networks of organizations sharing resources such as information, expertise and funding are seen as an effective manner in which to address sustainable development challenges.(Follow-up: see page 356) For further information about international NGO networks, in addition to the above addresses, contact the following:

Diane Lowrie, Global Tomorrow Coalition, 1325 G Street NW, Suite 915, Washington, D.C., USA 20007 or Dr. Edgar Wayburn or Michael McCloskey, Sierra Club, Earthcare Network, 330 Pennsylvania Avenue SE, Washington, D.C. USA 20003.

INTERNATIONAL PARKS FORUM OF
THE AMERICAS AND THE CARIBBEAN

At the 4th WWC, the National Parks and Conservation Association, in collaboration with the Canadian Parks and Wilderness Society, with 58 participants from 17 countries, initiated this new, network of NGOs to work for the protection and sound management of national parks in the Americas and Caribbeans. Regional coordinators have been named and organization is now under way.

Chairman Dr. Felix Nunez, President, Fundacion de Parques Nacionales Y Medio Ambiente, Apartado 6-6623, El Dorado, Panama; or Regional Coordinator, South America, Mr. Alfredo E. Ferreyros G., Asociacion de Ecologia y Conservation (ECCO), Vanderghen 560-2A, Lima 27, Peru or Regional Coordinator, Caribbean, Mr. Mark D. Griffith, Research Director, Environment Unit, Ministry of Employment, Labour Relations and Community Development, Government of Barbados, P.O. Box 722, Bridgetown, Barbados or Regional Coordinator North America, Mr. Paul Pritch ard, President, National Parks and Conservation Association, 1015 31st Street NW, Washington, D.C., USA 20007.

A CONSERVATION MEDIA STRATEGY

Norma Foster

Today's environmental issues affect all nations and all segments of society. As such, they need to be communicated, understood and consequently supported by more global constituencies and a wider range of the public. Communication of environment and development concerns is as vital as research and policy efforts.

Most major conservation conferences on the important global issues of our times use a traditional process of communicating, which often results in only minimal advance publicity. A basic form of communicating is usually via newsletters, announcements in journals and on-site speeches. These are essentially paper conferences that also result in minimal press coverage and little post-conference publicity.

These traditional conferences are often useful, but have a built-in limitation: only a limited number of people have access to the information and materials beforehand, and even fewer are able to participate in the rewarding personal and professional discussions that occur during the event itself. If the public is invited (which is seldom the case), prospective participants are usually drawn from a selected mailing list of people who are already committed to and/or informed of the issues.

To reach the public, conservation events should be planned as topical, exciting and effective occasions to which the media can respond. If the program is excellent, with a diversity of professionals and members of the public, the media will have a great opportunity to report on issues of vital importance to our future.

Our objective for the 4th World Wilderness Congress was to expand communication to the wider public by making use of many new techniques in the print, visual and electronic media. In addition, the 4th WWC (like all previous World Wilderness Congresses) was open to the public.

A communications plan was created 18 months prior to the 4th WWC. It incorporated precongress publicity, on-site media exposure and follow-up coverage. There was close liaison between fund-raising efforts and media exposure, especially in the precongress period. The intensive activity commenced 12 months prior, outlined on a four-phase flow chart. Volunteers were solicited nationally, through committees or contacts in numerous cities. Six months prior to the congress we concentrated efforts in the state of Colorado and city of Denver in addition to the national and international efforts under way.

All the latest techniques and facilities available to the print, electronic and visual media were utilized:

1. Public Relations/Communications—In the international, national and local areas, early contact was made with specific individuals, agencies, corporations and organizations, both governmental and private. Concentrated, persistent effort yielded rewarding support and involvement from all sectors. Formally requested welcoming letters and proclamations were received from the President of the United States, the Prime Minister of India, the Governor of Colorado, Mayor of Denver and the mayors of 12 neighboring cities. Art auctions and entertainment events were produced prior to and during the 4th WWC, to stimulate interest from the wider public and the media.

2. Advance Press Releases—Prior to the congress, important issues were covered on a monthly basis, released both through news wire services and targeted mailings. Coverage was obtained in national dailies and magazines throughout the United States and abroad.

3. Public Service Announcements—This is an important element for the general public. Celebrity endorsement and participation was offered by Richard Chamberlain, and public service announcements were produced for radio and television. Air time is donated to bona fide nonprofit organizations.

4. Promotional Video—A professionally produced and edited 14-minute video highlighted the history, current objectives, program and organization of the World Wilderness Congress. Time, services and duplication were largely donated, the product was used widely in all promotional activities and was transmitted via satellite to cable television stations in the United States.

5. Satellite—Two features of the 4th WWC, the opening ceremonies and the final public hearing of the World Commission on Environment and Development, were carried live via satellite and were made available free of charge to television for use in full or to be excerpted for news clips. Satellite time and transmission were mostly donated, and equipment fees were negotiated to a reasonable level.

6. Press Corps—During the congress, 75 journalists from various media requested and received interviews with leading figures.There were daily press conferences on important issues and personalities. Press releases were issued from an on-site computer to national news wire services and distributed to 1,750 newspaper, television and radio outlets. In the week of the 4th WWC, over 200 different articles appeared in daily newspapers in the United States and abroad, with follow-up articles appearing for a month afterward.

7. Film and Video—Film and professional broadcast video crews documented all major portions of the conference.

There is a close link between a successful media campaign and fund-raising. The visual elements recorded during the congress have stimulated numerous inquiries regarding their use in commercial and educational markets. In addition, with the extra attention and public participation in the congress, there was a greater market for memorabilia such as sportswear with the congress logo and a specially minted, commemorative silver coin, all of which were handled by a marketing company obtained by our agent.

Post-Congress Activity—Immediately following the 4th WWC, the Denver Declaration was presented to the U.S. Congress and formally entered into the Congressional Record of the Senate and House of Representatives. It was also entered into the permanent record of the United Nations after being presented during the General Assembly. Work is continuing with the U.S. Congress, with plans for a Joint Resolution incorporating the objectives of the Denver Declaration to be passed for World Environment Day in 1988. Long-term follow-up includes work by sponsoring organizations on the 48 Plenary Resolutions. Most importantly, an educational video series for colleges and universities is being prepared. Utilizing the information and discussion filmed at the 4th WWC, the series will present an overview of Worldwide Conservation. Marketing will be under the auspices of the International Wilderness Leadership Foundation.

Conservation activities are constantly underfunded. The cost of media and public relations is often seen as a barrier to increased communications. There are ways to achieve a great deal. For relatively small amounts of money, time, services and equipment were donated by professionals. Volunteers, less-trained but equally valuable, are available if you look and ask for help.By making efforts to research, plan for and use the innovative new technologies in communication, conservation will be more effective for your effort.

FOLLOW-UP
Charisma Communications, 8621 Wilshire Blvd., Suite 204
Beverly Hills, CA, USA 90211.

SCIENCE AND CONSERVATION

John C. Hendee

(Editor's note:) There were six technical sessions attended by scientists from many countries. The proceedings of individual sessions are available from program leaders. Conservation is replete with differences in belief about the causes of environmental problems and their likely solutions. Organizations and disciplines reflect these differences in their perspectives and priorities.

Increased dialogue among all these differing viewpoints, toward greater understanding and consensus, is a major purpose of the World Wilderness Congress. Differing views must be acknowledged and honored before protagonists can discuss them productively, rationally and diplomatically. Only then can lasting agreement be reached.

In such debate, expertise and evidence are needed to resolve questions of fact. Science can contribute important perspectives to worldwide conservation: evidence about the nature and degree of environmental problems; evidence about alternative solutions and their probable effects; descriptions of natural processes so as to better predict effects and thereby prescribe more effective mitigating actions.

With this in mind, and as a result of resolutions from the 3rd World Wilderness Congress in Scotland, the International Wilderness Leadership Foundation resolved to help further integrate science into public conservation.

The major goal of the science program of the 4th World Wilderness Congress was a renewed infusion of science and scientists into worldwide conservation, with two main purposes:

• To strengthen dialogue between scientists and other conservationists—the WWC process expanded collaboration through the attendance of more than 400 scientists, and their interaction with citizen environmentalists, resource managers, educators and other delegates; and,
• To strengthen involvement of scientists in conservation issues—scientific data and expertise were focused on worldwide conservation issues in more than 200 presentations by scientists complementing other views based on ideology, belief and conservation principles and values.

Through the people-to-people involvement of scientists with other conservationists at the congress, new personal contacts and friendships were formed that will grow into future collaborations spanning disciplines, perspectives and countries.

Distinguished scientists participated in all aspects of the congress. The plenary program featured presentations by scientists from Europe, Asia, Africa,

North and South America on global atmospheric and climate changes, population, land use, wildlife conservation and many other topics. Six scientific symposia were organized by leaders in their respective fields and addressed topics with technical papers, poster sessions, demonstrations and workshops. Each symposium will publish its own separate proceedings to make the information available to scientific disciplines as well as to conservationists. Persons interested in details of scientific symposia can order proceedings from the leaders at the addresses indicated. The symposia topics and leaders were:

ACID-RAIN IMPACTS ON WILDERNESS, PARKS AND NATURE RESERVES

Sponsored by: USDA Forest Service, U.S. Environmental Protection Agency, and U.S. National Park Service.

Program Leader: Dr. John D. McCrone, Coordinator, Cooperative Park Studies Unit, National Park Service, Clemson University, Clemson, South Carolina, USA 29631.
Associate Leaders: Dr. David Parsons, National Park Service and Dr. Ann Bartuska, U.S. Forest Service.

Forty leading scientists from Canada, Chile, Czechoslovakia, Mexico, Sweden and the United States addressed such topics as monitoring atmospheric pollution (including long-range transport and visibility), aquatic effects and vegetation effects.

Although termed "acid rain" because of its familiarity to the public, the related problem stems from many forms of atmospheric and air pollution, including wet and dry deposition, clouds, fog, particulate matter, ozone, sulfur dioxide, nitrogen oxides, organics and even carbon dioxide. Evidence presented that showed sensitive lakes in the eastern United States do not have stable chemistry and are continuing to acidify, a process which has been under way for 25 years. The fauna and flora of aquatic ecosystems in the eastern United States and Canada are being profoundly altered over large areas.

Strong evidence was also presented that vegetation effects and forest deterioration are taking place in many parts of the world, but it is difficult to show cause and effect relationships. There are only a few cases where tree death and forest decline can be definitively linked to air pollution. Clearly there are multiple and interactive stresses, both natural and anthropogenic that must be considered and studied. Only with long-term monitoring will we be able to separate natural variability from pollutant stress and thus more fully understand what is happening in natural ecosystems. Data presented on soil acidification in Sweden and vegetation change in Czechoslovakia clearly testified to the importance of such approaches.

The lack of scientific findings do not justify a lack of action in political and regulatory arenas. Throughout history man has had to act on the basis of information that was available at the time. Lack of action before all the facts are in may mean that we will eventually have to deal with processes that are irreversible. The importance of clean air was recognized by Chief Seattle of the American Indians who said in 1854: "The air is precious to the red man for all things share the same breath—the beast, the tree, the man—we all share the same breath. The white man does not seem to notice the air he breathes. . . if we sell you our land, you must keep it apart and sacred, as a place where even the white man can go to taste the wind that is sweetened by the meadow flowers."

DESIGNATION AND MANAGEMENT OF PARK
AND WILDERNESS RESERVES

Program Leaders: Dr. Edwin Krumpe, Director, Wilderness Resource Center, University of Idaho, Moscow, Idaho, USA 83843; and Mr. Paul Weingart, U.S. Forest Service.

The five sessions with 27 papers and 27 poster presentations consisted of a good variety of U.S. and international perspectives, agreeing that:

• Key ecosystems and biogeographical regions of the world still lack representation in park and wilderness reserves;
• With examples and data, the presentations and discussions highlighted that wilderness and park reserves should be managed to endure. The management must focus on influence both inside and external to the protected area;
• Park and wilderness problems and threats are amazingly similar around the world and involve population pressures; resource overconsumption, including logging, grazing, mining, uncontrolled tourism, hydropower development, settlement, introduction and imbalance by exotic plants and animals;and,
• The concept of diversity is a key to understanding natural areas and protection must include the preservation of genetic diversity from which great future benefits will be derived by humankind.

THE USE OF WILDERNESS FOR PERSONAL GROWTH,
THERAPY AND EDUCATION

Sponsored by: National Outdoor Leadership School
Program Leaders: Dr. Tim Easley, Chairman, Dept. of Forest Resources, University of New Brunswick, Bag Service #44555, Fredericton, New Brunswick, Canada E3B 6C2; and Dr. Joe Passineau, South Dakota State University.

This program consisted of 12 sessions offering 28 technical presentations and nine demonstrations and experiential workshops, ranging from presentations of theory about the effects and values of wilderness experiences to empirical studies of wilderness experience programs such as Outward Bound and the National Outdoor Leadership School. Recurring needs, themes, concepts and paradoxes emerged:

1. There is a need for additional theoretical models to explain the beneficial effects of wilderness and outdoor experiences and the continuum of personal growth. The need for theory is matched by the need for more empirical study and discussion to clarify and determine relationships between wilderness values, wilderness programs and wilderness benefits;

2. Wilderness resource managers must reflect the human effects of wilderness use in management to help facilitate such efforts. Scientific evidence is yet evolving, but the issue can be constructively addressed by expanding dialogue between wilderness managers, scientists, wilderness experience program participants and leaders;and,

3. There is great need for wilderness education to foster environmental awareness, sensitivity and skills among wilderness users so that appreciation and use of wilderness do not ultimately destroy it. Much could be accomplished with expanded cooperation between wilderness managers and existing environmental education organizations and networks, such as the Alliance for Environmental Education (AEE), the National Association of Environmental Educators (NAEE), the United Nations Environmental Program (UNEP) and existing outdoor leadership and wilderness experience programs.

POPULATION AND ENVIRONMENTAL STRESS
Program Leaders: Dr. Rupert Cutler, (Former) Executive Director, Population-Environment Balance, Inc.; and Dr. Robert Repetto, Senior Economist, World Resources Institute, 1735 New York Avenue, NW, Washington, D.C., USA 20006.

Lively debate occurred during four sessions with presentations by 12 prestigious authors. Conclusions:

• The global population problem results from an aggregation of national population problems and their different approaches to population stabilization;
• Internal and international migration of population doesn't solve population problems, it just changes the location;
• The world could cope with a slowly growing population synchronized with technical innovation, but population is growing much faster than such an optimum trajectory;
• The average number of children born to each woman in Africa today is 6.5;
• Fertility control efforts must be accompanied by improvement in the status of women, reduction in poverty and opportunities for employment;
• Illegal abortion is the leading cause of death in young women in Latin America and a major cause of death among poor women in North America;
• Birth control isn't population control—population control depends upon couples wanting to have small families; and,
• If we don't have the courage to require developing nations to lower their birth rates in exchange for food, we'll be guilty over time of increasing their suffering.

THE MAN AND BIOSPHERE (MAB) PROGRAM
Sponsored by: U.S. MAB, USDA Forest Service and UNESCO/MAB, PARIS

Program Leaders: Dr. William Gregg, Cochairman, US-MAB Project, USDI, National Park Service, Washington, D.C., USA 20240; and Dr. Stanley Krugman, Cochairman, US-MAB Project, USDA Forest Service. Adviser: Gonzalo Halffter. Investigador Nacional, Instituto de Ecologia; and Chairman, Mexican National Committee for Man and the Biosphere, MEXICO.

Sixteen papers by authors from nine countries presented an evolutionary history of the biosphere-reserve concept and offered status reports on implementation in different regions of the world. Sixteen additional case studies presented in poster sessions pointed out how the concept is being applied on the ground in Canada, Costa Rica, Mexico, Panama, the Philippines and the United States.

Some attendees reflected the perception that biosphere reserves are another form of national parks. Discussions clarified the more expansive function of biosphere reserves, which may integrate a national park into a broader region.

One of the papers explained how discovery of *Zeea diploperennis*, a wild perennial plant related to maize, stimulated the establishment of a large biosphere reserve in Mexico based on cooperation between scientists and local people. Only 1 percent of this Mexican biosphere reserve is in public ownership.

Another paper described the work of the Kuna and Embera people in building biosphere reserves to secure a productive future for indigenous people in tropical forests. The report included statements by tribal leaders that, although the biosphere reserve term was new to their vocabulary, the ethic it embodies has been a part of their culture for millennia.

Other papers documented that successful biosphere reserves are built on long-term commitment and full involvement of conservationists, scientists and those in economic sectors. The establishment of a global network of biosphere reserves—a large area combining the protection and use of natural environments—provides centers for understanding the coevolution of human societies and the natural environment. They are places where men and women of vision can develop alternative patterns of use which are ecologically sustainable, culturally appropriate and meet the needs and aspirations of local people. In this way, biosphere reserves provide a practical framework for galvanizing human investment and creativity toward a more promising common future.

OCEANIC WILDERNESS SEMINAR
Program Leader: Dr. Nancy Foster, Director, Protected Species and Habitat Conservation, Marine Estuaries Management NOAA-NOS, 1825 Connecticut Avenue, #174, Washington, D.C., USA 20235. Coleaders: Michelle Lemay and Annie Hillary, NOAA-NOS; Graeme Kelleher, Great Barrier Reef Marine Park

Authority; and, Harold Eidsvik, Parks Canada.

Seventy percent of the globe is covered with water, but less than 1 percent of that is included in marine-protected areas. Seventy percent of our oxygen is produced by marine phytoplankton, 70 percent of our population lives within 60 miles of the coastline and more than half the population in developing countries receives almost 50 percent of its animal protein from marine fisheries, yet little attention has been given to marine conservation.

After prompting by the World Wilderness Congress, an emerging debate on marine wilderness areas represents an important step in marine-resource management. The symposium considered several preliminary aspects:

• There is no reason why the concept of wilderness could not apply to the marine environment. The symposium's preliminary definition of such wilderness is: "Marine areas where little or no persistent evidence of human intrusion is present or permitted, so that natural processes will take place unaffected by human intervention."
• Even without this definition, there are examples of countries throughout the world that have designated areas that, in essence and probably in fact, would qualify as wilderness.
• Wilderness is at the highly protected end of the spectrum of protected marine areas, and is but one component in the broader framework of integrated marine conservation.
• These most highly protected marine wilderness areas should not be viewed in the negative sense—as places where resources are locked-up—but in the positive sense as a means to long-term replenishment of overexploited resources. They would be management models to assist in sustaining natural resources.
• Natural resource, economy and social systems are all interrelated; sound marine conservation will never be accomplished if one depends on only scientific data and ignores economics and people.
• Other aspects that are important to the concept of oceanic conservation include local marine-management projects on developing islands; voluntary conservation programs along the coasts of England, (managed without enabling legislation); the establishment of an extensive marine estuaries park in the Waddensea; and Antarctic wilderness, which is seriously threatened through unregulated fisheries, mineral exploration and development.

The concept of oceanic or marine wilderness is at the same place now as was that of terrestrial parks and wilderness one hundred years ago. An inadequate international framework for defining ocean wilderness, as well as a lack of institutional capability to protect ocean areas which may meet any set of defined criteria, are two specific shortcomings for protection of oceanic wilderness. The next step will be at the 1988 IUCN General Assembly in Costa Rica during which, at the meeting of the Commission on National Parks and Protected Areas, the concept of global marine wilderness will be discussed.

The content of the science program reflected the stature of the leading scientists present, and the proceedings will provide contributions advancing several fields of inquiry. The integration of science and scientists with other conservation disciplines was most striking. The synthesis between art and science was described by Dr. Joe Passineau, one of the science symposia leaders, as a merging of matters of the heart and matters of the head:

"Art and science applied to conservation have the same destination. Art, through the emotions, takes you there in a heartbeat, while science goes step-by-step, tracking the evidence patiently from source to distribution, and proving that which art, tracking through the heart and emotions, knew instantly. Each path of knowing is essential for the validation of the other. Together they create a balance, and in the center of that balance is truth. So it has been with integration of science and conservation at the 4th World Wilderness Congress."

THE ARTIST AND THE WILDERNESS ETHIC

David M. Lank

The famous English critic John Ruskin was inspiringly perceptive when, in the nineteenth century, he wrote: "Great nations write their autobiographies in three manuscripts: the book of their deeds, the book of their words, and the book of their art. Not one of these books can be understood unless we read the two others; but of the three the only trustworthy one is the last."

Future generations will judge us by our attitudes toward wilderness not only by our words and deeds, but also by our art. Artists therefore have as vital a role as any other person in giving tangible and lasting form to the wilderness ethic on which our survival as a world will increasingly depend.

At the 4th World Wilderness Congress, it was recognized that the artist has as much right to have input in discussions on the crisis of wilderness as does the scientist and the politician, the hunter and the conservationist. With the passage of a few months, I realize that what I should have said was, "The artist has as much OBLIGATION to have input" as any of the others.

Few artists make any real effort to have input. We see staggering amounts of wildlife art; we see very little wilderness art.

With the passage of the centuries we have witnessed an evolution of animal art that has sprung from totemic and magical inspiration, through an emphasis on animals in the service of man, with the pious blessing of Genesis I:28, through stiff scientific portraiture, down to our contemporary idolatrous worship of frozen detail. Overwhelmingly, today's artists are painting photographs, and art is suffering.

But artists—and their promoters—howl when the photographic stigma is leveled at their work. And yet, check for yourselves the number of times attention is called in promotional texts and self-laudatory articles to the "unbelievable," "extraordinary," "incredible" detail in so-and-so's work. By inference, the more detail the better the quality of art.

In 99 cases out of 100, it isn't art. It's photography—and bad photography at that. Any artist who has mastered sufficient technical training to put paint on canvas has the requisite skill to paint a photograph. Whether or not an actual photograph is used as the "inspiration" for a particular painting is not relevant. How else, other than in a photograph, can you capture in steel-edged detail every pinnion of a duck exploding off yet another pond? You certainly can't see such detail in real life, so why is minute detail referred to as "lifelike?"

To contradict my last statement, there is another way of seeing such detail. The word in French for a still life is *nature morte* directly translated, dead nature. Fifty million Frenchmen can't be wrong. The kind of detail we see in certain very successful and popular moose paintings can only be captured first on film, or sitting in front of a stuffed animal, gazing blindly through the dust slowly gathering over its glass eyes. You don't see that kind of detail in a Runguis; instead, you see the wilderness.

The current mania for animal portraiture is all too often a two-dimensional equivalent of a stuffed trophy over the fireplace. Both are monuments to the dead—inanimate but detailed. Life for a wild thing is not just a matter of breathing; they can do that in a zoo. Life only takes on its real meaning in wilderness. It is as if a portrait has been painted on a single piece of a giant jigsaw puzzle, and that one piece—a piece of animal art—is now deemed an end in itself. If the whole puzzle were looked at, that piece would be missing and we would spot it immediately. But when we look only at the piece, we seem oblivious to the fact that the whole puzzle is missing. That puzzle is wilderness.

As an investment counselor, part of my training is to try to anticipate trends before they become obvious. In the buzz words of my profession, I try to discount the future. Let me discount the future of animal art. I am predicting that, in spite of booming sales figures, startling secondary market prices and a proliferation of wildlife galleries and publications, animal art as currently practiced by the vast majority of wildlife artists is basically dead.

Why? Because it is basically photography, and photographers are doing it better. At least they make no pretense of being anything other than photographers, some of whom have raised the level of their craft to the stature of art. For most people, however, photography is not considered to be art. Thanks to the sophistication of today's cameras and long lenses, we all get the feeling that if only we had had the time to climb Mount Washington on a frosty morning at the right time, we too could have taken that perfect picture of the sunrise through the frost crystals. Through the sheer weight of numbers, with hundreds of millions of pictures being taken per year, some of the best pictures are going to be taken statistically by rank amateurs. There is an understandable tendency to consider photography more a question of timing than of talent. There is hope for us all; it is not inconceivable that every one of us could have a photo selected by Audubon Magazine.

What a significant thing it is that the photo editor of Audubon Magazine—with perhaps the most consistently stunning selection of pictures in print—has authored a long-overdue book on an artist who, half a century ago, proved that photographic detail is not an automatic criterion for excellence. Marty Hill, first in her own article in Audubon three years ago, and now in her book, *The Peerless Eye*, forces the art community to confront the towering genius of Bruno Liljefors, Sweden's incomparable gift to wilderness art.

Liljefors, I predict, will no longer by considered the past: He will be seen as the future. If this comes true, it will be not an evolution but a revolution—a turning back again—to the whole puzzle, to the wilderness ethic. Compare his loons with the latest limited edition art prints; compare his eiders with the usual duck stamp offerings.

My reference shelves are lined with coffee table books on "The Art of. . ." and you fill in the blank. They tend to share certain things in common. First, they were all written too soon. Secondly, they are flatteringly uncritical and usually written by someone who knows little about art or its history, but who obviously "knows what he likes."

Why are the artists only making statements about their art, rather than making a statement about the wilderness through their art? An exception is Paul Bosman, who has done it with his spectacular book on African elephants, in an appropriately large format, but which contains paintings of elephants no more than fractions of inches long in a vast environmental setting—the piece properly placed in the whole puzzle.

There are other artists who paint the whole puzzle. I name names because I feel their work should be seriously examined not just from a technical viewpoint, but from the perspective of the underlying ethos: Lanford Monroe, George McLean, Bob Kuhn, and Sweden's new Liljefors, Lars Jonnson.

There are others—many others—who could paint the whole puzzle. If artists are going to have a voice in the forming of a viable conservation and wilderness ethic, then they must do it.

FOLLOW-UP

ART AND CULTURE: International Leadership Foundation, c/o Fulcrum Inc., 350 Indiana St., Suite 510 Golden, CO , USA 80401

RESOLUTIONS

Resolutions passed by the Plenary Session of the 4th WWC:

Following are Resolutions titles and sponsors. For more detailed information and to assist with the implementation, please contact the person and/or organization listed.

GROUP A—ACHIEVING SUSTAINABLE DEVELOPMENT

WORLD COMMISSION ON ENVIRONMENT AND DEVELOPMENT
1. Report of the World Commission on Environment and Development. Global Tomorrow Coalition, 1325 G St. NW, Suite 915, Washington, D.C., USA 20005
2. World Conservation Strategy; National Conservation Strategies. IUCN, National Conservation Strategies, Dr. Kenton Miller, Avenue du Mont-Blanc, CH-1196 Gland, Switzerland
3. International Conservation Banking Programme or Facility. Michael Sweatman, IWLF, c/o World Resources Institute, 1735 New York Ave. NW, Washington, D.C., USA 20006
4. Population and Environmental Stress. Rupert Cutler, Population-Environment Stress Inc., 1325 G St. NW, Suite 1003, Washington, D.C., USA 20005

SUSTAINABLE DEVELOPMENT IN SPECIFIC REGIONS
5. Funding Sustainable Development in Tropical Regions. Sr. José M. Borrero, Fundacion para la Investigacion y Protection del Ambiente, Apartado Aereo 2741, Cali, Colombia, S.A.
6. Sustainable Development in Small Island States. Gabriel Charles, Chief Forest and Lands Officer, Ministry of Agriculture, Castries, St. Lucia, West Indies

ENVIRONMENTAL RIGHTS
7. Environmental Rights. Peter D. Glavovic, School of Law, University of Natal, Durban, South Africa

INDIGENOUS PEOPLES
8. Lands and Rights of Indigenous Peoples. Dana Guppy, Indigenia, 1314 NE 42nd, Room 208, Seattle, WA, USA 98105
9. Haida Gwaii Conservation Strategy. Council of the Haida Nation, Miles G. Richardson, P.O. Box 98, Skidegate, Haida Gwaii, Canada V0T 1S0

GROUP B: INCREASING SUPPORT

NON-GOVERNMENTAL ORGANIZATIONS
10. World Conservation Service. Ms. Joan Martin-Brown, UNEP, 1889 F St. NW, Washington, D.C., USA 20006
11. Worldwide NGO Cooperation. Dr. Edgar Wayburn, The Sierra Club, 730 Polk St., San Francisco, CA 94109
12. Earth Friendship Center Concept. Sarah Weaver Kipp and Clive Callaway, 621 Alexander Crest NW, Calgary, Alberta, Canada T2M 4B4

EDUCATION AND INFORMATION
13. Environmental Education and Training. For complete text and sponsors contact: IWLF, Colorado State University, Fort Collins, CO, USA 80523
14. Fund for Conservation Projects of Young Scientists and Students in Developing Countries. Arturo Gomez-Pompa, UC MEXUS, University of California, Riverside, CA, USA 92521
15. Cooperation on Use and Exchange of Data and Information. John Kineman, NOAA/NGDC E/GC-12, 325 Broadway, Boulder, CO, USA 80303
16. Conservation Inventory. IWLF, Colorado State University, Fort Collins, CO, USA 80523

GROUP C: IMPROVING ENVIRONMENTAL MANAGEMENT AND CONSERVATION

ENVIRONMENTAL MANAGEMENT
17. Environmental Restoration. David R. Brower, Earth Island Institute, 40 Stevenson Ave., Berkeley, CA, USA 94708
18. Pesticides, Herbicides and Sustainable Agriculture. Verne McLaren, World Wildlife Fund, P.O. Box 114, Robe, South Australia 5276, Australia
19. Waste Policy for Environmental Groups. Bill Shireman, Californians Against Waste, 8498 Sunblaze Way, Sacramento, CA, USA 95823
20. The California Recycling Act. Bill Shireman, Californians Against Waste, 8498 Sunblaze Way, Sacramento, CA, USA 95823

OCEAN CONSERVATION

21. Ocean Conservation. Dr. Nancy Foster, Office of Protected Resources, NOAA, 1825 Connecticutt Ave. #805, Washington, D.C., USA 20035

CONSERVATION (GENERAL)

22. Conservation on Private Lands. Kathleen Shea Abrams, National Parks and Conservation Association, Environmental and Urban Problems, Florida International University, North Miami, FL, USA 33181

23. U.S.-U.S.S.R. Cooperative Tropical Forest Pilot Project. Arnold Newman, ISPTR, 3931 Camino de La Cumbre, Sherman Oaks, CA, USA 91423

24. The Biosphere Reserve Programme. William Gregg, US-MAB Project Directorate, Depart. of the Interior, National Parks, Washington, D.C., USA 20240

25. Representation of Ecosystems in Protected Areas. George D. Davis, Wild Wings Foundation, Chevre Hill Farm, Wadhams, NY, USA 12990

CONSERVATION IN THE NEOTROPICS

26. Conservation in Jamaica. Karl Aiken, Natural History Society of Jamaica, P.O. Box 58, Mandeville, Jamaica

27. Conservation in Latin America. Frances Spivy-Weber, National Audubon Society, 645 Pennsylvania Ave SW, Washington, D.C., USA 20003

28. Protection of the Remaining Atlantic Coastal Rainforest of Brazil. Dr. Jose Pedro de Oliveira Costa, S.O.S. Atlantic Forest Foundation, Rua Conselheiro Carrao, Sao Paulo, SP 01328, Brazil

29. Creation of a Biosphere Reserve at Calakmul, Campeche, Mexico. Joann M. Andrews, PRONATURA-MEXICO, Calle 13 #203-A, G. G., Merida, Yucatan, Mexico

30. Puerto Rico and the U.S. Virgin Islands. Environmental Coalition of Puerto Rico, Ms. Cindy Gines, Calle 1 #1094, Urban Villa, Nevarez, Rio Piedras, Puerto Rico 00921

CONSERVATION IN OTHER REGIONS

31. Three Gorges Dam, China. V.C. Mohan, Asia-Pacific People's Environment Network, Sahabat Alam Malaysia, 37 Lorong Birch, Penang 10250, Malaysia

32. The Cairngorms Scotland Establishment of a World Heritage Site. Ian S. Gardiner, The Braids, 13 Tudor Drive, Otford near SevenOaks, Kent TN14 5QP, United Kingdom

GROUP D: PROTECTING WILDERNESS

WILDERNESS (GENERAL)

33. Definition and Recognition of Wilderness. Dr. John Hendee, Dean, College of Forestry, Wildlife and Range Sciences, University of Idaho, Moscow, ID, USA 83843

34. Recognition and Designation of Caves as Underground Wilderness. George

N. Huppert, American Cave Conservation Association, 1830 Green Bay St., La Crosse, WI, USA 54601
35. Desert Ecosystems. Jeff Widen, Coordinator, Desert Task Force, The Sierra Club, 3550 West 6th St. #323, Los Angeles, CA 90020
36. John Muir Commemoration and Memorial. Joe Passineau, Department of Horticulture, Forestry and Parks, South Dakota State University, Brookings, SD, USA 57007

ANTARCTICA
37. Antarctica. Jim Barnes, Antarctica Project, 218 D St. SE, Washington, D.C., USA 20003

WILDERNESS IN AUSTRALIA
38. Wilderness in Australia. Dr. Judy Lambert, The Wilderness Society, 179 Sydney Road, Fairlight, NSW 2094, Australia

WILDERNESS IN CANADA
39. Protection for the Temagami/Lady Evelyn Wilderness. Brian Back, The Temagami Wilderness Society, 204, Wedgewood Drive, Willowdale, Ontario, Canada M2M 2H9
40 Long-Term Protection for the Threatened Wilderness of Western Canada. Lisa Spellacy, Canadian Parks & Wilderness Society, RR7, Munn Road, Victoria, British Columbia, Canada V8X 3X3
41. Independent Inventory and Analysis of Remaining Old Growth Forest in British Columbia. Peter McAllister, Sierra Club of Western Canada, 2901 Seaview Road, Victoria, British Columbia, Canada V8N 1K9
42. Special Protection for Robson Bight. Peter McAllister, Sierra Club of Western Canada, 2901 Seaview Road, Victoria, British Columbia, Canada V8N 1K9
43. Proposed Khutzeymateen Grizzly Bear Sanctuary. Vicky Husband, Friends of Ecological Reserves, P.O. Box 10, Victoria, British Columbia, Canada V8X 4M6
44. Stikine Transnational Park. John J. Christian, Friends of the Stikine, 1405 Doran Road, North Vancouver, British Columbia, Canada V7K 1N1

WILDERNESS IN ITALY
45. Wilderness in Italy. Bianca Vetrino, Italian Wilderness Society, Regione Piedmonte Italy, Piazza S. Giovanni 4, Torino 10122, Italy

WILDERNESS IN THE USA
46. Full Protection for the Coastal Plain of the Arctic National Wildlife Refuge. Jack Hessian, Alaska Task Force, The Sierra Club, 241 East 5th Suite 205, Anchorage, AK, USA 99501
47. Tongass National Forest, Southeast Alaska. Bart Koehler, SEACC, P.O. Box 021692, Juneau, AK, USA 99805
48. Aerojet Land Swap. Charles S. Watson Jr., NORA, P.O. Box 1245, Carson City, NV, USA 89702

ABSTRACT OF ADDITIONAL PRESENTATIONS

Philip E. Austin

In the mid-nineteenth century, the United States began to realize that supposedly unlimited natural resources and land were indeed limited. A more scientific approach to the use of resources was needed, as well as a concern by higher education for the development, transmission and practical application of knowledge to particular problems. A manifestation of this was the establishment of land grant colleges throughout the U.S. The Agricultural College of Colorado, now called Colorado State University, was created in 1870 with a commitment to the protection and wise use of natural resources, which have come to be considered the lifeblood of humanity.

We have found that protection of our lands not only adds to quality of life, but also strengthens economic stability.

The CSU College of Forestry and Natural Resources has been a front-runner in education for natural resource conservation. Since 1916, when the U.S. Congress created the National Park Service, our university has served as the principal training ground for rangers and administrators for this agency. This tradition continues today.

Colorado State University also has a rich tradition of work in the international arena. Over one-third of the faculty have had international experience, many in Third World countries providing technical assistance involving the utilization and preservation of natural resources. Almost 800 international students representing 101 countries make unique contributions to our campus life. We're also proud of our university's instrumental role in developing the Peace Corps, for which the original feasibility was conducted by researchers on our campus.

Carmen Blondin

The designation of large marine ecosystems (LMEs) is an evolving scientific and socioeconomic process. Useful comparisons may be made of the different processes which have influenced large-scale change among LMEs. Management and conservation of LMEs, responding to strong environmental signals, will be enhanced by improved understanding of the physical factors which force biological change. Current global-scale efforts to improve the information base for sustained management of LMEs is meager. We have taken steps to improve the situation over the next few years by focusing efforts on regional marine ecosystem management, based on a better understanding of the productive capabilities of LMEs.

The shift that has occurred over the past decade in the United States from single-species research to multispecies orientation is attributed in large part to the standards of the Fisheries Management and Conservation Act of 1976. In addition, the National Oceanic and Atmospheric Agency (NOAA) has been mandated by the U.S. Congress to conduct research in support of the National Environmental Protection Act, the Marine Mammal Protection Act, the Endangered Species Act and the requirements of the Marine Protected Areas Program. Given the growing interest in the conservation and management of fishery resources, along with efforts to avoid further environmental degradation and to enhance the recovery of endangered and threatened species and preserve marine areas as a human responsibility for future generations, it is both timely and appropriate to broaden the focus of fisheries research and management to multispecies studies at different levels and from an ecosystem perspective.

Dhananjayan

A traditional story of India, presented in Katakali, the classical Indian dance: A traveller in the wilderness sees a deer about to give birth and follows her to her hiding place. All at once, a barrage of misfortunes, including a hunter with a bow and arrow, a lion and a forest fire beset the deer. As the traveller, bewildered, wonders what to do, an equally bizarre stream of natural accidents rescues the deer from her plight. The traveller watches the deer give birth to her fawn and marvels at the mysteries of divine providence.

Mayor Federico Peña

While it is absolutely critical that governments at whatever level—national, regional or local—be committed to conservation, the individual has a responsibility and role to play as well. If one thinks about the individual responsibility which we can take in local and global conservation, the consequences are staggering.

Each one of us has a responsibility to conserve a resource such as water. In Denver and Colorado we live in a semiarid environment where conservation and wise use of water is a high priority. Every individual must meet that responsibility whether it is deciding how to use water in his home or deciding how to use and allocate that water resource in his business. The same is true of land use, air pollution and the well-being of our mountain scenery.

Each of us as individuals must recognize that what we do has worldwide implications. Rivers leaving our cities, states and country, carrying pollution to the oceans have global implications. Our air pollution has global implications. While government has an absolutely critical role to play, the real answer and solution will be found by individuals.

Governor Roy Romer

The State of Colorado is constantly engaged in environmental policy issues. The key issues are air quality, water rights and agricultural production. For example, within the borders of Colorado are the headwaters of some of the nation's great rivers—the Rio Grande, the Arkansas, the Platte and the Colorado. If political boundaries were meant to enhance the efficient use of these resources, then John Wesley Powell was right to suggest that Western states should correspond to river basins. But that is not what happened. Thus, we must be mindful of how the use of our water in Colorado affects the citizens of other states and other countries. An elaborate structure has emerged to ensure that we do that.

Tom Thomas

There are two main aspects which must be addressed if the dilemma of worldwide conservation is ever to be solved. The first, as emphasized and demonstrated by the World Wilderness Congress, is to develop cross-communication between sectors and professions involved in different aspects of international environment and development. It is this type of cross-pollination which yields new ideas, effective programs and eventual success in our collective efforts.

The second, equally important aspect is represented by the youth of the world. Results of all conservation efforts will be carried out by today's youth. As I travel from one country to another and visit school systems, despite the critical importance of this simple issue, I find that conservation education is one topic that is either nonexistent or offered on an elective basis. If we are to win the conservation battle—and we must—the sooner we get young people exposed to conservation education and environmental values, the more effective our fight will be. Until we develop communication and education for the youth of the world, implementing our conservation programs and sustainable development policies.

Dr. Edgar Wayburn

The American conservation movement—or if you will, the American environmental movement—has come a long way in the past 40 years. It now encompasses a great variety of issues: national park establishment and protection; wildlife protection; wetlands preservation; logging and mining on public lands; energy production and conservation; nuclear energy; clean air and water; and management practices. These are all absolutely interconnected with the great public lands issues which have been our primary focus for the past 100 years.

In the past 20 years we have broadened our concerns and involvement in the arena of our activities. One by one, conservationists and conservation organizations have realized that no matter how many battles are won on American soil, the environmental war must be fought worldwide. Americans and their organizations are progressively taking increased interest and participation in what goes on outside the United States and are urging the U. S. government to do much more on the international scene than was done in the past.

Bruce E. White

The impact of the World Conservation Strategy has been great. While the concept of sustainability had long been a part of the language of resource managers and economists, definitions of sustainability were often not compatible. By integrating economic goals with those of environmental protection, the World Conservation Strategy (WCS) has provided the impetus for a series of new efforts.

To implement the WCS, the International Union for Conservation of Nature and Natural Resources has promoted the preparation of National Conservation Strategies (NCS). There are five elements essential to creation of effective NCS:
- Tailor strategies to local conditions;
- Utilize local expertise;
- Obtain the highest level of official sanction;
- Be comprehensive; and,
- Use participatory planning.

Key questions that need to be considered by planners and participants in NCS-like efforts are:

1. How can NCS most effectively address the goals of sustainable development? Should they serve as action plans for the environmental community or as an integral part of national development policy plans?

2. To what extent must the financial and industrial communities support strategies, and how can this be accomplished?

3. What changes must NGOs make in philosophy, funding strategies, educational programs, advocacy and staff expertise to effectively implement an NCS?

PRESENTERS

Ms. Susan Abbasi
Congressional Research Service
The Library of Congress, USA

Dr. George Archibald
Director
International Crane Foundation, USA

Dr. Philip Austin
President
Colorado State University, USA

Dr. Stephen Bacon
Vice President
Outward Bound International, USA

The Hon. James A. Baker, III
United States Secretary of the Treasury
Washington, D.C., USA

The Hon. Minister Patrick Balopi
Minister of Local Government and Lands
Gabarone, Republic of Botswana, Africa

Mr. Peter A.A. Berle
President, National Audubon Society
USA

Mr. Carmen Blondin
Deputy Assistant Administrator for
Fisheries Resource Management
National Oceanic and Atmospheric Administration
Washington, D.C., USA

Mr. Frank D. Boren
President
The Nature Conservancy, USA

Mr. Eddie Box, Sr.
Ute Tribal Leader
Ignacio, Colorado, USA

Mr. Nyle C. Brady
Senior Assistant Administrator for
Science and Technology
U.S. Agency for International Development (USAID)

Mr. Michael H. Brown, M.A.
Human Resources Consultant, USA

Gro Harlem Brundtland
Prime Minister of Norway
Chairman, World Commission on Environment and Development

Lord Michael Burghley
Executive Director
Emissary Foundation International, Canada

Mr. F. William Burley
Senior Associate
World Resources Institute, USA

Dr. Jose Pedro de Oliveira Costa
IUCN/WWF Advisory Committee, Brazil

Dr. M. Rupert Cutler
President
Defenders of Wildlife, USA

Mr. Raymond F. Dasmann
Professor of Environmental Studies
University of California, Santa Cruz, USA

Dhananjayan
Classical Dancer, India

Dr. Bernd von Droste
Director, Division of Ecological Sciences
UNESCO, MAB Program, France

Dr. Tim Easley
Chairman, Department of Forest Resources
University of New Brunswick, Canada

Dr. Harold Eidsvik
Chairman
Commission on National Parks
and Protected Areas, Canada

Dr. Nancy Foster
Chief, Marine and Estuarine
Management Division
National Oceanic and
Atmospheric Administration, USA

Ms. Norma Foster
Director
Charisma Communications
USA

Mr. Michael Fischer
Executive Director, Sierra Club
USA

Mr. George T. Frampton, Jr.
President
The Wilderness Society
USA

Mr. Patrick J. Galvin
Secretary, Environment and the Arts
Department of the Arts
Heritage and Environment, Australia

Dr. Alan Grainger
Gilbert White Fellow
Resources for the Future, USA

Dr. William Gregg, Jr.
Cochairman, U.S. Man
and Biosphere Programme
Biosphere Reserves

Mr. Liu Guangyun
Vice Minister of Forestry
People's Republic of China

Dr. Michael D. Gwynne
Global Environment
Monitoring System
United Nations Environment Programme
Kenya

Dr. Jay D. Hair
President
National Wildlife Federation, USA

Dr. Garrett Hardin
Department of Biological Sciences
University of California Santa Barbara
USA

Ms. Susan Hart
Eco-Link
Republic of South Africa

Dr. John C. Hendee
Dean, College of Forestry
Wildlife and Range Sciences
University of Idaho, USA

Ms. Yolanda Kakabadse
Executive Director
Fundacion Natura, Ecuador

Ms. Norma Kassi
Member of the Yukon Territorial
Legislative Assembly for the
Vuntat Gwich'in Nation, Old Crow
Yukon Territory, Canada

Mrs. Joyce M. Kelly
Past President, Defenders of Wildlife, USA
Former EPA and BLM, U.S. Government

Dr. Edwin Krumpe
Director, Wilderness Research Center
University of Idaho, USA

Mr. David M. Lank
Investment Banker,
Art Historian and Critic
Canada

Mr. Charles Lankester
Principal Development Adviser
United Nations Development Program, USA

Mr. George M. Leonard
Associate Deputy Chief
U.S. Forest Service

Dr. Walter J. Lusigi
Chief Technical Advisor
UNESCO/KALRES
Nairobi, Kenya

Jo Agquisho-Oren R. Lyons
Onondaga Nation, Haudenosaunee
Six Nations Iroquois Confederacy
Professor of American Studies
State University of New York at Buffalo, USA

Mrs. Joan Martin-Brown
Washington Liaison
United Nations Environment Programme
USA

Mr. J. Michael McCloskey
Chairman
The Sierra Club, USA

Dr. John D. McCrone
Coordinator, Cooperative Park Studies Unit
National Park Service, USA

The Hon. Thomas McMillan, P.C., M.P.
Minister of the Environment, Canada

Dr. Kenton Miller
(Former) Director General
International Union for the
Conservation of Nature and Natural Resources
Distinguished Fellow, World Resources Institute, USA

Dr. Irving Mintzer
Research Associate
World Resources Institute, USA

Ms. Lorraine Mintzmyer
Regional Director, Rocky Mountain Region
U.S. National Park Service

Dr. Hemanta R. Mishra
The King Mahendra Trust for
Nature Conservation, Nepal

Mr. Val Morin
Ecologist, Canada

Mr. William Penn Mott, Jr.
Director
U.S. National Park Service

Dr. Roderick Frazier Nash
Professor of History and Environmental Studies
University of California Santa Barbara, USA

Magqubu Ntombela
Elder, Zulu Nation
Republic of South Africa

Dr. Joe Passineau
Department of Horticulture, Forestry and Parks
South Dakota State University, USA

The Honorable Federico Peña
Mayor, City of Denver, Colorado, USA

Dr. Ian Player, DMS
Vice Chairman
Wilderness Leadership School
Republic of South Africa

Dr. Arturo Gómez-Pompa
UC-MEXUS
University of California at Riverside, USA

Dr. D. Jane Pratt
Chief, Environmental Operations and Strategy
The World Bank, USA

Mr. Robert Prescott-Allen
PADATA, Inc., Canada

Mr. Paul Pritchard
President
National Parks and Conservation Association, USA

Mr. Philip James Ratz
Executive Director
National Outdoor Leadership School, USA

Mr. William K. Reilly
President
World Wildlife Fund/
The Conservation Foundation
USA

Dr. Robert Repetto
Senior Economist
World Resources Institute
USA

Mr. David Rockefeller, USA

The Hon. Roy Romer
Governor, State of Colorado
USA

Mr. William D. Ruckleshaus
Washington, D.C., USA

Dr. Hind Sadek
Museum of Natural History for Children
Egypt
Director, WorldWIDE, USA

H.E. Dr. Emil Salim
Minister of State for
Population and the Environment
Indonesia

Dr. John A. Sanford
Jungian Analyst
San Diego, USA

Sri Kailash Sankhala
Director, Wildlife Reserves, India

Mr. M.A. Partha Sarathy
Chairman
IUCN Education Commission, India

Mr. Douglas Scott
The Sierra Club, USA

Ms. Jasmine Shah
Photographer, Producer
India

Ms. Heather Spalding
The Sierra Club, USA

Dr. James G. Speth
President
World Resources Institute, USA

Dr. Robert Staffanson
Director
American Indian Institute, USA

Mr. Nick Steele
Director, Bureau of Natural Resources
KwaZulu, Republic of South Africa

Mr. Maurice Strong, President
American Water Development Company
USA

Dr. R. Sukumar
Centre for Ecological Sciences
Indian Institute of Science, India

Mr. I. Michael Sweatman, FICA
Chairman
International Wilderness Leadership Foundation
Visiting Fellow
World Resources Institute
USA

Mr. Peter Thacher
Distinguished Fellow
World Resources Institute, USA

Dr. William Theobald
Director, Pacific Tropical Botanical Garden
Hawaii, USA

Mr. Tom D. Thomas
International Cooperation Specialist
U.S. National Park Service

Dr. Mostafa K. Tolba
Director
United Nations Environment Programme, Kenya

Mr. Russell Train
Chairman
World Wildlife Fund/The Conservation Foundation, USA

Ms. Dilnavaz Variava
Coordinator
Save Silent Valley Committee, India

Ms. Bianca Vetrino
Vice President, Piedmont Region
Natural Parks and
Territory Planning Department, Italy

Dr. Edgar Wayburn
The Sierra Club, USA

Dr. Paul Weingart
Director of Recreation
USDA Forest Service, SW Region, USA

Dr. Bruce E. White
Center for Policy Negotiations, USA

Dr. Roman I. Zlotin
Institute of Geography
USSR Academy of Sciences

USEFUL WORLDWIDE CONSERVATION ADDRESSES

The following represents a few of the many natural resource and conservation groups and agencies throughout the world, of whom participated in the 4th World Wilderness Congress. There are many others, both governmental and non-governmental, which we encourage you to also contact for more information on worldwide conservation.

AFRICA

Ministry of Local Government
and Lands
Government of Botswana
Private Bag 0042
Gabarone
Republic of Botswana

Kalahari Conservation Society
Botswana House
The Mall
P.O. Box 859
Gaborone
Republic of Botswana

Institute for Nature Conservation
B.P. 2757
Bujumbura
Burundi

Wildlife Conservation Organization
P.O. Box 386
Addis Ababa
Ethiopia

Environmental Protection Council
P.O. Box M
Accra 326
Ghana

United Nations Environment Program
Room C-106
P.O. Box 30552
Nairobi
Kenya

Environmental Liaison Center
P.O. Box 72641
Nairobi
Kenya

African Environment Network
P.O. Box 53844
Nairobi
Kenya

Wildlife Clubs of Kenya
P.O. Box 40658
Nairobi
Kenya

UNESCO Arid Lands Program
P.O. Box 417
Marsabit
Kenya

Department of Environment
Private Bag X447
Pretoria 0001
Republic of South Africa

Wilderness Leadership School
P.O. Box 53058
Yellowwood Park
Natal 4001
Republic of South Africa

Wildlife Society of South Africa
P.O. Box 44189
Linden Transvaal 2104
Republic of South Africa

South African Nature Foundation
P.O. Box 456
Stellenbosch Cape Province 7600
Repoublic of South Africa

KwaZulu Bureau of Natural Resources
Private Bag X23
Ulundi 3838
KwaZulu
Republic of South Africa

Natal Parks Board
P.O. Box 662
Pietermartizburg
Natal 3200
Republic of South Africa

International Professional
Hunters Association
P.O. Box 1317
Parklands 2121
Transvaal
Republic of South Africa

Eco Link
P.O. Box 727
White River
Transvaal 1240
Republic of South Africa

National Parks Board
Private Bag X402
Skukuza
Transvaal 1350
Republic of South Africa

Tourism and Travel Agencies
ORTPN. B. P. 905
Kigali
Rwanda

Ministry of Natural Resources
and Fisheries
State Avenue
Freetown
Sierra Leone

Wildlife Club of Uganda
P.O. Box 4596
Kampala
Uganda

Department of National Parks
and Wildlife
Private Bag 1
Chilanga
Zambia

Ministry of Forestry
Beijing
Peoples Republic of China

Center for Ecological Sciences
Indian Institute of Science
Bangalore 560 012
India

IUCN Education Commission
Hamsini 12th Cross Rajmahal
Bangalore
India

Bombay Natural History Society
32 B. Samachar Marg
Bombay 400 023
India

Department of Environment
Bikaner House
Shahjahan Road
New Delhi 110011
India

Department of National Parks
and Wildlife
P.O. Box 8365 Causeway
Harare
Zimbabwe

The Department of Natural Resources
Natural Resources Board
P.O. Box 8070 Causeway
Harare
Zimbabwe

Zimbabwe Wildlife
P.O. Box 3497
Harare
Zimbabwe

ASIA

Wildlife Preservation Society of India
G-28 Nizamuddin West
New Delhi 110013
India

Wildlife Reserves
21 Duleshwar Garden
Jaipur 302001
India

Ministry of State for Population
and Environment
Sekretariat Negara
Jalan Merdeka Barat #15 3rd Floor
Jakarta, Indonesia

Ministry of Forestry and
Nature Conservation
Jalan Ir. H. Juanda #9
Bogor, Indonesia

Center for Environmental Studies
Jalan Prof. Maas No. 3A
Medan, North Sumatra
Indonesia

Wildbird Society of Japan
Aoyama Flower Building
1-1-4 Shibuya, Shibuya-ka
Tokyo 150, Japan

Environment Agency
3-1-1 Kasumigaseki
Chiyoda-ku
Tokyo 100, Japan

National Institute for
Environmental Studies
16-2 Onogawa, Yatabe-cho
Tsukuba-gun, Ibaraki Pref. 305
Japan

Sahabat Alam Malaysia
37 Lorong Birch
10250 Penang
Malaysia

Environmental Protection
Society Malaysia
17 Jalan SS 2/53
Petaling Jaya
Malaysia

Malayan Nature Society
Persatuan Pencinta Alam
17, SS 2/53, Petaling Jaya
Selangor, Malaysia

The King Mahendra Trust for
Nature Conservation
P.O. Box 3712
Babar Mahal
Kathmandu, Nepal

National Resources Center
8th Floor Triumph Building
1610 Quezon Avenue
Quezon City, Deliman
Philippines

Philippine Federation for
Environmental Concern
13 Kapiligan Street
Quezon City, Philippines

Department of Wildlife Conservation
P.O. Box 1562
Colombo, Sri Lanka

Sri Lanka Environmental Federation
215, G-2/5, Park Road
Colombo 5
Sri Lanka

PACIFIC

Department of Home Affairs
and Environment
Parliament House
GPO Box 1252
Canberra A.C.T. 2601
Australia

Queensland National Parks
P.O. Box 190
Brisbane 4000
Australia

Australian Trust for
Conservation Volunteers
P.O. Box 423
Ballarat, Victoria 3350
Australia

Wilderness Society
179 Sydney Road
Fairflight, New South Wales 2094
Australia

Australian Conservation Foundation
672B Glenferrie Road
Hawthorn VIC 3122
Australia

Ecological Society of Australia
P.O. Box 1564
Canberra A.C.T. 2601
Australia

Australian National Parks Council
7a Powell Street
Killara New South Wales 2071
Australia

Great Barrier Reef Marine Park
G.P.O Box 791
Canberra A.C.T. 2601
Australia

Department of Conservation
P.O. Box 10-420
Wellington
New Zealand

New Zealand Ecological Society Inc.
P.O. Box 12-019
Wellington
New Zealand

The Environment and
Conservation Organizations Inc.
7 MacDonald Crescent
P.O. Box 11057
Wellington 1
New Zealand

Department of Environment
P.O. Box 6601
National Capital District
Boroko
Papua, New Guinea

Office of Environment and
Conservation
Central Government Offices
P.O.Wardstrip
Papua, New Guinea

Wau Ecology Institute
P.O. Box 77
Wau
Papua, New Guinea

SOUTH AMERICA

Ecology Institute
Calle Julio Llanos 3556
Barrio Poeta Lugones 2 seccion
5008 Cordoba
Argentina

Argentine Ecology Institute
Facultad de Ciencias,
Universidad de Buenos Aires
Pabellon 2, Nunez
Buenos Aires
Argentina

Bolivian Ecology Association
Apartdo 4923
La Paz
Bolivia

Bolivian Wildlife Society
Casilla 989
Lapaz
Bolivia

AGAPAN
Rua Jacino Gomes 39
Port Algero RS 90000
Brazil

Brazilian Institute for
Forest Development
Av. L-4 Norte
Setor de Areas Isoladas NT
S/N-Ed. Sede
CEP: 70.040, Brasilla D.F.
Brazil

National Institute for
Amazon Research
Estrada do Alexio, KM 4, 1.756
Caxio Postal 478
CEP: 69.000, Manaus, A.M.
Brazil

Department of Environmental
Conservation
Estrada da Vista Chinesa #741
20.531 Rio de Janeiro
Brazil

Gaucho Association for the Protection
of the Natural Environment
Jacintho Gomes 39
90000 Porto Alegre RS
Brazil

Department of Environment
Bandada 52, 7th Floor
Santiago
Chile

Institute of Ecology of Chile
Augustinas 641, Office 11
Santiago
Chile

National Institute for the Development
of Natural Renewable Resources and
the Environment
Diagonal 34, no. 5-18, Third Floor
Apartado Aereo 13458
Bogota, D.E.
Colombia

Colombian Ecological Society
Apartado Aero 8674
Bogata, D.E.
Columbia

Ministry of Natural Resources
and Energy
Santa Prisca 223
Quito
Ecuador

Fundacion Natura
Jorge Juan 481
P.O. Box 243
Quito
Ecuador

National Office of Natural
Resource Evaluation
#355 Calle 17
El Palomar, San Isdro
Apartado Postal 4992
Lima
Peru

Ecological Nature Group
Apartdo 3051
Lima 100
Peru

CENTRAL AMERICA

Belize Audubon Society
P.O. Box 6
Belize City
Belize

CATIE
Turrialba
Costa Rica

Fundacion Neotropica
Atdo. 236-1002
Paseo De Los Estudiantes
San José, Costa Rica

National Park Service of Costa Rica
Apartado 7473
San José, Costa Rica

Costa Rican Association for the Conservation of Nature
Apartado 8-3790
San José, Costa Rica

Honduran Ecology Association
Apartado T-250
Tegucigalpa D.C.
Honduras

Ministry of Natural Resources
Barrio Guacerique #1534
Tegucigalpa D.C.
Honduras

NORTH AMERICA

Environment Canada
Les Terrasses de la Chaudiere
10 Wellington Street
Hull, Quebec K1A 0H3
Canada

Canadian Wildlife Federation
1673 Carling Avenue
Ottawa, Ontario K2A 3Z1
Canada

Canadian Nature Federation
203-75 Albert Street
Ottawa, Ontario K1P 0L2
Canada

Canadian Wildlife Services
Place Vincent Massey
351 St. Joseph Blvd
Hull, Quebec K1A 0E7
Canada

IUCN Commission on National Parks
and Protected Areas
135 Dorothea Drive
Ottawa, Ontario K1V 7C6
Canada

Yukon Territorial Legislative
Assembly
for the Vantat Gwich'in Nation,
Old Crow
P.O. Box 2703
Whitehorse, Yukon Territory Y1A 2C6
Canada

Western Canada Wilderness
Committee
1520 West 6th Avenue
Vancouver, B.C. B6Z 2E2
Canada

Indigenous Survival International
47 Clarence Street Suite 300
Ottawa, Ontario K2A 1P8
Canada

Temagami Wilderness Society
204 Wedgewood Drive
Willowdale, Ontario M2M 2H9
Canada

World Wildlife Fund Canada
201-60 St. Clair Avenue East
Toronto, Ontario M4T 1N5
Canada

London Cross Cultural Learner Centre
533 Clarence St.
London, Ontario N6A 3N1
Canada

Secretariat of Urban Development
and Ecology
Teposteco 36 4th Floor
Colonia Navarte
Mexico 03020 D.F.

Instituto Mexicano de
Recursos Naturales Renovables
Av. Dr. Vertiz 724
Mexico 12 D.F.

African Wildlife Foundation
1717 Massachusetts Avenue, NW
Suite 602
Washington, D.C. 20036
United States of America

Massachusetts Audubon Society
Lincoln, Massachusetts 01773
United States of America

American Water Development
Company
1099 18th Street, Suite 2950
Denver, Colorado 80201
United States of America

American Parks and Wildlands
P.O. Box 97
Big Sky, Montana 59716
United States of America

American Indian Institute
P.O. Box 1388
Bozeman, Montana 59715
United States of America

Ansel Adams Gallery
1772 Alluvial Avenue
Fresno, California 93711
United States of America

The Antarctica Project
218 D Street, SE
Washington, D.C. 20003
United States of America

Aspen Rainforest Awareness Group
P.O. Box 10538
Aspen, Colorado 81612
United States of America

Colorado Environmental Coalition
2239 East Colfax Avenue
Denver, Colorado 80206
United States of America

Colorado Division of Wildlife
13539 Jackson Street
Denver, Colorado 80241
United States of America

Committee for International
Wolf Center
Route 2
P.O. Box 225A
Bovey, Minnesota 55709
United States of America

Defenders of Wildlife
1224 19th Street, NW
Washington, D.C. 20036
United States of America

Denver Audubon Society
2340 Fairfax Street
Denver, Colorado 80207
United States of America

Denver Botanic Gardens
909 York Street
Denver, Colorado 80206
United States of America

College of Forestry and
Natural Resources
Natural Resources Building
Colorado State University
Fort Collins, Colorado 80523
United States of America

American Wilderness Alliance
7600 East Arapahoe Road, Suite 114
Englewood, Colorado 80112
United States of America

Colorado Wildlife Federation
1560 Broadway, Suite 895
Denver, Colorado 80202
United States of America

College of Forestry, Wildlife
and Range Sciences
University of Idaho
Moscow, Idaho 83843
United States of America

Game Conservation International
P.O. Box 1744
San Antonio, Texas 78217
United States of America

International Institute for Environment
and Development (IIED)
1717 Massachusetts Avenue, NW
Suite 302
Washington, D.C. 20036
United States of America

Global Tomorrow Coalition
1325 G Street, NW, Suite 1003
Washington, D.C. 20005
United States of America

International Wilderness
Leadership Foundation
1224 Roberto Lane
Los Angeles, California 90077
United States of America

Rainforest Action Network
300 Broadway, Suite 28
San Francisco, California 94133
United States of America

United Nations Environment Program
1889 F Street, NW
Washington, D.C. 20006
United States of America

United Nations Environment Program
New York Liaison Office
Room DC2-0816 United Nations
New York, New York 10017
United States of America

Wilderness Vision Quest
6214 Hibbling
Springfield, Virginia 22150
United States of America

Earthwatch
680 Mount Auburn
P.O. Box 403
Watertown, Massachusetts 02272
United States of America

Emissary Foundation International
P.O. Box 489
Lyndon, Washington 98265
United States of America

Environmental Defense Fund
1616 P Street, NW
Washington, D.C. 20036
United States of America

Environmental Center
University of Colorado
UMC 331, Campus Box 207
Boulder, Colorado 80309
United States of America

Flintridge Foundation
1100 El Centro Street #103
South Pasadena, California 91030
United States of America

Green Earth Inc.
P.O. Box 229
Crestone, Colorado 81131
United States of America

International Crane Foundation
Baraboo, Wisconsin 53913
United States of America

Island Resources Foundation
1718 P Street, NW
Washington, D.C. 20036
United States of America

Keystone Center
P.O. Box 606
Keystone, Colorado 80435
United States of America

Manomet Bird Observatory
P.O. Box 936
Manomet, Massachusetts 02345
United States of America

Missouri Botanical Gardens
P.O. Box 299
St. Louis, Missouri 63110
United States of America

Morris Animal Foundation
3220 Cherryridge Road
Englewood, Colorado 80110
United States of America

Mzuri Wildlife Foundation
41 East Taylor Street
Reno, Nevada 89501
United States of America

National Audubon Society
950 Third Avenue
New York, New York 10022
United States of America

National Geographic Society
17th & M Street, NW
Washington, D.C. 20036
United States of America

National Oceanic and
Atmospheric Adminstration
1825 Connecticut Avenue, NW
Washington, D.C. 20235
United States of America

National Outdoor Leadership School
P.O. Box AA
Lander, Wyoming 82520
United States of America

National Park Service
P.O. Box 37127
Washington, D.C. 20013
United States of America

National Parks and
Conservation Association
1015 31st Street, NW
Washington, D.C. 20007
United States of America

The Nature Conservancy
1800 North Kent Street, Suite 800
Arlington, Virginia 22209
United States of America

Onondaga Nation
P.O. Box 200
Via Nedrow, New York 13120
United States of America

Pacific Tropical Botanical Garden
P.O. Box 340
Lawai, Kauai, Hawaii 96765
United States of America

Resources for The Future
1616 P Street, NW
Washington, D.C. 20036
United States of America

The Sierra Club
730 Polk Street
San Francisco, California 94108
United States of America

The Sierra Club
330 Pennsylvania Avenue, NW
Washington, D.C. 20001
United States of America

Southern Appalachian Conservancy
P.O. Box 3356
Kingsport, Tennessee 37664
United States of America

Thorne Ecological Institute
5370 Manhattan Circle Suite 104
Boulder, Colorado 80303
United States of America

The Trust for Public Lands
P.O. Box 9251
Santa Fe, New Mexico 87504
United States of America

U.S. Agency for International
Development
Room 4942 New State
Washington, D.C. 20523
United States of America

U.S. Forest Service
P.O. Box 2417
Washington, D.C. 20013
United States of America

Washington Wilderness
P.O. Box 45187
Seattle, Washington 98145
United States of America

The Wilderness Society
1400 I Street, NW
Washington, D.C. 20005
United States of America

Wilderness Therapy East
847 Sea Hawk Circle Suite 104
Virginia Beach, Virginia 23452
United States of America

The World Bank
Environmental Operations
1818 H Street
Washington, D.C. 20433
United States of America

World Resources Institute
1735 New York Avenue, NW
Washington, D.C. 20006
United States of America

World Wildlife Fund/
The Conservation Foundation
1250 24th Street, NW
Washington, D.C. 20037
United States of America

National Wildlife Foundation
1412 16th Street, NW
Washington, D.C. 20036
United States of America

Woodlands Institute
P.O. Box 907
Franklin, West Virginia 26807
United States of America

Outward Bound USA
384 Field Point Road
Greenwich, Connecticut 06830
United States of America

Sigurd Olson Environmental Institute
Northland College
Ashland, Wisconsin 54806
United States of America

American Forest Institute
54 Portsmouth Street
Concord, New Hampshire 03301
United States of America

Population Environment Balance
1325 G Street, NW Suite 1003
Washington, D.C. 20005
United States of America

The Whale Center
3929 Piedmont Avenue
Oakland, California 94611
United States of America

Zoological Society of San Diego
P.O. Box 551
San Diego, California 92112
United States of America

Partners for Livable Places
1429 21st Street, NW
Washington, D.C. 20036
United States of America

Wildlife Management Institute
1101 14th Street, NW Suite 725
Washington, D.C. 20005
United States of America

Friends of the Earth
530 7th Street, SE
Washington, D.C. 20003
United States of America

Greenpeace
1611 Connecticutt Avenue, NW
Washington, D.C. 20009
United States of America

World Environment Center
605 Third Avenue 17th Floor
New York, New York 10158
United States of America

Peace Corps
806 Connecticut Avenue, NW
Washington, D.C. 20526
United States of America

Youths for Environment and Service
111 South Patrick Street
Arlington, Virginia 22314
United States of America

Econet
3228 Sacramento Street
San Francisco, California 94115
United States of America

California Conservation Corps
P.O. Box 1380
San Luis Obispo, California 93406
United States of America

Involvement Corps
1515 Sunset Boulevard, Suite 108
Pacific Palisades, California 90272
United States of America

CARE
660 First Avenue
New York, New York 10016
United States of America

EUROPE

Department of Protected Landscape
Gottualdao NAM 10
96901 Banska Strainicci
Czechoslovakia

UNESCO, MAB Program
Division of Ecological Sciences
7, Place de Fontenoy
75700 Paris
France

French Federation of Societies for
Nature Protection
57, Rue Cuvier
75231 Paris Cedex 05
France

German Society for Environment
and Nature Protection
In der Raste 2
D-5300 Bonn 1
The Federal Republic of Germany

Environmental Protection
TOB02 U. 19
Budapest 111
Hungary

Hungarian Academy of Sciences
Roosevelt ter. 9
H-1394 Budapest
Hungary

Natural Parks and Territory
Planning Department
Piedmont Region
Commissioner to the Park
Torino 165
Italy

Foundation for the Environment
Viale Coni Zuvna 6
20144 Milan
Italy

Ministry of Agriculture and Fisheries
Division of Nature Protection
P.O. Box 20401
NL-2500 EK The Hague
The Netherlands

Waddenvereniging
Waddenhuis
Harlingen
The Netherlands

Council for Environmental Studies
University of Oslo
P.O. Box 1024
Blinderm
Oslo
Norway

Ministry of Environment
P.O. Box 8013, Oslo-Dep
Oslo 1
Norway

Swedish NGO Secretariat
Miljovard
Vallgatan 22 S-411 16
Gotegborg
Sweden

International Union for
the Conservation
of Nature and Natural Resources
Avenue du Mont-Blanc
CH-1196 Gland
Switzerland

World Commission on Environment
and Development
Palais Wilson
52 rue des Paquis
1201 Geneva
Switzerland

NGO Liaison Service
Palais des Nations
CH-1211 Geneva 10
Switzerland

World Wildlife Fund International
Avenue du Mont Blanc
CH-1196 Gland
Switzerland

Royal Society for Protection of Birds
The Lodge
Sandy
Bedfordshire
England United Kingdom

PANOS
8 Alfred Place
London WC1 E7E
England United Kingdom

World Wildlife Fund UK
Panda House
11-13 Ockford Road
Godalming Surrey GU7 1QU
England United Kingdom

The David Shepherd Foundation
P.O. Box 123
Guildford
Surrey GU1 3EW
England United Kingdom

Survival International
29 Craven Street
London WC2N 2NT
England United Kingdom

Department of Environment
Room A3-04
Romney House
43 Marsham Street
London SW1 3PY
England United Kingdom

The Conservation Society Ltd.
12a Guildford Street
Chersty
Surrey KT 16 9BQ
England United Kingdom

International Institute for Environment
and Development
3 Endsleigh Street
London WC1H 0DD
England United Kingdom

International Fur Trade Federation
69 Cannon Street
London EC4N 5AB
England United Kingdom

Conservation Monitoring Center
219 C Huntingdon Road
Cambridge CB3 0D1
England United Kingdom

International Council for
Bird Protection
219 C Huntingdon Road
Cambridge CB3 0D1
England United Kingdom

Center for Human Ecology
University of Edinburgh
Edinburgh EH8 9LN
Scotland United Kingdom

Scottish Wildlife Trust
25 Johnson Terrace
Edinburgh EH1 2NH
Scotland United Kingdom

Findhorn Foundation
The Park
Forres IV36 0T2
Scotland United Kingdom

USSR Academy of Sciences
Staromonetny Per. 29
Moscow 109017
USSR

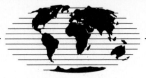

EXECUTIVE COMMITTEE AND ADVISERS

BOARD OF DIRECTORS
(INTERNATIONAL WILDERNESS LEADERSHIP FOUNDATION)
Michael Sweatman (Chairman); Dr. R.N. Cleaves; Michael Casey; Norma Foster; Dr. John Hendee; Vance G. Martin (President); Dr. Ian Player DMS; Sir Laurens van der Post CBE; Dielle Fleischmann; James Stewart.

EXECUTIVE COMMITTEE, 4th WWC
Dr. Jay Hughes, Chairman; Dean, College of Forestry and Natural Resources, Colorado State University;Mr. Vance G. Martin, Executive Director; President, International Wilderness Leadership Foundation; Dr. John Hendee, Vice Chairman, Science; Dean, College of Forestry, Wildlife and Range Sciences, University of Idaho; Dr. Ian Player, Honorary Int'l Chief Executive; Vice Chairman, Wilderness Leadership School; Mr. Michael Sweatman, Vice Chairman, Economics and Development; Chairman, International Wilderness Leadership Foundation; Mr. Tom Thomas, Vice Chairman, Int'l Education; USDI National Park Service; Mr. Peter Thacher Vice Chairman, International Affairs; Distinguished Fellow, World Resources Institute; Dr. Edgar Wayburn Vice Chairman, Citizen Environmental Affairs; Vice President, Sierra Club

SENIOR ADVISERS, 4th WWC

Dr. David Munro United Nations Environment Programme
Mr. M.A. Partha Sarathy Chairman, IUCN Education Commission
Mr. Maurice Strong President, American Water Development Corporation
Mr. Russell Train Chairman, World Wildlife Fund/The Conservation Foundation

RESOLUTIONS COMMITTEE, 4th WWC

Mr. Robert Prescott-Allen (Chairman) PADATA, Inc., Canada
Mr. George Furness, (Rapporteur) Conservation Treaty Support Fund, USA
Dr. Nancy Foster, NOAA-NOS, USA
Ms. Joyce Kelly, USA
Ms. Cynthia Cook, The World Bank, USA
Mr. Bill Worf, U.S. Forest Service
Mr. Kishore Rao, India
Mr. Gabriel Charles, West Indies
Dr. Edgar Wayburn, The Sierra Club, USA

HONORARY PATRONS, 4th WWC

Dr. Salim Ali, India
Mr. G. Ray Arnett, USA
Mrs. Thomas Bata, Canada
The Hon. Felipe Benavides, Peru
Mr. Richard Chamberlain, USA
Mr. Dan M. Galbreath, USA
Mr. Verne McLaren, Australia
Dr. Mateo Magarinos de Mello, Uruguay
Dr. Kenton Miller, IUCN
Mr. William Penn Mott, Jr., USA
Dr. Paulo Nogueira-Neto, Brazil
The Hon. Russell W. Peterson, USA
Mr. Gary Player, USA
Mr. Nathaniel P. Reed, USA
Mr. Edmund de Rothschild, UK
Mr. Wally Schirra, USA
The Hon. John Seiberling, USA
Mrs. Dielle Fleischmann Seignious, USA
Mr. Jeffrey R. Short, USA
Mr. James Stewart, USA
Dr. Mostafa K. Tolba, UNEP
The Hon. Russell Train, USA
Mr. Stewart L. Udall, USA
Sr. Alvaro Ugalde, Costa Rica
Mr. and Mrs. G. P. Van de Bovenkamp
Sir Laurens van der Post, UK

CONGRESS ADVISERS, 4th WWC

Adirondack Park Agency (USA)
AGAPAN (Brazil)
American Forest Institute
American Mining Congress
American Forestry Association
American Institute of Architects
American Society of Landscape Architects
American Wilderness Alliance
Canadian Wildlife Federation
Cathedral of St. John the Divine (USA)
CATIE (Costa Rica)
Colorado Dept. of Natural Resources
Colorado Division of Wildlife
Colorado State Forest Service
Colorado State University, College of Forestry and Natural Resources
Council for Environmental Studies (Norway)
Defenders of Wildlife (USA)
Game COIN (USA)
Global Tomorrow Coalition (USA)
Idaho Power Company
International Environmental Education Foundation (USA)
International Institute for Environment and Development (UK)
International Society of Tropical Foresters (USA)
International Union for the Conservation of Nature and Natural Resources
Laboratory of Ecology and Zoology University of Paris-South
Lorian Association (USA)
Ministry of Interior (Brazil)
Mzuri Wildlife Foundation (USA)
National Academy of Sciences (USA)
National Audubon Society (USA)
Natural Resources Council of America
National Council of Women (Kenya)
National Outdoor Leadership School (USA)
National Parks and Conservation Association (USA)
National Wildlife Federation (USA)
Natural Resources Defense Council (USA)
Outward Bound, Inc. (USA)
Partners for Livable Places (USA)
Population and Environment Balance
President's Commission on Americans Outdoors
PRODENA (Peru)

PRONATURA (Mexico)
Renewable Natural Resources Foundation (USA)
Sierra Club (USA)
Survival International
Tenneco, Inc.
UNESCO Arid Lands Program (Kenya)
United Nations Environment Programme
U.S. Dept. of Agriculture, Forest Service
U.S. Dept. of Commerce, National Oceanic and Atmospheric Association (NOAA)
U.S. Dept. of Interior, National Park Service; Fish and Wildlife Service; Bureau of Land Management
University of Idaho, College of Forestry Wildlife & Range Sciences
Wildlife Management Institute (USA)
Wilderness Foundation (UK)
Wilderness Society (USA)
Wilderness Leadership School (USA)
World Resources Institute (USA)
World Wildlife Fund (India, Australia)
World Wildlife Fund/The Conservation Foundation (USA)
Zoological Society of San Diego (USA)

It would be impossible to list all the individuals, corporations and organizations which gave freely of their time and resources to collaborate on the 4th World Wilderness Congress. The many thousands of hours of volunteer effort were complemented by hundreds of thousands of dollars of support-in-kind from many sources. In addition, we are most grateful for the significant financial support that was received from the following friends and supporters:

Tom and Odette Worrell, Ted and Sue Dalzell, Dick and Beverly Davis, Mrs. Alexander Haig, Genevieve di San Faustino, Ronald T. and Susan Lyman, Edmund de Rothschild, Gaylord Donnelly, Mr. and Mrs. Bayard Henry, Barbara Moore Rumsey, Dielle Fleischmann, Robert and Charlotte Baron, Peter Callaway, Jane Engel, Simon and Sarah Fraser, Jeffrey Short, John and Diana Slocum, Ralph and Muriel Stahl, John and Stephanie Christie.

Worrell Newspapers, Inc., International Fur Trade Federation, Jackson Hole Preserve Inc., Bothin Foundation, Adolph Coors Co., Edison Electric Institute, Armand G. Erpf Fund, Ford Foundation,Fulcrum, Inc., Gates Foundation, Safari South, Gulf Oil Corp., Island Foundations, Mzuri Wildlife Foundation, Ruth and Vernon Taylor Foundation, Times-Mirror Foundation, The Denver Post, World Wildlife Fund/The Conservation Foundation, Man and Biosphere Program, Ministry of Development Cooperation (Norway), Zoological Society of San Diego , The World Bank, A-Mark Financial Corp., Colorado National Bank, Maki Foundation, New-Land Foundation, German Marshall Fund, National Parks and Conservation Association, Wilderness Leadership School, Findhorn Foundation.

The International Wilderness Leadership Foundation is a U.S. not-for-profit foundation and sponsor of the WWC that welcomes any assistance and involvement you may wish to offer to worldwide conservation. For more information contact: The President, International Wilderness Leadership Foundation, c/o Fulcrum Inc., 350 Indiana Street, Suite 510, Golden, Colorado USA 80401.